Prolog:
A Relational Language and Its Applications

John Malpas

Prentice-Hall, Inc., Englewood Cliffs, New Jersey 07632

Library of Congress Cataloging-in-Publication Data

Malpas, John   (date)
  Prolog : a relational language and its applications.

  Bibliography: p.
  1. Prolog (Computer program language)   I. Title.
QA76.73.P76M35 1986   005.13'3   86-25551
ISBN 0-13-730805-1

Editorial/production supervision: Lisa Schulz Garboski
Interior design: John Malpas
Cover design: George Cornell
Manufacturing buyer: S. Gordon Osbourne

© 1987 by Prentice-Hall, Inc.
A division of Simon & Schuster
Englewood Cliffs, New Jersey 07632

UNIX is a trademark of AT&T Bell Laboratories.
Writer's Workbench, and Documenter's Workbench are trademarks of AT&T Information Systems.
VMS, VT-100, and DEC are trademarks of Digital Equipment Corporation.
MS-DOS is a trademark of Microsoft, Inc.
Knowledge Workbench is a trademark of Silogic, Inc.
Prolog-1 and Prolog-2 are trademarks of Expert Systems International, Inc.
Arity and Arity/Prolog are trademarks of Arity Corporation.
micro-PROLOG is a trademark of Logic Programming Associates Ltd.
Turbo Prolog is a trademark of Borland International, Inc.
IBM PC is a trademark of IBM Corporation.
Laserlink is a trademark of Urban Software.

Prentice-Hall International (UK) Limited, *London*
Prentice-Hall of Australia Pty. Limited, *Sydney*
Prentice-Hall Canada Inc., *Toronto*
Prentice-Hall Hispanoamericana, S.A., *Mexico*
Prentice-Hall of India Private Limited, *New Delhi*
Prentice-Hall of Japan, Inc., *Tokyo*
Prentice-Hall of Southeast Asia Pte. Ltd., *Singapore*
Editora Prentice-Hall do Brasil, Ltda., *Rio de Janeiro*

Contents

Preface

Intended Audience

"Introduction to Prolog and Its Applications" is directed at programmers who already know one or more programming languages, and who are interested in

1) Prolog,

2) logic programming, and

3) applications of artificial intelligence.

Result of reading the book

As a result of reading the book (and doing the exercises!), a reader should gain facility in both representing problems in Prolog and technical Prolog programming. To some extent, these skills are transferable to other computational formalisms now used in artificial intelligence. An attempt is made throughout the book to illustrate some of the interesting aspects of logic programming theory with practical code, and thereby to demonstrate the usefulness of theory. Readers who would like to pursue their interest in theory are referred to the Bibliographic Notes at the end of each chapter.

Read the book with a computer handy

To get the most benefit out of reading this book, it is suggested that the reader have a computer with a version of Prolog on it somewhere close by. This will allow experimentation with each new idea presented in the text. The book is intended primarily to stimulate the reader's imagination regarding how Prolog works and what to use it for. It is possible (but difficult) to learn Prolog from the book without a computer.

There are several places in the book where analogies are drawn to the C language. These analogies are simple, and should be comprehensible even to a reader who does not know C.

Subjects
Covered in
the Book

Chapter 0 introduces the basic theoretical notions of symbolic logic, logic programming, and Prolog. The history of symbolic logic is presented in Secs. 0.2 through 0.6, ending with a discussion of resolution theorem proving as it applies to Prolog. These sections will acquaint an unfamiliar reader with the rich heritage of logic from which Prolog comes. Many concepts and terms (such as *axiom* or *theory*) are introduced here in the context of symbolic logic, and are later used in the context of Prolog. A reader's appreciation for these concepts should deepen by seeing them in more than one context. It is not strictly necessary to read Chapter 0 in order to understand the rest of the book, nor is it necessary to know anything about symbolic logic to program in Prolog. Therefore, a reader anxious to learn the practical details of Prolog can skip Chap. 0 on the first reading.

Learning the
language

Someone unfamiliar with Prolog should be able to learn the language from Chaps. 1, 2, and 3. Chapter 1 covers facts, rules, and queries. It introduces a classification of types of relations that occur in the world, and shows how they can be represented in Prolog. Chapter 2 covers arithmetic, data structures, list processing, and ends with an overview of ways to represent a database. Chapter 3 begins with an extensive discussion of the Prolog execution model, and shows how the search space of a program can be controlled using "cut." A set of built-in predicates common to most versions of Prolog is also presented. Chapter 4 contrasts various approaches to the process of programming in Prolog. A reader who reads the book straight through should be well aware of the capabilities of the language by the end of Chap. 4.

Applications

Chapters 5-7 go on to explore specific applications of Prolog. Chapter 5 covers text manipulation tools, and presents a language translator (DEC-10 to/from micro-Prolog) and a query language interpreter. Chapter 6 discusses what it means to represent knowledge in a computer program, and provides an overview of some computational formalisms used for knowledge representation. It then covers the implementation of an *inheritance mechanism* in Prolog. Several applications of the inheritance mechanism are investigated, including a form-driven database query program that allows incremental refinement of queries. Chapter 7 deals with the user interface aspect of systems for expert consultation, and presents an interpreter that can explain how it arrived at its answers. The last example in Chap. 7 is an interpreter that can successfully evaluate queries that cause the usual Prolog interpreter to go into an infinite loop.

Examples of Code

An attempt is made throughout the book to provide enough concrete examples to illustrate the point being made, but not so many as to lose the reader in a sea of code. Often the examples of code in the seven chapters are kept simple on purpose to maximize their readability. Appendix II contains various supplementary programs for screen i/o, answer set collection, etc.

Compatible versions of Prolog

All examples conform to a highly portable subset of DEC-10 Prolog, which is completely compatible with what Clocksin and Mellish call "core Prolog." Specifically, the examples will run on the following versions of Prolog: CProlog, Quintus, Arity, Expert Systems International Prolog-1 and Prolog-2, UNSW Prolog, Prolog-86, Chalcedony Prolog, IF/Prolog, micro-Prolog or Sigma Prolog with the DEC-10 front end, etc. Many of the examples will run on Turbo Prolog. (In fact, all examples in the book were initially developed in CProlog, and then ported to several other versions.) An attempt was made to avoid the use of any version-specific constructs or features. Appendix IV is an explicit discussion of the differences between versions of Prolog; it may be a useful reference for porting a program from one version of Prolog to another.

Case Study

Appendix III contains a case study concerned with the scheduling of work in a manufacturing operation. This application requires some sophisticated problem solving methods, and naturally entails the use of many programming and representation techniques covered in the book. While the case study deals with a greatly simplified model of a manufacturing operation, it sets up a framework that can be expanded to the level of complexity necessary to represent a real operation. The purpose of the case study is to show how a problem of some consequence can be solved with Prolog.

There is a danger, however, in including a single case study. If the application area is too esoteric, it will leave readers unfamiliar with it cold. If the application area is too familiar, then the program will not appear to be doing anything significant, and may disappoint some readers. The area of manufacturing was selected to fall somewhere between the familiar and the esoteric. It should be accessible even for someone who does not have a background in manufacturing, and many of the techniques employed are appropriate to other areas.

There is another reason to include a case study from the area of manufacturing. Many people have the impression that Prolog is an impractical, academic language. They tend to ask questions like: "What can you really *do* with it?" An ineffective way to answer such questions is to mention all of the things that *could* be done with Prolog, to talk about academic research projects, or to imply that much of the really great work that has been done with Prolog is classified. A better answer is to point out real, commercial systems that have been built with Prolog, and there are several such systems in the area of manufacturing.

Navigating Through the Book

The book can be read straight through, but does not have to be: readers already familiar with Prolog may skip directly to the subjects they are interested in. The book is formatted with margin titles to make it easy to locate a section of interest. There is also a thorough index to aid readers in navigating through the book. Some basic technical terms are explained in the glossary in Appendix I.

Introduction

Why Learn Prolog?

There is no doubt that learning a new language requires a commitment of time and energy, so it is worthwhile to consider briefly why a programmer might be motivated to learn Prolog. It comes down to a question of what advantages Prolog might have over other languages for the development of applications.

View of the World Imposed by a Language

A programming language tends to impose a certain view of the world on its users. One manifestation of this imposition is that a programmer who has been using a language long enough to be infected by its world view will tend to find uses for those types of computation at which the language is adept, and avoid problems for which the language is not suited. Suppose we assume that the purpose of writing a computer program is either to 1) solve a problem, or 2) represent a system that exists in the world in such a way that the program can be used to simulate the behavior of the system. It would be convenient to be able to judge the world views imposed by various programming languages according to how well they serve this purpose. Such considerations are on the level of *meta software engineering*: given the purpose of programming stated above, what languages and tools will best serve it?

Semantics of programming languages

One way to approach the world view imposed by a programming language is through the *semantics* (meaning) of a construct of the language. To program with the constructs of a language requires thinking in terms of the semantics of those constructs; thus, semantics is a key to the thought processes of the programmer.

Programming languages can be classified by the nature of their semantics into three broad categories:

1) *procedural,*

2) *functional,* and

3) *relational.*

The meaning of a construct in a procedural language is defined in terms of the behavior of the computer when the construct is evaluated. Behavior might be either external (i.e. printing a message to the terminal) or internal (i.e. changing the value of a variable). The meaning of a construct in a functional language (i.e. a function call) is defined in terms of the value it returns. A function call can be read as a *declaration of its returned value.* The meaning of a construct in a relational language is defined as a relation that holds between individual entities or a class of entities. A relational construct can be read declaratively as an *assertion that the relation represented by the relation name holds between the arguments.*

The level of a language

Let us assume further that a programmer starting out to write a program has a *logical specification* that clearly describes the problem to be solved or the structure of the system to be represented. This assumption enables us to classify the world view of a programming language by its *level* with respect to the specification. A *low level language* has a world view close to that of the computer. A *high level language* has a world view closer to that of the specification. By this criterion, procedural languages tend to be low level. Because of the semantics of procedural language constructs, the programmer must think in terms of telling the computer how to behave. When using a procedural language, it requires a great deal of translation to turn the specification of a complex system into a working program. Functional languages are higher level than procedural languages, because the programmer is able to think in terms of computing values instead of behaviors, and values are often a part of the specification. Relational languages are on the highest level, because the semantics of relational language constructs is very close to that of a specification. The world view of an ideal relational language is the same as the world view of a logical specification, and so a minimum of translation is necessary to transform one into the other. With an ideal relational language, it becomes possible to write a program that is *structurally isomorphic* to its specification; that is, every variation in the form of the specification has a corresponding variation in the form of the program.

Advantage of thinking relationally

While Prolog is far from being an ideal relational language, it is close enough to enable a programmer to enjoy the benefits mentioned above. Using Prolog properly can elevate the world view of a programmer to the level of a specification. If a programmer is able to think totally in terms of the structure of relations without having to worry about the accuracy of a translation (implementation), then his or her time is freed for greater pursuits. A criticism sometimes leveled at Prolog is that it imposes a *logical* view of the world on the programmer; the truth is that *any* point of view can be expressed as a Prolog program. This is why there is active research in Prolog occurring in so many of the most interesting areas of computer science, such as natural language and expert systems. The most persuasive reason to learn Prolog is that it enables one to deal with these areas at a high level.

Acknowledgments

A reader familiar with the logic programming literature will recognize my indebtedness to the ideas of two researchers in particular, Bob Kowalski and Pat Hayes. Borges wrote a short story about the Arab scholar Averroes in Umayyad Spain, who took it upon himself to translate the works of Aristotle from Greek to Arabic. The story concerns what happened when he encountered the Greek words for "comedy" and "tragedy." Since there was no tradition of theatre in Islamic culture, the sense of a "comedy" or "tragedy" as a type of play was completely foreign to his experience. After much browbeating late one night, he ended up inventing his own meanings for the words that seemed to him consistent with the way that Aristotle used them, but were (from our point of view) completely incorrect. The process of doing research in order to write this book has left me very sympathetic to Averroes' plight. Some readers may discover that I have committed errors of interpretation similar to Averroes'.

People instrumental in the completion of this book include Ron Gombach, who helped me clarify ideas through innumerable discussions, and who decided to put Prolog to the test as a language for industrial applications at an early point. Many of the application examples in the book appear courtesy of Ron. Thanks are also due to John Struse, Richard Struse, and John Roseman, who lent me valuable cpu cycles when I had no machine of my own with which to learn Prolog, and to Bob Didner, who gave me the first opportunity to build a commercial application in Prolog. The support of Bill Jensen, Bill Roberson, and Keith Eisenstark of Structured Methods, Inc. was important to the development of the Prolog course from which this book emerged. Kathy O'Leary must be ackowledged for her patience in listening to endless explanations of Prolog during the development of the course. The criticism and suggestions of Patti Kahn, Jennifer Zimmerman, and Richard O'Keefe (all of Quintus Computer Systems, Inc.) were invaluable. The feedback of students who attended the Prolog course has had an important refining effect on the presentation of ideas contained in the book. The comments of readers of drafts of the book, including Doug DeGroot, Joe McDonough, Larry Lynch-Freshner, and Dave Smith, has greatly contributed to the final product. I would also like to ackowledge Bob Horn, David Johnson, and Patricia D'Andrade of the Lexington Conference, as well as Jack O'Leary and Karl Karlstrom, for their encouragement.

AT&T's Writer's Workbench was used to copy edit early drafts of the manuscript. The book was formatted with AT&T's Documenter's Workbench, including device independent troff, the tbl preprocessor for tables, and the pic preprocessor for figures. The index was automatically generated by Urban Software's Laserlink.

0

Logic, Logic Programming, and Prolog

0.1 Introducing Logic Programming

Logic
Programming
Defined

Logic programming is an approach to computer science in which the Horn clause form of *first order predicate logic* is used as a high level programming language. The study of symbolic logic goes back to the work of Aristotle in the fourth century B.C. First order predicate logic is a branch of symbolic logic that has evolved largely in the twentieth century. It is a universal, abstract language for representing knowledge and solving problems, and can be considered to be a general theory of relations. Logic programming is based on a subset of first order predicate logic, but is equally broad in scope. Logic programming allows a programmer to describe a situation with formulas of predicate logic, and then to use a *mechanical problem solver* (i.e. a procedure) to make inferences from the formulas. When using a logic programming language, the emphasis is on describing the structure of the application, instead of telling the computer what to do. Other concepts of computer science in areas such as relational database theory, software engineering, and knowledge representation, can all be described (and thereby implemented) in logic programs. In this way, logic programming is a potentially revolutionary influence on many aspects of computer science.

Prolog

For the most part, logic programming languages utilize a software technology based on Robinson's *resolution inference rule*. Prolog is the best known logic programming language, although there are others. The first Prolog was written by Alain Colmerauer and associates at the University of Marseilles in 1972, and nurtured at various European universities throughout the last decade. The language began to attract attention in the United States only after 1981, when the Japanese Ministry of International Trade and Development announced that their fifth generation project was to be based on logic programming software technology. Interest in Prolog has grown steadily since then. Prolog is now being used for applications by many government and business institutions in Europe, the United States, and Japan. There exists a decidedly international community of people developing the field of logic programming, in which Japanese researchers play a significant role.

An artificial intelligence language

Prolog is often referred to as an artificial intelligence language, but this designation is misleading in two ways. Lisp is the best known artificial intelligence language, and to throw Prolog into the same pot seems to invite all kinds of spurious comparisons regarding which (Lisp or Prolog) is better. In practical terms, each language has its own programming methodologies. The only imaginable way that one might be said to be "better" than the other is in terms of human factors such as readability, ease of use, etc. At this point, people in the American AI community still strongly favor Lisp. Their preference may not be due to deficiencies of Prolog *per se*, but rather because they are accustomed to Lisp.

A more important point is that the usefulness of Prolog is not limited to artificial intelligence. It has been appropriately applied to many conventional applications (software engineering, database interface, decision support) as well as AI applications (expert systems, natural language systems).

Simplicity of Prolog

Prolog is attractive as a programming language because of its simplicity (it has few lexicographical symbols). Prolog code is easy to read, which augurs well for productivity and ease of program maintenance. Because Prolog is based on the universal formalism of Horn clauses, Prolog source code is more immune to implementation dependencies than source code in other languages. Furthermore, implementations of Prolog tend to be uniform, so that a program written for one version can easily be ported to another. Finally, Prolog is straightforward to learn.

The Heritage of Logic

Logic programming comes out of the heritage of symbolic logic. To fully appreciate logic programming, it is useful to understand what symbolic logic is and how it developed. In Secs. 0.2 through 0.7, we consider the evolution of logic from the first codification of traditional logic, through modern predicate logic, to the beginnings of logic programming. In Secs. 0.8 through 0.11, we discuss the distinctive aspects of logic programming and Prolog as a software technology.

0.2 Traditional Logic

Aristotle

What is now known as "traditional logic" began at the time of Aristotle over 22 centuries ago. Aristotle attempted to codify into a scientific system the way that knowledge can be most effectively pursued through rational debate. His work is best understood as a theoretical study of successful reasoning techniques.

Laws of logic

Aristotle's point in codifying logic was to establish a standard whereby the correctness of a line of reasoning used in rational debate could be established. In describing Aristotle's logic, we use the word *statement* to indicate a complete thought that could be expressed in a simple English sentence. Aristotle's three laws of traditional logic (listed in Table 0-1) are an attempt to establish the constraints that should govern the introduction of a statement into a debate.

Laws of Traditional Logic
identity   A is A.   (a thing is always equal to itself; a statement implies itself)
contradiction   A is not not-A.   (a thing cannot both be and not be something; no statement is both true and false)
excluded middle   A is not both A and not-A.   (a thing either is or is not something; every statement is either truc or false)

Table 0-1

The laws can be understood as protecting the integrity of a statement. They establish that a statement must always have a single truth value, *true* or *false*, and this truth value cannot change to suit the needs of one of the participants in the debate. Once the truth value of a statement has been accepted, then the opposite truth value for the same statement cannot be accepted. If these laws are not followed (as, for instance, if both an initial statement A and a second statement that contradicts A are introduced), then any conclusion reached in the debate is not reliable.

Elements of a statement

Aristotle analyzed the form of a statement into the following elements:

Quantifier Subject Copula Predicate

so that, for instance, in the following statement:

```
All Americans are car-drivers.
```

"Americans" is the subject, "All" quantifies the subject, "car-drivers" is the predicate, and "are" is the copula. Alternatively, in:

```
Some taxi-drivers are not aggressive.
```

"taxi-drivers" is the subject, "Some" quantifies the subject, "not aggressive" is the predicate, and "are" is the copula.

Four statement forms

Traditional logic recognizes four possible statement forms, each characterizing a possible relationship between two classes. They are:

```
All S is P.
No S is P.
Some S is P.
Some S is not P.
```

where S stands for a subject class of items and P stands for a predicate class of items. "All" and "No" are known as *universal quantifiers* that refer to every element of the subject class; "Some" is known as an *existential quantifier* that refers to a subset of the subject class.

The syllogism

The *syllogism* is a set of rules governing what conclusions can be reached from a set of statements written in the four statement forms. For instance, it indicates that given the following two *premisses* (i.e. statements that are assumed to be true):

```
All Americans are car-drivers, and        (1)
All Californians are Americans            (2)
```

then the following *conclusion* is valid:

```
All Californians are car-drivers.         (3)
```

The process of reaching a conclusion from premisses is also called *making an inference*. Formally, an inference such as the above can take place only when the predicate class of one statement (i.e. "Americans" in (2)) matches the subject class of another (i.e. "Americans" in (1)). As a result of the inference, a new statement is formed out of the subject of one statement and the predicate of the other. The syllogism specifies different results for each type of quantification, so that, for instance, from:

```
All baseball players are gum-chewers, and   (4)
Some baseball players are from Boston        (5)
```

it specifies the conclusion:

```
Some (people) from Boston are gum-chewers.  (6)
```

The syllogism is primarily a logic of classes: the previous example referred to classes of baseball players, gum-chewers, and people from Boston. All syllogistic rules are based on the *transitivity* of class inclusion. Transitivity is a property of certain relationships, such as arithmetic equality: if it is known that $a = b$ and $b = c$, then it is also known that $a = c$ by transitivity. The inclusion of one class in another is also transitive: if class A is included in class B (as in "All baseball players are gum-chewers"), and class B is included in class C, then class A must be included in class C.

Each rule of the syllogism states a transition from premisses to a conclusion that is intuitively evident. When a complex argument is composed of many deductive steps, then the whole argument is logically valid (and hopefully comprehensible) if each step can be explained by a rule of the syllogism.

Propositions   Based on the syllogism, students of Aristotle were able to isolate principles of deductive inference operating on the more abstract level of *propositions*. A proposition is any statement that can be assigned a truth value (either *true* or *false*). A proposition is more general than a statement in the syllogism, because an expression such as

```
the unicorn XYZ exists
```

is a proposition, but not a syllogistic statement (i.e. it does not correspond to one of the four statement forms listed above).

The rules of deductive inference for propositions listed in Table 0-2 were derived after Aristotle's time by his disciples. The letters P and Q are variables that can represent any actual proposition.

Inference Rules	
Modus Ponendo Ponens	If P implies Q, and P is true, then Q is true.
Modus Tollendo Tollens	If P implies Q, and Q is false, then P is false.
Modus Ponendo Tollens	If P and Q are not both true, and P is true, then Q is false (exclusive "or").
Modus Tollendo Ponens (disjunctive syllogism)	If either P or Q is true, and P is not true, then Q is true (inclusive "or").

Table 0-2

These rules provide a much more general method of inference than the original syllogism, and constitute a first step toward a logic of propositions. Such a logic (i.e. the *propositional calculus*) was not fully developed until the nineteenth century.

Point of view associated with traditional logic

Philosophically, traditional logic is associated with the static world view of Hellenistic Greece. The notion of identity (or truth value) in this view does not allow change—once the identity of something has been established, it is immutable. The three laws of Table 0-1 express this idea concisely: a statement must have a truth value, and can only have one truth value. This point of view is not conducive to experimental science that seeks to account for change. Thus, Aristotelian logic began to fall out of favor in the seventeenth and eighteenth centuries when interest in experimental science was on the rise.

**Criticism of
the Syllogism**

For better or worse, Aristotle's approach to logic became so en-
trenched that no one even considered trying to improve on it until
the nineteenth century. Generations of students read Aristotle's
basic text on logic and learned the syllogism by rote. It is interesting
to note that Leibniz's (1646-1716) unpublished writings contain a
seed of doubt about the perfection of Aristotelian logic. Leibniz
found certain points where the syllogism seemed to be wrong or incomplete. Instead of alerting other scholars to these points, however,
he believed himself to have made an error (because Aristotle was
perfect!) and kept quiet.

But Leibniz also wrote about a vision of a new, universal language of
mathematical logic to replace the syllogism. He anticipated that
such a language would be able to solve philosophical problems in a
mechanical way, and thereby bring peace and harmony to the world.
He imagined a time when two people having a disagreement would,
instead of fighting, use this language to calculate the answer to their
problem.

*Inadequacy of
the syllogism*

The syllogism as a theory is overly complicated and incomplete. It is
a logic of classes, yet it contains no notion of the *complement* of a
class. (If A is a class, then the complement of A contains all items
not in A.) Thus, to make certain inferences, negatively defined
classes must be introduced, such as "the class of all non-car drivers."
There is no mechanism or notation within the syllogism to go from a
negatively defined class to a positively defined class.

The syllogism is intended to govern rational debate in natural
language, but is identified too closely with natural language. This
has led to absurd difficulties, in which logicians have denied the logical equivalence of two ways of saying the same thing. For instance, for most purposes,

```
All programmers are logicians.
```

means the same thing as

```
If someone is a programmer,
he or she is also a logician.
```

Unfortunately, the syllogism cannot deal with the second statement
at all, because it does not correspond to one of the four statement

forms. (A problem must be expressed in terms of the four statement forms to be solvable by the syllogism.)

The syllogism is *incomplete* in the sense that it cannot handle deductive inference dealing with the existence of a member of a class. Also, many of the forms of valid syllogistic inference are redundant and could be eliminated entirely without diminishing the strength of the syllogism as a deductive system.

All things considered, the syllogism is an interesting attempt at formalizing deductive thought. Symbolic logicians today regard it as a curiosity, unimportant to contemporary symbolic logic. The most amazing thing about the syllogism is the length of time that it was accepted unquestioningly as the normative form of all rational thought.

0.3 Early Development of Symbolic Logic

DeMorgan

The first step toward a logic of propositions, or *propositional calculus*, was taken by Aristotle's own disciples when they derived a set of inference rules applicable to propositions. The simplest and most important of these rules is *modus ponens*:

If P implies Q, and P is true, then Q is true.

Further developments in the evolution of propositional logic did not come until the English mathematician DeMorgan in the middle of the nineteenth century. DeMorgan criticized Aristotelian logic because it was written in natural language; he thought that the formal meaning of a syllogistic statement was confused by the semantics of natural language. He looked forward to a purely formal system of logic—that is, a language capable of manipulating symbols in a consistent manner irrespective of what meaning was ascribed to the symbols. He took algebraic notation as an example. In an expression such as x + y, x and y might be interpreted as something other than numerical quantities, and + might signify an operation other than addition. The rules for manipulating algebraic expressions, since they are completely syntactic (formal) in nature, continue to hold even when the symbols of algebra are interpreted differently. With regard to the syllogism, the word "is" in a statement such as all S is P had always been interpreted as the relationship of class inclusion (that is, the class P includes all elements of the set s). DeMorgan's inspiration was to free "is" from this meaning, and let it range over all relations that have the property of *transitivity*. In this way, he is responsible for introducing the general notion of *relation* as an abstract quality possessing any of various properties (for instance, *transitivity, symmetry*, and *reflexivity*).

Boole

The English mathematician Boole, a contemporary of DeMorgan, also contributed to the development of propositional logic. He thought that the essential character of logic is *form*, not content. He considered logic to be a sort of nonquantitative algebra of classes. Where Aristotelean logic had always been closely associated with philosophy, he took the position that logic should be associated instead with mathematics. Using familiar algebraic symbols, he showed how certain algebraic rules were equally applicable to numbers, sets, and the truth values of propositions.

Rules of Algebraic Manipulation		
$x + y$ = $y + x$		commutativity
$x * y$ = $y * x$		
$x + (y + z)$ = $(x + y) + z$		associativity
$x * (y * z)$ = $(x * y) * z$		
$x * (y + z)$ = $(x * y) + (x * z)$		distributivity

Table 0-3

Interpretations of algebraic rules

Consider the five rules that govern algebraic symbol manipulation given in Table 0-3. First, read each of the rules as if x and y possess their usual meanings as numerical variables, + denotes addition, and * denotes multiplication. For instance, if the value of x is 3 and the value of y is 4, then the value of both $x + y$ and $y + x$ is 7.

Now re-read the rules as if x and y are variables whose values are sets, + denotes the union of two sets, and * denotes the intersection of two sets. For instance, if the value of x is the set {1,2,3}, and the value of y is the set {3,4,5}, then the value of both $x + y$ and $y + x$ is the set {1,2,3,4,5}.

Finally, re-read the rules as if x and y are variables whose values are propositions, + denotes "or," * denotes "and," and = denotes logical equivalence. For instance, if the value of x is a proposition with a truth value of *true*, and the value of **y** is a proposition with a truth value of *false*, then the truth value of both **x + y** and **y + x** is *true*.

These rules constitute an internally consistent formal language, because they retain their validity through three different interpretations. (This language later came to be called *Boolean algebra*.) One more symbol can be added to the language for the set and truth value interpretations: ~, which is a unary operator placed before an expression. (A unary operator is one that takes a single argument.) In the set interpretation, ~ means "complement of," so that the expression

    ~(x * y)

indicates the complement of the intersection of two sets **x** and **y**, which consists of those elements that are either in **x** or in **y** but not in both.

In the propositional interpretation, ~ means "not," so that the above expression denotes the opposite of the truth value of **x * y** (i.e. the *exclusive or* of **x** and **y**).

If two ~'s are placed adjacent to one another, they cancel each other out. This behavior is expressed in the rule shown in Table 0-4:

Double Negation Rule		
~~x	=	x

Table 0-4

DeMorgan contributed two rules to this formal language that are applicable to the set and propositional interpretations. They are known as *DeMorgan's rules of duality* (Table 0-5):

DeMorgan's Rules		
~(x + y)	=	~x * ~y
~(x * y)	=	~x + ~y

Table 0-5

(Does the meaning of these rules correspond to your intuition in both the set and propositional interpretations?)

Truth Tables

The propositional interpretation of any expression in this language can be specified in a truth table. For instance, Table 0-6 gives the truth values of some simple expressions.

x	y	~x	~y	x * y	x + y	~(x * y)
T	T	F	F	T	T	F
T	F	F	T	F	T	T

Table 0-6

The second line of the table can be read as follows: if the value of **x** is a proposition whose truth value is *true* (written T), and the value of **y** is a proposition whose truth value is *false* (written F), then the truth value of ~**x** is *false*, the truth value of ~**y** is *true*, the truth value of **x** * **y** is *false*, the truth value of **x** + **y** is *true*, and the truth value of ~(**x** * **y**) is *true*.

Implication

An implication such as:

    if x then y

where **x** and **y** are truth values, can be expressed as:

    ~x + y

The exact meaning of this relationship is specified in Table 0-7.

x	y	~x + y
T	T	T
T	F	F
F	T	T
F	F	T

Table 0-7

It is interesting (if somewhat counterintuitive) to note if the truth value of **x** is *false*, **y** can be anything and truth value of the overall implication will still be *true*.

Frege and Peano

The era of modern symbolic logic began in earnest with the work of Gottlob Frege that appeared in 1879. Like his contemporary Peano, Frege sought to develop a purely formal logic language that could serve as the foundation of arithmetic. The essential problem for Frege and Peano was to find a logical treatment of the notion of *sequence*, so as to be able to deal formally with the set of numbers. Frege considered the work of Boole and DeMorgan confusing because they used the same notation (+, *, etc.) for both arithmetic and logic. Frege is responsible for the "begriffsschift" ("concept language"), a symbolic calculus capable of representing and manipulating pure logical forms that did not depend on numerical analogies.

Frege regarded the propositional interpretation of Boolean algebra as fundamental. In his version of propositional logic, from two primitive connectives, "implication" and "negation," all other connectives ("and," "or," etc.) can be derived.

A theory of relations

In syllogistic logic, a truth-valued statement is considered to be made up of the subject and the predicate (see Sec. 0.2). Another of Frege's innovations is to consider a truth-valued statement to be made up of a predicate and some number of *arguments*. To write such statements, he used a notation that is similar to the mathematical notation for functions. Frege made an analogy between the components of a statement and the components of a sentence of ordinary language such as:

```
You read the book.
```

The *arguments* are those words that can change while the expression remains meaningful. For instance, "book" might be replaced by "newspaper" or "You" might be replaced by "I," and the result will still be meaningful. The *predicate*, on the other hand, is that part of the expression that cannot be changed without sacrificing meaningfulness—consider what happens when "read" is replaced by "ate."

Frege's goal was to develop a general *theory of relations*. The analysis of a proposition into predicate and arguments is an essential feature of this theory. He also recognized that the theory requires a way to handle *quantification of variables* that occur as arguments to a predicate (see Sec. 0.5 below). After Frege, the general theory of relations came to be called *predicate logic*.

The Calculi

It is beyond the scope of this book to present a detailed history of the development of symbolic logic in the twentieth century. One of the factors that makes such a treatment almost impossible is that the notation of symbolic logic evolved just as fast as its substance. Almost every twentieth century logician used a different notation from every other logician, at least until recently when several notations have emerged as standard. An attempt was made to select the most "vanilla flavored" (and ascii printable!) of logic notations for use in the rest of this chapter.

Instead of a historical treatment, then, the next two sections are devoted to an informal overview of propositional logic and predicate logic. This is in preparation for a discussion of *resolution*, the basic inference rule of logic programming, in Sec. 0.6. The tone of the presentation is deliberately nonrigorous, and the reader is referred to works cited in the bibliographic notes at the end of the chapter for a complete treatment of any of these topics.

0.4 Propositional Logic

Propositions

In the conventional *lexicon* of propositional logic, the symbols A, B, C, etc. are used to represent *atomic propositions* (i.e. propositions that cannot be broken down into components). The significant characteristic of a proposition is its ability to denote a truth value of either *true* or *false*.

For some purposes, it is useful to imagine that one of these symbols stands for a proposition expressed in English. For instance, imagine that the symbol A stands for the English sentence:

The earth revolves around the sun.

We describe this situation by saying that the sentence is the *informal meaning* of A. Because the English sentence states something that we accept as true, by giving A this particular informal meaning, we thereby also give it a truth value of *true*. In general, propositional logic is concerned only with the truth values of symbols and formulas that are built up from those symbols. The fact that a particular symbol has an informal meaning is not directly relevant to propositional logic. The informal meanings of symbols become important, however, if we wish to apply the techniques of propositional logic to a particular field of knowledge.

Well-Formed Formulas

Propositional logic allows complex formulas to be built up by combining symbols representing atomic propositions with the logical connectives shown in Table 0-8:

Connectives	
Symbol	**Meaning**
~	*not*
&	*and*
v	*or*
-->	*implies*
<-->	*if and only if*

Table 0-8

A complex formula that includes logical connectives is known as a *well-formed formula* (wff). In the lexicon of propositional logic, the symbols p, q, and r are *propositional variables*. A propositional variable is used to represent a well-formed formula. A well-formed formula can be defined as follows:

1) a symbol representing an atomic proposition (such as A) is a wff;

2) if p and q are wffs, then so are:

Wff	**Read as:**
~p	*not* p
p & q	p *and* q
p v q	p *or* q
p --> q	*if* p *then* q; p *implies* q
p <--> q	p *if and only if* q; p *is equivalent to* q

Each of the expressions involving p and q above is referred to as a *statement form*. A statement form is an abstract specification of the syntax of an infinite number of wffs composed of symbols representing atomic propositions. A statement form is either a single propositional variable (such as p), or a combination of propositional variables joined together by the connectives. A well-formed formula that syntactically matches a statement form is called a *substitution instance* of the statement form. For instance, if A, B and C are symbols representing atomic propositions, then the following well-formed formula:

   A & (B v C)

is a substitution instance of any of the following statement forms:

(1)   p   (p stands for A & (B v C))

(2)   p & q   (p stands for A;
                             q stands for (B v C))

(3)   p & (r v q)   (p stands for A;
                             r stands for B;
                             q stands for C)

**Truth Value
of a Wff**

The form of a wff (that is, the way it is constructed from atomic propositions and logical connectives) is known as its *syntax*. The truth value of a wff is known as its *semantics* or *meaning*. It remains to consider the truth values of wffs that include logical connectives.

In a formal presentation of propositional logic, certain connectives are designated to be *primitive*, and their meanings are defined in a truth table. Then the meaning of the nonprimitive connectives is defined in terms of the primitive connectives. Suppose that ˜, &, and v are designated as primitive connectives. The meaning of these connectives is given in Table 0-9:

Meaning of ˜, &, and v				
p	q	˜p	p & q	p v q
T	T	F	T	T
T	F	F	F	T
F	T	T	F	T
F	F	T	F	F

Table 0-9

Once the meaning of these connectives has been established, then the meaning of --> and <--> can be defined in terms of them (Table 0-10):

Definition of --> and <-->		
Name	Notation	Definition
implication	p --> q	˜p v q
equivalence	p <--> q	(p & q) v (˜p & ˜q)

Table 0-10

A truth table (Table 0-11) for these connectives makes their meaning explicit:

Meaning of --> and <-->			
p	q	p --> q	p <--> q
T	T	T	T
T	F	F	F
F	T	T	F
F	F	T	T

Table 0-11

The truth value of a wff such as

        A & B   (*)

is only decidable with respect to a particular *interpretation*. An interpretation of a wff is an assignment of truth values to each atomic proposition that occurs in the wff. Suppose that under one interpretation, the truth value of A is *true* and the truth value of B is *true*; then the truth value of wff (*) under this interpretation will also be *true*. Under a different interpretation, the truth value of wff (*) might be *false*.

Semantic properties of wffs

Suppose there is a wff represented by the propositional variable p that is true with respect to a particular interpretation, I. The idea that interpretation I makes p *true* can be expressed in any of the following ways:

I *satisfies* p.

I *is a model of* p.

I *verifies* p.

p *is true in* I.

Tautologies and contradictions

There are some wffs that have definite truth values as a result of their syntactic form, regardless of the truth values of the atomic propositions of which they are composed. For instance, the truth value of the wff:

    A v ˜A

is *true*, no matter what the truth value of A. Such a wff is described as *valid*, and is known as a *tautology*.

On the other hand, the truth value of the wff:

    B & ˜B

is *false*, no matter what the truth value of B. Such a wff is described as *inconsistent*, and is known as a *contradiction*.

Theories and Axioms

In order to apply the techniques of propositional logic to a particular field of knowledge, we must first analyze the *structure* of that field. In performing this analysis, we are looking for atomic propositions that hold within the field, and for logical relationships that hold between these atomic propositions. After a suitable set of such atomic propositions has been isolated, we must then chose a symbol such as A, B, C, etc. to represent each proposition. After the symbols have been selected, the informal meaning of each symbol will be some atomic proposition in the field of knowledge. It is then possible to describe the logical relationships between these propositions with wffs constructed from the symbols. The set of wffs constructed for this purpose is called a *theory* of the field of knowledge, and each individual wff is called an *axiom*.

The point of the theory is to describe the relevant body of knowledge as economically as possible. If a theory successfully describes the field of knowledge, then all things known to be true in the field of knowledge will be *consequences* of the axioms of the theory, and no things known to be false in the field of knowledge will be consequences of the axioms. If all things known to be true in the field of knowledge are consequences of the theory, that theory is said to be *complete*.

As an example, consider the following very simple field of knowledge that concerns someone named David and his attitude toward logic. Everything we know about this field is contained in the following English sentences:

If David is interested in logic, then either he will sign up for Logic 101 next semester, or he is lazy.

If David has read books about logic on his own, then he is interested in logic.

David has read books about logic on his own.

David is not lazy.

From this knowledge, we can abstract the following propositions and choose symbols to represent them:

Proposition	Symbol
David is interested in logic.	D
David will sign up for Logic 101 next semester.	A
David is lazy.	B
David has read books about logic on his own.	C

That is, the proposition *David is interested in logic* is the informal meaning of the symbol D. We can now use these symbols to write axioms that describe what is known about the field of knowledge, and thereby construct a theory of the field of knowledge. Here is such a theory:

An example
theory

```
D --> A v B        (1)
C --> D            (2)
C                  (3)
~B                 (4)
```

Axiom (1) asserts that if D is *true*, then so is either A or B. Axiom (2) asserts that if C is *true*, then so is D. Axiom (3) asserts that C is *true*. Axiom (4) asserts that B is *false*.

Proof
Methods

There are techniques for propositional logic to *prove* whether or not a particular wff is a consequence of the axioms of a theory. Two methods can be used to accomplish this task, one based on the semantics (i.e. truth values) of the wffs involved, the other based on syntactic manipulation of the wffs.

Consider the example theory above. Suppose we want to find out if the following wff:

A

is a logical consequence of the axioms of the theory.

Semantic
methods of
proof

Using a simple semantic method, we examine all models of the set of axioms (a model is an interpretation under which every axiom is *true*). That is, we need to consider every possible assignment of truth values to the atomic propositions in the axioms (i.e. A, B, C, and D) that makes the axioms true. Notice that since axiom (3) asserts that C is *true*, C must be *true* under each of these interpretations. If A is *true* under all of these interpretations, then A is in fact a logical consequence of the theory.

Using an alternative semantic method, we look for a model of the set of axioms in which A is *false*. If such a model exists, then A is not a consequence of the theory.

Syntactic
methods of
proof

To use a syntactic method of proof, it is necessary to find a complete set of *inference rules*. A set of rules is complete if it enables one to derive every wff that is valid (i.e. every tautology that can be constructed from a finite number of propositional symbols). There are two generally accepted approaches to the construction of a complete set of rules.

The natural deduction approach (such as that advanced in Copi [1986]) involves many inference rules, each of which is relatively intuitive to understand. For instance, the rules of commutativity, double negation, distributivity, associativity, and *modus ponens* explained in Sec 0.3 above are all included as rules of inference. If a wff is a logical consequence of the axioms of a theory, a logician can demonstrate it to be so by application of the rules of inference to the axioms of the theory. Such a demonstration is called a *proof* of the wff. In a natural deduction system, the axioms of a theory are referred to as *premisses*, and the result of the application of a rule of inference is a *conclusion*. A proof is a series of steps; at each step, a rule of inference is applied to the premisses or to the preceding conclusions. The conclusion of the last step of the proof is the wff itself.

The axiom scheme approach (such as that advanced in Mendelson [1979] and Hamilton [1978]) uses only a single inference rule such as *modus ponens*. In addition to this rule, the system has a minimum number of *axiom schemes*, which are logically valid statement forms. An example of an axiom scheme is:

```
((~p --> ~q) --> (q --> p)
```

where p and q are propositional variables (Hamilton [1978] p. 28). Since p and q each stand for wffs, the axiom scheme stands for an infinite number of axioms that have the same syntactic form. If a wff is a logical consequence of the axioms of a theory, a clever logician can prove it by artful application of the axiom schemes and rule of inference to the axioms of the theory.

In general, the development of a complete rule set following an axiom scheme approach is more elegant than a natural deduction system because it relies on fewer rules, but a proof may be more difficult to follow for the same reason.

Algorithmic verification of a proof

An *algorithm* is a systematic way of solving a problem. An algorithm consists of 1) certain initial formulas, and 2) rules for the transformation of those formulas. The essential feature of an algorithm is that to apply it requires only the ability to recognize strings of symbols and to manipulate these strings according to a set of rules. The existence of a complete set of inference rules for propositional logic implies that there is an algorithm for checking the correctness of each step of a proof. Here, the axioms of the theory constitute the initial formulas of the algorithm, and the rules of inference constitute the transformation rules of the algorithm. A complete set of inference rules for propositional logic is referred to as *propositional calculus*. In general, a question such as: "Does this sequence of steps constitute a proof that this wff is a consequence of these axioms?" is decidable by means of an algorithm. Interestingly, the more fundamental question: "Is this wff a consequence of these axioms?" is decidable by an algorithm only in the case that the wff in question actually is a consequence of the axioms.

Metalanguage and Object Language

Logicians sometimes find it necessary to distinguish between the formal language they are studying and the language they use to discuss the formal language. The formal language itself is referred to as the *object language*, and the language used to discuss it is referred to as the *metalanguage*. The object language is so called because its statements may concern logical relationships between actual objects. The concern of the metalanguage includes the truth values of symbols used in the object language, the informal meaning of symbols used in the object language, properties of individual object language statements, properties of object language theories, and properties of the object language as a whole. In this section, propositional logic is the object language. To discuss propositional logic, we are using a subset of English as a metalanguage. Any statement about the properties of any aspect of the object language is a metalanguage statement. Here are some examples of metalanguage statements about a proposition A:

A *is true.*

A *is false.*

A v ~A *is logically valid.*

The informal meaning of A *is "It is raining today."*

A *is a logical consequence of the theory defined by axioms (1-4).*

Completeness and consistency of a theory

A theory is said to be *syntactically consistent* if it is not possible to derive a contradiction from the axioms of the theory. For instance, a theory from which it is possible to prove both p and ~p is inconsistent. A theory is said to be *complete* if every wff known to be *true* is provable by the axioms of the theory. Consistency and completeness are properties of a theory. A statement such as

The theory defined by axioms (1-4) is consistent and complete.

is a metalanguage statement.

0.5 Predicate Logic

Atomic Formulas

In propositional logic, the basic truth-valued object is an atomic proposition that cannot be subdivided into components in any way. The basic truth-valued object in predicate logic is an *atomic formula*. An atomic formula is composed of a *predicate symbol*, and *terms* that act as arguments to the predicate symbol. In general, the predicate symbol is the name of a *relation* that holds between the arguments. Because an atomic formula is itself constructed of other objects, it possesses much greater expressive power than an atomic proposition in propositional logic.

An atomic formula is written as a predicate symbol followed by some number of arguments inside parentheses. Each argument is a term. The general form of an atomic formula is:

```
P(t1, t2, ..., tn)
```

where `P` is a predicate symbol and `t1, t2, ..., tn` are terms.

"Term" defined

A term can be one of three things:

1) a constant;

2) a variable; or

3) the application of a function.

The application of a function is written as a function symbol followed by a list of arguments inside parentheses. Each argument is itself a term. The general form of the application of a function is:

```
f(t1, t2, ..., tn)
```

where `f` is a function symbol and `t1, t2, ..., tn` are terms.

The lexicon of predicate logic

In the conventional lexicon of predicate logic, the letters a, b, c are used as constant symbols, x, y, z are used as variable symbols, f, g, h are used as function symbols, and P, Q, R are used as predicate symbols. Symbols can be added to the lexicon as long as the intended use of each new symbol is explicitly stated.

Well-formed Formulas

The result of combining atomic formulas together with logical connectives is a *well-formed formula (wff)*. A well-formed formula can be defined as follows:

1) an atomic formula is a wff;

2) if A and B are wffs, then so are

Wff	Read as:
~A	*not* A
A & B	A *and* B
A v B	A *or* B
A --> B	A *implies* B
A <--> B	A *if and only if* B
∃x A	*there exists an* x *such that* A
∀x A	*for all* x, A

The meaning of the first six logical connectives is exactly as in propositional logic. The variable quantifiers ∃x and ∀x are new, however; their meaning is discussed below.

Truth Value of a Wff

As in propositional logic, the truth value of a wff of predicate logic depends on an interpretation. Because atomic formulas have terms, however, the interpretation of a wff of predicate logic is considerably more complex than the interpretation of a wff of propositional logic. An interpretation of the wff can only be made with respect to a particular *domain of interpretation*, which is the set of all possible values of terms that occur in the wff. The usual approach to explaining how an interpretation gives meaning to a wff is to start from the syntax of the wff, and work backward into the possible meanings of the wff (Figure 0-1). This approach emphasizes the independence of the formal system of predicate logic (and the wff itself) from any particular interpretation. Since, ultimately, we want to apply the techniques of predicate logic to some field of knowledge, we choose instead to explain how an interpretation gives meaning to a wff by starting from the meaning (i.e. knowledge about the field), and working forward to the possible wffs that could express that meaning.

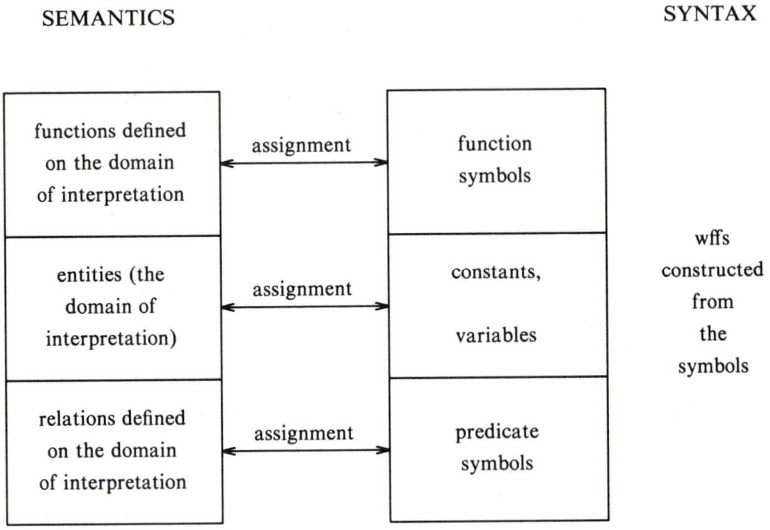

SEMANTICS   SYNTAX

Figure 0-1

Constructing a Theory of a Field of Knowledge

Applying predicate logic to a particular field of knowledge is similar to applying propositional logic, in that we begin by analyzing the *structure* of that field, then choose symbols to represent aspects of that structure, and finally write wffs using those symbols to describe the structure. As in propositional logic, the set of wffs that describe a field of knowledge is a theory of the field, and each individual wff is an axiom.

Analysis of the field

The analysis of the field of knowledge proceeds as follows. The first task is to isolate the set of significant entities in the field; this set is called the domain of interpretation. If the field is arithmetic, the domain of interpretation might be the natural numbers. The next task is to find what functions on members of the domain of interpretation are important, if any, and then to identify significant relations that hold between members of the domain of interpretation. The final task is to define the significant relations syntactically—that is, by means of axioms.

"Function"
defined

It will be useful at this point to state precisely what is meant by *function* and *relation*. A function is a mapping from *n* members of the domain of interpretation (where *n* is the number of arguments that the function takes) onto one member of the domain of interpretation. For instance, suppose that the field of knowledge we are concerned with is arithmetic, and the domain of interpretation is the set of natural numbers. "Times" is an important function in this field. The "times" function takes two arguments, and so is a mapping from two natural numbers onto one natural number. Consider a particular application of this function that maps the numbers "2" and "3" onto the number "6." The number "6" is the called the *value* of this application of the "times" function.

As another example, suppose that the field of knowledge is the relationships between someone named "Bob" and several of the people he talked to at a family reunion. The domain of interpretation is the set of people:

{Bob, Bob's cousin George, Bob's cousin Mick, Mick's girlfriend Nancy}

"Girlfriend of" is an important function in this field. The "girlfriend of" function takes one argument, and so is a mapping from one person to another person. A particular application of this function maps "Mick" onto "Nancy." "Mick" is the argument, and "Nancy" is the value of this application of the function.

"Relation"
defined

A relation is a mapping from *n* members of the domain of interpretation (where *n* is the number of arguments that the relation takes) onto a truth value (that is, onto a member of the set {*true, false*}). Suppose that the field of knowledge is arithmetic, and the domain of interpretation is the set of natural numbers. "Is greater than" is an important relation in this field. The "is greater than" relation takes two arguments, and so is a mapping from two natural numbers onto a truth value. Consider a particular instance of this relation that maps the numbers "2" and "3" onto *false*. *false* is the value of this instance of the "is greater than" relation. Another instance of the relation maps "3" and "2" onto *true*.

As another example, suppose that the field of knowledge is the relationships between the people at the reunion described above. "Is the cousin of" is an important relation in this field. The "is the cousin of" relation takes two arguments, and so is a mapping from two people onto a truth value. A particular instance of this relation maps "Bob" and "George" onto *true*. Another instance of the relation maps "George" and "Nancy" onto *false*. If the value of a particular instance of a relation is *true*, it is said that the relation *holds* between its arguments.

Representing entities and relations

Once we know the domain of interpretation for the field of knowledge being described, the next step is to choose symbols to represent members of that domain, and symbols to represent functions and relations defined on members of that domain. First, we choose a set of constant symbols such as a, b, c, etc. and assign a member of the domain to be the value of each constant symbol. Then we choose function symbols such as f or g for each important function. Note that a function symbol by itself cannot have a value; only the application of a function can have a value. The function represented by a function symbol is semantically defined by specifying the values of various applications of the function (that is, specifying instances of how the function maps n members of the domain, where n is its number of arguments, onto one member of the domain). Finally we choose predicate symbols such as P or Q for each important relation in the field. A predicate symbol by itself cannot have a value; an instance of the relation represented by a predicate symbol has a truth value. The relation represented by a predicate symbol is semantically defined by specifying the truth values of various instances of the relation (that is, specifying exactly how the relation maps n members of the domain, where n is its number of arguments, onto a truth value). An instance of a relation is represented by an atomic formula constructed from the chosen predicate, function, and constant symbols.

A concrete example of choosing symbols and defining functions and relations in this way will illustrate the concepts involved. The field of knowledge is the reunion, and the domain of interpretation is the set of people specified above. First we assign a member of the domain to be the value of several constant symbols:

The value of	a	is	Bob's cousin George
The value of	b	is	Bob
The value of	c	is	Bob's cousin Mick

We choose the symbol `f` for the function "girlfriend of," with one argument. This function is semantically defined by specifying that:

The value of	`f(c)`	is	Nancy

We choose the symbol `P` for the relation "is the cousin of," with two arguments. This relation is semantically defined by specifying that

The value of	`P(a, b)`	is	*true*
The value of	`P(b, a)`	is	*true*
The value of	`P(c, b)`	is	*true*
The value of	`P(b, c)`	is	*true*
The value of	`P(a, c)`	is	*false*
The value of	`P(c, a)`	is	*false*
The value of	`P(a, f(c))`	is	*false*
The value of	`P(f(c), a)`	is	*false*
The value of	`P(b, f(c))`	is	*false*
The value of	`P(f(c), b)`	is	*false*
The value of	`P(c, f(c))`	is	*false*
The value of	`P(f(c), c)`	is	*false*

Notice that each instance of the relation "is the cousin of" is represented by an atomic formula with a definite truth value. Wffs such as the following can be constructed from these atomic formulas:

```
P(a, b) & ~P(b, f(c))
```

The meaning of this wff is: *George is the cousin of Bob, and Bob is not the cousin of Nancy.* Since both atomic formulas that occur in this wff are *true*, the wff itself is also *true*. This wff could become an axiom in a theory of this field of knowledge. In constructing such a theory, we would try to find an economical set of axioms (i.e. wffs that are *true*) from which everything we know about the field follows as a consequence.

By going through this elaborate exercise of choosing symbols, defining functions and relations, etc., we have defined an interpretation under which the wff:

```
P(a, b) & ~P(b, f(c))
```

is *true*. It is now easy to state precisely what an interpretation of a wff is. An interpretation consists of four types of assignment:

1) Every constant in the wff is assigned to an element of the domain (i.e. the value of b is "Bob").

2) Every variable in the wff is assigned to an element of the domain (this is discussed in detail below).

3) Every application of a function in the wff is assigned to an element of the domain (i.e. the value of f(c) is "Nancy"). The set of such assignments for a particular function semantically defines that function.

4) Every atomic formula in the wff is assigned a truth value (i.e. the value of P(a, b) is *true*). The set of such assignments for a particular relation semantically defines that relation.

Since a theory is made up of a set of wffs, the interpretation of a theory consists of the same four types of assignment. It is important to bear in mind that within the bounds of a single domain of interpretation, there may be many possible interpretations of a particular wff. That is, the value of b might be "Bob" under one interpretation, "George" under another interpretation, etc. It should be clear from the discussion that the interpretation of a wff of predicate logic is considerably more complicated than the interpretation of a wff of propositional logic.

Variables as Terms

When a variable appears as a term in an atomic formula, it indicates that more than one member of the domain of interpretation might fill that spot. For instance, in the wff:

```
P(x, b)                (*)
```

the value of the variable x is some member of the domain of interpretation. In its present form, this wff cannot be assigned a truth value, because it is not clear how many values the variable x may have. The variable x is said to be *unquantified*.

Quantification
of a variable

If a variable occurs in a wff, it must be explicitly *quantified* before the wff can be assigned a truth value. There are two possible quantifications for a variable: *Existential quantification* indicates that there must exist at least one member of the domain of interpretation which, when substituted for the variable in the wff, will make the wff true. *Universal quantification* indicates that the wff will be true if any member of the domain of interpretation is substituted for the variable in the wff. Variable quantifiers are usually placed in front of a wff containing a variable, and the wff is referred to as the *scope* of the quantifier. The quantifier symbols in Table 0-12 are used:

Variable Quantification Symbols		
Symbol	**Quantification**	**Meaning**
∃x	existential	there exists one x
∀x	universal	for all x

Table 0-12

An existentially quantified version of wff (*) is:

    ∃x P(x, b)

This new wff *can* be assigned a truth value. Under the interpretation given above, it indicates that "there exists somebody who is Bob's cousin," which is *true* because both George and Mick are Bob's cousins.

A universally quantified version of wff (*) is:

    ∀x P(x, b)

This wff can also be assigned a truth value. Under the interpretation, it indicates that "for all x, x is Bob's cousin," or "every person is Bob's cousin," which is *false* because the value of **x** might be either Bob or Nancy.

Semantic
Properties of
Formulas

An interpretation of a wff that makes the wff true is called a *model* of the wff. Such an interpretation is said to *satisfy* the wff. Similarly, an interpretation of a theory in which all axioms are true is a model of the theory. As was just demonstrated, the example interpretation above is a model of the wff:

```
∃x P(x, b)
```

A wff or theory that is *true* under at least one interpretation is described as *satisfiable*; a wff or theory that is *false* under all interpretations is described as *unsatisfiable* or *inconsistent*. An example of an unsatisfiable wff is:

```
∃x P(x, b) & ~P(x, b)
```

A wff that is true under all possible interpretations is described as *valid*. An example of a valid wff is:

```
∃x P(x, b) v ~P(x, b)
```

A wff is a *consequence* of a theory if the wff is *true* in all models of the theory.

Semantic Properties of a Formula	
A wff is	**If it is**
valid	*true* under all interpretations
a consequence of a theory	*true* in all models of the theory
satisfiable	*true* under at least one interpretation
unsatisfiable	*true* under no interpretation

Table 0-13

Proof Methods

There are techniques for predicate logic to prove whether or not a particular wff is a consequence of the axioms of a theory. As in propositional logic, there are two methods of proof: one is based on the semantics of the wff and the axioms involved, and the other is based on syntactic manipulation of the axioms.

A simple method of semantic proof in propositional logic is to examine all models of the set of axioms; if the wff in question is *true* in each of these models, then the wff is a consequence of the theory. The equivalent method in predicate logic requires examining all models of the set of axioms in all possible domains of interpretation.

But since there are an infinite number of possible domains of interpretation, the task of examining all of them is impossible. Therefore, this method of proof is not tractable for predicate logic.

The alternative semantic approach involves looking for a model of the set of axioms in some domain of interpretation under which the wff in question is *false*. If such an interpretation exists, then the wff is not a consequence of the theory. Unfortunately, just because one is unable to find such an interpretation does not mean that the wff in question is a consequence of the theory.

To use a syntactic method of proof, it is necessary to find a complete set of inference rules. In Sec. 0.4 on propositional logic, two approaches to construction of a complete set of rules were mentioned: the natural deduction approach, and the axiom scheme approach. In order to make the natural deduction approach complete for predicate logic, additional inference rules need to be added to deal with wffs that include variable quantifiers (see Copi [1986]). In order to make the axiom scheme approach complete for predicate logic, additional axioms need to be added to deal with variable quantifiers (see Mendelson [1979] or Hamilton [1978]). A complete set of inference rules for predicate logic is referred to as *predicate calculus*.

Axiomatic Definition of a Relation

In the family reunion example above, we painstakingly built a semantic definition of the relation "is the cousin of" by assigning a truth value to every instance of the relation with respect to the domain of interpretation. As part of constructing a theory about a field of knowledge, we would like to be able to define a predicate by means of axioms—that is, syntactically. Such a definition is called an *axiomatization* or *axiomatic definition*. If the axiomatic definition of a relation is successful, then every instance of the relation that we regard as true with respect to the intended interpretation should be derivable as a consequence of the axioms by means of a syntactic method of proof. To make this point another way, the semantic definition of a relation should be derivable from its axiomatic definition by application of the rules of inference.

Example: the natural numbers

In the following example, the field of knowledge is arithmetic, and the domain of interpretation is limited to the natural numbers (i.e. positive integers including zero). (This discussion is not intended to be a thorough treatment of natural number theory; see Behnke et al. [1983] pp. 71-80.) Notice that, unlike the family reunion example, the domain of interpretation in this example is *infinite*. To be able to construct a theory about this field, it is necessary to to able to represent any natural number as a term. This is accomplished by introducing the constant symbol a and assigning it a value from the domain of interpretation:

The value of   a   is   0

and then by introducing the function "successor of," with one argument, that will be represented by the symbol s. The value of an application of this function is always its argument plus one. Thus:

The value of   s(a)   is   1
The value of   s(s(a))   is   2
The value of   s(s(s(a)))   is   3
          etc.

Recursive definition of a relation

Now consider the relation "is a natural number" with one argument, that will be represented by the symbol N. (Note: a relation that has only one argument is also called a *property*.) This relation can be defined by the following axioms:

```
N(a)                    (1)
∀x N(x) -> N(s(x))      (2)
```

Axiom (1) states that a is a natural number. Axiom (2) states that for every natural number x, the successor of x is also a natural number.

Using these axioms together with a complete set of rules of inference for predicate logic, it is possible to prove syntactically that the relation denoted by N holds for any term constructible from the constant symbol a and the function symbol s. The definition of N is said to be *recursive*, because, in axiom (2), whether one instance of the relation holds (i.e. that represented by N(s(x))) depends on whether another instance of the relation holds (i.e. that represented by N(x)). (Recursion is discussed in more detail in Sec. 1.6.)

Recursive enumerability

Axioms (1) and (2) provide a *constructive definition* of the set of natural numbers, in that any natural number can be constructed by repeated application of the inference rules to the axioms. The combination of a complete set of inference rules and the two axioms describes a *recursive algorithm*: it is an algorithm because it is composed of initial formulas and rules for transforming those formulas, and it is recursive because the axioms themselves are recursive. The set of natural numbers is said to be *recursively enumerable*, because it can be generated by a recursive algorithm. More generally, a set of terms (natural numbers or otherwise) that possess a certain property is recursively enumerable if the set can be generated by a recursive algorithm.

"Is greater than"

Another interesting relation in the field of arithmetic that can be defined axiomatically is "is greater than." This relation has two arguments, and will be represented by the symbol GT. "Is greater than" can be defined semantically as follows:

The value of	`GT(s(a), a)`	is	*true*
The value of	`GT(s(s(a)), a)`	is	*true*
etc.			
The value of	`GT(s(s(a)), s(a))`	is	*true*
The value of	`GT(s(s(s(a))), s(a))`	is	*true*
etc.			
The value of	`GT(a, a)`	is	*false*
The value of	`GT(a, s(a))`	is	*false*
The value of	`GT(s(a), s(a))`	is	*false*
etc.			

Here is an axiomatic definition of the relation that captures the sense of the semantic definition:

$$\forall x \ GT(s(x), x) \qquad\qquad (1)$$
$$\forall x \ \forall y \ GT(x, y) \rightarrow GT(s(x), y) \qquad\qquad (2)$$
$$\forall x \ {\sim}GT(x, s(x)) \qquad\qquad (3)$$
$$\forall x \ \forall y \ {\sim}GT(x, y) \rightarrow {\sim}GT(x, s(y)) \qquad\qquad (4)$$

Axiom (1) states that for every natural number x, the successor of x is greater than x. Axiom (2) states that for every number x and every number y, if x is greater than y, then the successor of x is also greater than y. Axiom (3) states that for every number x, x is not greater than the successor of x. Axiom (4) states that for every number x and every number y, if x is not greater than y, then the successor of x is not greater than y.

Using these axioms, it is possible to prove syntactically whether a specific instance of the "is greater than" relation is *true* or *false*. The definition is recursive, because, in axiom (2), whether one instance of the relation holds (i.e. that represented by `GT(s(x), y)`) depends on whether another instance of the relation holds (i.e. that represented by `GT(x, y)`).

Decidability of Properties

Mathematicians investigating the properties of numbers at the beginning of this century embraced the axiomatic method of defining the properties of numbers as a way of eliminating reliance on intuition. As a side effect of adopting the axiomatic method, however, they brought a more fundamental issue to the surface: there are certain properties of numbers that are, at the same time, 1) known to be true, and 2) undecidable (i.e. not provable from a finite set of axioms using a complete set of rules of inference).

Recursive decidability

Concern with the decidability of properties has produced the following results: A relation or property defined on an infinite domain of interpretation such as the natural numbers is *representable* in a first order theory only if it is recursive. A relation or property is *decidable* if there is a recursively enumerable set of terms possessing the property—that is, a set that can be generated by a recursive algorithm in a finite number of steps. Remember that a theory is said to be *complete* if everything known to be true about the field of knowledge it describes follows as a consequence from the axioms of the theory. Because there are properties of numbers that are both true and undecidable, no axiomatic theory of arithmetic can be complete.

Recursive computability

The nature of recursive decidability suggests the feasibility of a mechanical procedure—to be executed by either a human or a computer—capable of proving that a given wff is a consequence of a set of axioms, if in fact the wff is a consequence of the axioms. Should such a procedure exist, then the recursive decidability of a question such as: "Is this wff a consequence of these axioms?" is the same as its *recursive computability* by the procedure. Turing and others worked on the practical aspects of recursive computability. The "Turing machine" is an abstract system that provides a computational characterization of any recursive algorithm. Similarly, a logic programming language such as Prolog provides a computational characterization of whether a wff is a consequence of the axioms of a theory.

0.6 From Symbolic Logic to Logic Programming

Mechanization
of Proof
Procedures

After discovering the computability of logical consequence in an abstract sense, it is a natural step to want to mechanize the proof process on a computer. But as Robinson points out,

> "The problem of actually computing with a procedure whose original purpose had been only to supply an 'existence' proof...turned out to be disheartening"

(Robinson [1979] p. 292). Full predicate logic is a very expressive language. To implement the proof procedures of predicate calculus on a computer in a general way is combinatorially explosive. Researchers in the late fifties and early sixties began to look for computationally feasible ways of implementing proof procedures that would retain as much of the expressiveness of first order predicate logic as possible. They began to dream of the same type of general-purpose problem solving machine as Leibniz, but now in a practical way.

In the late fifties, Gilmore, Davis and Putnam, and Pravitz all began to work on the mechanization of a refutation proof technique developed by Herbrand in the thirties (see Siekmann and Wrightson [1983]). Building on Pravitz' work, Robinson came up with *resolution*, an inference rule appropriate for machine inference (Robinson [1965]). Early attempts at designing a problem solving algorithm based on resolution worked only for very small problems. Loveland, Kowalski, and Kuehner refined such algorithms with the techniques of *model elimination* (Loveland [1968]) and the *selection function* (Kowalski and Kuehner [1971]). In the early seventies, Colmerauer and Roussel brought this work together into a language based on resolution that they called PROLOG (for PROgramming in LOGic) (Roussel [1975]).

The following sections describe Herbrand interpretations, the clausal form of logic, and resolution. They show how logic programming evolved out of first order predicate calculus, and explain its refutation proof procedure.

Refutation
Procedures

From the definitions of validity and inconsistency in Sec. 0.5 above, it follows that a wff is *valid* with respect to a theory if and only if adding the negation of the wff to the theory makes the theory *inconsistent*. Semantically, a theory is inconsistent if there is no interpretation that satisfies all of the axioms of the theory. Syntactically, a theory is inconsistent if it is possible to derive a contradiction such as:

    A & ~A

from the theory. A *refutation procedure* is a special kind of proof procedure that takes advantage of this relationship between validity and inconsistency. The method of a refutation procedure is as follows: to prove that a wff is a consequence of the axioms of a theory, show that is is possible to derive a contradiction when the negation of the wff is added to the theory.

To provide a semantic explanation of a refutation proof procedure, we rely on a special domain of interpretation called the *Herbrand universe*. The Herbrand universe has the following property: a wff is a consequence of the axioms of a theory if there is no interpretation *of the Herbrand universe* in which the negation of the wff and the axioms of the theory are all *true*. Thus, to understand (semantically) why a wff is a consequence of a theory, we need only consider all interpretations of the Herbrand universe.

The Herbrand universe

The Herbrand universe of a theory is defined in terms of the symbols that occur in the theory. A *ground term* is either 1) a constant symbol or 2) the application of a function all of whose arguments are ground terms. The Herbrand universe of a theory consists of all ground terms constructible from the symbols that occur in the theory.

As an example, consider a first order theory constructed only from the following symbols: the constant symbols a, b, and c; the variable symbols x, y, and z; the predicate symbols P (with one argument) and Q (with two arguments); and no function symbols. Since there are no function symbols, the *Herbrand universe* of this theory consists of just the three constant symbols

    a   b   c

The Herbrand base

A *ground atomic formula* is an atomic formula containing no variables as arguments; that is, all arguments are ground terms. For instance, in the example theory, Q(a, b) is a ground atomic formula, whereas Q(x, b) is not. The *Herbrand base* of a theory is the set of all ground atomic formulas constructible from the symbols that occur in the theory. The Herbrand base of the example theory can be completely specified as:

```
P(a)        P(b)        P(c)
Q(a,a)      Q(a,b)      Q(a,c)
Q(b,a)      Q(b,b)      Q(b,c)
Q(c,a)      Q(c,b)      Q(c,c)
```

*Herbrand
interpretations*

The Herbrand universe is the domain of interpretation of a *Herbrand interpretation*. In a Herbrand interpretation of a theory, the value of each ground term is itself. In other words:

The value of   a   is   a
The value of   b   is   b
    etc.

In any particular Herbrand interpretation, each ground atomic formula in the Herbrand base denotes either *true* or *false*. There are only as many Herbrand interpretations of a given theory as there are possible assignments of truth values to the atomic formulas of its Herbrand base.

Here is one Herbrand interpretation of the Herbrand base specified above:

The value of   P(a)   is   *true*
The value of   P(b)   is   *true*
The value of   P(c)   is   *true*
The value of   Q(a,a)   is   *false*
The value of   Q(a,b)   is   *true*
The value of   Q(a,c)   is   *false*
The value of   Q(b,a)   is   *false*
The value of   Q(b,b)   is   *false*
The value of   Q(b,c)   is   *true*
The value of   Q(c,a)   is   *false*
The value of   Q(c,b)   is   *false*
The value of   Q(c,c)   is   *false*

Because there are twelve formulas in the Herbrand base, there are 2^{12} (4096) possible Herbrand interpretations.

A *Herbrand model* of a theory is a Herbrand interpretation under which each axiom of the theory is *true*.

Usefulness of
Herbrand
interpretations

Herbrand interpretations are useful because of the following property: On the level of the truth values of atomic propositions that occur in a particular theory, there is always a Herbrand interpretation corresponding to any conceivable non-Herbrand interpretation. (This property does not hold on the level of the values of terms that occur in a theory. In a non-Herbrand interpretation, the value of a constant symbol such as b will be some member of the domain of interpretation such as "Bob." In a Herbrand interpretation, the value a constant symbol such as b will always be itself.) This property of Herbrand interpretations enables the following leap of faith: If a wff is *true* under all Herbrand models of a theory, then it will be true under all models of the theory in all possible domains of interpretation, and is therefore a consequence of the theory.

Therefore, in semantic terms, we can imagine the refutation procedure proceeding as follows:

To find out if a wff is a consequence of a theory, negate the wff.

Try to discover a Herbrand model of the theory under which the negated wff is true.

If such a model exists, then the wff cannot be a consequence of the theory.

If such a model does not exist, then the wff is a consequence of the theory.

Clausal Form

The *clausal form* of predicate logic is a way of writing formulas that uses only the connectives &, v, and ˜. A *literal* is either a positive or a negative atomic formula. Each *clause* is a set of literals connected by v. Negative literals are placed at the end of the clause, and positive literals are placed at the beginning. A schematic view of a clause is

```
P1 v P2 v ... Pn v N1 v N2 v ... Nn
```

where P1...Pn are positive literals and N1...Nn are negative literals.

A clause can be understood as a generalization of the definition of implication (see Sec. 0.3). If A and B are both atomic formulas, then

```
A --> B
```

can also be written as

```
~A v B
```

Since ˜A is negative and B is positive, in clausal form this would be

```
B v ~A
```

Alternative
conclusions
and necessary
conditions

All positive atomic formulas in a clause are alternative conclusions, and all negative atomic formulas are necessary conditions. For instance, if C, D, E, and F are atomic formulas, then the clause

```
C v D v ~E v ~F
```

states that either C or D is true if E and F are both true. (To follow this reading of the conditions, it may be useful to review De Morgan's rules, which state that ˜E v ˜F is equivalent to ˜(E & F).)

The simplest clause has only one literal, either positive or negative. If a, b, and c are constants and Q is a predicate with two arguments, then

```
Q(a, b)
```

is a clause asserting that Q(a, b) is unconditionally true, and

```
~Q(b, c)
```

is a clause asserting that Q(b, c) is unconditionally false. A theory is expressed as a set of clauses, implicitly connected to one another by &.

Backward
arrow notation

Clauses can be written with a backward implication arrow between the positive and negative literals, and with commas connecting literals on both sides of the arrow. The backward arrow is read as "is implied by." Thus,

```
C, D <-- E, F
```

means the same as

```
C v D v ~E v ~F
```

Horn clauses

A *Horn clause* is a clause containing only one positive literal. The previous example is not a Horn clause because it has two positive literals, but the following clause is:

```
C v ~E v ~F v ~G
```

or in the arrow notation:

```
C <-- E, F, G
```

Resolution

Robinson came to the conclusion that an inference rule for the mechanization of proofs by computers need not be the same as inference rules used by human logicians. He found that inference rules such as *modus ponens* are deliberately weak, in order that each step of the proof procedure can be followed intuitively by a human being. He discovered a stronger inference rule, called *resolution*, that is difficult for humans to follow but efficient for machines. (The resolution rule is similar to the disjunctive syllogism rule; see Table 0-2.)

What makes the resolution rule useful for computation is that, by itself, it is a complete set of inference rules for the clausal form of predicate logic. In other words, using the resolution rule alone, it is possible to derive every consequence of a set of axioms expressed in clausal form.

The resolution rule

Resolution works as follows: two clauses can be resolved with one another if one of them contains a positive literal and the other contains a corresponding negative literal with the same predicate symbol and same number of arguments, and if the arguments of both literals can be *unified* (matched) with one another. Consider a theory composed of the following two clauses:

```
P(a) v ~Q(b, c)          (1)
Q(b, c) v ~R(b, c)       (2)
```

Since clause (1) contains the negative literal ~Q(b, c), and clause (2) contains a corresponding positive literal Q(b, c), and since the arguments of the two literals can be *unified* (that is, b unifies with b and c unifies with c), then clause (1) can be resolved with clause (2). The result of this resolution is clause (3) below. It is called the *resolvent*, and becomes a new clause in the theory:

```
P(a) v ~R(b, c)              (3)
```

After this resolution has been made, any of clauses (1), (2) or (3) can be used in future resolutions.

Clauses (4) and (5) below are not resolvable with one another because arguments to the Q literals do not unify:

```
P(a) v ~Q(b, c)              (4)
Q(c, c) v ~R(b, c)           (5)
```

Unification of variables

There are no explicit variable quantifications in clausal form. Implicitly, however, all variables are universally quantified. Thus, a clause such as:

```
Q(x, y) v ~R(x, y)
```

implies the quantifiers:

```
∀x ∀y ( Q(x, y) v ~R(x, y) )
```

When a variable occurs as an argument, it is unifiable with any constant. If a variable occurs more than once in a single clause, and the variable is unified with a constant as result of resolution, then the resolvent will contain the constant at each place that the variable appeared in the original clause. For instance, clauses (6) and (7) below,

```
P(a) v ~Q(a, b)              (6)
Q(x, y) v ~R(x, y)           (7)
```

are resolvable because the arguments to the Q literal unify. That is, the variable x unifies with the constant a and the variable y unifies with the constant b. Notice that in clause (8), the resolvent:

```
P(a) v ~R(a, b)              (8)
```

the variables in the R formula of clause (7) are replaced by constants.

The empty
clause

Consider the following two clauses:

```
P(a)                        (9)
~P(a)                       (10)
```

Clause (9) is a conclusion with no conditions, and clause (10) is a condition with no conclusion. The presence of clauses (9) and (10) in a theory is a *contradiction*. When clauses (9) and (10) resolve with one another, the resolvent is said to be the *empty clause*. If the result of the resolution of two clauses in a theory is the empty clause, then that theory must be inconsistent. In semantic terms, the ability to derive the empty clause means that there can be no Herbrand model of the theory.

An algorithm
based on
resolution

The basic problem is to prove whether a clause is or is not a consequence of a theory. Use of a refutation procedure (see above) as the basic method of proof simplifies this problem to that of discovering whether a theory is consistent or inconsistent. To be able to automate the discovery process, we would like to find an efficient algorithm based on the resolution rule that can detect the inconsistency of a set of clauses.

Suppose there is a theory expressed in clausal form. All of the clauses of this theory are consistent with one another except for one. The presence of this problem clause makes the theory as a whole inconsistent. Imagine some active agent (either human or machine) that randomly applies the resolution rule to the clauses of the theory. Each time resolution is applied, the resolvent is added to the theory. If the empty clause is generated, it means that the theory is inconsistent, and the active agent will stop. Because this theory is in fact inconsistent, the active agent may generate the empty clause, sooner or later, and thereby detect the inconsistency of the theory. But many of its resolutions will be either 1) redundant, or 2) irrelevant to the problem clause. To make an effective algorithm for detecting the inconsistency of a theory, it is necessary to constrain this process and keep it focused on areas most likely to yield an empty clause.

There is more than one *problem solving strategy* that can be pursued using the resolution rule. In the rest of this section, we examine a *top-down* (or *backward*) *strategy*. The strategy aims to detect whether a single clause, C, is a consequence of an existing set of clauses, *T*. The set of clauses *T* is assumed to be consistent. The algorithm works as follows. To begin with, the negation of the clause being tested, ~C, is added to the existing set of clauses, to form a new set of clauses, T' (i.e. T' consists of T plus $\sim$C). If the algorithm can derive the empty clause from T', then T' is inconsistent because of the presence of $\sim$C, and C must therefore be a consequence of T. An example will illustrate this process.

Example of top-down resolution

Suppose that the existing set of clauses is:

```
P(a) v ~Q(a, b)              (6)
Q(x, y) v ~R(x, y)           (7)
S(b)                         (11)
R(a, b)                      (12)
```

and that it is necessary to find out if

```
P(a)                         (13)
```

is a consequence of the existing set of clauses. The first step is to add the negation of P(a) to the rest of the clauses, to produce:

```
P(a) v ~Q(a, b)              (6)
Q(x, y) v ~R(x, y)           (7)
S(b)                         (11)
R(a, b)                      (12)
~P(a)                        (14)
```

The following two rules keep the resolution algorithm focused on the consequences of adding clause (14) to the existing set:

1) the first resolution to take place should involve the negated clause just added (i.e. clause (14)); and

2) each subsequent resolution should involve the resolvent of the last resolution (this prevents the algorithm from wandering aimlessly).

According to rule 1), the first resolution must involve clause (14). It resolves with clause (6) to produce

```
~Q(a, b)                     (15)
```

By rule 2), clause (15) must be used in the next resolution. Clause (15) resolves with clause (7) to produce

```
˜R(a, b)                              ( 16 )
```

(Notice that the variables in the original R formula were replaced by constants in clause (16).) Clause (16) resolves with clause (12) to produce the empty clause, which means that a contradiction has been detected. Since adding ˜P(a) to the existing set of clauses results in a contradiction, it follows that P(a) is a consequence of those clauses.

The problem solving strategy

The problem solving strategy just described can be characterized by the following properties: it is *top-down* because it starts with the negation of the conclusion (i.e. ˜P(a)), and works its way through the clauses of the theory until it can derive the empty clause. It is *depth first*, because the product of the last resolution is always used in the next resolution.

0.7 Development of Prolog

Development of Prolog

During the seventies, Prolog evolved from an esoteric European experiment to a robust language with a worldwide user base. There are two important aspects of the growth of the language during this period: 1) contributions to logic programming theory provided the conceptual apparatus necessary to use the language effectively; and 2) the development of improved implementation strategies provided efficient versions of the language.

Theory

Kowalski's work is vital to the development of logic programming theory. He first suggested how a logic language could be used as a programming language in Kowalski [1974]. With van Emden, he suggested two alternative ways to read logic programming code: *procedural* and *declarative* (van Emden and Kowalski [1976]; discussed in Sec. 0.8 below). He has expanded considerably on this theme since then, particularly in Kowalski [1979a]. His ideas have shaped much of the direction of logic programming research in the last several years. Other important contributors to logic programming theory include Apt (Apt and van Emden [1982]), Clark (Clark [1977]), and Bowen (Bowen and Kowalski [1982]).

Highlights of the Evolution of Prolog	
1879	Frege publishes "Begriffsschift"
1965	J.A. Robinson, "A Machine-Oriented Logic Based on the Resolution Principle"
1968	Loveland, "Mechanical Theorem Proving by Model Elimination"
1971	Kowalski and Kuehner, "Linear Selection with Resolution Function"
1973	Colmerauer at Marseilles writes first Prolog in Fortran (Roussel [1975])
1974	Kowalski, "Predicate Logic as a Programming Language"
1977	Warren and Pereira's DEC-10 Prolog interpreter/compiler, University of Edinburgh
1980	Micro-Prolog for PC's from Imperial College (Clark and McCabe [1985])
1981	Fifth generation project announced by ICOT in Japan, based on logic programming technology (Moto-oka et. al. [1981])

Table 0-14

Implementation   Colmerauer and Roussel's original version of Prolog was written in Fortran and ran extremely slowly. In 1977, Warren and Pereira completed their Prolog interpreter/compiler for the DEC-10 computer, and showed that Prolog can be as efficient as Lisp for large scale problem solving (Warren and Pereira [1977]). The algorithm used to implement DEC-10 Prolog is now known as a "Warren machine," and has served as a model for many of the subsequent implementations of Prolog (Tick and Warren [1984]). In 1980, Clark and McCabe completed a version of Prolog for micro computers that has since been used as a first programming language in junior high schools in the UK (Clark and McCabe [1985], Ennals [1984]).

Pereira wrote a Prolog interpreter in C for UNIX systems, and there are now several other UNIX Prologs (Pereira [1985]). Kahn and others have implemented a version of Prolog for Lisp machines (Kahn [1982]). Various commercial versions of the language are discussed in detail in Appendix IV.

ICOT

In 1981, the Japanese Ministry of International Trade and Industry (MITI) announced the creation of a special laboratory (the Institute for New Generation Computing Technology, or ICOT) to pursue the development of what they called *fifth generation* computing technology (Moto-oka et al. [1981]). To the surprise of many people in the American AI community, logic programming was chosen as the fundamental software technology of the fifth generation project. One aim of this project is the production of *knowledge information processing systems*. These are to be knowledge based systems capable of communicating with users in natural language or graphics, and able to assist users in a number of high level domains involving expertise. The net effect of such systems will be to put vast computational resources at the disposal of a wide segment of society, and to increase productivity in traditionally low productivity areas of industry.

*Logical
inferences per
second*

On the hardware side, the fifth generation project is responsible for the notion of LIPS (*logical inferences per second*) as a way of measuring the speed of a version of Prolog. One of ICOT's goals is to produce logic programming machines that run in the range of 1000-10000K LIPS. There is still a considerable gap between this goal and current versions of Prolog, as the following figures indicate. The original DEC-10 Prolog compiler can produce code that runs at 10K LIPS. Improvements to this compiler and faster hardware (a DEC-2060) bring this speed up to 35-40K LIPS. For the sake of comparison, interpreted micro-PROLOG runs at about 200 LIPS on a Z-80 machine, and interpreted C-Prolog runs at 1.5K LIPS on a Vax 11/780. ICOT's *Personal Sequential Inference Machine*, a computer with a special processor architecture optimized for Prolog, runs at 20-30K LIPS. Warren's latest Prolog compiler (Quintus Prolog) produces code that runs at 50K LIPS on a microprocessor-based workstation (Shapiro [1984]). At this point, there are rumored to be research machines in both the United States and Japan that run faster than 600K LIPS.

*Other
languages*

Logic programming does not begin and end with current versions of Prolog, however. Other logic programming languages have been invented, such as DUC (McDermott [1981]), ESP (Chikayama

[1983]), and HCPRVR (Simmons [1984]), as well as logic programming based shells such as APES (Hammond and Sergot [1984]). Currently there are several efforts underway to design a logic programming language capable of taking advantage of parallel machine architecture, including Parlog (Clark and Gregory [1985]), Concurrent Prolog (Shapiro [1983b]), and ICOT's KL1.

Features of Prolog

The Prolog language is a combination of powerful ideas, including:

1) the use of Horn clauses to represent knowledge;

2) descriptive style programming;

3) both declarative and procedural semantics; and

4) the ability to intersperse metalevel code with object level code.

These ideas are introduced in the rest of this chapter, and considered in a practical way in later chapters of the book.

0.8 Prolog Syntax

Before proceeding much further, it will be useful to examine how the Horn clause form of logic is written in Prolog. The examples below are deliberately trivial, but serve to demonstrate the principal ingredients of a Prolog program.

In a Horn clause, one conclusion is followed by zero or more conditions, which is written in Prolog as follows:

```
conclusion :-
    condition1,
    condition2, ...
    conditionN.
```

:- is read as "if," and , is read as "and," so the whole clause can be read:

The conclusion is true if
condition1 and condition2 and ... conditionN
are all true.

The principal component of a Prolog interpreter is a general-purpose problem solving mechanism based on the resolution rule. To utilize this mechanism, a programmer must describe a problem accurately in Prolog-style Horn clauses. Each clause asserts a relationship between terms, where a term is a symbol representing some entity in the world. By writing a query, a programmer can use the problem solving mechanism to find out if a particular atomic formula is a consequence of the currently asserted clauses.

An Example Prolog Program

The simplest Horn clause is the assertion of a fact, consisting of a conclusion followed by *no* conditions, for instance:

```
hacker(john).
```

which can be read:

> *John is a hacker.*

A *rule* is another form of Horn clause that shows the dependence of one fact on other facts. An example is:

```
has_stiff_neck(john) :- hacker(john).
```

which can be read:

> *John has a stiff neck if he is a hacker.*

Notice the direction of inference implied by this rule. If it is already known that John is a hacker, then the rule is provides the additional knowledge that John has a stiff neck. The word john is a constant symbol that indicates a specific entity within the universe of this program. This rule and fact contain *explicit* knowledge applicable only to john.

Using a variable instead of a constant

A Prolog *variable* is written as a word beginning with a capital letter. The "stiff neck" rule above can be generalized so that it applies to all hackers, by replacing the constant john with a variable:

```
has_stiff_neck(X) :- hacker(X).
```

which can be read:

> *If X is a hacker, he/she has a stiff neck.*

or:

> *All hackers have stiff necks.*

The variable X will match any constant, so this rule can be used to prove that any hacker has a stiff neck. Because this rule contains variables, it expresses knowledge implicitly applicable to all hackers.

Declarative style

Notice that these rules are simply declarations of relations that hold between entities. Prolog programs consist almost exclusively of such declarations, and there are none of the usual control constructs (*do, while, for, goto, etc.*) that specify how to execute a program. The programmer is able to leave many control decisions to the problem solving mechanism. Some database query languages (for example, SQL) are similarly declarative; the user needs to declare only what type of answer is required, and the query language interpreter decides how to supply it.

0.9 Horn Clauses to Represent Knowledge

Problem Solving

The ultimate purpose of writing a computer program is to make a tool that can be used to solve a problem in some application domain. (The phrase *application domain* refers to some discrete part of the world, or a field of knowledge). The *structure* of an application domain consists of its significant entities, functions, and relations. A successful computer program embodies the structure of its application domain in such a way that, when it is executed, its behavior will reflect some relevant aspect of that structure. For instance, a relation that holds between entities of an application domain should, by analogy, also hold between the symbols representing those entities in a program that embodies the domain.

Programming

The process of writing a computer program that embodies the structure of its application domain conventionally involves two steps:

1) The structure of the application domain must be analyzed and presented formally in a *logical specification* of the domain.

2) A program must be written to *implement* the structure described in the logical specification.

When the application language is Prolog, writing a program that embodies the structure of its application domain is essentially similar to constructing a theory in predicate logic (see Sec. 0.5). In particular, it involves the following steps:

1) The programmer analyzes the significant entities, functions, and relations in the application domain, and chooses symbols to represent each of them. (In the example above, the programmer chose the constant symbol `john` and the predicate symbols `has_stiff_neck` and `hacker`.)

2) The programmer defines each of the significant functions and relations semantically. In the case of a relation, this entails specifying which instances of it are *true* and which are *false*.

3) The programmer defines each relation axiomatically with Prolog clauses. (In the example above, the single clause `has_stiff_neck(X)   :-   hacker(X)` is an axiomatic definition of the relation "has_stiff_neck.") An axiomatic definition of a relation is successful if it captures the sense of the semantic definition. The set of axiomatic definitions of all significant relations in the application domain is a program that embodies the structure of the domain.

4) The programmer or user uses the Prolog interpreter to evaluate queries to the set of program clauses. The combination of the query, the set of program clauses, and the interpreter can be considered to be an *algorithm* for solving problems in the application domain in the following sense: the query and the program clauses are the initial formulas of the algorithm, and the interpreter contains the rules for transforming those formulas. The interpreter is an active agent that makes inferences from the program clauses, and thereby *realizes* or *unfolds* the relations defined by the program clauses. The interpreter's answer to a query reflects the structure of the application domain, and can be used to solve problems in the application domain.

Kowalski succinctly describes this kind of problem solving algorithm in the following "equation" (Kowalski [1979b]):

Algorithm = Logic + Control

"Logic" here means the part of a program that embodies the structure of the domain. When the programming language is Prolog, "logic" means the axiomatic definition of important relations of the application domain. "Control" means the procedure(s) capable of making inferences from (or realizing the meaning of) the "logic" part of the program. When the programming language is Prolog, a great deal of the "control" is taken care of by the interpreter.

The ability to *represent knowledge* about an application domain is one of the essential parts of many types of artificial intelligence programs. Knowledge about an application domain amounts to someone's analysis of the significant entities, functions, and relations of the domain. Writing a successful Prolog program thus necessarily involves representing knowledge about the domain, and Prolog clauses can be regarded as a *knowledge representation language*. The subject of knowledge representation is covered in depth in Chap. 6.

0.10 Semantics of Prolog

Three Semantic Models

The *semantics* (meaning) of a formula of symbolic logic refers to its truth value. The semantics of a constant symbol inside of a formula refers to its value with respect to a domain of interpretation. In computing, on the other hand, the semantics of a programming language construct usually refers to the behavior of the computer when the construct is evaluated. Because Prolog is both a logic language and a programming language, both notions of semantics are applicable.

There are three semantic models to explain the meaning of a Prolog program: the *declarative* model, the *procedural* model, and the *abstract machine* model. The existence of three semantic models gives Prolog great expressiveness.

The Declarative Model

The declarative semantic model of Prolog specifies the truth value of instances of relations. The word *declarative* is used because a Prolog clause *declares* that a relation holds between its arguments if all of the conditions of the clause are met. For instance, the following clause:

```
executive(Name, Salary) :-
    employee(Name, Salary),  Salary > 70000.
```

can be read as:

> *Anyone (*Name*) is an executive if*
> *he or she is an employee*
> *with a salary greater than $70,000.*

Read according to the declarative model, Prolog clauses are formulas of first order predicate logic written in Horn clause form. The only logical connectives that can occur are "if," "and," and "or." The order of conditions in a clause is not significant, since all conditions are understood to hold simultaneously. The set of clauses forming a Prolog program describes the relevant logical structure of its application domain.

The Procedural Model

According to the procedural semantic model of Prolog, the conditions of a clause specify a *process* to establish the truth value of the conclusion of the clause. That is, the conditions are understood as a series of steps that must be successfully evaluated for the relation specified in the conclusion of the clause to hold. A set of clauses with the same predicate name and the same number of arguments is understood as a *procedure*. A query with the same predicate name and same number of arguments as a procedure is understood to be a *call* to that procedure. For a query to succeed, the procedure it calls must be successfully evaluated. Each condition of a clause is also understood as a call to a procedure.

Read procedurally, the meaning of the "executive" clause above is that

> *One way to find an executive is:*
> *first, find an employee,*
> *then second, verify that the salary*
> *of the employee is greater than $70,000.*

The order in which conditions are evaluated is significant according to the procedural model.

The Abstract Machine Model

Read according to the declarative model, a Prolog program is a description of a logical structure. The Prolog interpreter is the active agent (i.e. procedure) capable of realizing the consequences of this description. The interpreter applies a problem solving strategy to evaluate a query against a set of Prolog clauses; its problem solving strategy can be characterized computationally by an *abstract machine*. A Prolog query together with the set of program clauses has a *computational meaning* in the sense that they trigger a certain behavior on the part of the Prolog interpreter. The abstract machine model specifies the meaning of a query and set of clauses in terms of abstract machine actions.

As discussed in Sec. 0.6, the actions of this machine can be explained as applications of the resolution inference rule. It is also possible to explain the actions of the machine in terms of stack operations. Such an explanation is offered in Chap. 3.

Uses of the Models

Each of the three semantic models has its strengths and weaknesses. The declarative model is closest to the semantics of predicate logic, and makes Prolog an effective language for representing knowledge.

The declarative model cannot adequately account for a clause in which the order of subgoals is important, however. An extreme example of such a clause is one that produces *output side effects* such as printing messages to the screen in a certain order. It is necessary to resort to the procedural model to explain the meaning of clauses of this sort.

Even the procedural model is not adequate to explain clauses that have *control side effects*, such as halting the evaluation of a query, or retracting a clause from the set of program clauses. The meaning of such clauses can only be explained in terms of the abstract machine model. The abstract machine model is the most precise of the three models, but is also the most implementation dependent.

The procedural and declarative models are discussed in Chap. 1. The abstract machine model is explained further in Chap. 3. Chapter 4 deals with how the three semantic models can influence programming practice.

0.11 Metalanguage/Object Language

Functions of the Metalanguage

Logic is usually studied through the vehicle of a *formal language*. Earlier in the chapter we considered two such languages, propositional logic and predicate logic. In the previous section, it was mentioned that Prolog is also a formal language when read according to the declarative semantic model. In order to discuss the properties of a formal language, it is necessary to use a language other than the formal language itself. Conventionally, the formal language is referred to as the *object language*, and the language used to discuss it is called the *metalanguage* (see Sec. 0.4).

The metalanguage performs two functions, one analytical, and one prescriptive. The analytical function of a metalanguage is to characterize object language statements by properties such as *tautology* or *contradiction*. It also allows the characterization of object language theories, and the object language itself, by properties such as *complete* or *consistent*. The three laws of logic (Table 0-1) are metalanguage statements about the nature of an object language.

The prescriptive function of the metalanguage is to establish the truth value of an object language statement that is neither a tautology nor a contradiction. (If an object language statement is neither a tautology or a contradiction, its truth value cannot be determined by rules of the object language alone.) The metalanguage is capable of asserting the truth value of an object language statement from a source of knowledge outside of the object language; i.e. from intuition, common sense, or knowledge of an application domain. In this way, the metalanguage is responsible for introducing the axioms of a theory that describes the structure of some application domain. Similarly, the ability to add a new clause to a Prolog program is a metalanguage function.

Syntactic relation between object language and metalanguage

In predicate logic, the simplest construct that can denote a truth value is an atomic formula. An atomic formula is composed of a predicate symbol and some number of terms, none of which is capable of denoting a truth value by itself. When a metalanguage statement describes a property of an object language statement, there is an important syntactic relation between the two: the object language statement acts as a *term* (i.e. a syntactic object that cannot denote a truth value) in the metalanguage statement. Consider the following metalanguage statement:

P(a, b) is provable.

In this example, "is provable" is a metalanguage predicate, and the object language statement P(a, b) is an argument to this predicate. By itself, the term P(a, b) has no truth value; its truth value comes from the metalanguage statement in which it is embedded. A metalanguage necessarily contains predicates (such as "is provable") that are not part of the object language.

Metalanguage of Prolog

The interaction between a user and the Prolog interpreter can be understood on the level of the object language or on the level of the metalanguage. On the level of the object language, when a user types in a query to the interpreter, he or she is implicitly asking the question:

Question implicit in a query

Does the relation described by this query hold?

But on the level of the metalanguage, the implicit question is:

Is the relation described by this query provable by means of the interpreter's problem solving strategy according to the clauses currently asserted?

The query itself is an object language statement, and "*provable by means of the ... strategy according to the clauses ...*" may be a property of that statement. The interpreter responds to a query by stating whether it succeeded or failed. There are two interpretations of this answer. On the level of the object language, it tells us whether the relation described by the query holds. On the level of the metalanguage, it tells us whether the relation is provable by means of the interpreter's strategy according to the currently asserted clauses.

How the question is answered

The interpreter evaluates a query as follows. If a clause matching the query is unconditionally asserted, then the query succeeds. If no clause matching the query is asserted, then the query fails. If a clause matching the query is conditionally asserted, then the query succeeds only if the interpreter can evaluate all of the conditions as true; otherwise, it fails. If the query contains a variable, then the interpreter will try to find values of the variable for which the relation described by the query holds.

The closed
world
assumption

If a query fails, it means that the interpreter was unable to prove it from the clauses that are currently asserted. Thus, Prolog is based on the assumption that an instance of a relation that cannot be proved is false. It does not distinguish between an unknown relation and a provably untrue relation. The set of currently asserted clauses is sometimes referred to as a *world*. The fact that Prolog acts as though the currently asserted clauses are the only source of knowledge is known as the *closed world assumption*.

Suppose that there is only one clause in the current program that asserts:

Someone is of French ancestry if their name is Delacroix.

If we write a query asking if Mr. Chevalier is of French ancestry, it will fail. On the level of the object language, the failure of the query means that Mr. Chevalier is not of French ancestry. On the level of the metalanguage, however, it means that whether or not Mr. Chevalier is of French ancestry is unprovable. Because of the closed world assumption, the actual meaning of the clause is that

Someone is of French ancestry **if and only if** *their name is Delacroix.*

The "only if" part of this meaning comes from the metalanguage. The closed world assumption is discussed further in Sec. 3.2.

Metalanguage
Predicates

It is possible to write a Prolog program that acts like a metalanguage predicate. The reason to write such a program is to override the implicit metalanguage meaning of a Prolog query either by 1) using a problem solving strategy other than the one used by the Prolog interpreter, or 2) using a source of knowledge other than the currently asserted clauses.

The classic metalanguage predicate is called "demo" (for "demonstrate") (Kowalski [1979a], Bowen and Kowlaski [1982], Miyachi et al. [1984]). One version of "demo" makes both the strategy and the source of knowledge explicit. It takes three arguments: a query to be evaluated, the name of a problem solving strategy to be used, and the name of world (i.e set of clauses). The conclusion of the "demo" predicate looks like:

```
demo(Query, Strategy, World) :-
    ...
```

If a call to "demo" succeeds, it means that:

The query (argument 1) is provable
by means of the problem solving strategy (argument 2),
according to the clauses in the world (argument 3).

In Sec. 7.5, an interpreter is implemented in Prolog that uses a problem solving strategy different from the Prolog interpreter's own strategy. This new interpreter can be considered to be a *metalanguage predicate*, because the metalanguage meaning of the answer to a query evaluated by this interpreter is slightly different from the metalanguage meaning of the same query evaluated by the normal Prolog interpreter. The ability to write a Prolog interpreter in Prolog demonstrates Prolog's extensibility.

0.12 Applications of Prolog

Prolog has been used to develop a number of artificial intelligence as well as conventional applications, some of which are mentioned below.

Relational Databases

Because the relational database model is a logical, well developed formalism, its representation in Prolog is straightforward. Prolog has proved particularly useful for user interfaces to relational databases. All types of query languages have been implemented in Prolog, including QBE, SQL, relational algebra (Li [1984]), and one similar to Visicalc (Kriwaczek [1982]). Various database interfaces are presented in Chaps. 3, 5 and 6.

Software Engineering

In the area of software engineering, researchers have shown that a logical specification of a system can be directly transformed into a logic program (Davis [1982], Kowalski [1984]).

Natural Language

Colmerauer originally invented Prolog to perform natural language processing. He designed a kind of top-down parser in Prolog for natural language that later came to be known as the Definite Clause

Grammar (DCG) formalism (Colmerauer [1978]). Dahl, Warren, Pereira and others have refined the DCG formalism and demonstrated its usefulness for natural language query systems (Dahl [1984], Pereira and Warren [1980] and [1983]). Pereira's CHAT-80 is an example of a natural language system based on the DCG formalism (Warren and Pereira [1981]).

A number of approaches to computational linguistics are converging on *unification* as the fundamental way of exchanging information (unification is the mechanism whereby variables are given values in Prolog). So-called *unification grammar formalisms* include GPSG (Gazdar [1980]), HPSG (Pollard [1984]), LFG (Kaplan and Bresnan [1984], Yasukawa [1983]), PATR-II (Shieber et al. [1983]), and FUG (Kay [1985]), as well as DCG.

There are several major natural language projects being developed in Prolog, including the Epistle project at IBM (McCord [1985]), and various projects at ICOT (Matsumoto [1984], Uehara et al. [1984a] and [1984b]).

Natural language processing is beyond the scope of this book, but basic top-down and bottom-up parsing techniques are discussed in Chap. 5.

Knowledge Representation

The concepts inherent in knowledge representation formalisms used in artificial intelligence, including:

semantic networks,

frames,

production rules, and

object oriented programming

can all be expressed in logic and implemented in logic programming. This subject is covered in depth in Chap. 6.

Expert Systems

One purpose of representing knowledge is to get it in a form that can be utilized by an expert system. Expert systems have been built with Prolog in a variety of areas, including equation solving (Bundy and Welham [1981]), medicine (Darvas [1980], Hammond [1984]), legislation (Sergot [1982], Cory et al. [1984]), law, architecture (Swinson [1980]), factory automation, circuit design (Uehara et al. [1983], Zaumen [1983]), microcode synthesis (Poe [1984]), financial analysis, and decision support (Kriwaczek [1982] and [1984]). Aspects of the user interface necessary for an expert system are discussed in Chap. 7.

Bibliographic Notes

On the subject of propositional and predicate logic, readable introductory texts include Hamilton [1978], Mendelson [1979], and Copi [1986]. Chang and Lee [1973] and Manna and Waldinger [1985] deal with the same subject in a way that is oriented toward computation. The philosophical point of view of traditional logic is best described in Horn [1983] and Taylor [1955]. For a history of the development of symbolic logic, see Nagel and Newman [1964], Boyer [1968], Hermes and Markwald [1974], van Hiejenoort [1967], Davis [1983], or particularly Robinson [1979] (i.e. the appendix entitled "Historical Notes").

The most thorough treatment of resolution is in Robinson [1979]. The subject is also covered in Chang and Lee [1973], Bundy [1983], and Kowalski [1979]. For the history of the development of logic programming, see Siekmann and Wrightson, [1983a] and [1983b]. The best presentations of logic programming theory are Kowalski [1979], Hogger [1984], and Lloyd [1984].

The Prolog language is covered in Clocksin and Mellish [1984], Clark and McCabe [1984], Hogger [1984], and Kluzniak and Szpakowicz [1985]. Clark and McCabe [1984] is best for actually learning to program in Prolog, although all examples are in micro-Prolog syntax. The implementation of Prolog is covered in Hogger [1984], Kluzniak and Szpakowicz [1985], and Campbell [1984]. For the view of the orthodox AI community toward Prolog, see Bobrow [1984].

The distinction between metalanguage and object language came originally from Hilbert (see Hilbert [1904]), and served as a way to avoid logical paradoxes. The issue of metalanguage in symbolic logic is mentioned in Nagle and Newman [1964], Reichenbach [1947] pp. 9-17, and Mendelson [1979] p. 32. Metalanguage in logic programming is discussed in Kowalski [1979], Bowen and Kowalski [1982], and Bowen [1985]. Miyachi et al. [1984] and Kitakami et al. [1984] use metalanguage predicates in an interesting way.

The semantics of logic programming languages is discussed in van Emden and Kowalski [1976], as well as all of the books on logic programming theory cited above. The importance of semantics to knowledge representation is emphasized in Hayes [1977], Hayes [1983], and Bundy [1983].

1

Facts and Rules

1.1 Using Prolog

**Invoking
Prolog**

Hopefully you have a computer with a version of Prolog on it close at hand while you are reading this book. If so, then your first task is to learn how to invoke the Prolog interpreter. It will be useful at this point to go in and out of Prolog enough times that you are thoroughly comfortable with the procedure. Unfortunately, each version of Prolog in each different environment has a unique way of being invoked. It is recommended that you consult your Prolog manual and find out how to:

**Basic
operations**

1) invoke Prolog from the operating system;

2) get out of Prolog;

3) use a text editor to make a Prolog program file;

4) load a Prolog program file while running Prolog; and

5) enter a program interactively while running Prolog.

After you are comfortable with these basic operations, go ahead and explore the particular capabilities of your version of Prolog. Look for the following:

*Special
capabilities of
some Prologs*

* a command to dump the current program into a file while inside Prolog;

* *a program editor that can be invoked while inside Prolog; or*

* *a command to compile (instead of interpret) a Prolog program file.*

Syntax of
Different
Versions of
Prolog

In the rest of the book, all examples of code are written in "core Prolog" syntax. The top level prompt looks like:

    ¦ ?-

Whenever you see the top level prompt, it means that the Prolog interpreter is in *command mode*, and is waiting for you to enter a query.

"Core Prolog" is a subset of the original DEC-10 version of the language, and has become a de facto standard simply because it is compatible with so many versions of Prolog. At the same time, different implementors of Prolog have taken the liberty of changing details of the language, as well as adding extensions. Appendix IV deals with the the specific details of some versions of Prolog. If an example in the book does not work on your version, you may be able to find out how to make it work by consulting Appendix IV.

*Prolog
interpreter*

Throughout the book, the phrase *Prolog interpreter* is used loosely to refer to *the Prolog problem solving machine*. A more accurate expression would be *Prolog run-time system* or *Prolog executor*. The Prolog interpreter is what actually executes a Prolog program.

1.2 Facts

Parts of a
Prolog
Program

A Prolog program consists of a set of *clauses*, and can be understood as a network of relations that hold between *terms*. Each term represents an entity in the world. A clause is either a *fact* or a *rule*. A fact is an assertion that a particular relation holds; it is written as a name followed by a list of terms (called *arguments*) inside of parentheses. A rule is a fact whose truth value depends on the truth values of other facts.

"predicate" vs. "procedure"

Sometimes the word *procedure* is used almost interchangeably with *predicate*, although there is a difference. Both a predicate and a procedure are identified by a predicate name and an arity (i.e. number of arguments). A predicate is the abstract sense of a relation that holds between a certain number of arguments. A procedure is a set of clauses whose heads have the same predicate name and same number of arguments. In Prolog, a predicate is defined (implemented) by a procedure.

Form of a Prolog Fact

A fact is a clause with no conditions. A fact is used to indicate a simple data relationship. The following fact expresses the idea that *Mary knows Bob:*

```
knows(mary, bob).
```

Syntactically, a fact is composed of a predicate name (knows) and a list of arguments inside of parentheses (mary, bob). It is up to the programmer how a Prolog fact should be read in a way that makes sense in English, but the predicate name usually expresses some kind of relationship between its arguments. Each argument to a fact must be a *term*. One type of term is an *atom*. An atom is a constant, and is usually written as a word beginning with a lower case letter. In the fact above, the terms mary and bob are both atoms.

Number of arguments

A predicate can have any number of arguments. The following fact indicates that the the Milford Plaza Hotel is located at 8th Ave. and 43rd St.:

```
%          Place             Ave  Street
location(milford_plaza_hotel, 8,   43).
```

The comment character is %, and the rest of a line following a % is treated as a comment. When a fact has many arguments, it is good programming practice to write a comment stating how to read it.

The fact below indicates that one possible mode of transportation from the World Trade Center to the Milford Plaza at 2PM is a taxi:

```
%               From  To            Via   At
transportation(wtc,  milford_plaza, taxi, 1400).
```

A database of
facts

The simplest Prolog program is a set of facts, informally referred to as a *database*. Here is a database of "knows" facts:

```
knows(mary, bob).
knows(sam, bob).
knows(sam, patricia).
```

Taken together, this set of facts defines the predicate "knows/2"— "knows" is the name of the predicate, and "2" is the *arity* (i.e. number of arguments) of the predicate.

Entering a
Program

A Prolog program, such as the "knows" database above, can be entered in one of two ways: 1) the program is created in a file by a text editor, and then *loaded* into Prolog; 2) the program can be entered directly from the terminal while inside Prolog. On a DEC-10 style version of Prolog, the way to enter a program directly is as follows:

```
| ?- consult(user).
        .
        .
        <type in program text>
        .
        .
        <type an end of file mark to return to command mode>
| ?-
```

Typing consult(user) puts the interpreter into *program insert mode*. Typing an end of file character brings it back to command mode, as indicated by the | ?- prompt.

1.3 Queries to a Database

Writing a
Query

Once a database of clauses has been consulted, you can write a *query* to it. A *simple query* consists of a predicate name followed by a list of arguments. (Another word for *query* is *goal*.) The | ?- prompt means that the interpreter is ready to evaluate a query.

If the "knows" database has been consulted, you can write a query to it such as:

```
| ?- knows(mary, bob).
```

This indicates the question: *Does Mary know Bob?* The interpreter looks up the corresponding fact in the "knows" database, and responds:

yes

Note: Throughout the book, the interpreter's answers are written in italic. This answer can be understood as: *Yes, Mary knows Bob.*

Queries with Constants

If a query has no variables in it, then the interpreter answers either

yes

or

no

A "yes" confirms that the interpreter was able to prove the query according to the set of clauses currently loaded. A "no" means that the interpreter was unable to prove the query.

Queries with Variables

A *variable* is a type of term written as a word beginning with an upper case letter, such as X or Who. If a query contains variables, the interpreter will try to find values of those variables for which the query is true. This query:

```
| ?- knows(mary, Who).
```

indicates the question: *Who does Mary know?*

Quantification of a variable in a query

A variable in a Prolog query is said to be *existentially quantified*. This means that a query with a variable is implicitly asking if there exists at least one value of the variable for which the query is true. With this in mind, the query above can be read as:

Does at least one person exist whom Mary knows?

The query will be true if such a person can be found in the current "knows" database.

Solving the
Query

The interpreter tries to *unify* (that is, to match) the arguments of the query with the arguments of facts in the "knows" database. In this case, the query succeeds on the first "knows" fact, because the atom mary in the query unifies with the atom mary in the fact, and the variable Who unifies with the atom bob in the fact. As a result of this process, the variable Who takes on the value of the atom bob, and the interpreter responds with

```
Who = bob
```

Instantiation

A variable is said to be *instantiated* when it is unified with a value during the evaluation of a query.

*More than one
answer*

The following query is designed to generate all people who know one another in the "knows" database.

```
| ?- knows(A, B).
A = mary
B = bob ;
```

Typing ; after the first answer is a way of rejecting that answer and causing the interpreter to look for another one:

```
A = sam
B = bob ;

A = sam
B = patricia ;

no
```

The interpreter found three answers to the query. The last response, *no*, means that the interpreter reached the end of the "knows" database, and is unable to find any further answers.

*Order of
answers*

Notice that the interpreter found answers from the "knows" database in exactly the same order that the facts were entered. After finding the first answer to the query, the interpreter keeps its place in the "knows" database. If the user types ; the interpreter begins looking for a new answer at the next "knows" clause. But if the user types a return, the interpreter gives up its place in the "knows" database and comes back to the top level prompt, ¦ ?-.

Duration of variables

A query lasts from the point that the user types it in and hits return until the top level prompt reappears. The duration of any variable in a query is the same as that of the query. Once a query has been evaluated and the interpreter has returned to the top level prompt, the variables in that query no longer exist.

Compound Queries

The queries shown thus far have all been simple queries. A compound query is composed of more than one simple query joined by commas. Each simple query in a compound query is known as a "subgoal." For a compound query as a whole to be true, each of its subgoals must be true. For instance, the following query:

```
¦ ?- knows(mary, X), knows(sam, X).
```

indicates the question: *Is there a person known by both Mary and Sam?* The same variable X appears in both subgoals of the query, which specifies that the second argument of each subgoal must be the same for the compound query to be true. The interpreter answers:

X = bob ;

no

The first answer, *X = bob*, indicates that Bob is known by both Mary and Sam. The second answer, *no*, indicates that Bob is the only person they both know.

Arguments as input and output

Writing a query is the only way to cause the Prolog interpreter to execute a program. Using a constant as an argument to a query (for instance, mary or sam in the last example) is a way of supplying an *input parameter* to the program. Any successful answer must unify with the constant. Using a variable as an argument to a query (for instance, X in the last example) is a way of asking for *output* from the program.

The _ Variable

_ is a special *anonymous variable* that instructs the interpreter to ignore the value of an argument. It unifies with anything, but does not print. Each occurrence of _ in a query is distinct from any other variable in the query.

For instance, the effect of typing the query:

```
| ?- knows(A, _).
```

is to get all possible values of the first argument to "knows," no matter what the second argument is:

```
A = mary ;

A = sam ;

A = sam ;

no
```

Why does the interpreter find the answer *A = sam* twice?

1.4 Rules

Facts vs. rules

A fact is an assertion that the relationship indicated by the predicate name holds between the arguments. A rule, on the other hand, is a fact whose truth value depends on the truth value of the conditions that form the *body* of the rule.

The Form of a Rule: Head :- Body.

The head of a rule is of the same form as a fact. It is followed by the symbol :- (read as *if*), and then by the body of the rule. Each condition in the body is referred to as a *subgoal*. For the head of a rule to be true, each subgoal in the body must be true. Thus, the set of subgoals in the body of a rule acts like a compound query.

```
        HEAD            if              BODY
    ---------------          ------------------------------

                         SUBGOAL      and      SUBGOAL

                         -----------          -----------

exec(Name, Sal)  :-  emp(Name, Sal) ,  Sal > 70000.
```

The head of a rule is similar to a macro that stands for the set of subgoals in its body. The process of proving a query to a rule is similar to performing a macro substitution.

Example rule

Suppose that the following "work_shift" database is asserted. Each fact states the shift on which an employee works.

```
%              Employee  Shift
work_shift(mary,     daytime).
work_shift(sam,      evening).
work_shift(bob,      evening).
work_shift(patricia, evening).
```

The following rule establishes that Bob knows Mary if they both work on the evening shift:

```
knows1(bob, mary) :-            % head
    work_shift(bob, evening),   % first subgoal of body
    work_shift(mary, evening).  % second subgoal of body
```

knows1(mary, bob) is the head of this rule. The body is composed of two "work_shift" subgoals. The comma between the subgoals is read as "and," so the whole rule can be read:

Bob knows Mary if
 Bob works on the evening shift and
 Mary works on the evening shift.

Querying a rule

Rules are queried in the same way that facts are. The following query asks who Bob knows:

```
| ?- knows1(bob, X).

X = mary
```

The success of this query depends on the success of all the subgoals in the body of the rule. The query will fail unless the interpreter can verify that both Bob and Mary work on the evening shift.

**Rule Defined
with Variables**

If the "knows" rule above is defined with variables instead of constants, it can be used to establish that any two people know one another if they work on the same shift:

```
knows2(A, B) :-
    work_shift(A, Shift),
    work_shift(B, Shift).
```

In the body of this rule, `Shift` is a variable that is shared between the two subgoals; it must have the same value in each subgoal. (The predicate is called "knows2" to distinguish it from previous predicates, "knows" and "knows1.")

The "knows2" rule is much more general than the earlier version ("knows1") defined with constants. A rule with variables can be thought of as implicitly defining a set of facts. For instance, "knows2" contains the same data as the following database of facts:

```
knows2(sam, bob).
knows2(sam, patricia).
knows2(bob, patricia).
```

Variable scope

The scope of a variable in a rule is limited to that rule. There are no global variables in Prolog. For instance, the variable names `A`, `B` and `Shift` used in the "knows2" rule could also be used in other rules in the same program without implying any connection.

*Quantification
of a variable
in a rule*

Variables that occur in the head of a rule (such as `A` or `B` in the "knows2" rule) are *universally quantified*. This means that a rule with variables in its head is true for any terms that meet the criteria specified by the body of the rule. On the other hand, variables that occur only in the body of a rule (such as `Shift`) are existentially quantified. With these quantifications in mind, the "knows2" rule can be read:

> *For any two people, `A` and `B`,*
> `A` *knows* `B` *if*
> > *there exists a shift at the plant, `Shift`,*
> > *such that*
> > `A` *works on `Shift`, and*
> > `B` *works on `Shift`.*

Consider the following queries to the "knows2" rule. What results do you expect from each? Do any of them produce more than one answer?

```
| ?- knows2(bob, X).

| ?- knows2(patricia, mary).

| ?- knows2(frank, Y).

| ?- knows2(Y, Z).
```

Explicit and implicit databases

"work_shift" is an *explicit database*, because it is composed of facts whose arguments are constants. "knows2" is an *implicit database*, because it is a rule defined with variables whose values depend on subgoals in its body. From the point of view of a user writing queries, it does not matter whether a database is implicit or explicit.

Example: The "travel" Database

Below is a database of "travel" facts each of which has four arguments. Each fact establishes that it is possible to travel via some carrier (first argument) from a starting city (second argument) to a destination city (third argument) on a certain type of transportation (fourth argument).

```
%        Carrier      Origin      Destination   Type
travel(amtrak,       new_york,   boston,       train).
travel(nj_transit,   new_york,   princeton,    train).
travel(amtrak,       boston,     portland,     train).
travel(greyhound,    boston,     portland,     bus).
travel(amtrak,       new_york,   washington,   train).
travel(peoples,      new_york,   washington,   plane).
travel(peoples,      burlington, new_york,     plane).
```

Together, this set of facts defines the predicate "travel/4," where "travel" is the name of the predicate, and "4" is the arity of the predicate.

"competitor" rule defined with variables

The "competitor" rule establishes that any two carriers are competitors if they both serve the same two cities.

```
competitor(Carrier1, Carrier2) :-
    travel(Carrier1, CityA, CityB, _),
    travel(Carrier2, CityA, CityB, _).
```

In the body of this rule, `CityA` and `CityB` are variables shared between the two travel subgoals. The `_` variable is used as the fourth argument of the two "travel" subgoals because the type of transportation is not needed to establish whether two carriers are competitors. The "competitor" rule can be read:

> *For any two carriers,* `Carrier1` *and* `Carrier2`,
> `Carrier1` *is a competitor of* `Carrier2` *if*
> > *there exist two cities,* `CityA` *and* `CityB`
> > *such that*
> > `Carrier1` *provides transportation*
> > *between* `CityA` *and* `CityB`, *and*
> > `Carrier2` *provides transportation*
> > *between* `CityA` *and* `CityB`.

Queries to
"competitor"

The following queries show how "competitor" can be used:

```
| ?- competitor(peoples, X).
X = amtrak

| ?- competitor(amtrak, nj_transit).
no
```

What results do you expect from the following query?

```
| ?- competitor(X, Y).
```

Indirect
Relations

The "can_travel" rule below establishes an indirect relation between two cities that holds if it is possible to travel from one city to the other through a third, intermediate city.

```
can_travel(CityA, CityC) :-
    travel(_, CityA, CityB, _),
    travel(_, CityB, CityC, _).
```

According to the "travel" database above, "can_travel" should hold between New York and Portland, because it is possible to travel from New York to Boston on Amtrak, and from Boston to Portland on Greyhound.

Picturing a relationship

The "can_travel" relation between New York and Portland can be pictured by representing each argument as a point and each predicate as an arc between points, as shown in Figure 1-1:

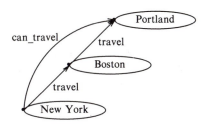

Figure 1-1

1.5 Procedures

Declarative and Procedural Semantics

The meaning of a Prolog clause can be understood either 1) *declaratively*, or 2) *procedurally*. Thus far in this chapter, only the declarative meaning has been considered. The declarative meaning emphasizes the static existence of relations. The order of subgoals in a rule does not affect the declarative meaning of the rule.

Procedural semantics

The procedural meaning of Prolog emphasizes the sequence of steps taken by the interpreter to evaluate a query. Thus, the order of subgoals in a rule is significant. A set of clauses with the same name and the same arity can be considered to be a *procedure*, in which case a query (or a subgoal in a rule) is a *procedure call*. When the interpreter evaluates a query against the clauses that make up the procedure, it considers clauses in the same order that they were asserted.

Two meanings
of the
"can_travel"
rule

Consider the "can_travel" rule above. It can be read declaratively as:

> *It is possible to travel between* CityA *and* CityC *if*
>   *one can travel from* CityA
>   *to an intermediate* CityB,
>   *and*
>   *one can travel from* CityB *to* CityC.

The same rule can be read procedurally as:

> *To find a way to travel between* CityA *and* CityC
>   *first*
>   *find a way to travel between* CityA *and*
>   *some intermediate* CityB,
>   *then*
>   *find a way to travel between* CityB *and* CityC.

**Two-rule
Version of
"can_travel"**

Below is a new version of "can_travel" made up of two rules. Clause (1) states that the "can_travel2" relation holds between two cities if there is a "travel" clause that establishes a direct connection between them. Clause (2) is the same as the earlier "can_travel" rule.

```
can_travel2(CityA, CityC) :-                    % (1)
    travel(_, CityA, CityC, _).

can_travel2(CityA, CityC) :-                    % (2)
    travel(_, CityA, CityB, _),
    travel(_, CityB, CityC, _).
```

There is an implicit "or" connective between the two rules. Together, the two rules can be read declaratively as:

> *It is possible to travel from* CityA *to* CityC *if either*
>   *1) there is a direct form of transportation*
>   *between the two cities,*
>   *or if*
>   *2) one can travel from* CityA *to some*
>   *intermediate* CityB, *and then travel*
>   *from* CityB *to* CityC.

or procedurally as:

To find a way to travel between CityA *and* CityC
either
1) find a direct form of transportation between the cities
or
2) find a form of transportation connecting CityA *with
an intermediate point* CityB, *and then
find a form of transportation from* CityB *to* CityC.

**Queries to
"can_travel2"**

In response to a query to "can_travel2," the interpreter first tries clause (1). If clause (1) fails, the interpreter goes on to try clause (2).

```
¦ ?- can_travel2(new_york, washington).
yes                         % answered by clause (1)
```

```
¦ ?- can_travel2(new_york, portland).
yes                         % answered by clause (2)
```

*How the query
is evaluated*

The evaluation of this last query can be thought of as equivalent to the following series of queries. Queries equivalent to the subgoals of a rule are indented.

```
¦ ?- can_travel2(new_york, portland).

    % first subgoal of first "can_travel2" rule:
    ¦ ?- travel(_, new_york, portland, _).
    no

    % first subgoal of second "can_travel2" rule:
    ¦ ?- travel(_, new_york, CityB, _).
    CityB = boston

    % second subgoal of second "can_travel2" rule:
    ¦ ?- travel(_, boston, portland, _).
    yes

yes
```

The last *yes* is the response to the original "can_travel2" query.

The Or Connective ;

In the bodies of rules considered thus far, subgoals have been connected by the "and" connective , (comma). It is also possible to connect subgoals (or sets of subgoals) with the "or" connective ; (semicolon). (¦ is an alternative "or" connective in some versions of Prolog.)

Compound queries using ;

Consider the following query:

```
¦ ?- a(X), b(X, Y) ; c(Z).
```

For this compound query to be true, either both subgoals a(X) and b(X, Y) must be true, or subgoal c(Z) must be true. If the a(X) subgoal fails, then the interpreter will skip over the b(X, Y) subgoal and try to evaluate the c(Z) subgoal.

Here is another example of how ; can be used:

```
¦ ?- wife(W, george), wealthy(W) ; wealthy(george).
```

The query will be true if either 1) George has a wife and his wife is wealthy, or 2) he is wealthy himself. If the wife(W, george) subgoal fails, then the interpreter will never try the wealthy(W) subgoal, but will go instead to the other side of ; and try the wealthy(george) subgoal.

Using , and ; Together

The "and" connective , groups subgoals together more tightly than the "or" connective ;. In the following examples, A, B and C stand for any subgoals. Parentheses in the right hand column indicate the implied grouping.

```
% this:              means the same as:
A ; B, C.            A ; (B, C).
A, B ; C.            (A, B) ; C.
A, B ; C, D.         (A, B) ; (C, D).
A ; B, C ; D.        A ; ((B, C) ; D).
```

Parentheses can always be used to change the implied grouping of subgoals combined with ; and ,.

Version of "can_travel" Utilizing ;

The "can_travel2" procedure can be redefined in a single rule by using the "or" connective, as follows:

```
can_travel3(CityA, CityC) :-
    travel(_, CityA, CityC, _)
    ;
    travel(_, CityA, CityB, _),
    travel(_, CityB, CityC, _).
```

Why use ;   When the interpreter sees this kind of construction, it translates it into two rules like the "can_travel" procedure on the previous page. In some situations, using ; has the effect of making code more readable, as it may save the trouble of writing two rules or writing a new predicate to handle a single decision.

1.6 Recursive Procedures

Recursion Defined

Recursion is an algorithmic technique often used in Prolog programming. Recursion can be used to achieve the same effect as an iterative control mechanism in a procedural language, such as a *while* loop. In a recursive rule, a more complicated case of the input arguments is defined in terms of a simpler case. For instance, here is a recursive set of instructions for eating marshmallows:

> *To eat N marshmallows:*
> *If N = 0, stop.*
> *If N > 0,*
> *swallow one marshmallow, then*
> *eat N - 1 marshmallows.*

Consider this to be a definition of the procedure "eat N marshmallows." "N" is the argument to the procedure, and stands for some integer. This procedure is recursive because the last line, "eat N - 1 marshmallows," is a call to the procedure itself. Notice that the argument to the recursive call, "N - 1," is simpler than the original argument, "N," in the sense that it is a smaller number. Thus, "eat N marshmallows" is a more complicated case, defined in terms of a simpler case of the same thing, "eat N - 1 marshmallows."

"Ancestor"

The classic example of a recursive definition in Prolog is the "ancestor" program, defined by two rules:

```
ancestor(A, B) :-                        % (1)
    parent(A, B).


ancestor(A, B) :-                        % (2)
    parent(C, B),
    ancestor(A, C).
```

Together, these rules define two ways that one person (**A**) can be the ancestor of another (**B**). According to clause (1), **A** is the ancestor of **B** if **A** is the parent of **B**. According to clause (2), **A** is the ancestor of **B** if **A** is also the ancestor of **B**'s parent, **C**. The relation described in the head of clause (2) depends on a simplified version of itself: the "ancestor" subgoal.

Queries to "ancestor"

Suppose that there is a "parent" database asserted:

```
parent(jb, lc).
parent(jb, gg).
parent(gg, wm).
```

The following queries show how "ancestor" is used:

```
% is jb the ancestor of gg?
¦ ?- ancestor(jb, gg).
yes                          % by clause (1)


% find all descendants of jb:
¦ ?- ancestor(jb, Z).
Z = lc ;                     % by clause (1)


Z = gg ;                     % by clause (1)


Z = wm ;                     % by clause (2) and clause (1)


no
```

Figure 1-2 is a *proof tree* showing how the "ancestor" relation holds between "jb" and "wm":

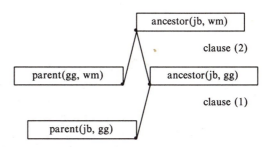

Figure 1-2

Each level of the diagram shows the application of one of the "ancestor" clauses. The first level shows that `ancestor(jb, wm)` can only be proved by clause (2), in which case it is necessary to prove both `parent(gg, wm)` and `ancestor(jb, gg)`. The second level shows that `ancestor(jb, gg)` can be proved by clause (1), in which case it is only necessary to prove `parent(jb, gg)`.

**Form of a
Recursive
Procedure**

Any recursive procedure must include at least one of each of the following components:

1) A nonrecursive clause defining the *base case* of the procedure—that is, where the recursion stops;

2) A recursive rule. In the body of this rule, the first subgoals generate new argument values. Then follows a recursive subgoal utilizing the new argument values.

In the "ancestor" procedure, clause (1) is the base case; once it has been satisfied, no further recursion will take place. Clause (2) is the recursive rule. This rule ascends one generation each time it is called. In the body of this rule, the `parent(C, B)` subgoal generates a value for the variable `C`. Then follows the recursive subgoal, `ancestor(A, C)`, that utilizes the new argument.

*Version of
"ancestor" that
does not work*

Below is a version of the "ancestor" procedure that does not work on most Prolog interpreters. "xancestor" is identical to "ancestor" except for the order of subgoals in the body of clause (2):

```
xancestor(A, B) :-              % (1)
    parent(A, B).

xancestor(A, B) :-              % (2)
    xancestor(A, C),
    parent(C, B).
```

The declarative meaning of this procedure is identical with that of "ancestor" above. But its procedural meaning is different in an important way. In "ancestor," the `parent(C, B)` subgoal of the recursive rule generates a value for the variable `C` that is then used by the recursive subgoal `ancestor(A, C)`. But in "xancestor," the variable `C` is uninstantiated at the point that the recursive subgoal `xancestor(A, C)` is evaluated. In practice, this means that when the interpreter tries to evaluate a query to "xancestor," it will find the correct answers, but then continue recursing until it runs out of memory:

```
| ?- xancestor(jb, Z).
Z = lc ;

Z = gg ;

Z = wm ;

warning: out of stack space.
```

The actions of the interpreter in trying to find a fourth answer to this query are shown in the proof tree in Figure 1-3:

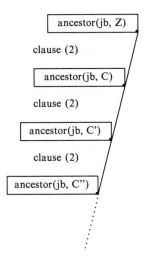

Figure 1-3

"xancestor" is known as a *left recursive procedure* because in clause (2), the recursive subgoal occurs first (i.e. it is *left* of the other subgoals). Due to the nature of the Prolog interpreter's problem solving strategy, it cannot safely handle left recursive procedures like this one.

| Recursive Version of "can_travel" | The recursive technique of "ancestor" can profitably be applied to the "can_travel" procedure. "can_travel4" below defines a relation that holds between two cities if it is possible to travel from one to the other through any number of intermediate cities. "can_travel4" is a recursive procedure very similar to the "ancestor" procedure. Assuming that the same "travel/4" database is asserted, "can_travel4" will hold in all of the same cases that "can_travel2" holds, but also in some additional cases (such as between Burlington and Portland via New York and Boston). |

```
can_travel4(CityA, CityB) :-                    % (1)
    travel(_, CityA, CityB, _).

can_travel4(CityA, CityB) :-                    % (2)
    travel(_, CityA, CityC, _),
    can_travel4(CityC, CityB).
```

Clause (2) is the recursive rule—it should move closer to the destination by one city each time it is called. Again, the relation described in the head of clause (2) depends on a simplified version of itself: the recursive subgoal. Clause (1) is the end condition, or base case. In the evaluation of a query, no further recursion occurs once clause (1) succeeds.

How a Query to "can_travel4" Is Evaluated

The proof tree in Figure 1-4 illustrates the evaluation of a query to "can_travel4":

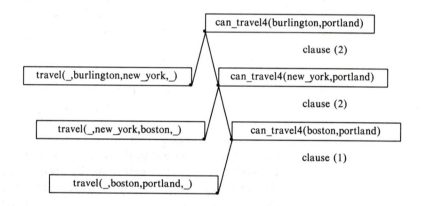

Figure 1-4

This diagram is be read in the same way as the previous proof tree.

1.7 Types of Relation

The Characterization of Relations

Writing Prolog programs involves using clauses to represent relations between terms. Terms are usually used to represent entities in the world. To program effectively, therefore, it is useful to analyze the properties of relations as they occur in the world, and then decide how to represent each type of relation with Prolog clauses. It is possible to instruct the Prolog interpreter to take advantage of the properties of a relation for the purpose of optimizing the evaluation of queries. For the sake of simplicity, only relations between two arguments (i.e. binary relations) are considered in the rest of this section, although the analysis can be extended to relations with more than two arguments.

Integrity constraints and properties

One of three possible integrity constraints holds between the arguments of any binary relation:

> *one-to-one*
> *one-to-many*
> *many-to-one*
> *many-to-many*

Furthermore, some relations can be characterized by the presence or absence of the following properties:

> *symmetry*   *(asymmetry)*
> *reflexivity*   *(irreflexivity)*
> *transitivity*   *(intransitivity)*

Each integrity constraint and property is considered in detail below.

One-to-One Integrity Constraints

In a binary relation governed by a *one-to-one integrity constraint* with arguments X and Y, for a given value of X, there is only one value of Y satisfying the relation, and for a given value of Y, there is only one value of X satisfying the relation. For instance, the relation between a person and his or her social security number is governed by a one-to-one integrity constraint:

```
ssn('Paula Smith', '347-22-5560').
```

(Note: any characters written between single quotes, such as 'Paula Smith' above, constitute a single atom.)

Application of an integrity constraint

Integrity constraints on a relation can be enforced either 1) when new instances of the relation (i.e. facts) are being asserted, or 2) when instances of the relation are being retrieved from the database.

Suppose that there is a data acquisition program that applies integrity constraints at the point that new facts are asserted. Suppose further that "ssn/2" is governed by a one-to-one integrity constraint, and that the above fact about Paula's social security number has already been asserted. If the user tries to enter another "ssn" fact about Paula Smith, say:

```
ssn('Paula Smith', '347-24-5561').
```

then the data acquisition program should object and refuse to assert the fact.

If it is known that a query should have only one answer, then it is possible to instruct the Prolog interpreter not to look for any further answers after the first has been found. In this case, the integrity constraint is applied by the program that retrieves data from the current set of clauses. Writing such a program involves the use of the special built-in predicate *cut* (covered in Chap. 3).

One-to-many Integrity Constraints

In a binary relation governed by a *one-to-many integrity constraint* with arguments X and Y, for a given value of X, there may be many values of Y satisfying the relation, but for a given value of Y, there is only one value of X satisfying the relation.

"father of" is an example of a relation governed by a one-to-many integrity constraint. It is possible for a father to have more than one child, but not vice versa.

```
%       One       Many
father(bill,      daniel).
father(bill,      kenneth).
father(geoffrey, bill).
```

Many-to-one Integrity Constraints

In a binary relation governed by a *many-to-one integrity constraint* with arguments X and Y, for a given value of X, there is only one value of Y satisfying the relation, but for a given value of Y, there may be many values of X satisfying the relation.

"native of" is an example of a relation governed by a many-to-one integrity constraint. A country has more than one native, but a person can be a native of only one country.

```
%           Many      One
native_of(jeremy,  america).
native_of(nancy,   america).
native_of(raoul,   france).
```

Many-to-many Integrity Constraints

In a binary relation governed by a *many-to-many integrity constraint* with arguments X and Y, for a given value of X, there may be many values of Y satisfying the relation, and for a given value of Y, there may be many values of X satisfying the relation.

For instance, here is a database of types of paper in the inventory of a printing company. The two arguments correspond to color and finish. Any combination of color and finish is permitted.

```
%      Color  Finish
paper(red,    vellum).
paper(white,  gloss).
paper(cream,  vellum).
paper(white,  smooth).
```

To say that a relation is governed by a many-to-many integrity constraint is like saying that it is governed by no integrity constraint at all. By default, the interpreter treats all predicates as if they are governed by a many-to-many integrity constraint.

Symmetry

A relation between two entities is *symmetric* when the role of one entity is interchangeable with the role of the other entity. If a Prolog predicate is symmetric, then the order of arguments in a query to the predicate is unimportant.

"sibling" is an example of a symmetric relation. If it is known that Jane is the sibling of Alice, then it can safely be assumed that Alice is the sibling of Jane. But consider a simple Prolog database of "sibling" facts:

```
sibling1(jane, alice).
sibling1(kathy, dorothy).
```

A query to this database with the arguments in the same order that they were asserted succeeds:

```
¦ ?- sibling1(jane, alice).
yes
```

But if the arguments are reversed, the query fails:

```
¦ ?- sibling1(alice, jane).
no
```

The failure shows that this implementation of the "sibling" relation is not symmetric.

Defining a symmetric relation

One way to make a symmetric "sibling" predicate is to write two rules that reference an explicit database. The explicit database is called "sib," and contains all data about Jane, Alice, Kathy, and Dorothy:

```
sib(jane, alice).
sib(kathy, dorothy).

sibling2(A, B) :- sib(A, B).          % (1)
sibling2(A, B) :- sib(B, A).          % (2)
```

Rule (1) of the "sibling2" predicate passes the arguments A and B through to the "sib" subgoal in the same order. Rule (2) reverses the order of the arguments. The following query:

```
¦ ?- sibling2(jane, alice).
yes
```

is solved by rule (1), whereas the same query with its arguments reversed:

```
¦ ?- sibling2(alice, jane).
yes
```

is solved by rule (2). Thus, "sibling2" behaves like a symmetric relation. What set of answers do you expect to be produced by the following query?

```
¦ ?- sibling2(X, Y).
```

Asymmetry

A relation that can never be symmetric is *asymmetric*. For instance, the relation between father and son is asymmetric. Certain relations, such as one person loving another, are not necessarily symmetric or asymmetric. By default, the interpreter treats all predicates as asymmetric, as with "sibling1" above.

Reflexivity and Irreflexivity

A relation that holds when both arguments are the same is *reflexive*. "Equal to" or "greater than or equal to" are examples of reflexive relations. A relation that does not hold when both arguments are the same is *irreflexive*. "Taller than" is an example of an irreflexive relation. By default, the interpreter treats predicates as if they are reflexive. Consider the "competitor" rule defined earlier:

```
competitor(C1, C2) :-
    travel(C1, CityA, CityB, _),
    travel(C2, CityA, CityB, _).
```

Since there is no condition that specifies C1 should be different from C2, "competitor" is reflexive by default. Thus, a query to "competitor" may prove that a carrier is its own competitor:

```
! ?- competitor(amtrak, amtrak).
yes
```

This is a nonsensical result, and it would be preferable if "competitor" were rewritten to be irreflexive (see Sec. 4.1).

Transitivity

A relation is *transitive* if it can hold between its arguments through a process of indirection. "Equal to" is an example of a transitive relation: if A is equal to B, and B is equal to C, then A must be equal to C. "Taller than" is also a transitive relation. In Prolog, transitive relations are usually implemented by recursive procedures, e.g. "ancestor" and "can_travel4."

Analysis of Common Relations

Table 1-1 below specifies the properties and constraints of some common relations.

Common Relations				
BINARY RELATION	PROPERTIES			INTEGRITY CONSTRAINT
	Symmetry	Reflexivity	Transitivity	
smaller than	asymmetric	irreflexive	transitive	many-many
equal to	symmetric	reflexive	transitive	many-many
can phone	symmetric	?	?	many-many
sibling	symmetric	irreflexive	transitive	many-many
father	asymmetric	irreflexive	intransitive	one-many
ancestor	asymmetric	irreflexive	transitive	many-many
wife	asymmetric	irreflexive	intransitive	one-one
teacher	?	irreflexive	intransitive	many-many
knows	symmetric	irreflexive	intransitive	many-many

Table 1-1

Bibliographic Notes

Many syntactic variations of Prolog have been invented. In addition to the family of Prologs that follow DEC-10 syntax, there is LM-Prolog (Kahn and Carlsson [1984]), Waterloo Prolog (Roberts [1977]), Prolog/KR (Nakashima [1984]), IC-Prolog (Clark et al. [1982]), micro-Prolog (Clark and McCabe [1984]), IBM Prolog, etc. Each of these has its own syntax. There currently exists a significant user community of only two Prolog syntaxes, however: DEC-10 and micro-Prolog. Of these two, the DEC-10 community is larger. The decision to use DEC-10 Prolog syntax for the examples in the book was based on this purely practical consideration.

Once one is familiar with the basic concepts of Prolog, it does not require much effort to translate code from one Prolog syntax to another. It is even possible to write a Prolog program to do the translation automatically; an example of such a program that translates between DEC-10 syntax and micro-Prolog syntax is presented in Chap. 5.

Readers who read Sec. 0.6 may find the discussion of variable quantification in a Prolog query in Sec. 1.3 to be confusing. In Sec. 1.3, it is stated that the variable Who in the query:

```
¦ ?- knows(mary, Who).
```

is existentially quantified. In Sec. 0.6 it is stated that all variables in a Horn clause are implicitly universally quantified. A Prolog query like the one above can be viewed as a Horn clause that consists of a condition with no conclusion. Recall from the discussion in Sec. 0.6 that the conditions in a Horn clause are negative atomic fomulas. In the example of top-down resolution in Sec. 0.6, clause (14) (i.e. ˜P(a)) is similarly a condition with no conclusion. Thus, we could write the Prolog query above in clausal form as

```
˜knows(mary, X)
```

or, making the quantification of X explicit:

$$\forall X \text{ ˜knows(mary, X)} \qquad (1)$$

i.e. *for all X, mary does not know X*, or *mary knows nobody*. Variable quantification always reverses across negation, so that (1) is logically equivalent to:

$$˜(\exists X \text{ knows(mary, X) }) \qquad (2)$$

i.e. *it is not true that there is some X whom mary knows*, or *mary knows nobody*. Both (1) and (2) capture the logical sense of the Prolog query. The query is more readable if we interpret it as (2), in which the variable is existentially quantified.

A thorough discussion of relation types and integrity constraints is in Reichenbach [1947], pp. 112-124.

Exercises

1. Run Prolog. Use "consult" to interactively add several clauses about your family, or some other application area you know well. Devise queries about the clauses you just entered, using both constants and variables.

2. Use an editor to create a text file called "travel." Enter the "travel" facts and the "can_travel" and "competitor" procedures from this chapter into this file. Run Prolog and load the file. Write a query to find out if you can go from New York to Burlington. Write a query to determine all pairs of companies that are competitors of each other. Write a query to find out if you can go by plane from Kansas City to Nashville.

3. Use the editor to create a Prolog program file called "group." Find out the names of your fellow classmates, and for each name, add a fact to the program that specifies which group (or department) that person is a member of—for example, Henry is in the network development group, Rosemary is in the compiler support group, etc.

Add a rule that specifies that one person knows another if they are both in the same group.

Load the program you just wrote. Write queries to extract the following information: Whom does Henry (or someone in your program) know? Whom does anybody know?

If the program does not produce the results you expect, leave Prolog and go back into the editor. Try to determine why the program is not working, and modify it so that it does work.

4. Conceptually, is the relationship of one person knowing another symmetric? Is it governed by a one-to-one, one-to-many, many-to-one, or many-to-many integrity constraint? What about the "knows" procedure that you just wrote? How might you change the "knows" procedure so that it corresponds to your analysis of the knowing relation?

5. Think of an transitive relation (like "can_travel4") that involves indirection, such as the ownership relationship between a company and its holding company, or the supply relationship between a manufacturing company and its parts suppliers.

Write a Prolog program that represents this relation, including all necessary facts and rules. Test your program to verify that it does what it should.

6. Should the "competitor" procedure be symmetric? Is it symmetric?

7. Begin designing your own "transportation advisor" program. Chose either a network of cities or a network of trains or buses within a city. You should be able to tell the system where you are and where you are going, and it will tell you which trains, buses, planes, etc. to take in order to get there.

2

Arithmetic and Data Structures

2.1 Arithmetic

Arithmetic
Expressions

Prolog has a set of *built-in predicates* that evaluate arithmetic expressions. (A built-in predicate is a procedure that comes with the Prolog interpreter.) The only time that an arithmetic expression will be evaluated in Prolog is when it occurs as an argument to one of these predicates.

An arithmetic expression is made up of integer numbers such as:

```
10   -3   2000
```

and the following set of operators:

```
+   -   *   /   mod
```

With the exception of unary minus, all of these are *infix operators*. An infix operator takes two arguments and is written in between its arguments with no parentheses. In the following list, X and Y stand for either numbers or other arithmetic expressions.

Arithmetic
operators
```
X + Y
X - Y
X * Y
-X
X / Y
X mod Y
```

Note: some versions of Prolog also have floating point numbers and the arithmetic operator `//` to perform integer division (see Appendix IV).

"is"

"is" is a built-in predicate that is also an infix operator. Its first argument is an uninstantiated variable or an integer, and its second argument is an arithmetic expression containing no uninstantiated variables. "is" unifies its first argument with the result of evaluating its second argument.

```
¦ ?- Y is 10 * 4.
Y = 40
```

```
¦ ?- 40 is 10 * 4.
yes
```

```
¦ ?- X is 50,  Y is X / 2.
X = 50
Y = 25
```

```
¦ ?- X is 3,  Y is (5*X)/2.
X = 3
Y = 7 ;

no
```

"is" is
determinate

The last example shows that "is" will produce at most one answer. A predicate that produces only one answer is called *determinate*.

Predicates for
Comparison

The following predicates are for arithmetic comparison. Each of them requires two arithmetic expressions as arguments. The arguments are evaluated before the comparison is performed.

>	*greater than*
<	*less than*
>=	*greater than or equal*
=<	*less than or equal*
=:=	*equal*
=\=	*not equal*

These predicates can be used as follows:

```
| ?- 12 =< 24.
yes

| ?- 50 =\= 50.
no
```

**Argument
Mode**

An argument in a query is considered to be input to the procedure if it is an atom or structure, and output from the procedure if it is a variable. An argument is called *bidirectional* if it can be used for either input or output in a query to a procedure. All rules and facts discussed in Chap. 1 are completely bidirectional.

The built-in predicates for arithmetic comparison, however, are not bidirectional: each argument must be an arithmetic expression without uninstantiated variables. If an uninstantiated variable is given as an argument to one of these predicates, the interpreter will produce an error message.

2.2 Data Structures

**Types of
Terms**

The arguments to a Prolog clause are known as *terms*. There are three types of terms:

constant	An atom (written as a word beginning with a lower case letter or any group of characters inside single quotes), or an integer.

variable	Written as a word begin-ning with a capital letter, as a word beginning with _, or as _ by itself.
compound term *(or structure)*	Written as name(arg1,..., argn), where arg1,...,argn are themselves terms.

Compound terms are similar to records

For readers familiar with Pascal or C, Prolog compound terms are analogous to *records* in Pascal, or *structures* in C—that is, they are programmer-defined arbitrarily complex objects. Following this ana-logy, the *name* and *arity* of the compound term indicate the record type, and the arguments to the compound term correspond to fields of the record. *Structure* is used informally to mean the same thing as *compound term*.

Examples of Compound Terms

The "customer" structure below contains information about a rental car customer, including name, daily rate, and number of days the car was rented. The "date" structure contains information about year, month and day. Both structures are arguments to a "transaction" fact:

```
transaction( customer(smith,29,4), date(86,4,22) ).
```

The "transaction" fact associates information about a customer tran-saction with the date on which it occurred. Note: by convention, structures are written with no space between their arguments, and facts, rules, subgoals, and queries are written with (at least) one space between each argument.

Rule to compute the total owed

Here is a rule that takes a "customer" structure as an argument, and returns the total owed by the customer (i.e daily rate times days rented):

```
%      +                      -
total( customer(_,Rate,Days), Owed) :-
    Owed is Rate * Days.
```

The comment line above the rule is a convention that indicates that the first argument to the "total/2" rule should be input (+) and the second argument should be output (−). Since the customer name is not needed inside of "total," the first argument of the structure is filled by "_".

The "total" rule can be queried as follows:

```
| ?- total( customer('B. Smith',29,4), T).
T = 116
```

What do you expect to happen if you write a query to "total" in which either `Rate` or `Days` is an uninstantiated variable?

Recursive Structures

A Prolog structure can be used in most of the same ways as a C structure. For instance, one way to keep a set of database records in memory is with a recursive data structure (similar to a singly linked list—see Aho et al. [1983]), where one argument in each record points to the next record. To make a recursive structure of "customer" records in Prolog, all that is necessary is to add an additional argument to the "customer" structure and make it point to the next record. Here is a recursive version of the "customer" structure called "cust":

```
cust(smith,29,4, cust(jones,40,5, cust(lee,29,1,end)))
1st record        2nd record        3rd record
```

Notice that each new record is more deeply nested inside of parentheses than the previous one. In the last record of the recursive structure, the fourth field contains the word end to signify that there are no further records.

Prolog recursive structures are somewhat easier to deal with than linked lists in a language like C, because the Prolog interpreter takes care of all of the pointer handling.

Procedure That Builds a Recursive Structure

Recursive structures can be used to describe various kinds of complex interrelationships between terms. For instance, "can_travel5" is a recursive procedure like "can_travel4," except that it builds a recursive "path/3" structure describing all intermediate cities visited on the way from an origin city to a destination city.

```
%        Company      Origin       Destination   Type
travel(amtrak,        new_york,    boston,        train).
travel(nj_transit,new_york,        princeton,     train).
travel(amtrak,        boston,      portland,      train).
travel(greyhound, boston,          portland,      bus).
travel(amtrak,        new_york,    washington,    train).
travel(peoples,       new_york,    washington,    plane).
travel(peoples,       burlington,  new_york,      plane).

can_travel5(A, B, path(A,Type,B) ) :-
    travel(_, A, B, Type).

can_travel5(A, B, path(A,Type,Rpath) ) :-
    travel(_, A, C, Type),
    can_travel5(C, B, Rpath).
```

*Queries to
"can_travel5"*

The following queries show how "can_travel5" is used.

```
| ?- can_travel5(new_york, boston, P).
P = path(new_york,train,boston)
```

The answer to this query indicates that there is a direct "path" from New York to Boston on the train.

```
| ?- can_travel5(new_york, portland, P).
P = path(new_york,train,
        path(boston,train,portland)) ;

P = path(new_york,train,
        path(boston,bus,portland))

| ?- can_travel5(burlington, portland, P).
P = path(burlington,plane,
        path(new_york,train,
            path(boston,train,portland)))
```

The answer to the last query indicates that there is a "path" from Burlington to Portland via New York and Boston.

2.3 Lists

Representing Lists with the "./2" Structure

"./2" is a special recursive structure used for representing lists of arbitrary length. "./2" takes two arguments: the first is any kind of term, and the second is either another "./2" structure or the special symbol [ ] that indicates the end of a list.

The following structure represents a list with one element, the atom `kathleen`:

```
.(kathleen,[])
```

This next example represents a list with three elements, `alpha`, `beta`, and `gamma`:

```
.(alpha,.(beta,.(gamma,[])))
```

The Bracket List Notation

Because it is cumbersome to write out lists in the form of "./2" structures, an alternative list notation exists. The elements of the list are written in between square brackets and separated by commas. In bracket notation, the previous two examples are written as:

```
[kathleen]
[alpha,beta,gamma]
```

Notice that it is not necessary to indicate the end of the list explicitly with "[]." The bracket notation and the "./2" notation for lists can be used interchangeably.

Representing a List of Arbitrary Length

Suppose it is necessary to indicate a list with two known elements, but with an indeterminate number of additional elements. Such a list can be represented in the "./2" structure notation simply by putting an uninstantiated variable as the second argument to the deepest "./2" structure:

```
.(one,.(two,X))
```

`.(two,X)` is the deepest "./2" structure, so the length of the overall list depends on the value of `X`. If

```
X = []
```

then the length of the overall list is two, but if

```
X = .(three,.(four,.(five,[])))
```

then the length of the overall list is five.

A List of Arbitrary Length in the Bracket Notation

There is an equivalent way to represent a list of indeterminate length using the bracket notation. The lexical symbol ¦ is used to separate specific elements on the front of the list from a variable representing the rest of the list. The previous example expressed in bracket notation becomes:

```
[one,two ¦ X]
```

Head and tail of a list

¦ divides this list into two parts: the *head* of the list, defined to be all elements in front of ¦ (in this case, the elements one and two), and the *tail* of the list, represented by the variable X. The head of a list is always explicit, and the tail of a list is implicit in the variable on the right hand side of ¦ .

If

```
X = []
```

then the length of the overall list is two, but if

```
X = [three,four,five]
```

then the length of the overall list is five.

In either notation, [ ] indicates an empty list.

Examples of Lists

Below are some examples of lists in the bracket notation. The second example illustrates a list of "phone/2" structures. The last example shows how the element of one list may itself be a list.

```
[representation, of, a, phrase]

[phone(jones,7279112), phone(rodriguez,9421001)]
```

```
[First|Rest]

[[a,b,c], [1,2] | R]
```

The Built-in Predicate "="

"=" is a built-in predicate written in infix notation that tests if its two arguments unify with one another. If one of the arguments contains uninstantiated variables, they will be instantiated if the unification succeeds. "=" is necessary to demonstrate pattern matching with lists below; first, however, consider the following queries that demonstrate how "=" works with nonlist arguments:

```
% unify X with "hello":
| ?- X = hello.
X = hello


% test if "hello" unifies with "goodbye":
| ?- hello = goodbye.
no


% unify two "customer" structures:
| ?- customer(smith,29,4) = customer(X,Y,Z).
X = smith
Y = 29
Z = 4
```

List Unification

The bracket list notation makes it easy to specify an arbitrary number of elements on the front of the list. Here follow some queries that show how different representations of lists unify with one another.

```
% take the first element off the front of a list:
| ?- [F|R] = [1,2,3,4,5].
F = 1
R = [2,3,4,5]


| ?- [F|R] = [a].
F = a
R = []
```

```
% take two elements off the front of a list:
¦ ?- [F1,F2¦R] = [a,b,c,d].
F1 = a
F2 = b
R = [c,d]


¦ ?- [F1,F2¦R] = [a].
no
```

The last query fails because [F1,F2¦R] will only match a list with two or more elements, and the list [a] contains one element.

Lists versus Simple Structures

The same information can often be represented equally well by a list or a simple structure. For instance, here are two representations of an entry in a dictionary:

[hana, flower]   list representation

d(hana, flower)   structure representation
                      ("d" means dictionary)

A useful rule of style is to always use a simple structure if the number of arguments is fixed. In the example above, no dictionary item will ever have more than two arguments, so the "d" structure is more appropriate. The list representation is most useful when the number of items to be represented is unknown.

2.4 Procedures Operating on Lists

Recursive Procedures to Process Lists

A recursive procedure is the easiest way to operate on each element of a list. A recursive procedure is applicable to a list of any length, and thus frees the programmer from having to know the exact length of the list to be processed ahead of time. A recursive procedure for list processing follows the same general form as other recursive procedures: clauses establishing the end conditions come first, followed by a clause that operates on the head of the list and then calls itself recursively with the tail of the list as an argument. An empty list usually constitutes an end condition.

Procedure to print each member of a list

"print_elements" is a simple example of a list processing procedure. "print_elements" takes a list as its single argument, and prints out each element of the list. "write" is a built-in predicate that prints its argument on the terminal. "nl" is a built-in predicate that prints a carriage return/line feed.

```
% base case when list is empty
print_elements([]).                          % (1)


% recursive rule.
print_elements([First|Rest]) :-              % (2)
    write(First), nl,        % operate on first element
    print_elements(Rest).    % recursive call
```

The following queries show how "print_elements" can be used.

```
| ?- print_elements([one, path(raleigh,nashville)]).
one
path(raleigh,nashville)
yes


| ?- print_elements([a,b,c]).
a
b
c
yes
```

Execution of a Query to "print_elements"

The execution of the previous query can be viewed as a sequence of nested procedure calls to "print_elements," each with a shorter list than the previous one. The proof tree in Figure 2-1 shows how the argument to "print_elements" shrinks on each successive call.

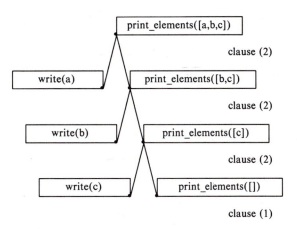

Figure 2-1

Notice that "print_elements" stops recursing when it reaches [ ] (the empty list).

Printing a List in Reverse Order

"rev_print" is almost identical to "print_elements" except that it prints the elements of a list in reverse order. This is accomplished simply by changing the order of the subgoals in the recursive rule, so that the procedure becomes *left recursive.*

```
%  end condition when list is empty
rev_print([]).                        % (1)

%  recursive rule.
rev_print([First|Rest]) :-            % (2)
    rev_print(Rest),        % recursive call
    write(First), nl.       % operate on first element

| ?- rev_print([a,b,c]).
c
b
a
yes
```

Figure 2-2 is a proof tree for the preceding query:

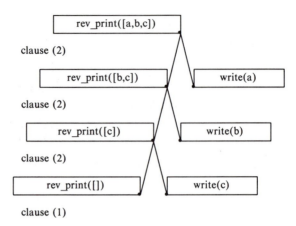

Figure 2-2

The Form of Arguments in the Head of a Rule

The form in which arguments are written in the head of a rule is a way of specifying the circumstances in which the rule applies, because the head of a rule must unify with the query before the interpreter will attempt to evaluate the body of the rule. For instance, the argument in the first "print_elements" rule will only unify with the empty list. The argument in the second rule will only unify with a list containing at least one element (i.e. First). Thus, the second rule will never be attempted if the input argument is the empty list.

It is good programming practice (that is, it results in efficient procedures) to use the form of arguments in the head of a rule to specify when that rule should be evaluated.

Examples of List Processing Procedures

"member" is a list processing procedure that takes two arguments. Its second argument is a list. A query to "member" is true if its first argument is an element in the list.

"member"

```
% base case: X is the first element of the list.
member(X, [X|Rest]).              % (1)

% X is not the first element of the list, so
% look for X in the rest of the list.
member(X, [Y|Rest]) :-            % (2)
    member(X, Rest).

%  is b a member of [a,b,c]?
| ?- member(b, [a,b,c]).
yes

| ?- member(b, b).
no

%  generate members of the list:
| ?- member(X, [1,2,3]).
X = 1 ;
X = 2 ;
X = 3 ;
no
```

Note that in the last query, the first argument is a variable that will unify with anything. This form of a query to "member" will generate each element of the list that is the second argument.

"findword"

"findword" is similar to "member," except that it ends if either the atom is found in the list, or if the list is empty. Notice how the form of arguments in the head of each clause is used to specify the circumstances in which that clause applies.

```
% base case #1: the list is empty
findword(Word, []) :-             % (1)
    write(Word),
    write(' not found'), nl.

% base case #2: Word unifies with first element
findword(Word, [Word|Rest]).      % (2)
```

```
%  recurse if Word does not unify with first element
findword(Word, [Xword¦Rest]) :-              % (3)
     findword(Word, Rest).
```

These queries show how "findword" can be used:

```
¦ ?- findword(the, [in,the,house]).
yes

¦ ?- findword(barn, [in,the,house]).
barn not found
yes

¦ ?- findword(X, [in,the,house]).
X = in ;
X = the ;
X = house
```

If the user types ; once again, what do you expect to happen?

"append"   In "append," all three arguments are lists. The first two arguments are appended together and returned in the third argument. "append" can also be used to divide a list given as the third argument into two sublists. "append" is a *reversible* procedure because all three of its arguments are bidirectional.

```
%  base case: first argument is empty
append([], List,  List).                      % (1)

%  Take X off the front of the first argument
%  and put onto the front of the third argument,
%  or vice versa:
append([X¦List1], List2, [X¦List3]) :-        % (2)
     append(List1, List2, List3).

¦ ?- append([a,b,c], [1,2], Y).
Y = [a,b,c,1,2]

¦ ?- append([a], X, [a,z,m,n]).
X = [z,m,n]
```

```
| ?- append(A, B, [1,2,3]).
```

A = [ ]
B = [1,2,3] ;

A = [1]
B = [2,3] ;

A = [1,2]
B = [3] ;

A = [1,2,3]
B = [] ;

no

Notice that the last query generated all possible ways of dividing the
list [1,2,3] into two lists.

"has_length"   "has_length" takes a list as its first argument, and returns the length
of the list in its second argument.

```
% base case: empty list has 0 elements.
has_length([], 0).                    % (1)

has_length([F|R], N) :-               % (2)
    has_length(R, N1),
    N is N1 + 1.

| ?- has_length([alpha,beta,gamma], Length).
```
Length = 3

```
| ?- has_length([[a,b],X], Length).
```
X = _1
Length = 2

Note that in the last query, the list [a,b] counts as one element,
and the uninstantiated variable X counts as one element.   _1 is the
internal designation of X. It is printed because X is uninstantiated
at the point that the query succeeds. A programmer cannot use such
an internal designation to refer to a variable.

2.5 Representations of a Database

There are several ways to represent a database in Prolog. These include:

1) a set of facts, where each fact corresponds to a database tuple;

2) a set of facts, where each fact corresponds to an attribute/key value pair;

3) a list of structures, where each structure corresponds to a tuple;

4) a linear recursive structure, where each structure corresponds to a tuple (i.e. like the "cust/4" structure); and

5) a recursive structure that is a binary tree, where each node of the tree corresponds to a tuple.

In the rest of this section, an "employee/4" database is represented according to each of the five ways. A query is given for each representation that finds all employees in department 100.

The simplest way of representing a database in Prolog is by asserting each tuple as a fact:

```
%              Name    Dept  Position   Salary
employee1(brian, 100,  operator, 20000).
employee1(nancy, 200,  acct_exec,71000).
employee1(ralph, 100,  manager,  71500).
```

The following query finds all employees in department 100:

```
¦ ?- employee1(N, 100, P, S).
N = brian
P = operator
S = 20000 ;

N = ralph
P = manager
S = 71500 ;

no
```

2) Attribute Fact Representation

Instead of asserting facts containing complete tuples, it is also possible to assert each attribute of a tuple as a separate fact. When necessary, the attributes can be brought together by a rule. One attribute must act as a key to join the others. The name attribute is a suitable key for the "employee" database. The first "employee" tuple could be represented by:

```
department(brian, 100).
position(brian, operator).
salary(brian, 20000).
```

All attributes for an employee can be brought together by a rule such as the following:

```
employee2(Name, Dept, Pos, Sal) :-
    department(Name, Dept),
    position(Name, Pos),
    salary(Name, Sal).
```

This rule defines an implicit database with the same form as the explicit "employee1" database above. With this rule defined, the same query will work:

```
| ?- employee2(N, 100, P, S).
N = brian
P = operator
S = 20000 ;

N = ralph
P = manager
S = 71500 ;

no
```

Attribute assertions are more flexible than tuple assertions, because new attributes can be added without rewriting the existing database. For instance, the rule below prescribes a "bonus" attribute of $1000 to all employees in Department 200.

```
bonus(Name, 1000) :- department(Name, 200).
```

Alternatively, a "years_of_service" attribute can be added for certain employees:

```
years_of_service(brian, 2).
years_of_service(nancy, 1).
```

Adding the "bonus" or "years_of_service" attributes has no effect on the "employee2" rule above.

3) List of Structures Representation

A database can also be conceived of as a *stream of tuples*, and represented in Prolog as a list of structures. Each member of the list is a tuple:

```
% Name Dep Pos      Sal
[e(brian,100,operator,20000),
 e(nancy,200,acct_exec,71000),
 e(ralph,100,manager,71500)]
```

The interesting thing about this style is that the stream of tuples need not ever be asserted into the current program. It might exist only as an argument that is shared between the various subgoals that process it.

The following procedure takes a list of tuples as its second argument and returns one tuple at a time in its first argument.

```
%  return the tuple on the front of the list.
%                 -              +
one_tuple_1( e(N,D,P,S), [e(N,D,P,S)¦Rest] ).

%  ignore the tuple on the front of the list,
%  and call "one_tuple" to get the next tuple
one_tuple_1( e(N,D,P,S), [e(_,_,_,_)¦Rest] ) :-
    one_tuple_1( e(N,D,P,S), Rest ).
```

Once "one_tuple_1" has been defined, it is a simple matter to write a query to find all employees in department 100. This query contains the entire database in its second argument.

```
¦ ?- one_tuple_1( e(N,100,P,S),
                  [e(brian,100,operator,20000),
                   e(nancy,200,acct_exec,71000),
                   e(ralph, 100, manager, 71500)]).
N = brian
P = operator
S = 20000 ;

N = ralph
P = manager
S = 71500 ;

no
```

4) Recursive Structure Representation

A variation on the list of structures representation is a recursive structure representation such as that used in the "cust" example in Sec. 2.2. The "e/4" structure used above is transformed into a recursive structure ("rs") by adding an extra argument that contains the rest of the database.

```
%  Name  Dep Pos       Sal     Rest of database
rs(brian,100,operator,20000,
    rs(nancy,200,acct_exec,71000,
        rs(ralph,100,manager,71500,end) ) )
```

Here is a version of "one_tuple" modified to handle a recursive data structure. "one_tuple_rs" returns an "e/4" structure as its first argument:

```
%   construct an "e" structure
%   from the top level of the recursive data structure:
%                 -              +
one_tuple_rs( e(N,D,P,S), rs(N,D,P,S, Rest) ).


%   ignore the top level of the recursive data
%   structure, and call "one_tuple_rs" to get
%   the next tuple from Rest:
one_tuple_rs( e(N,D,P,S), rs(_,_,_,_, Rest) ) :-
    one_tuple_rs( e(N,D,P,S), Rest ).
```

Again, once "one_tuple_rs" has been defined, it is simple to write a
query that finds all employees in department 100. The second argument to "one_tuple_rs" is the entire database.

```
¦ ?- one_tuple_rs( e(N,100,P,S),
                   rs(brian,100,operator,20000,
                      rs(nancy,200,acct_exec,71000,
                         rs(ralph,100,manager,71500,end)))).
N = brian
P = operator
S = 20000 ;

N = ralph
P = manager
S = 71500 ;

no
```

5) Binary Tree Representation

To take the recursive data structure idea one step further, it is possible to transform the "rs" structure into a binary tree structure ("bt")
by adding one more argument. The purpose of a binary tree is to
store a database in a sorted form. In this example, the database is
sorted on the name attribute.

The structure now requires six arguments:

```
bt(Name, Dept, Pos, Sal, Before, After)
```

Before is a branch of the tree containing all tuples alphabetically
before the current tuple, and After is a branch containing tuples
alphabetically after. Suppose that the tuple for "nancy" is the

topmost node in the tree. Then a binary tree sorted alphabetically by employee name can be pictured as in Figure 2-3:

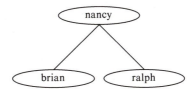

Figure 2-3

and written as:

```
bt(nancy,200,acct_exec,71000,
   bt(brian,100,operator,20000,end,end),
   bt(ralph,100,manager,71500,end,end)
   )
```

Here is a version of one_tuple for the binary tree representation:

```
%  ignore the top level of the binary tree;
%  call one_tuple_bt to get the next tuple in Before:
%              -              +
one_tuple_bt( e(N,D,P,S), bt(_,_,_,_, Before, After) ) :-
   one_tuple_bt( e(N,D,P,S), Before ).

%  return the tuple on the top level of the binary tree:
one_tuple_bt( e(N,D,P,S), bt(N,D,P,S, _, _) ).

%  ignore the top level of the binary tree;
%  call one_tuple_bt to get the next tuple in After:
one_tuple_bt( e(N,D,P,S), bt(_,_,_,_, Before, After) ) :-
   one_tuple_bt( e(N,D,P,S), After ).
```

Once "one_tuple_bt" has been defined, the following query will get all employees in department 100. The entire database is in the second argument.

```
¦ ?- one_tuple_bt( e(N,100,P,S),
                        bt(nancy,200,acct_exec,71000,
                            bt(brian,100,operator,20000,end,end),
                            bt(ralph,100,manager,71500,end,end)
                           )
                      ).
N = brian
P = operator
S = 20000 ;

N = ralph
P = manager
S = 71500 ;

no
```

Properties of
the binary tree
representation

One interesting property of the binary tree representation is that the "one_tuple_bt" procedure will always return tuples from the tree in sorted order, as this query demonstrates:

```
¦ ?- one_tuple_bt(Tuple,
                        bt(nancy,200,acct_exec,71000,
                            bt(brian,100,operator,20000,end,end),
                            bt(ralph,100,manager,71500,end,end)
                           )
                      ).
Tuple = e(brian,100,operator,20000) ;

Tuple = e(nancy,200,acct_exec,71000) ;

Tuple = e(ralph,100,manager,71500) ;

no
```

Evaluation of the Representations

The most important difference between the representations is that each one entails the use of a particular type of algorithm to access it. Specifically, tuple assertion and attribute assertion databases must be accessed by a backtracking algorithm, and databases represented as recursive data structures (including lists and binary trees) must be accessed by a recursive algorithm. The rules and queries in this section are simple examples of these algorithms. The binary tree representation has the advantage that the retrieval time for a particular tuple will usually be less than it would be in one of the other representations. Due to the sorted nature of the tree, fewer tuples need to be considered by the retrieval procedure on the way to finding a tuple of interest.

Bibliographic Notes

The notion of treating a database as a stream of tuples that can be represented by a recursive structure is from Kowalski [1984].

Exercises

1. Write a compound query that instantiates a variable X to 10, and then instantiates a variable Y to the result of multiplying X times 3.

Write the same compound query again, but add a third subgoal that tests the value of Y against 300. Can you explain the results of these two queries?

2. Write a rule to compute the area of a rectangle. It should have three arguments: base, height, and area. Write a series of queries to this rule using a variable and a number for each argument.

Is this program reversible (i.e. are the arguments bidirectional)?

3. Try a query to "append" that appends two existing lists together into a third list. Try another query that generates all possible combinations of sublists that can be formed from a list with ten elements.

4. Write a new version of "findword" that counts the number of occurrences of a word in a list.

5. Write a version of "has_length" that does not count the word "none" when it occurs as an element of a list. That is, the new version should return a count of 5 when given the following list:

```
[a, b, c, d, e]
```

but should return a count of 3 when given this list:

```
[a, none, c, d, none]
```

6. Could the "can_travel5" procedure be redefined to be symmetric?

7. Suppose that you have a list of "cust" structures like the following:

```
[cust(a,29,3), cust(b,29,6), cust(c,40,2)]
```

where the first argument of each structure is customer name, the second argument is daily rate, and the third argument is number of days. Write a rule to calculate the grand total of all customer receipts in the entire list.

8. Write a version of "ancestor" that returns a list of all intervening generations between an ancestor and a descendant. For instance, suppose that Henry is the father of Jack, Jack is the father of Richard, Richard is the father of Charles, and Charles is the father of Jane. A query about whether Henry is an ancestor of Jane should return a list showing how they are related; specifically,

```
[jack, richard, charles].
```

9. Write a version of "can_travel" that interfaces to the "transportation advisor" program you wrote for the exercise in Chap. 1. Add an argument to this procedure that returns a list of all points visited from the origin to the destination.

10. Write a recursive procedure that, given a database in the form of a binary tree, will convert it into a list of tuples.

11. Compare "xancestor" in Sec. 1.6 with "rev_print" in Sec. 2.4. Both procedures are left recursive. Why does "rev_print" work and "xancestor" not work? (Hint: examine how arguments are specified in the heads of clauses for both procedures.)

3

Controlling Execution

3.1 How Prolog Evaluates a Query

**Three
Semantic
Models**

In Chap. 0 we mentioned three distinct semantic models that can give meaning to Prolog code: the *declarative model*, the *procedural model*, and the *abstract machine model*. The declarative model specifies the meaning of a Prolog predicate as a definition of a static relation between terms. The order of the conditions in a rule is unimportant in this model. The procedural model specifies the meaning of a rule as a series of subprocedure calls, and therefore can explain rules in which the order of subgoals is significant. The abstract machine model is similar to behavioral semantic models of other programming languages. It specifies the behavior of the interpreter in response to the evaluation of a construct of the language. This model can accurately account for input/output and control side effects in Prolog programs.

The declarative and procedural models were discussed in Chap. 1. The following section explains the abstract machine model in terms of operations on a stack of active queries. We first examine how the abstract machine executes a Prolog program that contains no control side effects, then consider how control constructs such as *cut* and *repeat* affect the operation of the abstract machine.

**Evaluation of
a Query**

The operation of a Prolog interpreter can be understood as *a recursive cycle of unification (pattern matching) and subgoal evaluation.* Triggered by a query, the interpreter will descend as deep as necessary into the structure of the current program to find facts that validate the query, and then return having proved or failed to prove the query.

When a user types in a query to the interpreter, the query is *activated*. The interpreter searches through the currently asserted clauses for the first clause whose head unifies with the query. For a query to unify with the head of a clause, both must have the same predicate name and same arity, and all arguments of both must unify. Rules governing the unification of terms are given below.

Activating a matching clause

When a clause is found that unifies with the query, it is activated, and each of the subgoals in the body of the clause is evaluated in the same way as the original query. If the unifying clause has an empty body (that is, it is a fact), then the query succeeds immediately. If the interpreter fails to find a clause in the database that unifies with a goal, it backtracks: it returns to the last successful subgoal, undoes the instantiation of any variable that was made as a result of the success of this subgoal, and begins looking for the head of another clause in the current set of clauses that unifies with this subgoal.

Success

If the interpreter successfully evaluates the user's query, it prints out the values of any variables in the query that were instantiated as a result of the evaluation process, or the word *yes* if there were no variables. If the user types ; after the interpreter has found an answer, it has the effect of rejecting the answer. The interpreter backtracks and looks for an alternative answer.

Rules Governing Unification of Terms

The unification of two terms is governed by the following rules. All examples use the built-in predicate = that tries to unify its two arguments.

1) A variable unifies with a constant or a structure; as a result, the variable becomes instantiated to the constant or structure.

```
! ?- X  =  joan.
X = joan
```

2) A variable unifies with a variable; both variables become the same variable.

```
¦ ?- X = Y.
X = _1
Y = _1
```

(_1 is the internal name of both X and Y.)

3) _ unifies with anything.

```
¦ ?- joan = _.
```

4) A constant unifies with a constant, if they are identical.

```
¦ ?- joan = joan.
yes
```

5) A structure unifies with a structure if the structure names are the same, and if the arguments can be unified.

```
¦ ?- father(george) = father(X).
X = george
```

The "uncle" Example

To illustrate this discussion of the query evaluation process, we use the following simple program made up of a "father" database, a "brother" database, and an "uncle" rule.

```
father(bill, daniel).
father(bill, kenneth).

brother(daniel, kenneth).
brother(john, bill).

uncle(U, N) :-
    brother(U, B),
    father(B, N).
```

For the rest of the section, we alternately focus on the actions of the interpreter in general, and the specific events in the evaluation of a query to the "uncle" rule.

**The Query Is
Activated**

When the user types in a query, it is placed on top of the *active query stack* and is said to be *activated*. Consider the following query to the "uncle" program:

```
| ?- uncle(john, W).
```

The diagram below is a snapshot of the state of the interpreter just after the query "uncle(john, W)" is activated.

(1)

- Active Queries -   **- Program Clauses -**


```
?- uncle(john, W).
```

As soon as there is a query on the stack, the interpreter locates the set of clauses that have the same predicate name and same number of arguments as the query. If there are no such clauses, the query fails. The diagram below shows the query pointing to the beginning of the set of "uncle" clauses:

(2)

- Active Queries -   **- Program Clauses -**


```
?- uncle(john, W).        -------->    uncle(U, N) :-
                                          brother(U, B),
                                          father(B, N).
```

**Unification of
the Query**

The interpreter considers the first clause in the set of "uncle" clauses, and attempts to unify each argument of the query with each argument of this clause. In this case, the "uncle" query successfully unifies with the head of the "uncle" rule. As a result of the unification, U is instantiated to john, and W and N become the same, uninstantiated variable. Once a variable in the head of a rule has been unified with another term, *every instance* of that variable in the rule is similarly affected. The following diagram shows the state of the interpreter just after this unification.

(3)

- Active Queries -   - Program Clauses -

?- uncle(john, W).   -------->   uncle(john, W) :-
                                          brother(john, B),
                                          father(B, W).

Evaluating the Body of a Clause

After a query has been unified with the head of a clause, the interpreter considers the body of the clause. If the body of the clause is *empty* (that is, the clause is a fact), then the query succeeds immediately. If the body of the clause is not empty, then the interpreter places each subgoal in the body on the query stack in turn and evaluates it. If all subgoals in the body of the clause can be evaluated successfully, then the original query succeeds.

The body of the "uncle" rule

The body of the "uncle" rule consists of the compound query `brother(john, B), father(B, W)`. The first subgoal, `bother(john, B)`, is placed on the query stack, as shown below:

(4)

- Active Queries -   - Program Clauses -

?- uncle(john, W).   -------->   uncle(john, W) :-
                                          brother(john, B),
                                          father(B, W).

?- brother(john, B).   -------->   brother(daniel, kenneth).
                                       brother(john, bill).

The new query, `brother(john, B)`, is now the active query. The original "uncle" query is still there, however, waiting for the evaluation of the body of the "uncle" rule to complete. The "brother" query is now pointing to the beginning of the set of "brother" clauses.

If unification fails, go on to the next clause

If the attempted unification of a query with the head of a clause fails, then the interpreter goes on to consider the next clause in the set of relevant clauses. This process continues until a clause is found that can be unified with the query. If the interpreter reaches the end of the set of clauses without having found a unifiable clause, then the query fails.

The interpreter tries to unify the subgoal `brother(john, B)` with the clause `brother(daniel, kenneth)` and fails, because `john` does not unify with `daniel`. At this point, the interpreter moves ahead to consider the next clause in the set of "brother" clauses:

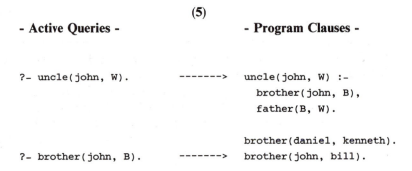

(5)

- Active Queries -   **- Program Clauses -**

```
?- uncle(john, W).        ------->   uncle(john, W) :-
                                       brother(john, B),
                                       father(B, W).

                                     brother(daniel, kenneth).
?- brother(john, B).      ------->   brother(john, bill).
```

The query `brother(john, B)` does unify with the clause `brother(john, bill)`, with the result that `B` is instantiated to `bill`. After this successful unification, the state of the interpreter is:

(6)

- Active Queries -   **- Program Clauses -**

```
?- uncle(john, W).        ------->   uncle(john, W) :-
                                       brother(john, bill),
                                       father(bill, W).

                                     brother(daniel, kenneth).
?- brother(john, bill).   ---->      brother(john, bill).
```

Notice that every occurrence of the variable `B` in the "uncle" rule assumed the value `bill` as a result of the last unification.

The "brother"
subgoal
succeeds

The clause `brother(john, bill)` is a fact (it has an empty body), so the "brother" subgoal immediately succeeds. The interpreter now places the second subgoal in the "uncle" rule, `father(bill, W)`, on top of the stack.

(7)

- Active Queries -   **- Program Clauses -**

```
?- uncle(john, W).          ------->   uncle(john, W) :-
                                          brother(john, bill),
                                          father(bill, W).

                                       brother(daniel, kenneth).
?- brother(john, bill).     ---->      brother(john, bill).

?- father(bill, W).         ------->   father(bill, daniel).
                                       father(bill, kenneth).
```

**Evaluating
the "father"
Subgoal**

The interpreter tries to unify the subgoal `father(bill, W)` with
the clause `father(bill, daniel)` and succeeds, with the result
that `W` is instantiated to `daniel`. The state of the interpreter is
now:

(8)

- Active Queries -   **- Program Clauses -**

```
?- uncle(john, daniel).     ---->      uncle(john, daniel) :-
                                          brother(john,bill),
                                          father(bill,daniel).

                                       brother(daniel, kenneth).
?- brother(john, bill).     ---->      brother(john, bill).

?- father(bill, daniel).    --->       father(bill, daniel).
                                       father(bill, kenneth).
```

Since `father(bill, daniel)` is a fact, the "father" query
succeeds immediately. There are no more subgoals in the body of
the "uncle" rule, so the original "uncle" query succeeds. The interpreter prints the value of `W`:

W = daniel

Note that the entire stack of active queries is still in place after the
first answer is found.

**Failure and
Backtracking**

If the active query reaches the end of the set of relevant clauses, it fails. If the active query is part of a compound query (i.e. a list of subgoals) and is not the first subgoal in the compound query, then the interpreter *backtracks* to reconsider the previous subgoal in the compound query. If the active query is the first subgoal in a compound query, then when it fails, the compound query fails as well. When the interpreter backtracks, all variable instantiations made by the last active query are undone.

*Causing
backtracking
with ;*

After the interpreter has found a single answer to a query, the user may ask for another one by typing ;. ; rejects the answer just given, and causes the interpreter to backtrack and search for another. Specifically, ; causes the *most recently activated query* (i.e. the query on top of the stack) to fail at its current location in the set of relevant clauses. If variables were instantiated by the last success of this query, these instantiations are undone. The interpreter begins reevaluating the query at the next available clause.

*Another
answer from
the "uncle"
query*

Suppose that the user types in ; after seeing the first answer to the "uncle" query, W = daniel. The "father" subgoal on top of the stack is made to fail, and the instantiation of the variable W caused by the last success of this subgoal is undone. The interpreter starts trying to unify the subgoal again at the next available "father" clause:

(9)

- Active Queries -		- Program Clauses -
?- uncle(john, W).	------>	uncle(john, W) :-
		brother(john, bill),
		father(bill, W).
		brother(daniel, kenneth).
?- brother(john, bill).	---->	brother(john, bill).
		father(bill, daniel).
?- father(bill, W).	------>	father(bill, kenneth).

The interpreter unifies the subgoal `father(bill, W)` with the clause `father(bill, kenneth)`, with the result that W is instantiated to `kenneth`. The state of the interpreter is now:

(10)

- Active Queries -		- Program Clauses -
?- uncle(john, kenneth).	--->	uncle(john, kenneth) :- brother(john,bill), father(bill,kenneth).
		brother(daniel, kenneth).
?- brother(john, bill).	---->	brother(john, bill).
		father(bill, daniel).
?- father(bill, kenneth).	-->	father(bill, kenneth).

At this point, the "uncle" query succeeds again. The interpreter prints the new value of W:

    W = kenneth

Looking for a Third Answer

Suppose that the user types ; once more, rejecting the last solution and causing the interpreter to look for an additional answer. This causes the "father" subgoal to fail, and the instantiation of the variable W to kenneth is undone. But now the "father" subgoal has reached the end of the set of "father" clauses:

(11)

- Active Queries -		- Program Clauses -
?- uncle(john, W).	--------->	uncle(john, W) :- brother(john,bill), father(bill,W).
		brother(daniel, kenneth).
?- brother(john, bill).	---->	brother(john, bill).
		father(bill, daniel). father(bill, kenneth).
?- father(bill, W).	-------->	

At this point, the "father" query fails and is removed from the stack. Then the interpreter backtracks to the previous subgoal in the compound query, brother(john, B). Backtracking causes the last success of the "brother" subgoal to fail and the instantiation of the variable B to be undone. However, the "brother" query has now reached the end of the set of "brother" clauses:

(12)

- Active Queries -   **- Program Clauses -**

```
?- uncle(john, W).      ---------->    uncle(john, W) :-
                                           brother(john,B),
                                           father(B,W).

                                       brother(daniel, kenneth).
                                       brother(john, bill).
?- brother(john, B).    ------->
```

So the "brother" subgoal fails and is removed from the stack. Since this was the first subgoal in the body of the "uncle" rule, the "uncle" rule fails. The interpreter backtracks and looks for another "uncle" clause. But at this point, the "uncle" query has reached the end of the set of "uncle" clauses:

(13)

- Active Queries -   **- Program Clauses -**

```
                                       uncle(john, W) :-
                                           brother(john,B),
                                           father(B,W).
?- uncle(john, W).      ---------->
```

So the "uncle" query fails and is removed from the stack. The interpreter responds with

no

to acknowledge that it can find no more answers, and returns to the top level prompt.

Looking for Nonexistent Answers

A more complex example will show how the interpreter sometimes wastes time looking for answers that do not exist. The "register" rule below specifies which people must register for the selective service system.

```
age(brian, 18).
age(mike, 17).
age(steve, 18).

male(brian).
male(mike).
male(steve).

register(X) :-
    male(X), age(X,Y), Y = 18.
```

Evaluation of a Query to "register"

Suppose a user enters the following query:

```
| ?- register(W).
```

The following diagrams illustrate the steps taken by the interpreter to evaluate the query.

(1)

- Active Queries -   **- Program Clauses -**

```
?- register(W).        ------------>    register(W) :-
                                            male(W), age(W,Y), Y = 18.
```

(2)

- Active Queries -   **- Program Clauses -**

```
?- register(W).        ------------>    register(W) :-
                                            male(W), age(W,Y), Y = 18.

?- male(W).            ---------------->  male(brian).
                                          male(mike).
                                          male(steve).
```

(3)

- Active Queries -   **- Program Clauses -**

```
?- register(brian).      -------->    register(brian) :-
                                         male(brian), age(brian,Y),
                                         Y = 18.

?- male(brian).          ----------->  male(brian).
                                       male(mike).
                                       male(steve).

?- age(brian, Y).        ---------->   age(brian, 18).
                                       age(mike, 17).
                                       age(steve, 18).
```

---

(4)

- Active Queries -   **- Program Clauses -**

```
?- register(brian).      -------->    register(brian) :-
                                         male(brian), age(brian,18),
                                         18 = 18.

?- male(brian).          ----------->  male(brian).
                                       male(mike).
                                       male(steve).

?- age(brian, 18).       --------->    age(brian, 18).
                                       age(mike, 17).
                                       age(steve, 18).

?- 18 = 18.
```

At this point the query succeeds, and the interpreter prints

```
W = brian
```

Another answer   But consider what happens if the user types ; to ask for another answer:

(5)

- Active Queries -   **- Program Clauses -**

?- register(brian).   --------->   register(brian) :-
                                          male(brian), age(brian,Y),
                                          Y = 18.

?- male(brian).   ------------>   male(brian).
                                       male(mike).
                                       male(steve).

                                       age(brian, 18).
?- age(brian, Y).   --------->   age(mike, 17).
                                       age(steve, 18).

---

(6)

- Active Queries -   **- Program Clauses -**

?- register(brian).   --------->   register(brian) :-
                                          male(brian), age(brian,Y),
                                          Y = 18.

?- male(brian).   ------------>   male(brian).
                                       male(mike).
                                       male(steve).

                                       age(brian, 18).
                                       age(mike, 17).
?- age(brian, Y).   --------->   age(steve, 18).

(7)

- Active Queries -   **- Program Clauses -**

```
?- register(brian).      -------->    register(brian) :-
                                         male(brian), age(brian,Y),
                                         Y = 18.

?- male(brian).          ------------>    male(brian).
                                          male(mike).
                                          male(steve).

                                          age(brian, 18).
                                          age(mike, 17).
                                          age(steve, 18).
?- age(brian, Y).        ---------->
```

---

(8)

- Active Queries -   **- Program Clauses -**

```
?- register(W).          ------------>    register(W) :-
                                          male(W), age(W,Y), Y = 18.

                                          male(brian).
?- male(W).              --------------->    male(mike).
                                          male(steve).
```

From this point on, the query will not succeed when W is instantiated
to mike because he is only seventeen, but it will succeed again when
W is instantiated to steve.

*Useless search
for an
alternative age*

Notice how much time the interpreter spends looking for an alternative age for Brian. Intuitively, we recognize that the relationship
between a person and their age is a many-to-one relationship, and
would not expect to find a second age for Brian. The Prolog interpreter, however, mechanically plows through the rest of the "age" database after Brian's age has already been found. If the "age" database is large, this search could take up a considerable amount of
time. The next section discusses how to eliminate this kind of useless
search by means of the built-in predicate "cut."

**Viewing
Program
Execution
Automatically**

All versions of Prolog have *debugging facilities* that enable you to watch the interpreter as it evaluates a query. The exact nature of these facilities is different in each version, however, so you should consult your manual or Appendix IV to find out what facilities your version has and how to use them. If the debugging facilities of your Prolog are not adequate, there is a program in Chap. 7 called "vis" (for *visible Prolog*) that provides a highly detailed level of debugging information. So, when you need to know exactly what the interpreter is doing when it evaluates a query (i.e. to find out where it is going wrong, or if it is wasting time), you can:

1) draw detailed active query diagrams describing the steps taken by the interpreter, like the ones in this chapter;

2) use your interpreter's debugging facilities to watch the program execute; or

3) enter the "vis" program from Sec. 7.3, and use it to watch the program execute.

3.2 The Cut

**Search Space
of a Query**

The *search space* of a query is the set of all possible answers considered by the interpreter during the evaluation of a query. In the previous section, the full search spaces of queries to "uncle" and "register" were explored. Clearly, part of the search space for the "register" query—when the interpreter is trying to find a second age for Brian—does not contribute to the program's ability to find correct answers, and could be eliminated to make the program more efficient.

**The Cut
Stops
Backtracking**

The cut (!) is a special built-in predicate that instructs the interpreter not to backtrack beyond the point at which it occurs. The cut is used primarily to reduce the size of the search space of a query. Cut should be used with discretion, however. It has no clear declarative meaning (i.e. it is always true), so using it means sacrificing some of the clarity of a program. The presence of cut can disrupt the execution of a program in unexpected ways.

The cut has two distinct effects: one on a compound query, and one on a set of clauses forming a procedure.

Effect of Cut on a Compound Query

Consider a situation where a cut is one of the subgoals in a compound query. After the interpreter has passed the cut, it will no longer be able to backtrack to those subgoals that came before the cut. Thus, the cut has the effect of committing the interpreter to the values of any variables that were instantiated to the left of it.

Here is an example of a compound query with a cut:

```
¦ ?- a(X), b(Y), !, c(X, Y, Z).
```

In the evaluation of this query, the interpreter passes through the cut only if both the a(X) and the b(Y) subgoals are successful. Once the cut has been passed, then should the "c" subgoal fail with the current values of X and Y, the interpreter will not backtrack to reconsider subgoals "a" and "b."

This compound query has no declarative meaning. Procedurally, however, it may be read as:

> *Get a value of* X *from "a,"*
> *and a value of* Y *from "b,"*
> *then evaluate* c(X,Y,Z).

Effect of Cut on a Procedure

Suppose the interpreter is backtracking through a set of clauses that form a procedure. One of the clauses has a cut in its body. If the interpreter reaches that cut, it will not be able to backtrack to consider other clauses in the set.

"a" procedure without cut

As an example, consider the following "a" procedure both with and without a cut. Without a cut, "a" is defined as:

```
a(1) :-
    write('one').
a(X) :-
    d(X),
    write('two').
a(3) :-
    write('three').

d('2a').
d('2b').
```

A query to "a" will produce the following answers:

```
| ?- a(N).
one
N = 1 ;

two
N = 2a ;

two
N = 2b ;

three
N = 3 ;

no
```

At the point that the second answer is produced, the state of the interpreter is as follows:

- **Active Queries** -   - **Program Clauses** -

```
                                        a(1) :-
                                           write('one').
?- a('2a').        --------------->     a('2a') :-
                                           d('2a'),
                                           write('two').
                                        a(3) :-
                                           write('three').


?- d('2a').        --------------->     d('2a').
                                        d('2b').
```

"a1" procedure
with cut

Here is an alternative version of "a," called "a1," with a cut in the middle of the second rule:

```
a1(1) :-
    write('one').
a1(X) :-
    d(X),
    !,                  % cut
    write('two').
a1(3) :-
    write('three').

d('2a').
d('2b').
```

Consider what happens when the interpreter evaluates the following query to "a1."

```
¦ ?- a1(N).
one
N = 1 ;
```

When the user types ;, the interpreter backtracks and begins evaluating the body of the second "a1" rule. The "d" subgoal instantiates X to 2a, the interpreter passes through the cut, and then the "write" subgoal writes the word *two* on the screen:

two
$N = 2a$;

The behavior of the interpreter in producing these first two answers is exactly the same as it is for the query to "a" above; the effect of the cut has not appeared yet. But consider what happens when the user asks for a third answer. The interpreter tries to backtrack from the `write(two)` subgoal. Because of the effect of cut on a compound query, however, it cannot backtrack to the "d(X)" subgoal to get another value of "X." Because of the effect of cut on a set of clauses, the interpreter will not go on to consider the third "a1" rule. Thus, there are no more answers, and the interpreter answers:

no

Because of the cut, the state of the interpreter after the second answer is as follows:

- Active Queries -   **- Program Clauses -**

```
                                        a1(1) :-
                                          write('one').
                                        a1(X) :-
                                          d(X),
                                          !,
                                          write('two').
                                        a1(3) :-
                                          write('three').
?- a1(N).        ----------------->
```

```
                                        d('2a').
                                        d('2b').
?- d(X).         ------------------>
```

**Cut as a
Subgoal in a
Compound
Query**

Here follow several examples of how cut can be used. Using cut as the last subgoal in a compound query insures that the query will only find one answer:

```
| ?- uncle(john, W), !.
W = daniel ;

no
```

Cut to Make a Procedure Determinate

A *determinate* procedure is one that the interpreter knows has no further answers. Cut can often be used to make a procedure determinate. For instance, putting cut at the end of each rule in a recursive list processing procedure prevents the interpreter from wasting time looking for additional answers once the end of the list has been encountered; the cut signals the interpreter that the procedure is determinate. Here is a determinate version of "member" called "membercheck":

```
membercheck(X, [X|Rest]) :- !.
membercheck(X, [Y|Rest]) :-
    !, membercheck(X, Rest).

| ?- membercheck(c, [a,b,c,d]).
yes
```

However, the cuts in this procedure prevent it from being used to generate all of the elements of a list:

```
| ?- membercheck(X, [a,b,c,d]).
X = a ;

no
```

Cut to Eliminate Part of the Search Space

In the "register" program discussed earlier, we discovered that the interpreter wastes time looking for more than one age for the same person. There are two views of this problem: 1) part of the search space of a query to "register" is useless, and could be eliminated without impairing the program's ability to produce all correct answers; or 2) "age" should be governed by a one-to-many integrity constraint, but instead it is governed by a many-to-many integrity constraint by default. The question is: how can cut be used to define a new version of "register" that can produce all the same answers as the original version but without wasting time looking for multiple ages? A related question is: how can cut be used to make a version of "age" that is governed by a many-to-one integrity constraint?

Stop after one answer

Let us start with the simpler problem of how to write a query to "age" that produces just one answer. Whatever solution we come up with to this problem may be useful in a future version of "register."

The obvious way to write a query to "age" that produces just one answer is a compound query in which the second subgoal is a cut. This works well if the first argument to "age" (the name) is a constant and the second argument (the age) is a variable:

```
age(brian, 18).
age(mike, 17).
age(steve, 18).

¦ ?- age(brian, Y), !.
Y = 18 ;

no
```

Note that the query refuses to look for an additional age for Brian.

However, if the first argument to "age" is a variable and the second argument is a constant, this approach prevents the interpreter from finding valid answers to the query:

```
¦ ?- age(X, 18), !.
X = brian ;

no
```

There is more than one eighteen-year-old person in the database, but because of the cut, this query will generate only the first one. Thus, the answer set of the program is *incomplete*.

Cut as a subgoal of "register"

Let us consider what happens if this same kind of compound query (that is, "age" subgoal plus cut) is put into the body of the "register" rule.

```
register2(X) :-
     male(X), age(X,Y), !, Y = 18.
```

A query to "register2" works well when the argument is a constant:

```
| ?- register2(brian).
yes

| ?- register2(mike).
no
```

but not so well when the argument is a variable:

```
| ?- register2(X).
X = brian ;

no
```

The query fails to generate the answer X = steve, so again the answer set of the program is incomplete.

Isolating the Effect of Cut

What is needed is a way to *isolate the effect of the cut*. We want to preserve the effect of the cut on the "age" subgoal, but eliminate its effect on the compound query that forms the body of the "register" rule. This can be accomplished by moving the cut out of the "register" rule to a lower level, such as into the "age" database itself. We construct an "xage" database in which each clause is a rule with a cut as its only subgoal.

```
xage(brian, 18) :- !.
xage(mike, 17) :- !.
xage(steve, 18) :- !.

register3(X) :-
    male(X), xage(X,Y), Y == 18.
```

A query to "register3" now works well when the argument is either a constant or a variable:

```
| ?- register3(mike).
no
```

```
| ?- register3(X).
X = brian ;

X = steve ;

no
```

Because there is a cut in each "xage" rule, the interpreter will not attempt to find more than one age for anybody. Thus, the useless part of the search space has been eliminated without affecting the completeness of the answer set—the second query found both Brian and Steve.

However, the cure for "register" has had a drastic side effect on "xage." A simple query to "xage" with variables cannot generate all of the people and ages in the database:

```
| ?- xage(X, Y).
X = brian
Y = 18 ;

no
```

The answer set is clearly incomplete. There are other answers in the database, but the interpreter will not find them because of the cuts. Using cuts in this way demodularizes a program, in the sense that any rule or compound query that attempts to use "xage" as a subgoal will also be affected by the cuts inside "xage." Ideally, one should never have to be concerned about how a cut in a subprocedure will affect a procedure that calls that subprocedure.

A General-purpose Rule to Isolate the Effect of Cut

A more flexible approach is to leave the "age" database in its original cut-free form, and write a special rule just to isolate the effect of the cut. "once" is a rule that takes a query as an argument. Its body consists of two subgoals: the query, and a cut. When "once" is evaluated, the cut insures that only one answer to the query is found. When "once" occurs in a compound query, the interpreter can backtrack over it; thus it does not have the same effect on a compound query as a cut does. Here is the definition of "once," and a version of "register" that uses it:

```
once(P) :-
    P, !.

register4(X) :-
    male(X), once(age(X,Y)), Y == 18 .


¦ ?- register4(brian).
yes


¦ ?- register4(X).
X = brian ;

X = steve ;

no
```

If the use of "once" seems obscure, remember that the argument to a predicate can be a structure. In the query to "once," `age(X,Y)` is a structure. `age(X,Y)` is transformed into a subgoal inside of "once."

The "register4" program meets our requirements in all ways. Because of the cut in "once," the interpreter will not waste time trying to find extra ages for anybody. The "age" database is free of cuts and so can be used for purposes other than the "register4" rule (i.e. its modularity is preserved). Since there is no cut directly in the body of "register4," the answer set of a query to "register4" will be complete.

3.3 Negation as Failure

Negative Information

Information regarding facts that are not true, or relations that do not hold, is referred to as *negative information*. Negative information is not usually stored explicitly in a Prolog program. Instead, all information not in the current set of clauses is assumed to be false, as if the following rule were always operative:

If a clause P *is not currently asserted, then the negation of* P *is currently asserted.*

The Closed World Assumption

In practical terms, this means that the interpreter is unable to distinguish between an *unknown* clause and a *provably untrue* clause. The rule above is known as the *closed world assumption*. The set of clauses currently asserted is referred to as a *world*. It is a *closed world* because the interpreter behaves as if it contains all possible knowledge. The closed world assumption is a result of the implicit metalanguage predicate governing the meaning of a Prolog query (see Sec. 0.9).

If and Only If

Because of the closed world assumption, a set of clauses defining a relation have a metalanguage meaning that is slightly different from their object language meaning. As an illustration, suppose that only the following three "executive" clauses are asserted:

```
executive(george).
executive(harry).
executive(nancy).
```

On the level of the object language, these three clauses mean:

X *is an executive if*
    X *is* George, *or*
    X *is* Harry, *or*
    X *is* Nancy.

But because of the closed world assumption, the meaning of these three clauses on the level of the metalanguage is actually:

X *is an executive* **if and only if**
    X *is* George, *or*
    X *is* Harry, *or*
    X *is* Nancy.

The "only if" part of this meaning is a result of the closed world assumption.

**The Open
World
Assumption**

An alternative to the closed world assumption for handling unknown information is the *open world assumption*:

> *If a clause* P *is not currently asserted,
> then* P *is neither true nor false.*

According to the open world assumption, a query might have any one of three possible truth values: *true*, *false*, or *unknown*. If a query is evaluated as unknown, the program might take some special action such as consulting an alternative source of knowledge. A Prolog interpreter is governed by the closed world assumption by default, so a program must be written explicitly to behave in accordance with the open world assumption. Writing such a program amounts to changing the implicit metalanguage predicate governing the meaning of a query.

**Explicit
Negation**

"not" (or "\+" in some versions of Prolog) is a built-in predicate that takes a query as an argument, evaluates it, and then reverses its truth value. If the query succeeds, then the "not" of the query fails, and if the query fails, then the "not" of the query succeeds. The following query:

```
¦ ?- not(father(peter, X)).                    % (1)
```

will be true only if

```
¦ ?- father(peter, X).                         % (2)
```

fails.

*Variable
quantification
in a "not"
query*

As discussed in Sec. 1.3, the variable X in query (2) above is *existentially* quantified; query (2) indicates the question:

> *Does there exist some* X *for whom Peter is the father?*

The variable X in query (1), on the other hand, is *universally* quantified. This query indicates the question:

Is Peter not the father of anybody?
(or: For all x, is Peter not the father of x?)

To verify this point, note that it requires only one value of **x** (representing someone for whom Peter actually is the father) to make query (1) fail. Note that the quantification of a variable always reverses (i.e. goes from existential to universal, or vice versa) when a clause is negated.

Example of
"not"

Here is a rule that defines a rural dweller as someone who is neither an urban dweller nor a suburban dweller.

```
urban_dweller(jake).

suburban_dweller(susan).

rural_dweller(X) :-
    not(urban_dweller(X)),
    not(suburban_dweller(X)).
```

What answer do you expect from the following query?

```
| ?- rural_dweller(bill).
```

An Open
World
Procedure

Here is a simple example of a procedure that behaves in accordance with the open world assumption. A query can have three possible truth values: *true, false* or *unknown.* False statements must be explicitly asserted into the current program as facts of the form `false(X)`, where **X** itself is a fact. If a statement cannot be proved either true or false, it is assumed to be unknown.

```
prove(P) :-
    P, write('**true'), nl, !.

prove(P) :-
    false(P), write('**false'), nl, !.

prove(P) :-
    not(P),
    not(false(P)),
    write('**unknown'), nl.
```

Assume that the following facts are asserted:

```
father(philip, charles).        % a positive fact
false(father(charles, X)).      % a negative fact
```

The following queries show how "prove" can be used:

```
! ?- prove(father(philip, ann)).
**unknown
yes

! ?- prove(father(philip, X)).
**true
X = charles
```

What answer do you expect from this query?

```
! ?- prove(father(charles, mary)).
```

3.4 Built-in Predicates for Input/Output

**Input/Output
Side Effects**

Prolog provides certain built-in predicates for input and output. Each of these predicates produces an *input/output side effect*. That is, when a query to one of these predicates is evaluated, it has some permanent effect on the environment, such as printing a message to the screen or reading a word from a file.

Each of the input/output predicates has a clear procedural meaning. However, like cut, these predicates have no declarative meaning.

Each of them is *determinate*, in the sense that a query to one of them will succeed only once.

`put(X)`   X is an integer whose value is an ascii code. "put" puts a character corresponding to X onto the current output stream.

`write(X)`   "write" writes a term onto the current output stream.

`nl`   "nl" writes a carriage return/line feed onto the current output stream.

`get0(X)`   "get0" unifies X with the ascii code of the next character in the current input stream.

`read(X)`   "read" unifies X with the next term on the current input stream, as delimited by a fullstop (a period followed by either a space or a new-line). Example:

```
¦ ?- read(X).
hello.
X = hello
```

Note that the period entered by the user is not included in the value of X.

Example Query Using "read"

Here is a complicated compound query that uses "read." Suppose that the following database of languages is asserted, and that a user who speaks French answers questions posed by the compound query below.

```
language(italian).
language(german).
language(japanese).
language(french).
language(english).
```

```
¦ ?- language(L),
      write('Do you speak '), write(L), write('?'), nl,
      read(A),
      A = yes,
      !,
      write('Aha! So you speak '),
      write(L), write('!'), nl.
```

Do you speak italian?
no.
Do you speak german?
no.
Do you speak japanese?
no.
Do you speak french?
yes.
Aha! So you speak french!

L = french
A = yes

*A
backtracking
algorithm*

The compound query asks the user if he or she speaks Italian, then "reads" the user's answer into variable A. If the user types in no, then the A = yes subgoal fails, and the interpreter backtracks to get a new language. This user finally answered *yes* to the question about French, so the interpreter passed through the cut and printed some additional messages. The cut insures that the query will end after the first *yes* answer; this is why the user was never asked about English.

This compound query is based on a *backtracking algorithm*, so called because the interpreter backtracks its way through the "language" database. In the initial loop, the interpreter goes back and forth between getting a new language and asking if the user speaks that language. There are two ways out of this loop: 1) the compound query fails when there are no more languages in the language database; or 2) execution passes over the cut (never to return) if the user types in yes.

3.5 Built-in Predicates for File Control

Prolog has a sense of the *current input stream* (where input predicates look to for characters) and the *current output stream* (where output predicates put characters). By default, both streams are associated with the user's terminal. The following predicates enable a programmer to associate either stream with a file.

see(F)

F must be a filename. If there is a readable file of that name, it is opened for input and associated with the current input stream, so that any calls to input predicates such as "read," "get0," etc. will take characters from this file.

seeing(F)

This predicate unifies "F" with the name of the file currently associated with the current input stream. If the current input stream is the user's terminal, F is unified with user.

seen

If a file was associated with the current input stream by means of "see/1," then this predicate closes that file and associates the current input stream again with the user's terminal. Example:

```
¦ ?- see('ap.data'),        % open the file for input
     read(R),               % read a term
     write(R),              % process the term
     seen.                  % close the file
```

tell(F)

F must be a filename. This file is created or opened for output and associated with the current output stream, so that any calls to output predicates such as "write," "put," etc. will put characters into this file.

telling(F)

This predicate instantiates F to the name of the file currently associated with the current output stream. If the current output stream is the user's terminal, F is instantiated to user.

told

If a file was associated with the current output stream by means of "tell/1," then this predicate closes that file and associates the current output stream again with the user's terminal.

3.6 Testing the Type of a Term

Prolog provides certain built-in predicates for testing the *type* of a term.

var(X)

"var" is true if its argument is an uninstantiated variable. Examples:

```
| ?- var(X).
yes

| ?- X = london,  var(X).
no
```

In the next example, "true" is a built-in predicate that always succeeds. It is often used as a placeholder in an "or" (;) construct.

```
write_default(X) :-
    ( var(X), X = 'warning: variable' ; true ),
    write(X), nl.

| ?- write_default(hello).
hello
yes

| ?- write_default(X).
warning: variable
yes
```

nonvar(X)

"nonvar" is true if its argument is any kind of term besides an uninstantiated variable. Example:

```
| ?- X = [paris,london,new_york,tokyo],  nonvar(X).
yes
```

integer(X)

"integer" is true if its argument is an integer constant or a variable instantiated to an integer.

atom(X)

"atom" is true if its argument is a noninteger constant. Examples:

```
| ?- atom(17).
no

| ?- atom(father(X)).
no

| ?- atom(paris).
yes
```

Using "var" and "nonvar"

With "var" and nonvar," it is possible to implement a front-end procedure for the "age" database that imposes a many-to-one integrity constraint at retrieval time:

```
%   Many   One
age(brian, 18).
age(mike,  17).
age(steve, 18).


%  Many-to-one Age
mo_age(Name, Age) :-              % (1)
    nonvar(Name),
    age(Name, Age), !.     % cut.

mo_age(Name, Age) :-              % (2)
    var(Name),
    age(Name, Age).        % no cut.
```

If the Name argument in a query to "mo_age" is instantiated, then the query will be answered by rule (1). The cut after the "age" subgoal in this rule ensures that the query will not spend time looking for an additional age after the first one has been found. On the other hand, if the Name argument is uninstantiated, then the query will be answered by rule (2). There is no cut in rule (2), so the query is capable of backtracking through the whole "age" database. The following examples illustrate this behavior.

```
| ?- mo_age(brian, X).
X = 18 ;          %  answer from rule (1)

no
```

```
| ?- mo_age(Who, 18).
Who = brian ;      %  answers from rule (2)

Who = steve ;

no
```

We can now write a version of "register" based on "mo_age," called "register5." A query to "register5" will always find the complete answer set without wasting time looking for alternative ages. Use of the "mo_age" procedure preserves the modularity of both "age" and "register5."

```
register5(X) :-
    male(X), mo_age(X,Y), Y = 18.

| ?- register5(X).
X = brian ;

X = steve ;

no
```

3.7 Manipulating the Current Program

There are several built-in predicates that enable the current set of clauses to be changed under program control.

assert(X)   "assert" adds a clause, X, to the current program. Example:

```
| ?- assert(king(louis, france)).
yes

| ?- king(louis, X).
X = france
```

asserta(X)   "asserta" adds a clause, X, to the current program as the *first* clause of a procedure.

assertz(X)   "assertz" adds a clause, X, to the current program as the *last* clause of a procedure.

retract(C)   "retract" removes the first clause in the current program that unifies
                      with C. Warning: "retract" is a way of *destructively assigning*
                      clauses, and should be used with care. Example:

```
¦ ?- retract(king(louis, france)).
yes

¦ ?- king(louis, X).
no
```

**Updating the
Value of a
Fact**
                      _____

                      Here is a short program that uses "assert" and "retract" to destruc-
                      tively assign the value of a fact containing the current hour.

```
time(10).

changetime :-
    time(H), NewH is H + 1,
    retract(time(H)), assert(time(NewH)).
```

                      Each time that "changetime" is queried, the hour advances by one:

```
¦ ?- changetime.
yes

¦ ?- time(X).
X = 11

¦ ?- changetime.
yes

¦ ?- time(X).
X = 12
```

**A
Backtracking
Algorithm
Using
"assert"**
                      _____

                      Here is another compound query that asks the user about languages.
                      This one asserts facts about the user as it is being evaluated.

```
language(italian).
language(german).
language(japanese).
language(french).
language(english).
```

```
¦ ?- write('Enter your name: '),
    read(Username),
    language(L),
    write('Do you speak '), write(L), write('?'), nl,
    read(yes),
    assert( speaks(Username, L) ),
    fail.
```

Enter your name: brian
Do you speak italian?
no.
Do you speak german?
no.
Do you speak japanese?
yes.
Do you speak french?
no.
Do you speak english?
yes.

no


```
¦ ?- speaks(brian, Y).
```

Y = japanese ;

Y = english ;

no

The compound query asks for the user's name at the top. Two subgoals in the earlier version, read(A) and A = yes, are consolidated into read(yes) which will only be true if the user types in yes. If the user admits speaking a language, then a fact of the form speaks(Username, L) is asserted. "fail" is a built-in predicate that always fails. The "fail" subgoal causes the interpreter to backtrack to get a new language. This process continues until there are no languages left, at which point the compound query as a whole fails.

At the end of the session above, there is a query to "speaks" to display the clauses that were asserted as a result of the compound query. In spite of the ultimate failure of the compound query, it produced a permanent effect on the current program by asserting two "speaks" facts.

How could the compound query be made into a rule?

**A Procedure
That Learns
from the User**

"loc" is a predicate that associates the name of a place with its street
address. Given the name of a place, "loc" will try to look up its address in the "location" database. However, "loc" behaves in accordance with the *open world assumption* in the sense that it does not
simply fail if it is unable to find a place in the "location" database.
Instead, it switches to a different strategy, and consults the user as
an *alternative source of knowledge.* "loc" learns from its own experience by asserting new answers into the current program.

```
location(whitehorse, 8, 11).
location(urban_software, 8, 42).
location(milford_plaza, 8 , 43).
location(penn_station, 7, 32).

loc(X, Ave, Street) :-
    location(X, Ave, Street), !.

loc(X, Ave, Street) :-
    nonvar(X), var(Ave), var(Street),
    write('-- this '), write(X), nl,
    write('what avenue is it near? (Ave# + period) '),
    read(Ave),
    write('what street? (Street# + period) '),
    read(Street).
    assert(location(X, Ave, Street)).
```

The following queries show how "loc" can be used:

```
| ?- loc(whitehorse, Ave, St).
Ave = 8
St = 11
```

```
¦ ?- loc(grand_central, Ave, St).
-- this grand_central
what avenue is it near? (Ave# + period) lexington.
what street? (Street# + period) 42.
Ave = lexington
St = 42


¦ ?- loc(grand_central, Ave, St).
Ave = lexington
St = 42
```

Notice that in the second query, the user was prompted for the address of grand_central. The user typed in lexington and 42, and then the interpreter reported these same values as answers to the query. When the same query is run again, "loc" knows the address of grand_central.

Integrity constraint governing "loc"

Is the relation between a place and its street address governed by a one-to-one, one-to-many, or many-to-many integrity constraint? The way it is currently defined, what integrity constraint is implicitly governing the "loc" rule?

Could you write a new version of "loc" that does something useful in response to a query like:

```
¦ ?- loc(What, 8, 21).
```

if there is nothing in the "location" database on 8th Avenue and 21st Street?

A Self-modifying Program

As a final example of the use of "assert" and "retract," consider the following program that maintains a database of terminals. When "change" is executed, it prompts the user for information and updates the terminal database.

```
terminal(vt220, connected).
terminal(tvi950, connected).
terminal(beehive, connected).
terminal(pc, unconnected).
terminal(wyse, connected).

change_terminal :-
    write('terminal? '),
    read(T),
    write('new condition? '),
    read(C),
    retract(terminal(T, _)),
    assert(terminal(T, C)).


%  example session:

| ?- terminal(vt220, Status).
Status = connected

| ?- change_terminal.
terminal? vt220.
new condition? unconnected
yes

| ?- terminal(vt220, Status).
Status = unconnected
```

3.8 Comparators

X = Y

(Unify.) If both arguments are instantiated, this predicate tests if they are equal. If one is instantiated and the other is not, the uninstantiated one becomes instantiated to the value of the other. If both are uninstantiated variables, they become the same variable.

X == Y

This predicate succeeds if its arguments are exactly the same. It will fail with two different uninstantiated variables. Examples:

```
¦ ?- X == X.
yes

¦ ?- X == Y.
no

¦ ?- X == alpha.
no

¦ ?- alpha == alpha.
yes
```

X \== Y   This predicate fails if its arguments are exactly the same, and succeeds otherwise. Example:

```
¦ ?- alpha \== beta.
yes

¦ ?- X \== alpha.
yes

¦ ?- alpha \== alpha.
no
```

3.9 Other Built-in Predicates

S =.. L   The predicate "=.." is known as *univ*. S is a term. L is a list. This predicate converts a list into a term, or vice versa. If the length of the list is greater than one, then it makes a structure out of the list; the first element in the list becomes the name of the structure, and all other elements in the list become arguments of the structure. Examples:

```
¦ ?- father(george, leo) =.. List.
List = [father, george, leo]

¦ ?- S =.. [flight, 450, san_francisco, los_angeles].
S = flight(450, san_francisco, los_angeles)
```

name(X, L)   X is an atom. L is a list of ascii character codes. If X is instantiated, then "name" breaks it up into a list of character codes. If L is instantiated, then "name" makes a constant out of the list of character codes in L. Examples:

```
| ?- name(help, L).
L = [104, 101, 108, 112]

| ?- name(X, [103, 101, 111, 114, 103, 101]).
X = george

| ?- name(X, [50, 51, 52]), integer(X).
X = 234
```

Note that "name" can be used to convert an integer or a floating point number into character codes, and vice versa.

**A Useful
Input Routine:
"getfield"**

As an input routine, "read" has a limited usefulness because it will only read a single Prolog term followed by a period. The built-in predicate "name" enables us to write a more flexible input routine, "getfield," that reads all characters up to a newline. "getfield" takes a single argument: an uninstantiated variable that will be instantiated with whatever the user types in. If the first character entered by the user is a newline (i.e. the user just hits return), then "getfield" will leave its argument uninstantiated.

"getfield" uses "getchars" to get a list of characters. "getchars" is based on a one character look-ahead scheme. Its first argument is the previous character read, and it returns a list of characters in its second argument. If the first argument is an ascii 10 (i.e. newline), "getchars" returns an empty list. Otherwise, it uses "get0" to get one more character and then recurses to get the rest of the characters on the line.

```
%          -
getfield(Field) :-
    get0(C),                        % if C is newline,
    (    C = 10                      % leave Field uninst.
         ;
         getchars(C, List),          % get chars until newline
         name(Field, List)           % convert List into atom
    ), !.


%  return empty list if prev char is newline:
%          +   -
getchars(10, []) :- !.
getchars(C, [C|Rest]) :-
    get0(C1), getchars(C1, Rest), !.



| ?- getfield(X).
frank smith                         % user enters a value here
X = 'frank smith'



| ?- getfield(X).
                                    % user hits return here
X = _1
```

clause(H,B)   H must be instantiated to the head of a clause. "clause" finds a currently asserted clause whose head unifies with H, and unifies B with the body of the clause. If the clause is a fact, then B is instantiated to the word **true**. Examples:

```
travel(amtrak, ny, boston, train).

can_travel(CityA, CityC) :-
    travel(_, CityA, CityB, _),
    travel(_, CityB, CityC, _).
```

```
| ?- clause(travel(amtrak, Y, Z, train), B).
Y = ny
Z = boston
B = true


| ?- clause(can_travel(X, Y), B).
X = _0
Y = _1
B = (travel(_2, _0, _3, _4), travel(_5, _3, _1, _6))
```

repeat
This predicate generates an infinite number of backtracking choices. It behaves as if defined by:

```
repeat.
repeat :- repeat.
```

This query will read an entire file of terms from "ap.data," writing each one to the screen:

```
| ?- see('ap.data'),      % open the file for input
     repeat,
     read(R),             % read a term
     write(R),            % process the term
     R = end_of_file,     % test for eof
     !,
     seen.                % close the file
```

The only normal way out of this loop is for the `R = end_of_file` condition to succeed, in which case the cut will prevent further backtracking.

findall(E,Q,L)
"findall" is a built-in predicate found in many versions of Prolog that computes all of the answers to a query and returns them in a list. `L` is the list of answers. `E` is the specification of the form of an element of `L`, and can be any kind of term. `Q` is the query.

As an example, suppose that the "language/1" database is asserted as in Sec. 3.7. The following call to "findall" constructs a list of all languages:

```
| ?- findall(L, language(L), List).
List = [italian,german,japanese,french,english]
```

Thus, the effect of "findall" is to map one kind of representation (facts) onto another (lists).

In the following example `E` is the structure `serves(Company,B)`, which is constructed from data supplied by the query `travel(Company, A, B, train)`.

```
travel(amtrak,      new_york,   boston,      train).
travel(nj_transit,new_york,     princeton,   train).
travel(amtrak,      boston,     portland,    train).
travel(greyhound, boston,       portland,    bus ).
travel(amtrak,      new_york,   washington,  train).
travel(peoples,     new_york,   washington,  plane).
travel(peoples,     burlington, new_york,    plane).

| ?- findall( serves(Company,B),
              travel(Company,A,B,train),
       L ).
L = [serves(amtrak,boston),
     serves(nj_trans,princeton),
     serves(amtrak,portland),
     serves(amtrak,washington)] ;

no
```

Note: a version of "findall" is given in Appendix II. Some versions of Prolog have the built-in predicates "bagof" and "setof" that are used for similar purposes.

3.10 Operators

Extensibility of Prolog Syntax

The outward form of Prolog syntax is extensible in the sense that a predicate or structure that takes one or two arguments can be declared as an *operator*. This is accomplished by a call to the built-in predicate "op/3."

A predicate or structure with two arguments can be declared to be an infix operator. An infix operator is written in between its arguments with no parentheses. A predicate or structure with one argument can be declared to be either a prefix or a postfix operator.

Prolog comes with certain operators already defined. "is" is an example of a built-in predicate that is an operator. "+," "-," etc. are structures that are operators.

`op(Precedence,Type,Name)`

Name, the third argument to "op," must be an atom. A call to "op" declares `Name` as an operator. `Precedence` is a number used to disambiguate expressions involving more than one operator (the exact scale of permissible numbers depends on the version of Prolog). For instance, if the "+" operator has a higher precedence than the "*" operator, then the following three expressions are equivalent:

```
X+Y*Z
X+(Y*Z)
+(X,*(Y,Z))
```

Parentheses can always be used in such situations to force an operator precedence.

Type can have one of the following values:

infix types:	xfx	xfy	yfx
prefix types:	fx	fy	
postfix types:	xf	yf	

A Left Associative Infix Operator: "+"

The "+" operator behaves as if it was declared an operator with the following line:

```
! ?- op(500, yfx, +).
yes
```

The type `yfx` specifies that "+" is left associative. Thus, an expression such as:

```
A+B+C+D              i.e. +(+(+(A, B), C), D)
```

can be pictured as a tree growing down to the left (Figure 3-1):

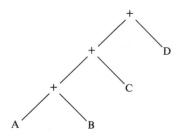

Figure 3-1

A Right
Associative
Infix
Operator: ","

The "," operator behaves as if it was declared:

```
¦ ?- op( 1000, xfy, ,).
yes
```

The type **xfy** specifies that "," is right associative. An expression
such as:

A,B,C,D   i.e. ,(A, ,(B, ,(C, D)))

can be pictured as a tree growing to the right (Figure 3-2):

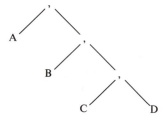

Figure 3-2

A Non-
Associative
Infix Operator

The type **xfx** specifies that an operator is neither left nor right associative. "mod" is an example of an operator of this type. Thus, an
expression such as the following, where one "mod" expression acts as
the argument to another:

```
¦ ?- X is 120 mod 50 mod 5.
```

is illegal, and will cause a syntax error.

Declaring Operators

If you write a procedure with one or two arguments that you plan to use frequently, you may want to declare the procedure name as an operator. The most important criterion for such a decision is the readability of the program. Some operators contribute to readability, but use of many obscure operators can result in a program that is impossible for anyone (including its author) to understand.

As an example, the following command declares "knows" as an infix predicate:

```
| ?- op(750, xfx, knows).
yes
```

At this point, "knows" facts can be asserted into the current program in infix form:

```
jake knows betty.
susan knows mary.
```

and queries to this database can also be written in infix form:

```
| ?- X knows mary.
X = susan
```

The -> Conditional

As another example of operators, consider the predicate "->" defined below. "->" is used by some Prolog programmers as a conditional construct to augment the standard "or" connector, ;. The first argument to "->" is the subgoal A. The second argument is an "or" expression, B ; C. If the A subgoal can be successfully evaluated, then the B subgoal is evaluated, and the C subgoal is ignored. If the A subgoal fails, then the C subgoal is evaluated, and the B subgoal is ignored.

```
| ?- op(1101, xfy, ->).
yes
```

```
% read: "If A then B, else C."
(A -> B ; C) :-  A, !, B.
(A -> B ; C) :-  C.


employee(jane).
employee(sally).
executive(sally).


¦ ?- employee(X),
     ( executive(X) -> write('do not') ; write('do') ),
     write(' invite '), write(X), nl,
     fail.


do invite jane
do not invite sally
no
```

3.11 Converting a Procedural Algorithm to Prolog

Backtracking
vs. Recursion

There are various algorithmic techniques in Prolog that produce the same effect as an iterative loop in a procedural language. The choice of a technique depends primarily on how the data to be processed is represented (Table 3-1). If the data is represented in the form of a list (or another kind of recursive structure), then a recursive algorithm is necessary. If the data is represented as a database of facts, then a backtracking algorithm is necessary.

Representation	Algorithm
facts	backtracking
recursive structure (e.g. a list)	recursion

Table 3-1

A "while"
Loop

As an example, consider the pseudo-code specification of a program that reads "employee/4" records and adds up all of the salaries paid by a particular department. Each "employee/4" record has fields for name, department number, position, and salary.

> *While not at end of "employee/4" database,*
>   *get record;*
>   *if department field contains department of interest*
>   *add salary field to subtotal.*
>
> *At end of database, print subtotal.*

Recursion

Suppose that the "employee" database is represented as a list of records:

```
% Name     Dept    Position      Salary
[e(brian,  100,    operator,     20000),
  e(nancy,  200,    acct_exec,    71000),
  e(ralph,  100,    manager,      71500),
  e(fred,   100,    tech,         29000),
  e(susan,  300,    programmer,   35000)]
```

"rtotal_sal" is a recursive procedure that has three arguments: a list of "e" structures, the department number of interest, and the total salaries paid by that department. The first "rtotal_sal" clause is the end condition. It specifies that recursion should stop when the list of "e" structures is empty. The second clause handles the case when the department field of the first record in the list contains the department of interest. The third clause handles the case when the department field of the first record in the list does not contain the department of interest.

```
rtotal_sal([], _, 0).

% Department field matches:
rtotal_sal([e(_,Dept,_,Sal)|R], Dept, Total) :-
    rtotal_sal(R, Dept, Subtotal),
    Total is Sal + Subtotal.

% Department field does not match:
rtotal_sal([e(_,XDept,_,Sal)|R], Dept, Total) :-
    XDept \== Dept,
    rtotal_sal(R, Dept, Total).
```

The following query will compute the total salary paid by department 100:

```
| ?- rtotal_sal([e(brian,100,operator,20000),
                 e(nancy,200,acct_exec,71000),
                 e(ralph,100,manager,71500),
                 e(fred,100,tech,29000),
                 e(susan,300,programmer,35000)],
                 100, Total).

Total = 120500
```

Backtracking

Suppose there is a database of "employee/4" facts. The "total_sal" procedure below will compute the total salaries paid by a certain department by means of backtracking. The first "total_sal" rule gets a new "employee" fact each time through the loop, retracts the old subtotal, computes a new one, and asserts it in a "running_total" fact. (Note that if the "retract" subgoal were not evaluated through "once," the procedure might backtrack to "retract" and remove the "running_total" fact it just asserted, and continue oscillating between "assert" and "retract.") When there are no further "employee" facts, the first rule fails completely. Thus, the first "total_sal" rule is only there for the side effects it produces on the current program. The second "total_sal" rule simply returns the value of the last subtotal that was asserted in the "running_total" fact, and resets "running_total" to zero.

```
%          Name   Dept Position    Salary
employee(brian,   100, operator,   20000).
employee(nancy,   200, acct_exec,  71000).
employee(ralph,   100, manager,    71500).
employee(fred,    100, tech,       29000).
employee(susan,   300, programmer, 35000).
```

```
running_total(0).

total_sal(Dept, Total) :-                                % (1)
    employee(_, Dept, _, Salary),
    once( retract( running_total(Subtotal) ) ),
    Total is Salary + Subtotal,
    assert( running_total(Total) ),
    fail.

total_sal(_, Total) :-                                   % (2)
    retract( running_total(Total) ),
    assert( running_total(0) ).

! ?- total_sal(100, Total).
Total = 120500
```

Note: Because "running_total/1" is asserted and retracted continually by this program, it has some of the character of a *global variable*.

Using "findall"

"findall" can be used to build a list of all salaries for "employee" facts that have the required department. Once this list exists, the "sum_up" procedure will add them together and return the total.

```
sum_up([], 0).
sum_up([X|R], Total) :-
    sum_up(R, Subtotal),
    Total is X + Subtotal.
```

The query to compute the total is as follows:

```
! ?- findall(S, employee(N,100,P,S), List),
     sum_up(List, Total).
List = [20000, 71500, 29000]
Total = 120500
```

The solution based on "findall" is more general-purpose (and reuseable) than the solution based on the "total_sal" rule above.

Bibliographic Notes

There are various ways to explain the method of the Prolog problem solver; see particularly Colmerauer [1985] and Kowalski [1979]. Implementations of Prolog are discussed in Campbell [1984] and Tick and Warren [1984].

The notion of negation as failure comes originally from Clark [1977]. The closed world assumption is discussed in Reiter [1978] and Nicolas and Gallaire [1978].

There are many papers that warn about the insidious nature of cut. Among the most interesting is O'Keefe [1985]. Kowalski [1984] discusses the dangers of using "assert" and "retract." His attitude is more forgiving toward "assert" than toward "retract," because asserting a new clause while a program is running has some of the character of *lemma generation* (a proof technique in predicate calculus). Hogger [1984] and Kowalski [1984] both compare backtracking and recursive algorithms. Naish [1985] provides an overview of "findall"-like predicates.

Exercises

1. Run Prolog and enter the "travel/4" facts of Sec. 1.4. Write a compound query using a cut that finds just one city to which Amtrak goes from New York, and then finds all of the cities to which Amtrak goes from that city.

2. Write a reversible version of the rectangle procedure of Chapter 2 Exercise 2 using "var(X)" and "nonvar(X)." If any two of the three arguments are instantiated, the procedure should be able to calculate a value for the third argument.

3. Assume the following databases are asserted:

```
age(mary, 16).
age(brian, 17).
age(keith, 15).
age(susan, 15).
```

```
drivers_training(keith).
drivers_training(mary).
drivers_training(brian).
```

Evaluate each of the following compound queries with respect to both 1) the completeness of its answer set, and 2) its efficiency. Consider a compound query to be efficient if it does not spend time looking for a second age for someone.

```
¦ ?- drivers_training(X), age(X, Y), Y >= 16.          % A

¦ ?- drivers_training(X), !, age(X, Y), Y >= 16.       % B

¦ ?- drivers_training(X), age(X, Y), !, Y >= 16.       % C

¦ ?- drivers_training(X), once(age(X, Y)), Y >= 16.    % D
```

Refer to the "age" and "drivers_training" databases above. Write a procedure called "license" that specifies that someone can get a license if they are 16 or older and have taken driver's training, or if they are 17 or older.

4. Think of several relationships that can be described negatively, such as:

A taxi connects A *to* B *if*
  A *and* B *are addresses in New York, and*
  neither a bus nor a train connects A *to* B.

The machine is in a normal condition if
  no annunciators are on.

X *is an AT&T customer if*
  X *has a phone, and*
  X *is neither an MCI customer nor a Sprint customer.*

Write a Prolog rule representing one of these relationship using "not."

5. Write a compound query using "repeat" that asks the user for the names of his or her classmates, and asserts each name into the database in the form

```
classmate(Name).
```

When the user types in the word "end," the query should stop asking for additional classmates, and print out the names of all classmates just entered.

6. Choose some way to represent a database of credit card transactions, where each record contains the spender's name, the transaction type, and the amount. Write a procedure that returns the sum of all transactions associated with a particular spender.

7. Use the debugger to examine the execution of your travel advisor program.

8. Transform the "travel" database into a list of structures. Write a version of "can_travel" that works with this list of structures.

9. Write a version of the "group" program you wrote for Chapter 1 Exercise 3 that asks the user for input when it fails to find an answer in the "group" database.

Use "var(X)," "nonvar(X)," and cut to modify this procedure so that no backtracking will occur if the name argument is not a variable (i.e. one person can be in only one group). If the name argument is a variable, then backtracking may occur.

10. Use the input/output predicates to make a "user friendly" front end to some program you have already written.

11. Define -- and --> to be operators, and rewrite the "can_travel5" procedure of Sec. 2.2 so that it returns answers in the following form:

```
travel(amtrak,    new_york,    boston,      train).
travel(amtrak,    boston,      portland,    train).

¦ ?- can_travel5(new_york, portland, P).
P = new_york--train-->boston--train-->portland
```

4

Approaches to Prolog Programming

Introduction

The first four chapters introduced the elements of Prolog, and provided some examples of Prolog programming style. This chapter contains some concrete suggestions regarding how to think about the programming process. Chapters 5, 6, and 7 consider specific applications of Prolog.

Three Views of a Prolog Program

Broadly speaking, there are three possible *views* a programmer might take of a Prolog program. There is a *relational view* in which the program appears to be a set of mutually defined, possibly very complex relations between terms. There is a *data stream view* in which each procedure relates two or more input/output streams with one another. Here, the set of answers that unfolds from the internal structure of the program over time in response to a query can be considered to be an output data stream. (The word *stream* is used in the loose sense of a sequence of items.) Finally, there is a *behavioral view* in which the program exists just to produce a set of extralogical behaviors, such as getting input, printing messages, etc. These behaviors also unfold from the internal structure of the program over time in response to a query.

The relational view

The view that one uses in order to develop a particular component of a program depends on what aspect of that component is specified (see Table 4-1). The relational view is appropriate if the structure of an application is well understood. The task of programming consists of defining each relation axiomatically (see Secs. 0.9 and 6.1). Input/output streams and program behaviors are the results of queries to a relation; if the relation is implemented correctly, then the input/output streams and behaviors will also be correct.

The data stream view

The data stream view is appropriate if only the nature of an output stream (i.e. an answer set) is known. The task of programming involves inducing an internal program structure capable of producing the desired output stream. If the order of answers in the output stream is important, then explicitly procedural considerations will be involved in the design of the program.

The behavioral view

The behavioral view is appropriate if only the desired behavior of the program is known. The task of programming involves inducing an internal program structure capable of producing this behavior. The design of such a program must necessarily involve procedural and side effect considerations.

Nature of Specification and Type of Programming Required			
What is Known			**Type of Programming**
Structure of System	**Output Datastream**	**Program Behavior**	
known	?	?	define relations axiomatically
unknown	known	?	induce program structure that will produce data stream
unknown	?	known	induce program structure that will produce behavior

Table 4-1

Coexistence of the views

The three views are not mutually exclusive, but amount to different ways of thinking about the process of programming. As a matter of style, it is recommended that you approach the development of a program from either the relational or data stream view, and resort to the behavioral view only when absolutely necessary. The reason for this is that using the behavioral view exclusively often leads to code that is unreadable, unmaintainable, and unportable between versions of Prolog.

4.1 The Relational View

According to the relational view, the basic task of writing an application program is to analyze the significant entities and relations in the application, choose symbols to represent all such entities and relations, and then define each relation with Prolog clauses. Chapter 1 mentioned the classification of relations according to *integrity constraints* (many-to-many, one-to-many, many-to-one, and one-to-one) and *properties* (symmetric/asymmetric, reflexive/irreflexive, transitive/intransitive). Once a relation has been accurately defined with all of its properties and integrity constraints, it can be used as an independent module in the definition of other relations. A good example of this approach is found in Sec. 3.3. A front-end procedure for the "age" database is defined (called "mo_age") that imposes a many-to-one integrity constraint, and then the "register" rule is defined in terms of "mo_age." "mo_age" and "register" are independent of each other, because no additional code is necessary inside of "register" to compensate for the inefficiency or control side effects of "om_age."

Picturing
Relations

It is often helpful when analyzing a binary relation to draw a picture of it, in which each relation is represented by an arc and each term by a point. This kind of picture shows how all terms are related. A symmetric relationship between two terms appears as a double pointed arrow, as shown in Figure 4-1:

Figure 4-1

and an asymmetric relation is pictured as a single pointed arrow, as in Figure 4-2:

Figure 4-2

Accordingly, an asymmetric transitive relation across several levels of indirection comes out looking like a downward growing tree (Figure 4-3):

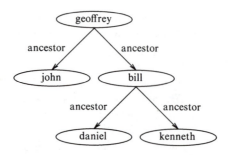

Figure 4-3

A relation that is both symmetric and transitive, such as "travel," would be pictured as in Figure 4-4:

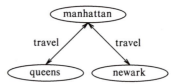

Figure 4-4

**Acquisition
Time Integrity
Constraints**

An integrity constraint can be applied to a relation either at acquisition time, or at retrieval time.

With the closed world assumption in mind, an integrity constraint is a characteristic of the particular set of clauses asserted in the current program. For example, if there is only one "father" fact in the current program, i.e.

```
father(bill, daniel).    % (1)
```

then the "father" relation is implicitly governed by a *one-to-one* constraint. For any query to "father" in which the first argument is the constant "bill," there is only one possible value of the second argument. The same is true for any query in which the second argument is the constant "daniel." But as soon as a fact is added for another of Bill's children:

```
father(bill, kenneth).     % (2)
```

then the "father" relation becomes implicitly *one-to-many* by the closed world assumption. Should another "father" fact with "daniel" as its second argument inadvertently creep into the current program:

```
father(william, daniel).  % (3)
```

then the "father" relation is implicitly *many-to-many*.

If a program is going to depend on the closed world assumption for integrity constraints, then each constraint must be enforced at the point that new clauses are added to the program.

**Retrieval
Time Integrity
Constraints**

Enforcing an integrity constraint by a front-end procedure at retrieval time is a way to optimize the execution of Prolog queries. The most direct way to enforce a one-to-one constraint is to write a procedure that looks up a fact and then goes through a cut. Here is a one-to-one version of father:

```
oo_father(F, C) :-
    father(F, C), !.
```

Because of the cut, any query to "oo_father" will only be able to get one answer. A procedure that enforces a one-to-many constraint on "father" can be written following the model of "mo_age" in Sec. 3.3:

```
father(bill, daniel).
father(bill, kenneth).

%  find the father of a specific child:
%          One   Many
om_father(F,   C) :-            % (1)
    nonvar(C),
    father(F, C), !.           % cut.
```

```
%  find all children of a specific father,
%  or all father/child pairs in the database:
om_father(F, C) :-             % (2)
    var(C),
    father(F, C).              % no cut.
```

This query:

```
| ?- om_father(X, daniel).
X = bill ;

no
```

is answered by rule (1). These queries:

```
| ?- om_father(bill, Y).
Y = daniel ;

Y = kenneth ;

no
```

```
| ?- om_father(X, Y).
X = bill
Y = daniel ;

X = bill
Y = kenneth ;

  ...
```

are answered by rule (2).

Using cut to enforce integrity constraints in a procedure is a safe way to eliminate superfluous parts of its search space.

Implementation of Relation Properties

As mentioned in Sec. 1.5, a binary relation implemented in Prolog has the default properties of *reflexivity*, *asymmetry*, and *intransitivity*. The simplest way to implement a property other than one of the default properties is by explicitly adding facts to establish the property. For example, suppose that the only "sibling" facts in the current program are:

```
sibling(alice, jane).
sibling(dorothy, kathy).
```

Then we can make the "sibling" relation symmetric simply by asserting additional "sibling" facts with the arguments reversed:

```
sibling(jane, alice).
sibling(kathy, dorothy).
```

In this way, the symmetry of the "sibling" relation could be maintained by a data acquisition program that adds two new "sibling" facts for every one entered. The transitivity of a relation like "ancestor" could be maintained in a similar and equally cumbersome fashion.

The alternative to representing every instance of a relation as a fact is to use a procedure to establish the symmetry, irreflexivity, or transitivity of a relation. Thus, the "sibling2" procedure in Sec. 1.3 establishes the symmetry of the sibling relation, and the recursive "ancestor" procedure establishes the transitivity of the "ancestor" relation. Implementing a relation property with a procedure instead of by asserting facts conserves resources tremendously. The following sections deal with the implementation of relation properties not covered in Chap. 1.

Irreflexivity

In Sec. 1.3 we mentioned that the "knows2" relation is inappropriately reflexive, because a query like the following succeeds:

```
| ?- knows2(mary, mary).
yes
```

The "knows" relation can be made irreflexive by adding one more subgoal:

```
knows3(A, B) :-
    work_shift(A, Shift),
    work_shift(B, Shift),
    A \== B.
```

A Symmetric and Transitive Relation

A problem not adequately solved yet is how to represent a relation that is both symmetric and transitive. In Sec. 1.5, we considered a version of the "can_travel" called "can_travel4" that is transitive but not symmetric; i.e. it will allow you to travel from New York to Boston but not from Boston to New York. The data (i.e. the database of "travel/4" facts) was carefully chosen to keep it free of cycles. For instance, there was a "travel" fact connecting Burlington with New York, and New York with Boston, but none connecting Boston to Burlington. Lack of symmetry and the necessity for cycle-free data are severe limitations of "can_travel4." We would like to write a version of "can_travel" that is symmetric and can handle any kind of data.

First Attempt

One approach to this problem is to make the "travel" database symmetric, using the same method that was used for "sibling," and then reference it inside of a recursive version of "can_travel." The "can_travel" rule should inherit this symmetry automatically. We also add the A \== B subgoal to make the relation irreflexive; this should eliminate some erroneous answers. The result is called "tsi_travel1" (for *transitive, symmetric, irreflexive* travel):

```
%  Either one Mode connects A to B:
tsi_travel1(A, B, m(Mode,B)) :-
    A \== B,
    s_travel(A, B, Mode).

%  Or more than one Mode connects A to B:
tsi_travel1(A, B, m(Mode1,C,Mode2)) :-
    A \== B,
    s_travel(A, C, Mode1),
    tsi_travel1(C, B, Mode2).
```

```
%  Symmetric front end to the "travel" database
s_travel(A, B, Mode) :- travel(A, B, Mode).
s_travel(A, B, Mode) :- travel(B, A, Mode).

%      From      To      Via
travel(manhattan, newark, bus).
travel(manhattan, queens, lirr).
```

Note that "travel" is an explicit database where the actual data is kept. For simplicity, this version of "travel" does not have an argument for the name of the carrier. When we try a query to "tsi_travel1" regarding how to go from Newark to Queens, the first answer is acceptable:

```
¦ ?- tsi_travel1(newark, queens, M).
M = m(bus,manhattan, m(lirr,queens)) ;
```

but there seem to be an infinite number of additional answers of dubious value:

```
M = m(bus,manhattan, m(bus,newark,
    m(bus,manhattan, m(lirr,queens)))) ;

M = m(bus,manhattan, m(bus,newark,
    m(bus,manhattan, m(bus,newark,
     m(bus,manhattan, m(lirr,queens)))))) ;

M = m(bus,manhattan, m(bus,newark,
    m(bus,manhattan, m(bus,newark,
     m(bus,manhattan, m(bus,newark,
      m(bus,manhattan, m(lirr,queens)))))))) ;

    . . .
```

Each time we ask for another answer, the procedure goes from Manhattan to Newark one more time before finally going out to Queens on the Long Island Railroad! Because "s_travel" is symmetric, the data is now inherently cyclic. The query to "tsi_travel1" gets lost in a cycle.

Second Attempt

One way to eliminate the oscillation between Newark and Manhattan is to assume that if there is a direct connection between point **A** and point **B**, then there is no reason to look for any further answers. In other words, when the first "tsi_travel" rule succeeds, there should be a cut to prevent the second rule from being tried. Let us ignore temporarily the possible ill effects of this cut, and find out if its presence will eliminate the oscillation problem. The new program is called "tsi_travel2":

```
% Either one Mode connects A to B:
tsi_travel2(A, B, m(Mode,B)) :-
    A \== B,
    s_travel(A, B, Mode), !.        % add cut!

% Or more than one Mode connects A to B:
tsi_travel2(A, B, m(Mode1,C,Mode2)) :-
    A \== B,
    s_travel(A, C, Mode1),
    tsi_travel2(C, B, Mode2).
```

If "s_travel" and "travel" are defined as above, the same query behaves reasonably:

```
| ?- tsi_travel2(newark, queens, M).
M = m(bus,manhattan, m(lirr,queens)) ;

no
```

Intuitively, there should only be one answer to this query, and the program has found it.

But suppose we add just a few new facts to the "travel" database, to get a more regional picture of available transportation. The following "travel" facts:

```
travel(manhattan, newark,    bus).
travel(manhattan, queens,    lirr).
travel(newark,    bronx,     limousine).
travel(bronx,     queens,    bus).
travel(manhattan, bronx,     subway).
travel(newark,    princeton, limousine).
travel(manhattan, princeton, bus).
```

can be represented in a map (Figure 4-5):

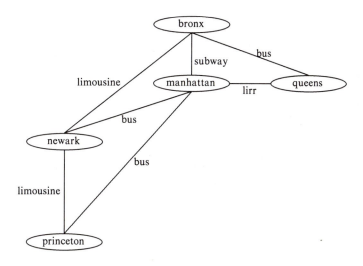

Figure 4-5

With the expanded database, the results of the same query to "tsi_travel2" are not encouraging:

```
| ?- tsi_travel2(newark, queens, M).
M = m(limousine,bronx, m(bus,queens)) ;

M = m(limousine,princeton, m(limousine,newark,
      m(limousine,bronx, m(bus,queens)))) ;

M = m(limousine,princeton, m(limousine,newark,
      m(limousine,princeton, m(limousine,newark,
      m(limousine,bronx, m(bus,queens)))))) ;
 ...
```

It seems that the cut we added solves the oscillation problem only when there are only two entries in the "travel" database. Furthermore, the cut is dangerous in the sense that it could eliminate valid answers: if there were more than one form of transportation that directly connected two points, "tsi_travel2" would only be able to find the first one. The answer set is also incomplete. Because "tsi_travel2" starts oscillating back and forth to Princeton in a limousine, it will never find the most obvious route to Queens through Manhattan.

Again, the data contains cycles, and the query is getting lost in one of them. When you discover cyclic data like this that sabotages a program, there are generally two ways to deal with it: 1) carefully screen all data so as to be sure that it contains no cycles, or 2) make the program immune to cycles. The second solution is preferable for a number of practical reasons. What is needed here is a way to prevent "tsi_travel" from going back to a place where it has already been.

Saving a List of Places Visited

The third version of "tsi_travel" uses a new strategy to avoid getting lost in an oscillation: it keeps a list of places visited, and refuses to return to a place already visited.

The first argument of "tsi_travel3" is a list of all places visited so far. In "tsi_travel3" rule (2), after the "s_travel" subgoal generates a new intermediate point C, the "member" subgoal checks that C is not in the list of places already visited. If C is a new place, it is added to the front of the list in the recursive call to "tsi_travel," so that C will be an invalid intermediate point for any further recursive calls. There is a front-end procedure called "travel3" to translate the original three arguments into four arguments required by "tsi_travel3." In the first call to "tsi_travel3," the starting point A is added to the list of places already visited. "s_travel" and "travel" are the same as above.

```
%  Front end to "tsi_travel3"
%       +  +  _
travel3(A, B, M) :-
    tsi_travel3([A], A, B, M).        % add A to Trail

%  Either one Mode connects A to B:
%               +     + +  _
tsi_travel3(Trail, A, B, m(Mode,B)) :-          % (1)
    A \== B,
    s_travel(A, B, Mode).
```

```
%  Or more than one Mode connects A to B:
%             +      +  +   _
tsi_travel3(Trail, A, B, m(Mode1,C,Mode2)) :-   % (2)
    A \== B,
    s_travel(A, C, Mode1),          % generate C
    not( member(C, Trail) ),        % test C
    tsi_travel3([C|Trail], C, B, Mode2).
```

Let us see how it does with the same query:

```
¦ ?- tsi_travel3(newark, queens, M).
M = m(limousine,bronx, m(bus,queens)) ;

M = m(limousine,bronx,
    m(subway,manhattan, m(lirr,queens))) ;

M = m(limousine,princeton,
    m(bus,manhattan, m(lirr,queens))) ;

M = m(limousine,princeton, m(bus,manhattan,
    m(subway,bronx, m(bus,queens)))) ;

M = m(bus,manhattan, m(lirr,queens)) ;

M = m(bus,manhattan,
    m(subway,bronx, m(bus,queens))) ;


no
```

If you study the map above, you will notice that this program gets *all* valid answers, including the most reasonable answer (taking a bus to Manhattan and the LIRR to Queens). So, "tsi_travel3" is a success because:

1) it is demonstrably symmetric, transitive, and irreflexive;

2) a query to it produces a *complete* answer set; and

3) a query about how to go from Queens to Newark will produce the mirror image of the answer set of a query about how to go from Newark to Queens.

The next step in the evolution of this program might be to assign weights to each direct connection between points corresponding to the *time* or *distance* between them. The program could chose the best route between two places on the basis of the shortest time, least distance, or some combination of factors. (See Exercise 1 at the end of the chapter.)

4.2 The Data Stream View

From Output Data Stream to Program

According to the *data stream* view, the answer set (or output data stream) of a program unfolds from the internal structure of that program as a result of writing a query to the program. If the desired answer set of a needed program is known, then writing the program is a matter of inducing an internal program structure that will produce the answer set. The purpose of the program is to produce the answer set, and it does not matter how it accomplishes this purpose. The program may produce its answer set in response to an input data stream supplied at the time the program is run (i.e. as a argument of the query), or by referencing other clauses in the current program. Once a program has been written that produces the specified answer set, it can be used as a module in the definition of other programs.

In Chap. 3 we discussed two basic families of algorithms used in Prolog programs: backtracking algorithms and recursive algorithms. For many types of problems, backtracking and recursion are equally effective. In the rest of this section, we demonstrate the data stream view with examples of both.

The answer set of a program is a set of values returned by the program under circumstances specified by 1) the query, and 2) the set of all clauses currently asserted. As a trivial example, suppose that the specification of the answer set is that when the department code number is 100, the program should return the employee names Brian and Ralph. A minimum program that meets this specification consists of two clauses:

```
employee(brian, 100).
employee(ralph, 100).
```

and the query:

```
| ?- employee(Name, 100).
```

that produces the values:

N = brian ;

N = ralph

**Ordered
Answer Sets**

An important characteristic of answer sets is whether the order in which the answers are returned is significant. As far as we know, there is no significance to the order of answers from the "employee" program above. But consider a program whose answer set is an ordered set of four-bit binary numbers from 0000 to 1111. The following query:

*Binary number
generator*

```
! ?- number(A,B,C,D).                % (1)
```

should return with its variables instantiated to the *digits* of a binary number. Each time the user types ; the query should produce the next binary number in the sequence. The first answer we expect is:

A = 0
B = 0
C = 0
D = 0 ;

the next answer is:

A = 0
B = 0
C = 0
D = 1 ;

and so on. The simplest way to produce this answer set is to define an ordered set of "number" facts:

```
number(0,0,0,0).
number(0,0,0,1).
number(0,0,1,0).
number(0,0,1,1).
number(0,1,0,0).
    ...
number(1,1,1,1).
```

Query (1) above will backtrack its way through these facts, returning the desired answers. But it is possible to produce the same results with a much more compact procedure.

The answer set amounts to an alternating pattern of ones and zeros, so the place to start is with a simple procedure that returns either a one or a zero:

```
digit(0).
digit(1).
```

Then we can write a "bin_number" (for "binary number") rule that calls "digit" four times:

```
bin_number(A,B,C,D) :-
    digit(A), digit(B), digit(C), digit(D).
```

You should be able to imagine the results of a query to this rule. The rule is doing the same job as four nested *while* loops in a procedural language:

```
A = 0
while A <= 1  begin
    B = 0
    while B <= 1  begin
        C = 0
        while C <= 1  begin
            D = 0
            while D <= 1  begin

                print A B C D

                D = D + 1
            end
            C = C + 1
        end
        B = B + 1
    end
    A = A + 1
end
```

The answer set has exactly sixteen entries. As it stands now, the "bin_number" rule will fail if the user requests another answer when A, B, C, and D are all instantiated to 1.

Generating an Infinite Set

Suppose that we specify that the answer set of the preceding program should be *infinite*, repeating the same pattern of sixteen answers over and over again. Once it reaches four ones, it should go back to four zeros and keep counting. "bin_number" can be modified to produce such an infinite set by adding one more subgoal:

```
inf_bin_number(A,B,C,D) :-
    repeat,
    digit(A), digit(B), digit(C), digit(D).
```

The `repeat` subgoal works as follows: imagine that the user types `;` for another answer when `A`, `B`, `C`, and `D` are all instantiated to `1`. The interpreter backtracks leftward from `digit(D)` until it encounters `repeat`, then starts over again with `A`, `B`, `C`, and `D` all instantiated to zero.

An Ecological Process

In this example, each answer is a statement about the relative balance of the predator and prey populations in a hypothetical ecological situation. The two populations are related to one another as follows:

> *An increase in the prey population causes an increase in the predator population in the next time period (because there is more for the predators to eat);*

> *An increase in the predator population causes a decrease in the prey population in the next time period (because there are more predators to eat the prey);*

> *A decrease in the prey population causes a decrease in the predator population in the next time period (because there is less for the predators to eat); and*

> *A decrease in the predator population causes an increase in the prey population in the next time period (because there are less predators to eat the prey);*

and so on. We want an infinite answer set that keeps going around and around this cycle.

A Backtracking Version

The simplest way to produce this answer set is with four facts describing the relative populations of prey and predators, one for each phase of the cycle. The order in which the facts are written is important, for it should be analogous to the order of phases in the cycle. The first argument of each "population" fact below describes the prey, and the second argument describes the predators:

```
%            Prey        Predators
population(increase,  no_change).
population(no_change, increase).
population(decrease,  no_change).
population(no_change, decrease).
```

Once this "population" database has been defined, the following compound query will go around the cycle for ever:

```
¦ ?- repeat, population(Prey, Predators).
Prey = increase
Predators = no_change ;

Prey = no_change
Predators = increase ;

Prey = decrease
Predators = no_change ;

Prey = no_change
Predators = decrease ;

Prey = increase
Predators = no_change ;
```

and so on. The pattern of the answers corresponds to the temporal phases of the system.

A Recursive Version

It is also possible to produce this answer set using a recursive procedure. We start by establishing a database of *state transitions* in the ecological model. The first argument to each "transition" fact is a "p" structure representing the prey/predator balance in the current state, and the second argument is a "p" structure representing the prey/predator balance in the next state. The assumption is that the situation in the current state causes the situation in the next state.

```
%               Current State          Next State
%               Prey      Predators    Prey      Predators
transition( p(increase, no_change), p(no_change,increase)  ).
transition( p(no_change,increase),  p(decrease, no_change) ).
transition( p(decrease, no_change), p(no_change,decrease)  ).
transition( p(no_change,decrease),  p(increase, no_change) ).
```

"rpop" (for "recursive population") is a procedure that takes a "p" structure representing an initial state of the prey/predator balance as its first argument, and returns a "p" structure representing a later state in its second argument.

```
%     variable names:
%     Cprey   Current prey population
%     Cpred   Current predator population
%     Nprey   Prey population in next period
%     Npred   Predator population in next period

%     +               _
rpop( p(Cprey,Cpred), p(Nprey,Npred) ) :-        % (1)
     transition( p(Cprey,Cpred), p(Nprey,Npred)).

rpop( p(Cprey,Cpred), p(Nprey1,Npred1) ) :-      % (2)
     transition( p(Cprey,Cpred), p(Nprey0,Npred0)),
     rpop( p(Nprey0,Npred0), p(Nprey1,Npred1) ).
```

Rule (1) just looks up the "transition" fact that has the required first argument, and returns the second argument of the fact. Rule (2) looks up this same "transition" fact, but then recurses using the second argument from the fact as the first argument to "rpop." Let us try a query to "rpop" beginning at the point that the prey are decreasing:

```
¦ ?- rpop( p(decrease, _), p(Prey, Pred) ).
Prey = no_change
Pred = decrease ;              % Phase 1

Prey = increase
Pred = no_change ;             % Phase 2
```

```
Prey = no_change
Pred = increase ;              % Phase 3


Prey = decrease
Pred = no_change ;             % Phase 4


Prey = no_change
Pred = decrease ;              % Phase 5,
                               % same as 1
```

In the recursive "rpop" procedure, the order of the answers does not
depend on the order that the "transition" facts are defined (unlike the
backtracking "population" procedure), because of the pattern
matching that occurs in each "transition" fact. Instead, each fact expresses a causal relation between two states. In a more elaborate
program, each "transition" fact could be expanded into a rule. For
instance, a "transition" rule might not let the predator population increase if the local sheriff's department is encouraging hunters to
shoot the predators. Another rule might let the prey population increase only if there is enough food and water:

```
%              Current State           Next State
%              Prey        Predators    Prey        Predators
transition( p(no_change,decrease),  p(increase, no_change) ) :-
    current_season(Season),
    sufficient_food(prey, Season),
    sufficient_water(Season).
```

Both the backtracking and recursive versions of this program produce an infinite answer set. The recursive version, however, uses
more memory, and will terminate when the interpreter runs out of
stack space on some versions of Prolog.

*Description of
the answer set*

The answer set of a query to "population" or "rpop" can be described
as follows: it is a cycle of four phases, and we are interested in two
answers that travel around this cycle offset by one phase from one
another. The order of answers returned by the query maps the flow
of time.

Scheduling a Manufacturing Operation

The final example below is concerned with scheduling jobs through a
manufacturing operation. The answer set of this program also consists of a cyclic pattern, but the number of phases in this cycle is

equal to the number of stations in the manufacturing process. Each answer from the program is a list describing the whereabouts of all jobs in the factory at a particular point in time.

For simplicity, suppose that the manufacturing process is made up of only three processing stations, called `station1`, `station2`, and `station3`. Suppose that there are three jobs, `A`, `B`, and `C`, to be processed. During a time period, a station can process only a single job. Whenever the time period changes, all jobs are moved ahead to the next station. Before a job is moved into the first station to be processed, it is classified as undone. After a job has been completely processed, it is classified as done. The answer set can be depicted as in Table 4-2:

Movement of Jobs Over Time			
	job A	job B	job C
time 1	undone	undone	undone
time 2	station 1	undone	undone
time 3	station 2	station 1	undone
time 4	station 3	station 2	station 1
time 5	done	station 3	station 2
time 6	done	done	station 3
time 7	done	done	done

Table 4-2

The program to produce this answer set uses an unusual recursive algorithm. To begin with, we need to represent the transitions between undone (the state of a job before being processed), the three stations of the process, and done (the state of a job after being processed):

```
%              From    To
transition(undone,    undone).
transition(undone,    station1).
transition(station1, station2).
transition(station2, station3).
transition(station3, done).
transition(done,      done).
```

The first "transition" fact is necessary to keep a job undone until there is room for it at station1. The last fact keeps a job done after it has been processed. "workflow" is a procedure that takes a list of jobs as its first argument, and returns a list of "at" structures describing the whereabouts of each job.

```
% variable names:
% A, B     jobs
% S1, S2   processing stations

%        List of jobs     Locations of jobs
%          +                -
workflow([A,B|Rest],      [at(A,S1),at(B,S2)|Jobs]) :-
    transition(S2, S1),
    workflow([B|Rest], [at(B,S2)|Jobs]).

% Last job in list:
workflow([A],             [at(A,S1)]) :-
    transition(_, S1).
```

The "transition" subgoal backtracks through the "transition" facts to show the movement of one job through the manufacturing process. The "workflow" procedure recursively sets up as many "transition" subgoals as there are jobs in the input list. It also insures that the position of a job will always be one station behind the job ahead of it in the input list. We give it three jobs to process in the following query:

```
| ?- workflow([jobA,jobB,jobC], T).
T = [at(jobA,undone), at(jobB,undone), at(jobC,undone)] ;

T = [at(jobA,station1),at(jobB,undone), at(jobC,undone)] ;

T = [at(jobA,station2),at(jobB,station1),at(jobC,undone)] ;
```

```
T = [at(jobA,station3),at(jobB,station2),at(jobC,station1)] ;

T = [at(jobA,done),     at(jobB,station3),at(jobC,station2)] ;

T = [at(jobA,done),     at(jobB,done),      at(jobC,station3)] ;

T = [at(jobA,done),     at(jobB,done),      at(jobC,done)]
```

Needless to say, this is a model of a fairly simple process. However, the approach used here can be extended by turning the "transition" facts into rules. For instance, the flow of work from station 1 to station 2 might depend on the presence of machine operators at station 1. The case study in Appendix III treats the scheduling of a manufacturing operation in more detail.

Pros and Cons of the Data Stream View

One advantage of the data stream view is that the programmer is always focused on the correctness and completeness of the answers being produced by the program. Using the relational view, it is possible to write a program that looks like an accurate structural description of the application, but that fails to produce a useful answer set. An example of such a program is "tsi_travel1" in Sec. 4.1. Considered from the data stream view, such a program is a complete failure.

Two programs are interchangeable according to the data stream view if they produce the same answer set, regardless of the internal structure of either. Thinking about programs in this way simplifies top-down development of a complex program. Suppose that a program can be broken down into discrete components, and that the answer set that must be produced by each component is known. Early in the development of the program, a component might be implemented by a set of facts. Later, the component can be replaced by a procedure that takes account of additional conditions or subtleties of the answer set.

If the order of an answer set is important, then it is necessary to bear the procedural semantic model in mind when writing a program. A Prolog program can be viewed as an *axiomatic definition of its answer set*, where each clause of the program is equivalent to an axiom. Viewed procedurally, a clause is a sequence of steps necessary to generate or constrain a member of the answer set. Together, the clauses constitute a way of *defining* a member of the set, and of *constructing* the set as a whole.

4.3 The Behavioral View

A programmer who writes a program for its behavioral side effects, to the exclusion of any relational or answer set considerations, is using the *behavioral view*. An example of a program written according to the behavioral view is "loc" in Sec. 3.5. When this program cannot find the location of something in the "location" database, it does not simply fail, but asks the user to supply the location. Other examples of programs written from the behavioral view in Chap. 3 include "change_terminal" (Sec. 3.5) and the compound query about languages (Sec. 3.6).

In general, it is a good programming practice not to use side effects in an ad-hoc way. Instead, try to concentrate all side effects into general-purpose rules, and leave application-specific code as free of them as possible. Clauses that are purely declarative (i.e. are free of side effects) are easy to read and maintain. Code that is highly application-specific is likely to change more frequently than other kinds of code; therefore, the more purely declarative it is, the better.

"loc," "change_terminal" (both in Sec. 3.7), and other similar programs are bad examples in this regard, because they are application-specific procedures that depend on predicates with behavioral side effects.

There are programming situations, however, which require a program to behave in a way that is not obtainable from simple queries to Prolog databases. The user interface component of a large program usually falls into this category, as it is unreasonable to expect a user to type in Prolog queries in order to be able to use a program. Another example of such a situation is the behavior exhibited by "loc": when it cannot find an answer in the "location" database, it asks the user for it, and then adds the answer to the database.

With the previous discussion in mind, suppose we write a general-purpose procedure that uses the same approach to unknown information as "loc." The new procedure is called "find_or_ask," because if it fails to find the required data in some database, it will ask the user for it. "find_or_ask" will only work with relations and attributes declared to be *askable* by an "askable" clause.

"find_or_ask" takes a query as its argument, and tries to evaluate it. If the query succeeds, "find_or_ask" simply returns the result. If the query fails, "find_or_ask" checks a special "askable" database to see if it should ask the user for the answer. If the predicate is in the "askable" database, then "find_or_ask" prompts the user for the missing information, asserts the query as a fact into the current program, and returns the value entered by the user. If the predicate is not "askable," then "find_or_ask" fails.

```
find_or_ask(Query):-
    Query.


find_or_ask(Query) :-
    askable(Query, Prompt, Value),
    var(Value),
    write(Query), nl,
    write(Prompt), write(' '),
    read(Value),
    assert(Query).


%         Fact                Prompt              Variable
askable(travel(A,B,Mode), 'enter the mode:', Mode) :-
    nonvar(A), nonvar(B).

travel(manhattan, queens, lirr).
```

"find_or_ask" can be used as follows:

```
| ?- find_or_ask(travel(manhattan, queens, M)).    % (1)
M = lirr


| ?- find_or_ask(travel(manhattan, brooklyn, M)).  % (2)
travel(manhattan, brooklyn, _0)
enter the mode: subway
M = subway
```

```
¦ ?- find_or_ask(travel(manhattan, brooklyn, M)).  % (3)
M = subway
```

Query (2) shows what happens when "find_or_ask" is used to ask how to travel between two unknown places. Note that at the time of query (3), the fact `travel(manhattan, brooklyn, subway)` has already been asserted, and so the procedure does not ask the user for anything.

Evaluation of the Behavioral View

One problem with the behavioral view is that it tends to lead to code that is complicated and undisciplined. It is possible to write a program that is just as hard to understand as the worst examples of procedural language programming, if one uses predicates with behavioral side effects indiscriminately. The relational and answer set views, however, are inherently more disciplined, and so go a long way toward protecting a programmer (and a program) from such confusion. Therefore, it is recommended that you resort to the behavioral view only when the other two views are clearly inadequate. When you do use it, try to isolate side effects into general mechanisms like "find_or_ask," instead of adding them to application-specific clauses.

A final warning: a program with many behavioral side effects tends to be more susceptible to differences between versions of Prolog, and therefore difficult to port.

Bibliographic Notes

The technique for controlling search by maintaining a list of visited nodes (as is done in "tsi_travel3") is fully explored in Nilsson [1980].

The "find_or_ask" procedure in this chapter was inspired by the *query-the-user* facility of the APES language (Hammond and Sergot [1984]).

Exercises

1. Suppose that the "travel" database of Sec. 4.1 had one more argument containing the number of miles between the two cities. Write a program based on "tsi_travel3" that returns the shortest path between two cities.

There are two approaches to solving this problem, one based on recursion and the other on backtracking.

Recursive solution

The recursive approach uses "findall" to collect all solutions to a query to "tsi_travel3" in a list, and then sorts them to find the solution with the shortest path. Many versions of Prolog have a built-in predicate called "keysort," which takes a list of "-/2" structures as an argument, and returns a list sorted according to the value of the first argument of each "-/2" structure. "-" is an infix operator. Here is an example query to "keysort":

```
! ?- keysort([6-hello, 3-m(ny,plane,la), 2-[one]], X).
X = [2-[one], 3-m(ny,plane,la), 6-hello]
```

In order to use "keysort," it will be necessary to change "tsi_travel3" so that it returns a "-/2" structure as its fourth argument. The first argument of this structure will be a number of miles, and the second argument will be the "m" structure describing the path between two cities. Suppose that the trip from Newark to the Bronx by limousine is 25 miles, and the trip from the Bronx to Queens by bus is 10 miles. Then "tsi_travel3" should return the following answer:

```
! ?- tsi_travel3(newark, queens, M).
M = 35-m(limousine,bronx, m(bus,queens))
```

Once the list of answers to a query to "tsi_travel3" has been sorted, the answer on the front of the sorted list will be the shortest route.

Backtracking solution

In the backtracking approach, an extra argument should be added to "tsi_travel3" which contains the number of miles associated with a certain path between two cities. A front-end procedure needs to be written, called for instance "best_path," which has the same arguments as "tsi_travel3," and which calls "tsi_travel3" as one of its subgoals. "best_path" needs a global variable fact, called for instance "optimum/2," in much the same way that "total_sal" in Sec. 3.11 needs a "running_total" fact. The first argument of "optimum" is an "m" structure describing the path between two cities, and the second argument is the number of miles implied by that path. The first thing "best_path" should do is assert an "optimum" fact that has an impossibly large number of miles, such as:

```
optimum(_, 100000).
```

Then "best_path" should run a query to "tsi_travel3," and compare the miles returned by the query with the miles argument of the "optimum" fact. If the miles returned by the query is less than the miles in the "optimum" fact, the procedure should retract the "optimum" fact and assert a new one that has the miles and path returned by the query to "tsi_travel3." "best_path" should backtrack through all answers to the query to "tsi_travel3" in this way, so that when there are no further answers, whatever path is in the current "optimum" fact will be the shortest path.

Which of the two solutions will be easier to read as a program? Which will execute faster? Which will use less memory? Which approach to Prolog programming (i.e. relational, data stream, or behavioral) is inherent in each solution?

2. In the example of the use of "find_or_ask," the "askable" fact covers the case when the origin and destination of a "travel" clause are known, but the mode of transportation between them is unknown. Could another "askable" fact be added for the case when the destination and mode of transportation are known, but the origin is unknown?

In its present form, "find_or_ask" can deal with a single unknown quantity in the query it evaluates. Can you write a new version of "find_or_ask" that can handle more than one unknown quantity in its query? For instance, it should be able to respond to a query to "travel" in which the mode of transportation is known, but both the origin and the destination are unknown. Can you imagine programming situations in which this new version of "find_or_ask" would be useful?

5

Text Processing

Introduction

Lexical Analysis and Parsing

Because of its strong pattern matching ability, Prolog is a useful language for many kinds of text processing applications, including report generators, stream editors, and language translators. Text processing programs are discussed in some detail in this chapter, because they constitute a practical and immediate use for Prolog.

The job performed by a text processing program can be divided into two phases. In the first phase, called *lexical analysis*, the input text is converted from its external form into some internal representation. In the second phase, the internal representation of the text is analyzed or processed in some way. A *parser* is a procedure that looks for high level syntactic patterns (objects) in the internal representation of a text.

Contents of this chapter

In the first sections of this chapter, we present a basic lexical analysis procedure in Prolog, and then go on to consider examples of two different types of parsers: *top-down parsers*, and *bottom-up parsers*. The example parsers operate with a grammar that covers a simple subset of English. Full natural language processing is beyond the scope of this book; however, these simple parsers give some idea of the design problems that come up in any natural language system.

Two applications of parsers are discussed at the end of the chapter. The first translates a Prolog program from DEC-10 syntax to micro-Prolog core syntax, and vice versa. The second is a database query language that takes queries written in an English-like language and transforms them into Prolog queries.

Parsing Strategies and Problem Solving Strategies

One reason that parsers are so interesting is that there is a close analogy between *parsing strategies* and *problem solving strategies* in general. By default, a Prolog interpreter uses a *backward-chaining* problem solving strategy: it starts from a hypothesis (the query), breaks it into sub-hypotheses (the subgoals of a rule), breaks each sub-hypothesis into further sub-hypotheses, and so on. When it encounters sub-hypotheses that cannot be broken down further (i.e. facts), it has confirmed the original hypothesis. An alternative is a *forward-chaining* strategy, such as is used in the OPS-5 language: it starts from facts, and looks for conclusions that follow from the facts. Then it looks for further conclusions that follow from the first conclusions, and so on until it reaches a goal conclusion.

A top-down parser is based on a backward-chaining strategy (like Prolog), and a bottom-up parser is based on a forward-chaining strategy (like OPS-5). In general, a top-down parser is more efficient than a bottom-up parser, but there are certain grammar constructs that can only be implemented by a bottom-up parser. Since Prolog itself is based on a backward-chaining strategy, it is straightforward to implement a top-down parser in Prolog. The implementation of a bottom-up parser is slightly more complicated, for it requires using Prolog in a procedural way to do forward-chaining. There are other problems for which a forward-chaining strategy is more appropriate.

5.1 A Lexical Analyzer

A lexical analyzer identifies patterns of characters in an input stream, and produces a stream of tokens. Each token represents one of the patterns. The set of tokens produced by the lexical analyzer constitutes an internal representation of the input stream (see Figure 5-1).

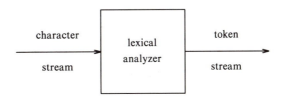

Figure 5-1

"readsent"

The lexical analyzer described here, called "readsent," is modeled closely on a program in Clocksin and Mellish [1984], p. 104 (used with permission). "readsent" identifies *words* and *punctuation marks* in the input stream. It gets one sentence at a time, and returns the list of words in the sentence. A word is defined as a set of letters delimited by blanks or other nonvalid characters. Punctuation marks such as comma and period are treated as words by themselves. A sentence is defined as a series of words delimited by a fullstop punctuation mark (i.e. period, question mark, or exclamation point). Because a newline character is treated like blank space, a sentence can span more than one line.

"readsent" uses two built-in predicates: "get0," that gets one character code from the current input stream, and "name," that converts a list of character codes into an atom. Here is the code for "readsent."

```
% variable names:
%    Lw = list of words
%    W,W1  = single word
%    Lc = list of characters
%    C,C1 = single characters
%         -
readsent([W|Lw]) :-          % read a sentence
    get0(C),
    readword(C, W, C1),
    restsent(W, C1, Lw), !.
```

```
% prev word and next char are input; read rest of sentence.
%          +   +   _
restsent(W, _, []) :-
    fullstop(W), !. % end if prev word was a fullstop.
restsent(W, C, [W1|Lw]) :-
    readword(C, W1, C1),
    restsent(W1, C1, Lw).

% take initial char, read a word, give back next char.
%             +   _   _
readword(C, W, C1) :-
    punctuation(C),
    !,
    name(W, [C]),        % construct a word from the char C.
    get0(C1).
readword(C, W, C1) :-
    valid_char(C),
    !,
    get0(C2),
    restword(C2, Lc, C1),   % get further chars.
    name(W, [C|Lc]).        % construct a word.
readword(C, W, C1) :-
    get0(C2),         % C is not acceptable. Get new char;
    readword(C2, W, C1).    % and try again.

% fill out a word, until an unacceptable char is encountered.
%            +    _        _
restword(C, [C|Lc], C1) :-    % aggregate chars into list
    valid_char(C),
    !,
    get0(C2),
    restword(C2, Lc, C1).
restword(C, [], C).           % end word if C is not a valid char
```

```
% characters that stand by themselves as words:
punctuation(44).           % ,
punctuation(59).           % ;
punctuation(58).           % :
punctuation(63).           % ?
punctuation(33).           % !
punctuation(46).           % .

% spans of chars that are valid:
valid_char(I) :- I > 96, I < 123.    % a-z
valid_char(I) :- I > 64, I < 91.     % A-Z
valid_char(I) :- I > 47, I < 58.     % 0-9

% punctuation marks that terminate a sentence:
fullstop('.').
fullstop('!').
fullstop('?').
```

Algorithm of "readsent"

The algorithm of "readsent" is based on a one character look-ahead scheme. "readsent" starts by getting one character (C) from the input stream, and then passes it to the "readword" procedure. "readword" tests the input character (C) to see if it is a punctuation mark. If it is, "readword" calls "name" to turn it into a word (W), then gets another character (C1) from the input stream. "readword" returns the word (W) as its second argument and the new character (C1) as its third argument. If the original character (C) is not a punctuation mark, then the next "readword" clause tests to see if it is a valid character (i.e. a-z, A-Z, or 0-9). If it is, "readword" calls "restword" to get a list of the rest of the characters in that word (Lc), and then calls "name" to turn the list ([C|Lc]) into a word (W). If, however, the original character (C) was not a valid character, then control drops through to the third "readword" clause. This clause ignores the invalid character (C), gets a new character (C2), and calls "readword" over again with the new character as first argument.

The other procedures, "restword" and "restsent," are similar to "readword." The first clause of "restsent" checks whether the last word found is a fullstop punctuation mark. If it is, "restsent" passes through a cut and succeeds, thereby causing "readsent" to succeed.

"readsent" can be used in a query such as:

```
| ?- write('enter sentence'), nl, readsent(X).
enter sentence
The cow jumped over the moon.

X = ['The', cow, jumped, over, the, moon, '.']
```

According to the current definition, "readsent" simply ignores characters like – or $, as is evident in the following query:

```
| ?- write('enter soc. sec. number and period: '),
     readsent(X).

enter soc. sec. number and period: 123-45-678.

X = ['123', '45', '678', '.']
```

How could you modify "readsent" to accept these characters as valid characters, or as punctuation marks?

5.2 A Top-down Parser

"obj"

A parser is a routine that recognizes syntactic objects in a stream of tokens. The top-down parser presented here, called "obj," takes a list of words and the name of some higher level syntactic object as input. The parser succeeds if it finds words forming the required syntactic object on the front of the list of words; otherwise it fails. The grammar for "obj" is a simple subset of English. The syntactic objects it recognizes are all parts of English sentences, such as "sentence," "verb phrase," or "article."

*"obj" is both
dictionary and
grammar*

In parsing terminology, a *terminal* is an input token, and a *nonterminal* is a syntactic object made up of some combination of terminals or nonterminals. The set of terminals known to a parser is called its *dictionary*. The components of each nonterminal are specified in a *grammar rule*, and the set of grammar rules known to the parser constitutes its *grammar*.

The simple grammar we are concerned with here can be specified in schematic form as:

```
sentence    --> nounphrase  verbphrase
nounphrase --> article  noun
verbphrase --> verb  nounphrase
```

where the arrow is read as "is composed of." In the implementation of this parser, each terminal in the dictionary is represented by an "obj" fact, and each nonterminal in the grammar is represented by an "obj" rule.

```
% variable names:
%    I = input list of tokens
%    O,R = output list of tokens

%    nonterminals:
%    In  Out  Name
obj(I,  O,    sentence) :-
    obj(I, R, nounphrase),
    obj(R, O, verbphrase).
obj(I,  O,    nounphrase) :-
    obj(I, R, article),
    obj(R, O, noun).
obj(I,  O,    verbphrase) :-
    obj(I, R, verb),
    obj(R, O, nounphrase).

%    terminals:
%    In          Out  Name
obj([the|R],    R,    article).
obj([cow|R],    R,    noun).
obj([tail|R],   R,    noun).
obj([shakes|R],R,    verb).
obj([walks|R], R,    verb).
```

Notice that the form of the nonterminal "obj" rules follows the form of the grammar rules exactly.

Using "obj"

The first argument to "obj" is an input list of tokens. The third argument is the name of the object being defined. The second argument constitutes whatever part of the list is left over after the terminal or nonterminal has been taken off the front of the input list. The function of the arguments is clearly shown by this query:

```
¦ ?- obj([cow, horse, goat], Leftover, noun).
Leftover = [horse, goat]
```

The query asks: *is it possible to take a noun off the front of the list*
[cow, horse, goat], *and if so, what part of the list is left over?*
The answer to the query indicates that it is possible, and that the list
[horse, goat] is left over. The query confirmed that the word
cow is a noun.

In a similar way, a query to "obj" will confirm or deny that a list of
words forms a nonterminal:

```
¦ ?- obj([the, cow, '.'], L, verbphrase).
no


¦ ?- obj([the, cow, '.'], L, nounphrase).
L = ['.']                    %  success


¦ ?- obj([the, cow, shakes, the, tail], L, sentence).
L = []                       %  success
```

Using "obj" Backward

All of the arguments to "obj" are bidirectional. This means that
queries to "obj" can also generate whatever syntactic objects can be
derived from an input list of tokens, or even generate all possible sentences in the dictionary and grammar:

```
%  analyze an input list:
¦ ?- obj([the, tail], L, Object).   % (1)
L = [tail]
Object = article ;


L = []
Object = nounphrase ;


no
```

```
%  generate all sentences:
| ?- obj(X, [], sentence).          % (2)
X = [the, cow, shakes, the, cow] ;

X = [the, cow, shakes, the, tail] ;

X = [the, cow, walks, the, cow] ;

X = [the, cow, walks, the, tail] ;

X = [the, tail, shakes, the, cow] ;

X = [the, tail, shakes, the, tail] ;

X = [the, tail, walks, the, cow] ;

X = [the, tail, walks, the, tail] ;


no
```

Note that in query (2) above, `[]` in the second argument specifies that the empty list must be left over after parsing.

The sentences generated by the parser are syntactically correct, but not necessarily *semantically correct*. It is able to produce a nonsensical sentence such as `[the, cow, walks, the, tail]`.

What results do you expect from the following query?

```
| ?- obj(A, B, C).
```

Extending the Grammar

The grammar can be extended in many ways. An interesting extension involves changing the definition of a noun phrase so that it allows any number of adjectives between an article and a noun. Once adjectives such as `big` and `strong` are added to the dictionary, the extended version of "obj" should be able to parse a noun phrase like `the big strong cow`.

If there is more than one grammar rule defining the same nonterminal, this parser acts just like the Prolog interpreter: it tries to parse the input list according to first rule, but if it fails, it tries the next rule, and so on. It is possible to allow adjectives in a noun phrase by defining one rule for the case in which there are no adjectives in the noun phrase, another rule for the case in which there is one adjective in the noun phrase, another rule for two adjectives, and so on:

```
nounphrase --> article noun
nounphrase --> article adjective noun
nounphrase --> article adjective adjective noun
    ...
```

This approach gets tedious quickly. A better strategy is to define an intermediate object (called "adjs") in such a way that it can represent any number of adjectives. "adjs" can be defined by two rules. The first rule takes one adjective off the front of the input list, then recursively calls "adjs" to look for more adjectives in the rest of the list. The second rule takes no words off the input list, establishing that an "adjs" can be composed of no words.

```
adjs       --> adjective adjs       (1)
adjs       -->                      (2)
```

This definition of "adjs" is *right recursive*, because in the first rule, the recursive call to "adjs" is the rightmost component of the rule. The second "adjs" rule is an *empty production*, because it has no components.

Once "adjs" has been defined, it is possible to define a new version of a noun phrase in terms of it:

```
nounphrase --> article adjs noun
```

Implementation of the extended grammar

The extended grammar is implemented by the "obj2" procedure below.

```
%    nonterminals:
obj2(I, O, sentence) :-
    obj2(I, R, nounphrase),
    obj2(R, O, verbphrase).
```

```
obj2(I, O, verbphrase) :-
    obj2(I, R, verb),
    obj2(R, O, nounphrase).

obj2(I, O, nounphrase) :-
    obj2(I, R, article),
    obj2(R, R1, adjs),
    obj2(R1,O, noun).

obj2(I, O, adjs) :-
    obj2(I, R, adjective),
    obj2(R, O, adjs).

obj2(I, I, adjs).

%    terminals:
obj2([big|R], R, adjective).
obj2([strong|R], R, adjective).
obj2([brown|R], R, adjective).

obj2([the|R], R, article).
obj2([cow|R], R, noun).
obj2([tail|R], R, noun).
obj2([shakes|R], R, verb).
obj2([walks|R], R, verb).
```

Note that the second "adjs" clause always succeeds because it has no
conditions. It copies whatever list comes in the first argument into
its second argument.

"obj2" is capable of parsing a sentence that includes a noun phrase
with any number of adjectives:

```
! ?- obj2([the, big, strong, brown, cow, shakes,
          the, big, tail], L, sentence).
L = []
```

What behavior do you expect from the following query?

```
! ?- obj2(X, [], sentence).
```

If the "obj" procedure is intended to generate valid sentences, then is the behavior of the last query acceptable? How could the program be modified to be a better sentence generator?

Method of a Top-down Parser

A top-down parser like "obj" or "obj2" proceeds by assuming a hypothesis and then testing the consequences of the hypothesis against the data found in the input list. The initial hypothesis might be that a "sentence" nonterminal can be located in the input list. According to the grammar rule for a "sentence," this hypothesis is broken down into two sub-hypotheses: that a "nounphrase" and a "verbphrase" can be found in the input list. These two hypotheses are in turn broken down into further sub-hypotheses. The process of breaking down a hypothesis into sub-hypotheses continues until the parser encounters a terminal, at which point it tries to verify the existence of the terminal on the front of the input list. The hierarchy of nonterminals and terminals implied by the grammar of "obj2" is pictured in Figure 5-2.

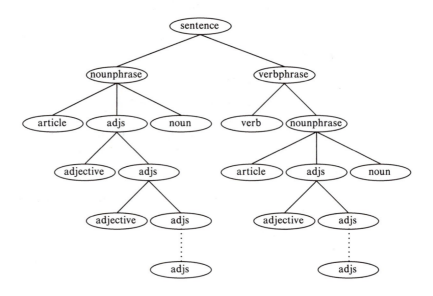

Figure 5-2

5.3 A Bottom-up Parser

**Method of a
Bottom-up
Parser**

A *bottom-up parser* uses a different technique to do the same job as a top-down parser. Bottom-up parsers work up from the data to simple syntactic objects, and then on to more complex syntactic objects. Where a top-down parser is primarily *hypothesis driven* (i.e. the decisions it makes are based on its current hypothesis), a bottom-up parser is *data driven* (i.e. the decisions it makes are based on the data at hand).

There are several strategies that a bottom-up parser might follow. The bottom-up parser described here, "bup_obj," starts by taking a word off the input list. From the dictionary, it finds out what type of terminal this word is. Then it looks through the grammar rules defining nonterminals to see if any of these rules begin with the terminal just identified.

Suppose that the grammar of "bup_obj" is composed of the same three rules:

```
sentence    --> nounphrase verbphrase
nounphrase --> article noun
verbphrase --> verb nounphrase
```

To begin with, the parser finds an "article" at the beginning of the input word list. It looks for a rule whose first component is an "article," and finds a "nounphrase." It then tries to find all remaining components of a "nounphrase." In this case, there is only one: a "noun." If the parser finds a "noun" as the next terminal on the input list, it has successfully identified a "nounphrase." It will then go on to look for another object whose first component is a "nounphrase." If the next terminal it finds is not a "noun," however, it rejects the hypothesis that the words on the front of the input list make up a "nounphrase," and goes back to search for another grammar rule whose first component is an "article."

The parser continues to look for successively higher nonterminals in this way, until it reaches some *goal nonterminal* (such as a "sentence"), at which point it stops. Without a goal nonterminal, the parser would keep going forever.

Form of a "bup_obj" Rule

The bottom-up parser is implemented as a single procedure called "bup_obj." Some of the "bup_obj" rules define terminals, and some define nonterminals. A "bup_obj" rule takes the following form:

```
         Input              First component
         wordlist           of this object

                  Output          Name of   Goal
                  wordlist        object    nonterminal
         bup_obj(Input, Output,   First,  Name,     Goal) :-

            %   subgoals to find other components of this object:
            bup_obj(_, _, terminal, _, Second),
            bup_obj(_, _, terminal, _, Third),
            ...
            %   subgoal to find a nonterminal that has
            %   this object as its first component:
            bup_obj(_, _, Name, _, Goal).
```

Arguments to "bup_obj"

The first argument to "bup_obj" is the input list of words. The second argument is whatever is left of the input list after the parser has attained its goal. The third argument is the name of the first component of the nonterminal defined by this rule. (This component must already have been found for the rule to be called.) If the rule defines a terminal, the third argument is the constant `terminal`. The fourth argument is the name of the object being defined in this rule. The fifth argument is the goal nonterminal; when the goal nonterminal is reached, the parsing procedure stops.

Evaluation of a "bub_obj" rule

At the point that the head of a "bup_obj" rule unifies with a query, the first component of the object defined by that rule has already been found. If the object defined by the rule is a nonterminal, then the body of the rule contains calls to "bup_obj" to find the other components of the object. The last subgoal of each "bup_obj" rule is an *ascending subgoal*; it looks for another nonterminal that has the object defined by this rule as its first component. Thus, the fourth argument in the head of the rule (`Name`) becomes the third argument in the ascending subgoal.

Here is the implementation of "bup_obj."

```
%  end condition when goal is reached:
bup_obj(I, I, Goal, _, Goal) :- !.

%  terminals:
%          +        _ +         _         +
bup_obj([the|R], O, terminal, article, Goal) :-
    bup_obj(R, O, article, _, Goal).

bup_obj([cow|R], O, terminal, noun, Goal) :-
    bup_obj(R, O, noun, _, Goal).

bup_obj([tail|R], O, terminal, noun, Goal) :-
    bup_obj(R, O, noun, _, Goal).

bup_obj([shakes|R], O, terminal, verb, Goal) :-
    bup_obj(R, O, verb, _, Goal).

bup_obj([walks|R], O, terminal, verb, Goal) :-
    bup_obj(R, O, verb, _, Goal).

%   nonterminals:
% sentence  -->  nounphrase verbphrase
%       + _ +            _          +
bup_obj(I, O, nounphrase, sentence, Goal) :-
    bup_obj(I, R, terminal, _, verbphrase),
    bup_obj(R, O, sentence, _, Goal).

% nounphrase  -->  article noun
bup_obj(I, O, article, nounphrase, Goal) :-
    bup_obj(I, R, terminal, _, noun),
    bup_obj(R, O, nounphrase, _, Goal).

% verbphrase  -->  verb nounphrase
bup_obj(I, O, verb, verbphrase, Goal) :-
    bup_obj(I, R, terminal, _, nounphrase),
    bup_obj(R, O, verbphrase, _, Goal).
```

Analysis of
the Parsing
Process

The following query parses a simple sentence.

```
| ?- bup_obj([the, cow, shakes, the, tail],
                O, terminal, _, sentence).
O = []
```

How to read
the diagrams

It is interesting to examine the actions of the parser in response to this query in more detail. Figures 5-3 through 5-9 show various stages in the parsing of the sentence. Each downward pointing arrow represents the start of a new parsing process with the object pointed to by the arrow as its goal. For instance, the initial query starts a parsing process to find a sentence, represented in the picture by an arrow pointing downward at the box labeled "sentence." Each upward pointing arrow represents the actions of an ascending subgoal in one of the "bup_obj" rules.

sentence

article
"the"

Figure 5-3

State 1 (Figure 5-3): a "sentence" is the goal of this process. The parser takes the off the input stream, and finds out that it is an "article."

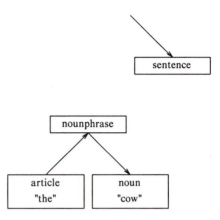

Figure 5-4

State 2 (Figure 5-4): the parser finds that an "article" is the first component of a "nounphrase," and then starts another parsing process to find a "noun" on the input list. It succeeds with cow.

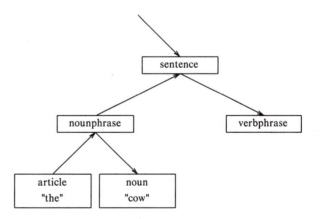

Figure 5-5

State 3 (Figure 5-5): the parser finds that a "nounphrase" is the first component of a "sentence," and then starts another parsing process to find a "verbphase."

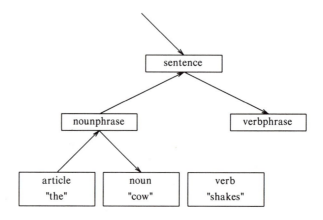

Figure 5-6

State 4 (Figure 5-6): the parser takes `shakes` off the input list, and finds out that it is a "verb."

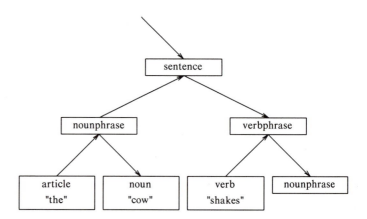

Figure 5-7

State 5 (Figure 5-7): the parser finds that a "verb" is the first component of a "verbphrase," and then starts another parsing process to find a "nounphrase."

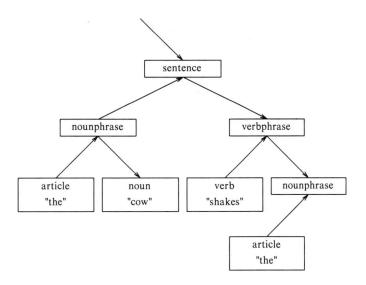

Figure 5-8

State 6 (Figure 5-8): the parser takes "the" off the input list, looks up that it is an article, and finds that an article is the first component of a nounphrase.

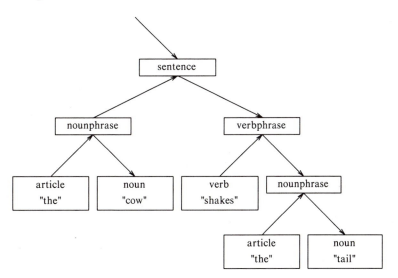

Figure 5-9

State 7 (Figure 5-9): the parser starts another parsing process to find a "noun," which succeeds with "tail." This causes the "nounphrase" process to succeed, which causes the "verbphrase" process to succeed, and which in turn causes the original "sentence" process to succeed.

Left Recursive Rules

In the "obj2" parser, we modified the definition of a "nounphrase" so that it can contain any number of adjectives, by means of a right recursive definition of "adjs":

```
adjs        --> adjective adjs
adjs        -->
```

This same definition cannot be implemented by "bup_obj," because a bottom-up parser cannot handle empty productions. However, a bottom-up parser can handle *left recursive* grammar rules that would cause a top-down parser to go into an infinite loop. Here is a definition of "nounphrase" based on left recursion that allows any number of adjectives:

```
nounphrase --> article adjsnoun      (1)

adjsnoun    --> adjs noun            (2)
adjsnoun    --> noun                 (3)

adjs        --> adjs adjective       (4)
adjs        --> adjective            (5)
```

In this grammar, an "adjs" is left recursively defined to be one or more "adjective" (i.e. "adjs" comes before "adjective" in rule (4)). There is a new intermediate object, "adjsnoun," that is either a noun by itself (by rule (3)), or any number of adjectives followed by a noun (by rule (2)). Rule (1) defines a "nounphrase" as an "article" followed by an "adjsnoun." This grammar is implemented by the "bup_obj2" procedure below.

```
% end condition when goal is reached:
bup_obj2(I, I, Goal, _, Goal) :- !.

% terminals:
%         +          _ +         _          +
bup_obj2([the|R], O, terminal, article, Goal) :-
    bup_obj2(R, O, article, _, Goal).

bup_obj2([cow|R], O, terminal, noun, Goal) :-
    bup_obj2(R, O, noun, _, Goal).

bup_obj2([tail|R], O, terminal, noun, Goal) :-
    bup_obj2(R, O, noun, _, Goal).

bup_obj2([big|R], O, terminal, adjective, Goal) :-
    bup_obj2(R, O, adjective, _, Goal).

bup_obj2([strong|R], O, terminal, adjective, Goal) :-
    bup_obj2(R, O, adjective, _, Goal).

% nonterminals:
% nounphrase -->  article adjsnoun
bup_obj2(I, O, article, nounphrase, Goal) :-
    bup_obj2(I, R, terminal, _, adjsnoun),
    bup_obj2(R, O, nounphrase, _, Goal).

% adjs       --> adjs adjective
bup_obj2(I, O, adjs, adjs, Goal) :-
    bup_obj2(I, R, terminal, _, adjective),
    bup_obj2(R, O, adjs, _, Goal).

% adjs       --> adjective
bup_obj2(I, O, adjective, adjs, Goal) :-
    bup_obj2(I, O, adjs, _, Goal).

% adjsnoun   --> adjs noun
bup_obj2(I, O, adjs, adjsnoun, Goal) :-
    bup_obj2(I, R, terminal, _, noun),
    bup_obj2(R, O, adjsnoun, _, Goal).
```

```
%  adjsnoun   --> noun
bup_obj2(I, O, noun, adjsnoun, Goal) :-
       bup_obj2(I, O, adjsnoun, _, Goal).
```

**Action of the
Left-recursive
Rule**

The left recursive "adjs" rule works as follows. When the parser
takes an "adjective" off the input list, it finds that an "adjective" is
the first component of an "adjs." For each additional "adjective" in
the input list, the parser goes through the "adjs" rule again. When
the parser fails to find another "adjective" on the input list, it looks
for another rule whose first component is an "adjs," and finds an
"adjsnoun." If the next word in the input list is a "noun," then it successfully identifies an "adjsnoun."

*A Query to
"bup_obj2"*

This query shows that "bup_obj2" can parse a "nounphrase" containing any number of adjectives:

```
| ?- bup_obj2([the, big, brown, cow], [],
               terminal, _, nounphrase).
yes
```

The parsing process is illustrated in Figures 5-10 through 5-15.

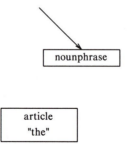

Figure 5-10

State 1 (Figure 5-10): a "nounphrase" is the goal of this process.
The parser takes the off the input stream, and finds out that it is an
"article."

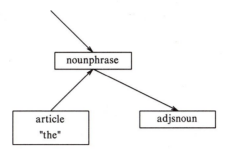

Figure 5-11

State 2 (Figure 5-11): the parser finds that an "article" is the first component of a "nounphrase," and then starts another parsing process to find an "adjsnoun."

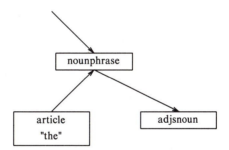

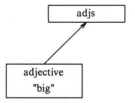

Figure 5-12

State 3 (Figure 5-12): the parser takes an "adjective" off the input stream, and finds that an "adjective" is the first component of an "adjs" (by the second "adjs" rule).

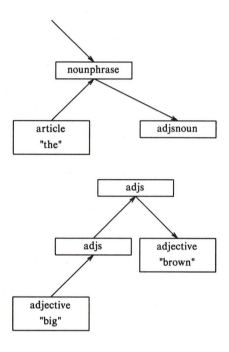

Figure 5-13

State 4 (Figure 5-13): the parser finds that an "adjs" is the first component of an "adjs" (by the first "adjs" rule), and then starts another parsing process to find an "adjective." It succeeds with "brown."

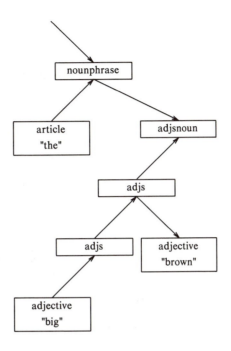

Figure 5-14

State 5 (Figure 5-14): the parser finds that an "adjs" is the first component of an "adjs" (second rule), but fails to find another adjective on the input stream. It backtracks and finds that an "adjs" is also the first element of an adjsnoun.

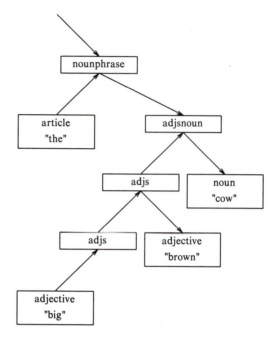

Figure 5-15

State 6 (Figure 5-15): the parser starts a parsing process to find a "noun," which succeeds with cow. This causes the "adjsnoun" process to succeed, which in turn causes the "nounphrase" process to succeed.

How do you suppose the bottom-up parser will behave when asked to *generate* sentences, in a query like:

```
 ?- bup_obj2(X, [], terminal, _, sentence).
```

Uses of Parsers

The example parsers "obj" and "bup_obj" are capable only of checking the syntax of an input sentence. ("obj" is also capable of generating sentences as long as the grammar contains no recursive rules.) In most of the example queries, the parser takes a sentence as input, and then confirms or denies whether the sentence is parsable. A more critical application of a parser is translating one language into another. This is the type of task done by a compiler, a query language, or a machine translation program.

In Sec. 5.4 we present a simple compiler that translates a Prolog program written in DEC-10 syntax into micro-Prolog core syntax. Unlike the DEC-10 front end that comes with micro-Prolog, this program can work in batch mode on an input file, producing an output file containing the translation. The same program will also translate a program written in micro-Prolog core syntax into DEC-10 syntax. This program may be useful if you have been writing programs in one of the two languages, and want to port them to the other language.

In Sec. 5.5 we present a simple query language interpreter that translates queries like

```
show employee name and employee salary
where department is 100.
```

into Prolog queries, and then executes the Prolog queries.

Top-down parsers like "obj" above form the basis of both the translator and the query language. Either of them could also be based on a bottom-up parser like "bup_obj." Top-down parsers are used because they are simpler than bottom-up parsers for the types of grammars needed.

5.4 DEC-10 to micro-Prolog Translator

Syntax of
micro-Prolog

micro-Prolog is a version of Prolog that is available on many smaller computers. The basic syntax of micro-Prolog, called *core syntax*, is considerably different from the DEC-10 syntax used in this book. The program presented below, called "d_to_m," is a translator from DEC-10 syntax to micro-Prolog core syntax or vice versa. This program has several purposes:

1) it shows off how a single Prolog program can be used to translate in either direction between two languages, provided that the languages are structurally similar;

2) it equates the components of DEC-10 Prolog to the components of micro-Prolog for readers who are interested in both languages; and

3) it can be used to port a program written in one language to the other.

Components of micro-Prolog

The terms of micro-Prolog consist of variables and constants; there are no structures. Any word beginning with one of the characters X, Y, Z, x, y, z, or _ is a variable. The most important syntactic object in micro-Prolog is a list, which is written as a set of terms between parentheses, separated by blanks (not commas). micro-Prolog has the same list constructor symbol, ¦, as DEC-10 Prolog (see Table 5-1).

Lists	
DEC-10	**micro-Prolog**
`[a,b,c]`	`(a  b  c)`
`[X¦Y]`	`(X ¦ Y)`
`[one,two¦R]`	`(one two ¦ _R)`

Table 5-1

In micro-Prolog, an expression representing a relation is written as a list, in which the first element of the list is the predicate name, and the other elements are arguments (see Table 5-2).

Relations	
DEC-10	**micro-Prolog**
`father(philip, charles)`	`(father philip charles)`

Table 5-2

A clause is written as a list of such relational expressions, in which the first element constitutes the head and the other elements constitute the body. A fact is such a list with only one relational expression in it (see Table 5-3).

Clauses	
DEC-10	**micro-Prolog**

`knows(X, Y) :-`
`    works(X, Z),`
`    works(Y, Z).`
	`((knows X Y)`
	`(works X Z) (works Y Z))`

`father(philip, charles).`	`((father philip charles))`

Table 5-3

It should be apparent how structurally similar the two languages are. In many cases, an expression of one language has an exact counterpart in the other. The most important way that they differ is with respect to built-in predicates. For the sake of simplicity, built-in predicates were omitted from "d_to_m."

Implementation of "d_to_m"

"d_to_m" is implemented as a top-down parser. Unlike "obj," "d_to_m" has five arguments. The first argument is the name of the terminal or nonterminal defined by this clause. If the program is translating from DEC-10 syntax to micro-Prolog syntax, then the second argument is the input list (a DEC-10 expression), the third argument is whatever is left over from the input list, and the fourth argument contains the output list (a micro-Prolog expression). If the program is translating from micro-Prolog syntax to DEC-10 syntax, then the fourth argument is the input list (a micro-Prolog expression), the fifth argument whatever is left over from the input list, and the second argument contains the output list (a DEC-10 expression).

```
% variable name conventions:
%   Id          input DEC-10 expression
%   Im          input micro-Prolog expression
%   Od,Rd,Rd1   output DEC-10 expressions
%   Om,Rm,Rm1   output micro-Prolog expressions
%
% comments show:
% nonterminal --> DEC-10 components // micro-Prolog components
```

```
%  terminals:

%    +    ?          ?    ?            ?
d_to_m(atom, [Word|Od], Od, [Word|Om],  Om) :-
  atom(Word).

d_to_m(var,  [DWord|Od], Od, [MWord|Om],  Om) :-
  (    nonvar(DWord),            % direction: DEC to MP
       name(DWord, [C|Rest]),
       uppercase(C),
       % put '_' on the front of DWord to make a MP var:
       name(MWord, ['_',C|Rest])
       ;
       nonvar(MWord),            % direction: MP to DEC
       name(MWord, [C|Rest]),
       % capitalize first letter to make a DEC variable:
       capitalize(C, CapC),
       name(DWord, [CapC|Rest])
  ).

% list --> [] // ()
d_to_m(list, ['[', ']'|Od], Od, ['(', ')'|Om], Om).


% nonterminals:

% list --> [ args ] // ( args )
d_to_m(list, ['['|Id], Od, ['('|Im], Om) :-
  d_to_m(args, Id, [']'|Od], Im, [')'|Om]).

% list --> [args|var] // (args|var)
d_to_m(list, ['['|Id], Od, ['('|Im], Om) :-
  d_to_m(args, Id, ['|'|Rd], Im, ['|'|Rm]),
  d_to_m(var,  Rd, [']'|Od], Rm, [')'|Om]).

% clause --> relation :- relations. // ( relation relations )
d_to_m(clause, Id, Od, ['('|Im], Om ) :-
  d_to_m(relation,  Id, [':-'|Rd1], Im, Rm1),
  d_to_m(relations, Rd1, ['.'|Od],   Rm1, [')'|Om]).
```

```
%  clause --> relation . // ( relation )
d_to_m(clause, Id, Od, ['('|Im], Om) :-
   d_to_m(relation, Id, ['.'|Od], Im, [')'|Om]).

%  relations --> relation , relations // relation relations
d_to_m(relations, Id, Od, Im, Om) :-
   d_to_m(relation,  Id,  [','|Rd1], Im,  Rm1),
   d_to_m(relations, Rd1, Od,        Rm1, Om).

%  relations --> relation // relation
d_to_m(relations, Id, Od, Im, Om) :-
   d_to_m(relation, Id, Od, Im, Om).

%  relation --> atom ( args ) // ( atom args )
d_to_m(relation, Id, Od, ['('|Im], Om) :-
   d_to_m(atom, Id,  ['('|Rd1], Im,  Rm1),
   d_to_m(args, Rd1, [')'|Od],  Rm1, ''|Om]).

%  relation --> atom // ( atom )
d_to_m(relation, Id, Od, ['('|Im], Om) :-
   d_to_m(atom, Id, Od, Im, [')'|Om]).

%  args --> arg , args // arg args
d_to_m(args, Id, Od, Im, Om) :-
   d_to_m(arg,  Id, [','|Rd], Im, Rm),
   d_to_m(args, Rd, Od, Rm, Om).

%  args --> arg // arg
d_to_m(args, Id, Od, Im, Om) :-
   d_to_m(arg, Id, Od, Im, Om).
```

```
% arg --> var ; atom ; list
d_to_m(arg, Id, Od, Im, Om) :-
  d_to_m(var, Id, Od, Im, Om),
  ;
  d_to_m(atom, Id, Od, Im, Om),
  ;
  d_to_m(list, Id, Od, Im, Om).
```

Using "d_to_m"

Let us give "d_to_m" a simple fact in DEC-10 syntax and see what output it produces. The fact:

```
father(philip, charles).
```

can be decomposed into a list of words:

```
[father, '(', philip, charles, ')', '.']
```

and then parsed:

```
¦ ?- d_to_m(clause,
            [father, '(', philip, charles, ')', '.'], [],
            MP, []).
MP = ['(', '(', father, philip, charles, ')', ')']
```

Out of list notation, the answer is:

```
((father philip charles))
```

Alternatively, the micro-Prolog rule:

```
((member X (Y¦Z)) (member X Z))
```

can be decomposed into:

```
['(', '(', member, X, '(', Y, '¦', Z, ')', ')',
 '(', member, X,Z ')', ')']
```

and then parsed:

```
¦ ?- d_to_m(clause, DEC, [],
       ['(', '(', member, X, '(', Y, '¦', Z, ')', ')',
       '(', member, X, Z, ')', ')'],
       []).
DEC = [member, '(', X, ',', '[', 'Y', '¦', 'Z', ']', ')',
       ':-', member, '(', X, ',', Z, ')', '.']
```

Out of list notation, the answer is:

```
member(X, [Y¦Z]) :- member(X, Z).
```

**Improving the
User
Interface**

One problem with the queries above is that they required the pains-
taking translation of a language expression into a list of elements.
We have already used a program that could automate this tedious
task: the lexical analyzer "readsent" discussed at the beginning of the
chapter. Before "readsent" can be used to input Prolog code,
however, lexicographical symbols such as , and ; need to be added
to its "punctuation" database.

A procedure that prints each element of a list would also be convenient for viewing the output of the parser. "print_exp" performs
this function:

```
print_exp([]) :- nl.
print_exp([X¦Y]) :-
    write(X), write(' '), print_exp(Y).
```

Now we can use "d_to_m" in the following compound query:

```
¦ ?- write('enter DEC-10 clause:'), nl,
    readsent(DEC),
    d_to_m(clause, DEC, [], MP, []),
    print_exp(MP),
    fail.

enter DEC-10 clause:
father(philip, charles).
((father philip charles))
no
```

The subgoal `fail` at the end of the query is there to suppress the
printing of variable values.

The version of "d_to_m" above cannot handle any of the following syntactic features of DEC-10 Prolog:

1) structures;

2) prefix, infix, or postfix operators; or

3) most built-in predicates.

These are precisely the features that are *not* structurally similar between the two languages. Therefore, to extend "d_to_m" to handle these features would require adding rules applicable to translation in one direction only. For instance, since micro-Prolog does not have general-purpose structures like DEC-10 Prolog (note: micro-Prolog has *tuples*, but they cannot be nested in the same way that structures can), a micro-Prolog programmer would use a list in many of the situations that a DEC-10 programmer would use a structure. So, if "d_to_m" were being used to translate from DEC-10 to micro-Prolog, it should convert every DEC-10 structure into a micro-Prolog list. But an ambiguity arises if "d_to_m" is being used to translate micro-Prolog to DEC-10: when it encounters a micro-Prolog list, should it convert it into a DEC-10 list or a DEC-10 structure? If the rule equating a DEC-10 structure with a micro-Prolog list were allowed to be completely bidirectional, then "d_to_m" would have two ways to parse every micro-Prolog list.

The safest, if tedious, solution to this problem is to *declare* ahead of time the names and arities of all DEC-10 structures used in the program. Then, when "d_to_m" encounters a micro-Prolog list while translating micro-Prolog to DEC-10, it will consult a database of DEC-10 structures to determine if this particular micro-Prolog list should be translated into a DEC-10 structure or a DEC-10 list. Here is an extension to "d_to_m" that implements this method of handling structures.

```
%   database of DEC-10 structures:
%          Name      Arity
structure(customer, 3).
structure(path,     3).
```

```
%   convert micro-Prolog list to DEC-10 structure:
%   structure_or_list --> atom ( args ) // ( atom args )
d_to_m(structure_or_list, Id, Od, Im, Om) :-
  find_valid_structure(Id, Od, Im, Om).

%                            -              -    +              -
find_valid_structure([Name,'('|Rd], Od, ['(',Name|Rm], Om) :-
  var(Rd),         % direction: MP to DEC
  atom(Name),
  % check that Name is the name of a DEC-10 structure:
  structure(Name, Arity),
  % get args off the front of Rm:
  d_to_m(args, Rd, [')'|Od], Rm, [')'|Om]),
  % check that number of args is correct:
  length(Rm, Rmlength), length([')'|Om], Omlength),
  Arity is Rmlength - Omlength.

%   convert DEC-10 structure to micro-Prolog list:
%   structure_or_list --> atom ( args ) // ( atom args )
d_to_m(structure_or_list, [Name,'('|Rd], Od, ['(',Name|Rm], Om) :-
  var(Rm),         % direction: DEC to MP
  atom(Name),
  d_to_m(args, Rd, [')'|Od], Rm, [')'|Om]),

%   convert micro-Prolog list to DEC-10 list or vice versa:
%   structure_or_list -->  list // list
d_to_m(structure_or_list, Id, Od, Im, Om) :-
  not( find_valid_structure(Id, Od, Im, Om) ),
  d_to_m(list, Id, Od, Im, Om).

%   arg --> var ; atom ; structure_or_list
d_to_m(arg, Id, Od, Im, Om) :-
  d_to_m(var, Id, Od, Im, Om),
  ;
  d_to_m(atom, Id, Od, Im, Om),
  ;
  d_to_m(structure_or_list, Id, Od, Im, Om).
```

The following queries illustrate how this extension to "d_to_m" works.

```
| ?- repeat,
    write('enter micro-Prolog structure or list:'), nl,
    readsent(MP),
    once( d_to_m(structure_or_list, DEC, [], MP, []) ),
    print_exp(DEC), nl,
    fail.
```

enter micro-Prolog structure or list:
(one two three)
[one, two, three]

enter micro-Prolog structure or list:
(customer smith compact week)
customer(smith, compact, week)

enter micro-Prolog structure or list:
(path new_york boston)
[path, new_york, boston]

The last example did not make a "path" structure because the arity of "path" was declared to be three.

Other features of DEC-10 Prolog such as operators and built-in predicates could be implemented in a way similar to structures.

5.5 A Query Language

The next application of a parser is a program that translates statements of an English-like database query language into Prolog queries, then runs the queries and prints the answers. The translation involved is more complicated than that of "d_to_m," because the two languages involved are not structurally similar.

Specifying the Schema of a Database

Before the English-like query language can be used on a database, it must have explicit knowledge of the number and names of that database's arguments. Such knowledge allows a user to refer to predicate arguments by name. Suppose that we will be querying the following databases:

```
employee(brian, 100, operator, 20000).
employee(nancy, 200, acct_exec, 71000).
employee(ralph, 100, manager, 71500).

department(100, data_processing, ralph).
department(200, sales, jb).
```

The name of a database (and the names of its arguments) to be queried are specified in a "schema" fact:

```
%  interface to "employee" and "department" databases:
%       Pred name    Argument names
schema(employee,  [name, code, position, salary]).
schema(department, [code, name, manager]).
```

The program also relies on "schema" facts for the number of arguments in each Prolog database. The above facts contain the implicit information that the "employee" database has four arguments and the "department" database has three.

Once the query language has knowledge of the schemas of the "employee" and "department" databases, it can interpret queries such as:

```
show employee name and department manager
where employee code is department code.
```

In response to that query, it generates the following output:

```
employee name  brian    department manager  ralph
employee name  nancy    department manager  jb
employee name  ralph    department manager  ralph
```

Implementation Strategy

The work that needs to be done by this query language can be divided into three phrases. In the first phase, a top-down parser translates a statement of the query language into a list of "t" (for "triple") structures. Each "t" structure contains a predicate name, an argument name, and an uninstantiated variable to hold the argument value. If two values are supposed to be equivalent (such as employee code and department code in the example query above), the value variables of two different "t" structures are unified. In the second phase, the list of "t" structures is transformed into a compound Prolog query. In the third phase, the query is executed and variable values are printed out.

For example, in the first phase, the query above is parsed into the following list of "t" structures :

```
[t(employee,    name,    N),
 t(department, manager, M),
 t(department, code,    C),
 t(employee,    code,    C)]
```

In the second phase, this list is transformed into a compound query:

```
employee(N, C, _, _),  department(C, _, M)
```

In the third phase, the compound query is executed, and a call to "print_tlist" prints the required values:

```
| ?- print_tlist([t(employee,name,brian),
                   t(department,manager,ralph)]).
employee name  brian   department manager  ralph
```

An advantage of this approach is that the list of "t" structures acts as an interface between the query language parser and the rest of the program. If the second phase of the program works reliably (i.e. the part that translates the list of structures into a Prolog query), then any procedure that produces a list of "t" structures can be used as a front end.

Grammar of the Query Language

The full grammar of the query language is given in Table 5-4.

Grammar of the Query Language		
Nonterminals:		
statement	->	command pa_list qualification
pa_list	->	pa connective pa_list
pa_list	->	pa
pa	->	predicate argument
qualification	->	pronoun pa relation pa
qualification	->	
Terminals:		
command	->	"show"
connective	->	"and"
pronoun	->	"where"
pronoun	->	"if"
relation	->	"is"
relation	->	"equals"
predicate	->	*(defined in a "schema" fact)*
argument	->	*(any word)*

Table 5-4

In this form, this language is too simple to be of much practical use. The only relation it knows about is *equality* between two database attribute values; it is not able to test for equality between an attribute value and a constant. It would be convenient to have additional relations such as *inequality*, or *greater than* (for numerical values), and commands besides *show* such as *sort* or *sum*. It is possible to extend the language presented here to include all of these features.

"qobj"

"qobj" works similarly to the "obj" program described in Sec. 5.2.

```
% variable name conventions:
%  P            = predicate name
%  A            = argument name
%  V            = argument value
%  Valuelist    = list of argument values
%  Tlist, Printlist, Qlist =
%                  [t(P,A,V), t(P,A,V), ...]
%  I            = input list of words
%  R, R1, O     = leftover list of words
```

```
% nonterminals:
qobj(I, O, statement, Tlist, Printlist) :-
    qobj(I, R, command, _, _),
    qobj(R, R1, pa_list, Printlist, _),
    qobj(R1, O, qualification, Qlist, _),
    append(Printlist, Qlist, Tlist).


qobj(I, O, pa_list, [t(P,A,V)|Tlist], _) :-
    qobj(I, R, pa, t(P,A,V), _),
    qobj(R, R1, connective, _, _),
    qobj(R1, O, pa_list, Tlist, _).
qobj(I, O, pa_list, [t(P,A,V)], _) :-
    qobj(I, O, pa, t(P,A,V), _).


qobj(I, O, pa, t(P,A,V), _) :-
    % generate a unique variable, V
    qobj(I, R, predicate, P, _),
    qobj(R, O, argument, A, _).


% unify V in 1st "pa" with V in 2nd "pa"
qobj(I,O,qualification, [t(P1,A1,V), t(P2,A2,V)],_) :-
    qobj(I, R, adv_pronoun, _, _),
    qobj(R, R1, pa, t(P1,A1,V), _),
    qobj(R1, R2, relation, _, _),
    qobj(R2, O, pa, t(P2,A2,V), _).
qobj(I, I, qualification, [], _).     % empty production.


% terminals:
qobj([show|R],    R, command, _, _).
qobj([P|R],       R, predicate, P, _) :- predicate(P, _).
qobj([Argname|R],R, argument, Argname, _).
qobj([is|R],      R, relation, _, _).
qobj([equals|R], R, relation, _, _).
qobj([and|R],     R, connective, _, _).
qobj([where|R],  R, adv_pronoun, _, _).
qobj([if|R],      R, adv_pronoun, _, _).


predicate(Pname, Arity) :-
    schema(Pname, List), length(List, Arity).
```

Algorithm of "qobj"

"qobj" has two more arguments than "obj" does. The fourth argument returns the results of the parsing process. For instance, when a "pa" (predicate and argument) is found, the parser returns a predicate-argument-value structure:

```
t(P,A,V)
```

A list of such structures is built up by the nonterminals "pa_list" and "qualification," and joined together into one list in the nonterminal "statement." The list of structures returned by "statement" contains all arguments that need to be referenced in the final Prolog query. The fifth argument to "qobj" is only used by the "statement" rule; it is a list of all structures that need to be printed after the Prolog query has been executed.

Output of the parser

We can test the parser by seeing what output it generates from an example query.

```
! ?- qobj(
      [show, employee, name, and, department, manager,
       where, employee, code, is, department, code],
      [], statement, Tlist, Printlist).

  Tlist = [t(employee, name, _613),
           t(department, manager, _642),
           t(employee, code, _668),
           t(department, code, _668)]

  Printlist = [t(employee, name, _613),
               t(department, manager, _642)]
```

Notice that the structures in `Printlist` are only those referred to in the "pa_list" following the "show" command. Thus, `Printlist` is a subset of `Tlist`. `Tlist` contains every "pa" mentioned in the entire query. As a result of the "qualification" rule, the same variable (`_668`) appears in both the employee code structure and the department code structure.

"make_plists"

The next task is to move each set of "t" structures with the same predicate name into a list consisting of the predicate name followed by argument name/value pairs. Each argument name/value pair is called an `AVpair` and is written as a `p(Name, Value)` structure. The resulting list of such structures is called a `Plist`.

As an example, suppose that the following two "t" structures occur in the `Tlist` coming out of the parser:

```
[t(employee,name,_1), t(employee,code,_2)]
```

then the following `Plist` will be generated:

```
[employee, p(name,_1), p(code,_2)]
```

The "make_plists" procedure takes `Tlist` from "qobj" as an input argument, and produces a list of `Plists`, one for each distinct predicate occurring in `Tlist`. "make_plists" keeps track of which predicates it has already processed in its second argument, `Donelist`. When "make_plists" finds an unprocessed predicate, it calls "build_AVpairs" to make "p" structures from all of the "t" structures in `Tlist` that contain that predicate. The call to "unify_vars" transforms the resulting list of "p" structures as follows: value variables are unified whenever the argument name is the same. Thus, if the following two "p" structures occur in `AVpairs1` (the input to "unify_vars"):

```
[p(name, _50), ...p(name, _65)]
```

then the uninstantiated variables will be unified in `AVpairs2` (the output of "unify_vars"):

```
[p(name, _50), ...p(name, _50)
```

This step is necessary to preserve whatever variable unifications were made by the parser.

```
% variable name conventions:
%  P        = predicate name
%  A        = argument name
%  V        = argument value (uninstantiated variable)
%  Tlist    = [t(P,A,V), t(P,A,V), ...]
%  AVpairs  = [p(A,V), p(A,V),...]
%  Plist    = [P, p(A,V), p(A,V), ...]
%  Plists   = a list in which each element is a Plist
```

```
% make_plists:
% transform list of t(P,A,V) structures
% into P + list of p(A,V) structures.
%           +              +          -
make_plists([],                 _,        []).

% skip  t(P,A,V)  if P is in Donelist:
make_plists([t(P,A,V)|Tlist], Donelist, Plists) :-
    member(P, Donelist),
     !, make_plists(Tlist, Donelist, Plists).

% otherwise, process P:
make_plists([t(P,A,V)|Tlist], Donelist,
            [[P|AVpairs2]|Plists]) :-
    build_AVpairs(P, [t(P,A,V)|Tlist], AVpairs1),
    unify_vars(AVpairs1, AVpairs2),
    % add P to Donelist:
    !, make_plists(Tlist, [P|Donelist], Plists).

% build_AVpairs:
% build a list of p(A,V) structures for one predicate.
%              +     +    -
build_AVpairs(_,    [], []).

%  P (1st arg) matches P in  t(P,A,V),
%  so add p(A,V) to AVpairs list:
build_AVpairs(P, [t(P,A,V)|Tlist],
              [p(A,V)|AVpairs]) :-
    !, build_AVpairs(P, Tlist, AVpairs).

%  P1 does not match P2, so skip ahead:
build_AVpairs(P1, [t(P2,A,V)|Tlist], AVpairs) :-
    !, build_AVpairs(P1, Tlist, AVpairs).


%            +                        -
unify_vars([],                  []).

unify_vars([p(A,V)|In_AVpairs], [p(A,V)|Out_AVpairs]) :-
    % "member" unifies V with V when A matches A:
    member(p(A,V), In_AVpairs),
     !, unify_vars(In_AVpairs, Out_AVpairs).
```

```
unify_vars([p(A,V)|In_AVpairs], [p(A,V)|Out_AVpairs]) :-
    %   if "member" fails, proceed to next pair:
    !, unify_vars(In_AVpairs, Out_AVpairs).
```

Output of "make_plists"

Let us see what "make_plists" does with the output of the previous query to "qobj."

```
| ?- make_plists(
    [t(employee, name, _613),
     t(department, manager, _642),
     t(employee, code, _668),
     t(department, code, _668)],
    [], Plists).
```

```
Plists = [[employee, p(name, _613), p(code, _668)],
          [department, p(manager, _642), p(code, _668)]]
```

"make_plists" consolidated the list of "t" structures into two `Plists`.

"construct_qlists"

The next task is to find out from the "schema" database the number of arguments of each predicate for which there is a `Plist`. An argument list needs to be constructed for each predicate. This list should contain the argument value variables from `Plist` in their correct positions, and new variables in all other positions. For instance, we want to transform the following `Plist`:

```
[employee, p(salary, _25)]
```

into a new list consisting of the predicate name followed by the same number of arguments as in the "employee" database:

```
[employee, _, _, _, _25]
```

Notice that the value variable associated with the salary argument is in the correct (fourth) position for a query to "employee." The transformed `Plist` is called a `Qlist`, and will later become a Prolog query.

"construct_qlists" is a procedure that takes the list of `Plists` from "make_plists" and returns a list of `Qlists`. "construct_qlists" looks up the "schema" for the predicate in each `Plist`, and gets back `Argnames`, the list of argument names associated with that predicate. It then calls "make_valuelist," which returns `Valuelist`, a list of just as many variables as there are names in the `Argnames` list. A `Qlist` is constructed by adding the predicate name onto the front of `Valuelist`.

"find_arg_pair" is a procedure called by "make_valuelist." It takes an argument name and a list of "p" structures as input. If it can locate the argument name in a member of the list, it returns the corresponding variable. Otherwise, it returns a new variable.

```
% variable name conventions:
%  Argnames      = list of argument names
%  V, V1, V2     = argument values
%  Valuelist     = list of argument values
%  AVpairs       = [p(A,V), ...]
%  Plist         = [P, p(A,V), p(A,V), ...]
%  Plists        = a list in which each element is a Plist
%  Qlist         = [P, V1, V2, ... VN]
%  Qlists        = a list in which each element is a Qlist

%  construct_qlists: construct a list of qlists.
%                    +    -
construct_qlists([], []).

construct_qlists([[P¦AVpairs]¦R],
                 [[P¦Valuelist]¦Qlists]) :-
    schema(P, Argnames),
    make_valuelist(Argnames, AVpairs, Valuelist),
    !, construct_qlists(R, Qlists).

%  make_valuelist:
%  look up each A from Argnames list in the AVpairs list;
%  return list of Values.
%               +           +         -
make_valuelist([],          _,        []).

make_valuelist([A¦Argnames], AVpairs, [V¦Valuelist]) :-
    find_arg_pair(A, V, AVpairs),
    !, make_valuelist(Argnames, AVpairs, Valuelist).
```

```
%  find_arg_pair:
%  If A (1st arg) is found in the AVpairs list,
%  return V (2nd arg).
%  Otherwise, return _ (2nd arg).
find_arg_pair(_, _, []).


%                 +   _   +
find_arg_pair(A, V, [p(A,V)|AVpairs]) :- !.
find_arg_pair(A, V, [p(NotA,_)|AVpairs]) :-
      !, find_arg_pair(A, V, AVpairs).
```

Output of "construct_qlists"

Here is a query to "construct_qlists" that takes **Plists**, the output of the previous query to "make_plists," as its input.

```
| ?- construct_qlists(
        [[employee, p(name, _613), p(code, _668)],
         [department, p(manager, _642), p(code, _668)]],
        Qlists).

Qlists = [[employee, _613, _668, _868, _885],
          [department, _668, _922, _642]]
```

Notice the position of each variable in the **Qlist** output. **_668**, the variable associated with code, appears in both **Qlists** and so will act as a shared variable in the final compound query.

"list_to_clause"

It is necessary to use the built-in predicate "=.." (see Sec. 3.9) to convert **Qlists** into the subgoals of a compound query. "list_to_clause" is a procedure that takes care of this conversion for any number of **Qlists**. The subgoals of a compound query are joined together by the infix operator **,** . This means that if "=.." gets a compound query as its first argument, it turns **,** into the first word of its output list:

```
| ?- (father(X,Y), father(Y,Z)) =.. List.
List = [,, father(X,Y), father(Y,Z)]
```

Note: the first element of **List** is a comma; it is followed by a comma to separate it from the next element, **father(X,Y)**. "list_to_clause" rules (2) and (3) handle compound queries.

```
% variable name conventions:
%  Tlist, Printlist = [t(P,A,V), t(P,A,V), ...]
%  Qlist         = [Predicate, Arg1, Arg2, ... ArgN]
%  Qlists        = a list in which each element is a Qlist

%  transform a list of Qlists into clause notation.
%  exactly one Qlist:
%                     +            -
list_to_clause([Qlist], Clause) :-              (1)
    Clause =.. Qlist, !.


%  exactly two Qlists:
list_to_clause([Qlist1, Qlist2], Clause3) :-    (2)
    Clause1 =.. Qlist1,
    Clause2 =.. Qlist2,
    %  join together Clause1 and Clause2 with ','
    Clause3 =.. [,, Clause1, Clause2], !.


%  more than two Qlists:
list_to_clause([Qlist1|Qlists], Clause3) :-     (3)
    Clause1 =.. Qlist1,
    list_to_clause(Qlists, Clause2),
    %  join together Clause1 and Clause2 with ','
    Clause3 =.. [,, Clause1, Clause2], !.
```

Output of
"list_to_clause"

When "list_to_clause" is executed with the output of "construct_qlists" as input, it produces the following output:

```
¦ ?- list_to_clause(
        [[employee, _613, _668, _868, _885],
         [department, _668, _922, _642]],
        Query).

Query = employee(_613, _668, _868, _885),
        department(_668, _922, _642)
```

Now consider what will happen when the Query above is executed.

```
¦ ?- Query = (employee(_613, _668, _868, _885),
      department(_668, _922, _642)),
      Query.

Query = (employee(brian, 100, operator, 2000),
          department(100, data_processing, ralph)) ;

Query = (employee(nancy, 200, acct_exec, 71000),
          department(200, sales, jb)) ;


  . . .
```

"print_tlist"

All that remains to be done is to print the required predicate names, argument names, and variable values. The parser returned a list of "t" structures to be printed in a variable called "Printlist." The "print_tlist" procedure prints out such a list:

```
print_tlist([]) :- nl, !.
print_tlist([t(P,A,V)¦Printlist]) :-
    write(P), write(' '),
    write(A), write('  '),
    write(V), write('   '),
    !, print_tlist(Printlist).
```

The following query shows how "print_tlist" is used.

```
¦ ?- print_tlist([t(employee,position,acct_exec),
                   t(department,name,sales)]).

employee position  acct_exec   department name   sales
yes
```

Putting the Parts Together

The "query" rule below combines all of the parts of the query language program.

```
query :-
    readsent(S),
    qobj(S, [], statement, Tlist, Printlist),
    !,
    make_plists(Tlist, [], Plists),
    construct_qlists(Plists, Qlists),
    list_to_clause(Qlists, Query),
    Query,
    print_tlist(Printlist).
```

Notice that each subgoal after "readsent" takes a list as input, transforms it in some way, and passes the transformed list on to the next subgoal. "qobj" produces both `Tlist`, which serves as input to "make_plists," and `Printlist`, which is an input argument to "print_tlist." The cut after "qobj" ensures that the query contained in S is parsed only once.

An interpreter

"ql" is a rule based on "query" that can answer an infinite number of queries from the user. Each time, the user is prompted by *?*. Once "ql" is activated, it acts like an interpreter for the query language. An example "ql" session is shown below.

```
% query language interpreter.
ql :-
    repeat, write('? '), query, fail.

! ?- ql.
? show employee name.

employee name   brian
employee name   nancy
employee name   ralph


? show employee name and employee salary
where employee name is department manager.

employee name   ralph   employee salary   71500

?
    . . .
```

Bibliographic Notes

Parsing strategies in general are discussed in Aho and Ullman [1979]. The analogy between parsing and deduction is made in Pereira and Warren [1983]. Matsumoto [1984] presents a flexible bottom-up parsing system implemented in Prolog. The implementation of conventional database query languages in Prolog is thoroughly discussed in Li [1984].

Exercises

1. Write a query to "readsent," and type in a sentence. What happens if the sentence you enter spans more than one line? What happens if the sentence does not end with a period? What happens if you enter more than one sentence on one line, each ending with a period?

2. Write a new predicate, "getline," which is the same as "readsent" except that it collects all of the words (including fullstops) on a single line, and returns them in a list.

3. Write a compound query that uses "readsent" to get a sentence from the user, and then uses "obj" (Sec. 5.2) to parse the sentence.

Write a query that generates all possible sentences from the words now in the dictionary.

Use the debugging facilities to watch what happens when you parse several noun phrases, both with and without adjectives.

Try other extensions to this grammar, such as

    1) transitive and intransitive verbs,

    2) adverbs, or

    3) compound verbs.

4. Write a compound query that uses "readsent" to get a nounphrase from the user, and then uses "bup_obj" (Sec. 5.3) to parse it.

Use the debugging facilities to watch what happens when you parse several noun phrases. Enter the same phrases you used in exercise 3, and compare the results of this trace with the trace of the top-down parser.

Under what circumstances is left recursion in a bottom-up parser more efficient than right recursion in a top-down parser?

5. Write a query in the query language syntax to show just the names of all department managers. Write a query to show the salaries and names of department managers.

6. Write a version of "readsent" that can read a Prolog clause and convert it into a suitable form for "d_to_m." Is there a way to handle the :- operator so that it comes out as a word by itself?

7. Interface the query language to other databases you already have.

8. Add additional features to the query language, such as other relations besides "is," or a "sum" command. "sum" should be able to compute the total value of one field for an entire database, provided that field is numeric.

6

Knowledge Representation

6.1 Representing Knowledge in Prolog

Many artificial intelligence applications require the ability to *represent knowledge* about the world. To understand how Prolog can serve this purpose, it is worthwhile to consider some of the characteristics of representational formalisms in general.

Predicate Calculus

We use the word *system* to refer to some limited part of the world. Knowledge about a system is equivalent to an analysis of the structure of the system.

As discussed in Sec. 0.5, first order predicate calculus is an example of a representational formalism, because it is possible to describe the structure of a system with an axiomatic theory of predicate logic. Several trivial examples of such theories are given in Sec. 0.5. A complete set of inference rules allows a logician to derive the consequences of an axiomatic theory. The formal meaning of an axiomatic theory is the set of all consequences that can be derived from it using valid rules of inference. An *interpretation of a theory* is an assignment of each symbol that occurs in the theory to some component (i.e. an entity, function, or relation) of the system. A theory accurately describes a system if all of the consequences of the theory are true in the system, given a suitable interpretation.

Computational Formalisms

A number of *computational formalisms* have been invented for the purpose of representing knowledge, although most of them are not as expressive as first order predicate calculus. The comments below apply in a general way to most available computational formalisms. A computational formalism consists of two parts:

  1) a descriptive language; and

  2) a set of procedures capable of realizing the formal meaning of a description written in the descriptive language. This set of procedures is sometimes referred to as the *process structure* of the formalism.

Formal meaning of a description

Representing knowledge about a system with a computational formalism amounts to describing the relevant aspects of the structure of the system in its descriptive language. The formal meaning of a description of a system is whatever answers or behaviors the process structure of the formalism can produce on the basis of that description. (The formal meaning of a description is analogous to the set of consequences of an axiomatic theory of predicate calculus, and the process structure of a formalism is analogous to a set of inference rules.)

The formal meaning of a description is a product of (and is therefore limited by) the process structure of the formalism. Some formalisms allow a programmer to add new procedures to the process structure, and thereby extend the range of possible formal meanings of the descriptive language.

The ultimate purpose of representing knowledge about a system is to obtain a program whose behavior reflects the structure of the system in some relevant aspect. If such a program is successful, it is able to solve problems that occur within the system, or to simulate the behavior of the system.

Prolog is an example of such a formalism. Using Prolog to represent knowledge is discussed in the rest of this section, and other formalisms are discussed in subsequent sections of this chapter.

Prolog as a Computational Formalism

Prolog's descriptive language is the Horn clause form of predicate logic. Prolog's process structure consists of the interpreter augmented by certain built-in predicates (such as "is/2") and perhaps by certain general-purpose procedures (such as "findall/3"). A Prolog program can represent knowledge about a system in much the same way that an axiomatic theory of predicate logic can describe a field of knowledge. (To make this comparison explicit, each Prolog clause in the program is equivalent to an axiom, and the program as a whole is equivalent to a theory.) The formal meaning of a Prolog program is the set of true instances of relations derivable by the interpreter from the clauses of the program.

Process of representing knowledge

The process of representing knowledge in a Prolog program may involve the following steps:

1) Someone familiar with the system analyzes its structure in order to identify all significant entities and important relations that hold between those entities.

2) The programmer chooses symbols to represent each entity and each relation.

3) Someone familiar with the system defines each relation semantically. This entails identifying which instances of the relation are *true* and which are *false*.

4) The programmer defines each relation axiomatically with Prolog clauses. An axiomatic definition of a relation is correct if the Prolog interpreter can derive every true instance of the relation from it.

Once knowledge of a system has been described in a Prolog program, a user can extract that knowledge by writing suitable queries, or by means of a more elaborate user interface.

Example of representing knowledge

As an example, suppose that the system is interpersonal relationships at a factory. The foreman, who knows the system intimately, analyzes it into the following components: Each employee (i.e. Mary Kravitz, Bob Jones, Sam Finkle, and Patricia Hendricks) is a significant entity. Each shift (i.e. day and evening) is a significant entity. The relation between an employee and their shift is important. The relation between two employees who know one another is important.

The programmer chooses the following symbols for these entities and relations:

`mary`, `bob`, `sam`, and `patricia` are employees;

`daytime` and `evening` are shifts;

`work_shift` is the relation between an employee and their shift; and

`knows` is the relation between two employees who know one another.

The foreman defines the "work_shift" relation semantically by stating that the following instances of it are true:

```
work_shift(mary,     daytime)
work_shift(sam,      evening)
work_shift(bob,      evening)
work_shift(patricia, evening)
```

and that all other instances of it are false. The foreman defines the "knows" relation by stating that any two people who work on the same shift know one another. It follows that the following instances of the "knows" relation are true:

```
knows(sam, bob)
knows(bob, sam)
knows(sam, patricia)
knows(patricia, sam)
knows(bob, patricia)
knows(patricia, bob)
```

and that all other instances of it are false. Armed with these semantic definitions, the programmer defines the "work_shift" relation axiomatically by including each true instance of it as a fact:

```
%            Employee  Shift
work_shift(mary,     daytime).
work_shift(sam,      evening).
work_shift(bob,      evening).
work_shift(patricia, evening).
```

but is able to define the "knows" relation with a rule that refers to the "work_shift" relation:

```
knows(A, B) :-
    work_shift(A, Shift),
    work_shift(B, Shift),
    A \== B.
```

Verifying that these axiomatic definitions are correct is a matter of demonstrating that the Prolog interpreter can derive every true instance of each relation from them (see Sec. 1.4).

Formal Meaning

The symbols that are used to represent entities and relations in such a Prolog program have both a *formal* meaning in terms of other symbols, and an *external* meaning that associates them with components of the system being represented. To appreciate the strength of Prolog as a formalism, it is worthwhile to consider the exact nature of both types of meaning.

The formal meaning of a symbol that occurs in a Prolog program is a product of 1) the descriptive clauses of the program, and 2) Prolog's process structure. Consider the formal meaning of a relation symbol (i.e. a predicate name) in a Prolog program. Formally, a relation is a mapping of n nonvariable terms, where n is arity of the relation, onto a truth value (see Sec. 0.5). In a Prolog program, a relation is defined axiomatically by a set of Prolog clauses. The interpreter is a procedure capable of deriving the true instances of a relation from the clauses that define it (in this sense, the interpreter realizes the meaning of an axiomatic definition of a relation). The formal meaning of a relation symbol is the set of true instances of the relation derivable by the interpreter from clauses in the program.

Similarly, the formal meaning of a term that has no variables in it (i.e. a constant or a structure with no variables) is the set of true instances of relations in which it can occur.

External Meaning

In order to be able to represent knowledge about the world in a Prolog program, symbols in the program (i.e. constants, predicate names, and structure names) must have an *external meaning* that associates them with components of the system being represented. This level of meaning exists in the minds of programmers and users of the program, and is similar to the denotative meaning of words in natural language. In the example above, the programmer chose the symbol `mary` to represent the employee Mary Kravitz; thus, Mary Kravitz is the external meaning of `mary`.

To make the difference between the formal and external meanings of symbols clear, consider the following clause:

```
knows(patricia, bob).
```

The formal meaning of the relation symbol `knows` is the set of true instances of the "knows/2" relation. Part of the formal meaning of the constant symbol `patricia` is that it is something that can occur as the first argument of a true instance of the "knows/2" relation. In the example above, the intended external meaning of `knows` is the familiarity of two people who see one another in a social context, and the intended external meaning of `patricia` is Patricia Hendricks. (In terms of predicate logic, the external meaning of a constant symbol is its value under an interpretation; see Sec. 0.5.) The Prolog interpreter realizes the formal meaning of a symbol; we, as programmers and users of the program, must supply the external meaning.

Figure 6-1 shows how external meanings link the symbols in a program to the components of the system being represented.

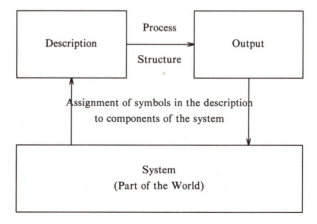

Figure 6-1

A program intended to represent knowledge about a system is successful if a user can extract that knowledge from the program and apply it in a useful way to the system. That is, the behavior and output of the program should reflect the structure of the system. If a user finds that the output of the program violates his or her understanding of the system, then the program has failed.

From the point of view of a user, the intended external meaning of symbols that appear in the output is the key to the knowledge embodied in the program. Thus, if the external meaning that the user applies to symbols in the output of the program is not the same as the external meaning that the programmer intended, the program may appear to fail.

As an example, consider someone who must use a computerized card catalog system in a library for the first time. The program prompts this person for *type of book?* without giving any indication of what might be meant by type. The user, becoming panic stricken, tries to think of what to enter: nonfiction? foreign? red? He finally decides to try nonfiction, but the program complains *"nonfiction" is not a valid type*. This user knows the structure of the card catalog system, and assumes that this structure is correctly embodied in the program. To be able to use the program, however, he must discover what meaning the programmer intended for the symbol type.

As another example, consider a user interacting with an expert system that purports to be able to analyze a person's personality. According to the advertising literature, the program embodies both a theory of personality and an analysis technique. At the end of a session, the program tells this user that he is "inflexible," but he does not think of himself as "inflexible." Is he wrong? Without knowing the external meaning that the authors of the program intended for the symbol "inflexible," the user has two choices: 1) he can dismiss the expert system as not very intelligent after all, or 2) he can assume that the program knows what it is talking about, and search for some way to see himself as "inflexible," thereby making the the program's diagnosis correct.

The external meanings of symbols are a treacherous aspect of any knowledge representation program, because there is almost always more than one possible external meaning for a given symbol. Symbols which are themselves ambiguous English words (such as type) are the worst offenders. The best way to narrow down the possible external meanings of a symbol is to make the relations in which the symbol occurs more precise. For example, the external meaning of the symbol *mary* in the following true instance of the "work_shift/2" relation:

```
work_shift(mary, daytime)
```

might be any one of a number of people whose first name is "Mary." Adding a social security number to the definition of the relation, however:

```
work_shift(mary, 121-76-7720, daytime)
```

severely limits the number of people named "Mary" to whom the symbol `mary` can refer, if this instance of the "work_shift/3" relation is true.

Representing Knowledge in C

To illustrate exactly what advantages a computational formalism gives a programmer for the task of representing knowledge, it is useful to consider how to write a program to represent knowledge in a procedural language such as C. C itself is not a computational formalism. To use C to represent knowledge, therefore, it is necessary to implement a formalism within C. In a typical C program, this entails:

1) defining data structures, instances of which will be used to describe the structure of a system; and

2) writing procedures to perform computations on instances of the data structures—that is, to give some formal meaning to the descriptions.

A naive C programmer tends to invent a new formalism for each different application (i.e. each system to be represented). As a result, the type of formal meaning realized by the procedures in a program is quite specific to the system being represented. Notice how different this is from Prolog: a relation symbol in a Prolog program has the same type of formal meaning no matter which system is being represented. The biggest disadvantage to inventing a new formalism for each application is that someone trying to read the program must learn both its formalism and the description of the system embodied in its data structures.

On the other hand, an experienced C programmer will invent a formalism for one application and then try to reuse it as much as possible in other applications, simply because this saves so much maintenance effort. It is possible to implement quite powerful formalisms in C. The UNIX tool "yacc" is an example, as are the implementations of Prolog written in C.

Extending Prolog

The view of Prolog as a formalism for representing knowledge presented above is too simplistic, because neither side effects nor the procedural semantics of Prolog have been taken into account. It is worthwhile at this point to define Prolog's descriptive language and Prolog's process structure more precisely.

Clauses with no side effects have a clear declarative meaning, and should be considered to be part of Prolog's descriptive language. Side effects (such as cut, "assert," "retract," "fail," etc.) are strictly procedural elements of Prolog that are used to control the interpreter's problem solving strategy. Therefore, clauses that include side effects make sense only when read procedurally. Certain general-purpose procedures, such as "findall," perform computations that are not possible in Prolog without the use of side effects, and can therefore be considered to *augment* Prolog's process structure.

The interesting thing about "findall" is that, although side effects are utilized in the bodies of the rules that define it, a call to "findall" has a declarative meaning. That is, a call to "findall" declares the relation between a query and all answers to that query that can be derived from the current program. It was stated above that the process structure of a formalism is the set of procedures capable of realizing the formal meaning of a description written in the formalism's descriptive language. Adding "findall" to Prolog's process structure extends the range of possible formal meanings of Prolog's descriptive language. A call to "findall" is a descriptive element that can occur as a subgoal in an otherwise declarative clause without disturbing the declarative semantics of that clause. There is nothing application-specific about "findall," and once it is implemented, it can be reused in many application programs.

When side effects are used in application-specific clauses, however, the distinction between Prolog's descriptive language and Prolog's process structure disappears. Clauses of this type may also be considered to augment Prolog's process structure, but in an application-specific way. In one sense, a programmer who writes such clauses is inventing a formalism specifically for an application, much as a naive C programmer invents a new formalism for each application. Such clauses are not reusable from application to application, and tend to undermine Prolog as a formalism.

In order to maintain the clarity of Prolog as a formalism, it is good programming practice to:

1) make all application-specific clauses purely declarative, and

2) isolate the computations that can only be accomplished with side effects into general-purpose procedures.

The issue of Prolog programming style is discussed further in Sec. 7.5.

Other Computational Formalisms

Computational formalisms for knowledge representation other than Prolog include semantic networks, frames, and object oriented programming. These formalisms are discussed in the following sections.

The conceptual overhead of predicate logic as a representational language is limited to the following two *ontological assumptions* (i.e. assumptions about what exists):

1) entities exist; and

2) relations between entities exist.

Prolog, because of its close relationship with predicate logic, is based on the same assumptions. Each of the other formalisms comes with certain built-in concepts (such as *inheritance, defaults, objects*, etc.) for the purpose of organizing knowledge. The advantage of these concepts is that they enable certain kinds of knowledge to be easily described. The disadvantage of these concepts is that they may tend to impose a certain view of the world on the programmer, and there may be kinds of knowledge that they are incapable of describing. Prolog is a more general computational formalism than the others precisely because it is free of built-in concepts. But ideally, we would like the best of both worlds: we would like to be able to use knowledge representation concepts when they are appropriate, but not to be forced to use them in all situations. This can be accomplished by describing a knowledge representation concept from another formalism in Prolog's descriptive language, and augmenting

Prolog's process structure with procedures that can realize the meaning of the description. The net effect of such an extension should be to augment the expressiveness of Prolog as a formalism, and provide the programmer with additional tools with which to organize knowledge.

Inheritance

Inheritance is an example of a concept deeply embedded in both the frame formalism and the object oriented formalism. Inheritance can be considered to be a weak inference rule that allows a specific frame or class to acquire information from a general frame or class. Information acquired by inheritance often plays the role of a *default value* in the specific frame or class. Later in the chapter, we discuss in detail how Prolog can be extended to include inheritance.

6.2 Semantic Networks

Nodes and
Arcs

In a semantic network, entities and classes of entities are identified with *nodes*, and relations between entities are identified with *arcs joining the nodes*. An arc connected to a single node establishes a *property* of that node. A semantic network allows inference along paths described by certain types of arcs. For example, in the network pictured in Figure 6-2, the node bird has the property flies. Because the node canary is connected to the node bird by an is a arc, it is possible to infer that the node canary also has the property flies.

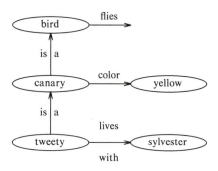

Figure 6-2

Semantic network drawings are a useful way to picture binary relations and properties. Notice the similarity between this picture and the arc-point pictures of relations in Chaps. 1 and 2.

An essential concept of the semantic network formalism is that of *hierarchy*, which makes it particularly adept at representing taxonomies of knowledge. Each level of the taxonomy is represented by a node connected by is a arcs to higher and lower levels. For instance, in the example shown in Figure 6-2, bird is the highest level of the taxonomy, and on the next level down might be various types of birds.

Problems result, however, if the programmer does not enforce the proper separation of levels of the taxonomy. In the example shown in Figure 6-3, the programmer divided the rock node (representing all rocks) into three subclasses:

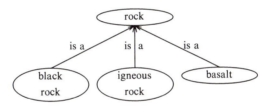

Figure 6-3

It is true that black rocks, igneous rocks, and basalt rocks are all types of rock, but organizing them in this way leads to more confusion than clarity. The three sub-classifications are not on the same level, and certain rocks can fall into more than one category simultaneously. This example points out that if the programmer has not analyzed the structure of a system correctly, no organizing concept will help.

A Semantic
Network as a
Prolog
Program

If we view a semantic network as a description of relations that hold between entities, then it is a straightforward matter to implement it in Prolog. The following program expresses the structure of the bird example shown in Figure 6-2:

```
is_a(canary, bird).
is_a(tweety, canary).

lives_with(sylvester, tweety).

flies(bird).
flies(X) :- is_a(X, Y), flies(Y).

color(canary, yellow).
color(X, Y) :- is_a(X, Z), color(Z, Y).
```

The second "color" clause enables the inference that `tweety` is yellow, because `tweety` is a canary, and any entity that is a canary is yellow. An inference can take place wherever there is an "is_a" arc between two nodes on the diagram. "is_a" represents a relation of either class inclusion (i.e. the class of canaries is included in the class of birds) or class membership (`tweety` is a member of the class of canaries).

6.3 Frames

Representing Knowledge about Situations

Minsky originated the concept of a *frame* as a way to represent knowledge about situations (Minsky [1973]). Each frame contains *slots* that identify the type of situation or specify the parameters of a particular situation. For instance, a frame description of a party situation might have a *type* slot whose value will identify the type of party. It might also have *time* and *place* slots the values of which will be the parameters of a particular party. The frame formalism can be viewed as a generalization of the semantic network formalism. *Hierarchy* is one of the essential concepts of the frame formalism, so it is also useful for representing taxonomies of knowledge.

An expression in a frame language such as FRL (Goldstein [1979]) declares the existence of a frame. In the following example, there are three frames mentioned, `ACTIVITY`, `MEETING`, and `MEETING_38`. `ACTIVITY` is the most general frame, `MEETING` is a more specific frame describing a kind of `ACTIVITY`, and `MEETING_38` is the most specific frame describing a particular `MEETING`. `MEETING` is known as a *subframe* of `ACTIVITY`, and `MEETING-38` is a subframe of `MEETING`.

```
(MEETING                                      name of frame
(A KIND OF ($VALUE (ACTIVITY)))               slot names and values
(TIME        ($DEFAULT (WED AT 2PM)))         (default values are
(PLACE       ($DEFAULT (BOARD ROOM)))         inherited by subframes)
)
```

```
(MEETING-38                                   name of frame
(A KIND OF ($VALUE (MEETING)))                slot names and values
(ATTENDEES ($VALUE (RONALD)
                   (CINDY)
                   (FRED)))
)
```

Inheritance of Slot Values

Another essential concept of the frame formalism is that of *inheritance*. It is possible to specify that if a slot in one frame is not specifically filled, the frame will *inherit a default value* of that slot from a superior frame. Inheritance of slot values is enabled between two frames by the presence of an A KIND OF slot in one frame that is filled by the name of the other frame. For example, the TIME and PLACE slots in the MEETING frame are inherited by the MEETING_38 frame. The A KIND OF slot in a frame language is similar to the is a arc in a semantic network, in that it represents a relation of class inclusion or class membership.

Evaluation of the Frame Formalism

A frame is best understood as a kind of data structure, and inheritance between frames is realized by procedures that access instances of the data structure (Goldstein [1979] p. 31). If the frame language does not provide the kind of inference that a programmer needs, then the programmer can write a new procedure to implement the inference. In the worst case, this means that each possible inference must be coded explicitly. To really understand the meaning of a frame language program, it is necessary to juxtapose expressions in the frame language against procedures that implement inferences between the frames. This can become quite complicated, since the procedures are written in a language other than the frame language.

The following Prolog program expresses the structure implied by the MEETING example above.

```
a_kind_of(meeting, activity).
a_kind_of(meeting_38, meeting).

%  slot values local to meeting:
meeting(time, 'Wed at 2pm').
meeting(place, 'Board Room').

%  slot values local to meeting_38:
meeting_38(attendees, [ronald,cindy,fred]).    % (1)

%  inheritance rule
meeting_38(Attribute, Value) :-                    % (2)
    a_kind_of(meeting_38, Frame),
    Subgoal =.. [Frame, Attribute, Value],
    Subgoal.
```

Note that both "meeting" and "meeting_38" are attribute assertion databases (Sec. 2.5). "meeting" is related to "meeting_38" by the fact a_kind_of(meeting_38, meeting). The inheritance rule enables "meeting_38" to inherit any attribute value from "meeting." When we ask for the time of "meeting_38":

```
| ?- meeting_38(time, X).
X = 'Wed at 2pm'
```

the answer comes from "meeting" by means of the inheritance rule.

Contradictory
facts

Imagine that "meeting_38" was originally scheduled at the default time (Wednesday at 2PM), but that it must be rescheduled for some reason. Consider what happens if a contradictory "time" attribute is added to "meeting_38."

```
meeting_38(time, 'Thurs at 9am').
```

The "meeting_38" frame now has two values in its time slot—the local value and the inherited value:

```
| ?- meeting_38(time, X).
```

X = 'Thurs at 9am';

X = 'Wed at 2pm';

no

The problem here is that "meeting_38" is intended to be a description of an actual meeting, and a meeting occurs only once. That is, the relationship between a meeting and the time it occurred should be governed by a one-to-one integrity constraint. With the program in its current form, however, the query returns two times. The `Thurs at 9am` value of time should override the default `Wed at 2pm` value, so that a query like the one above will return only `Thurs at 9am`.

Disabling Inheritance

This problem is solved in the program below. The cut in the first "meeting_38" rule ensures that if "meeting_38" has a local value of a slot, it will not be able to inherit a value of that same slot from "meeting."

```
a_kind_of(meeting, activity).
a_kind_of(m_38, meeting).

%  slot values of meeting:
meeting(time, 'Wed at 2pm').
meeting(place, 'Board Room').

%  local rule
meeting_38(Attribute, Value) :-
    m_38(Attribute, Value), !.

%  inheritance rule
meeting_38(Attribute, Value) :-
    a_kind_of(m_38, Frame),
    Subgoal =.. [Frame, Attribute, Value],
    Subgoal.

%  slot values local to meeting_38:
m_38(attendees, [ronald,cindy,fred]).
m_38(time, 'Thurs at 9am').
```

All attributes that are local to "meeting_38" are now stored in the "m_38" database. The first "meeting_38" rule checks if there is a "m_38" clause that has the required attribute. If there is, then the value is returned and the cut prevents any further answers. If no "m_38" clause exists, then the second "meeting_38" rule looks for the required attribute in the "meeting" database. A query about time now finds only a single answer:

```
| ?- meeting_38(time, X).

X = 'Thurs at 9am' ;      % from "m_38"

no


| ?- meeting_38(place, X).

X = 'Board Room' ;        % from "meeting"

no
```

6.4 Object Oriented Programming

Objects and Messages

In an object oriented programming language such as Smalltalk-80, an *object* is the fundamental computational entity. The only way to perform a computation is to *send a message to an object*. Objects are organized by *class*. An object is an *instance* of a class. The definition of a class determines the structure of its objects. A typical program is organized into a hierarchy of classes. *Class* is analogous to a data structure in a procedural language, and *object* is analogous to an instance of a data structure (i.e. a variable).

Definition of a class

The definition of a class may include four types of components:

1) *messages* (requests for computation), understood by all instances of the class;

2) *methods* (attached procedures), common to all objects of a class;

3) *class variables*, the values of which are common to all objects of a class; and

4) *instance variables* (analogous to "slots" in the frame formalism), the values of which are unique to a particular object.

Inheritance

The set of messages that an object understands define its *interface* (i.e. all possible ways of referring to the object). For each message, there is an associated *method* (i.e. procedure) that performs the computations necessary to answer the message. Messages (and the methods used to answer them) are inherited from class to class in the

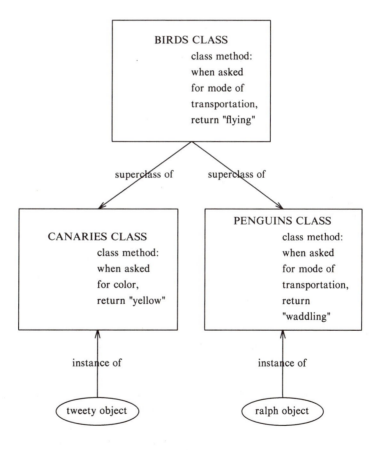

Figure 6-4

following way: if a message is sent to an instance of a class, and the message is not defined for that class, the message is passed on to the *superclass* of that class (i.e. the class above it in the hierarchy). Thus, a class inherits all of the messages defined in its superclass or above. If an inherited message is redefined in a class, the local definition *overrides* the inherited definition for that class.

Figure 6-4 depicts the hierarchy of classes in a program concerned with types of birds.

If a message is sent to the "ralph" object asking about the mode of transportation, it is handled by a method of the PENGUINS class, and the answer `waddling` is returned. But if the same message is sent to the "tweety" object, there is no class method of the CANARIES class that can handle this message, so it is passed on to BIRDS, the superclass of CANARIES. The message is handled by a class method of the BIRDS class, and the answer `flying` is returned.

The object oriented programming formalism can be understood as both 1) a generalization of the notion of abstract data types; and 2) a refinement of the frame formalism. It is worth considering both views in detail.

Object Oriented Programming in terms of Abstract Data Types

Most programming languages characterize variables by *type*. The type of a variable specifies the domain of values that it may hold, as well as the set of operations that can be performed on it. A language provides a set of *primitive data types* such as integers, floating point numbers, characters, etc. Associated with each type are *operators* for manipulating variables of that type, such as addition, subtraction, etc. The fact that variables must be declared by type constrains the way a programmer can use a variable. In languages with strong type checking, the compiler will object if an operator intended for a variable of one type is applied to a variable of another type.

Abstract data types

Many languages allow the definition of complex data types based on the primitive types. Examples of complex data types include *structures* in C, and *records* in Pascal. The language itself does not provide operators to manipulate variables of a complex data type, but allows a programmer to define *procedures* that can manipulate such variables. In this way, the notion of a *procedure* is a generalization of the notion of an *operator*. The combination of 1) a complex data type, and 2) all procedures that can act on variables of that type is known as an *abstract data type*. An example of an abstract data type implemented in C is an array of structures used to hold the records of a database, together with procedures to look up, add, delete, or change elements of this array.

The concept of *class* in the object oriented formalism can be understood as *abstract data type*. An *object* is an instance (i.e. variable) of a complex data type, and the set of messages that an object understands are operators that are applicable to a variable of that type.

If we consider the birds example above from the point of view of abstract data types, the BIRDS class is an abstract data type, and the method of answering a question regarding mode of transportation is one of its operators. This operator can be used by any of the other abstract data types that are under BIRDS in the hierarchy, i.e. CANARIES, PENGUINS, etc. As it happens, PENGUINS has its own local operator for answering a question about mode of transportation.

Object Oriented Programming in terms of the Frame Formalism

The object oriented formalism can also be considered a refinement of the frame formalism. Where the frame formalism makes no distinction between a class/subclass relationship and a class/instance relationship (i.e. A KIND OF is a relation that can hold either between two classes or between a class and an instance), these two types of relationship are orthogonal in the object oriented formalism. For instance, if the meeting example in Sec. 6.2 were implemented in Smalltalk, MEETING would be a class, ACTIVITY would be the superclass of MEETING, but MEETING_38 would be an instance of MEETING.

6.5 An Inheritance Mechanism in Prolog

Inheritance in the Other Formalisms

The frame formalism allows slot values of a general frame to be inherited by an specific frame. Inheritance is disabled when a slot value is added to the specific frame, thus overriding the inherited slot value. Similarly, the object oriented formalism allows the messages (and associated methods) of a general class to be inherited by a specific class. Inheritance is disabled when a message is defined for a specific class, overriding the inherited message. The concept of inheritance gives these formalisms great expressive power for representing taxonomies of knowledge, and, in Kowalski's words:

> "... encourage us ... to reason by comparing new occasions with preconceived stereotypes" (Kowalski [1986] p. 4).

Inheritance in Prolog

Thus far in the chapter, we have considered several ad-hoc ways of implementing inheritance in Prolog. For instance, in the second meeting example, inheritance is accomplished by the following procedure:

```
%   local rule
meeting_38(Attribute, Value) :-
    m_38(Attribute, Value), !.

%   inheritance rule
meeting_38(Attribute, Value) :-
    a_kind_of(m_38, Frame),
    Subgoal =.. [Frame,Attribute,Value],
    Subgoal.
```

This approach results in a contorted expression of the structure of the system being represented. It also suffers from two limitations: 1) it is only applicable to databases in the attribute assertion form `Frame(Attribute,Value)`; and 2) the cut in the first rule prevents "meeting_38" from having more than one local value of an attribute. It would be convenient to have a general mechanism for describing inheritance in Prolog that does not suffer from these limitations.

States of Knowledge

According to Hayes (Hayes [1979] pp. 54-56), inheritance can be considered to be a type of inference that occurs between *states of knowledge*. To clarify what he means, let us apply a full interpretation to the symbols in the meeting example. Suppose that weekly meetings between Ronald, Cindy, and Fred regularly occur on Wednesday at 2PM. We could say that Wednesday at 2PM is the *default* time for the weekly meeting between these people. When a particular weekly meeting, "meeting_38," is first planned, everyone involved assumes that it will take place at the usual time. On Wednesday morning, however, Fred finds out that he must go away that afternoon, and asks for "meeting_38" to be rescheduled. All participants agree to reschedule the meeting on Thursday at 9AM. The rescheduling changed the state of knowledge of these people regarding their weekly meeting. In the new state of knowledge, the default time of the meeting is overridden by the new time.

In the frame representation of this situation, the states of knowledge involved—before and after Fred's actions—are implicit. Any representation of the situation will be clearer if the states of knowledge are made explicit. This can be accomplished by naming the states of knowledge, and adding an extra parameter to each relation in the representation that ties it to the state of knowledge in which it holds. The relationship *between* states of knowledge should also be made explicit; then inheritance of information from a general state of knowledge to a specific state of knowledge can be realized by a general-purpose procedure.

The rest of this chapter is concerned with the implementation and applications of a general-purpose inheritance mechanism in Prolog. The mechanism is based on explicit references to states of knowledge. It enables a programmer to represent the structure of systems that involve inheritance (such as the meeting example) without having to use control side effects in application-specific clauses. The mechanism is an extension to Prolog's process structure, and should contribute to the expressiveness of the language.

Overview of the Inheritance Mechanism

The *inheritance mechanism* is a technique for representing multiple states of knowledge, where a specific state can inherit information from a general state. A clause is attached to a state by adding the name of the state as the first argument of the head of the clause; all other arguments remain the same. The relationship between a general state and a specific state is asserted by a "child_of/2" fact. Inheritance of clauses between states is realized by the "send" procedure. "send" can be understood declaratively as a relation that holds between a state of knowledge and a query if the query can be proved from clauses associated with that state.

To use the inheritance mechanism, the primary analytical task is to determine a hierarchy of states of knowledge. The relationship of states to one another can be understood as a tree in which each state is a node. Suppose there are two states, A and B. If state B is a child node of state A in the tree, then B inherits all clauses associated with A except those that are explicitly *refuted* in B.

Suppose that uppermost in a particular tree is a state called employees. It contains information that is generally applicable to all
employees, such as the locations of departments, names of department managers, etc. The employees state has two child states,
salaried employees and contract employees. The
salaried employees state contains a database of salaried employees together with information applicable to salaried employees,
such as which tax form they receive at the end of the year. The
contract employees state contains a database of contract employees together with information applicable to contract employees.
This tree of states can be pictured as in Figure 6-5:

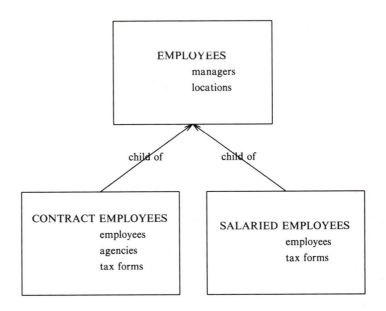

Figure 6-5

*Analogy with
object oriented
programming*

In the terminology of object oriented programming, information is
extracted from a state by *sending a message* to the state. If a message is sent to the contract employees state requesting information about tax forms, the response to the message will come from the
state itself. But if a message is sent to the contract employees
state requesting information about a department manager, this state

cannot answer it and so will pass it on to its parent state, employees. The response to the message will come from the employees state.

Answers
returned by
"send"

The "send" procedure is used to extract information from a state.
The inheritance mechanism imposes no integrity constraints of its
own, so that a query to "send" can return a set of answers derived
from more than one state. For instance, suppose that associated with
the `salaried employees` state there is a database of department
meetings only for salaried employees, and associated with the employees state there is a database of department meetings for all
employees. A query requesting information about department meetings directed to the `salaried employees` state will first return
department meetings for salaried employees only, and then department meetings for all employees.

Asserting the
Tree of
States

The relation of states to one another is described in a "child_of" database. For instance, to implement the example above, one "child_of"
fact specifies that `salaried employees` is a child of employees, and another fact specifies that `contract employees` is
a child of `employees`. The association of a Prolog clause with a
state is effected by adding an extra argument containing the name of
the state.

Here is a version of the employee example.

```
%  the tree of states:
child_of(salaried, employees).
child_of(contract, employees).



%  clauses associated with "employees":
%             State     Dept  Location
dept_location(employees, 100,  '2nd floor Annex').
dept_location(employees, 200,  'Building 4073').

%             State     Dept  Manager
dept_manager(employees, 100,  smith).
dept_manager(employees, 200,  rodriguez).

%  meeting for all employees in dept. 100:
dept_meeting(employees, 100, 'Tues Jan 22 Room 235').
```

```
% clauses associated with "salaried":
%   State      Name       Dept  Salary
emp(salaried, howe,       100,  55000).
emp(salaried, listvisky, 100,  40000).
emp(salaried, upton,      200,  35000).

%          State    Form
tax_form(salaried, w2).

% meeting only for salaried employees in dept. 100:
dept_meeting(salaried, 100, 'Mon Jan 21 Room 201').


% clauses associated only with "contract":
%   State      Name       Dept  Salary
emp(contract, lewis,   100, not_applicable).
emp(contract, bertoli, 200, not_applicable).

%          State    Form
tax_form(contract, 1099).
```

The "send" Procedure

The inheritance of clauses between a state and its child states is realized by the "send" procedure. "send" takes two arguments: 1) the name of the state to which the query is directed, and 2) a Prolog query without a state name argument. The following call to "send" asks for the tax form that contract employees should receive:

```
| ?- send(contract, tax_form(Form)).
Form = 1099 ;


no
```

Notice that "send" could find only one answer to the query tax_form(Form). The following call to "send" asks for the manager of contract employees in department 100. It shows that the contract state inherits clauses from the employees state.

```
! ?- send(contract, dept_manager(100, Who)).
Who =  smith ;

no
```

Redirecting a
query

If "send" cannot solve the query in the target state, it redirects the query to the parent of the target state. If the query fails again in the parent state, "send" redirects the query to the parent of the parent, and so on until the uppermost state is reached.

The query below asks for meetings that are for salaried employees in department 100. It shows that the "send" procedure can return answers from more than one state.

```
! ?- send(salaried, dept_meeting(100, M)).
M = 'Mon Jan 21 Room 201' ;        % from salaried

M = 'Tues Jan 22 Room 235' ;       % from employees

no
```

Refutation of a Clause

Suppose that, in a rash act of discrimination, the company decides to move all contract employees in Department 100 into the basement of the Annex. This amounts to a change in the structure of the system, and will require a corresponding change in the description of the system. This change might be effected by destructively recoding the relevant databases. But there is another way to effect the change with the minimum disruption of existing databases—by adding a new "dept_location" fact to the contract state, and refuting the old one:

```
dept_location(contract, 100, 'Basement Annex').
refute(contract,
       dept_location(employees,100,'2nd floor Annex')).
```

contract is the state where the refutation occurs, and dept_location(employees,100,'2nd floor Annex') is the refuted clause. After these clauses have been added, a request for information about this location directed at contract returns the new value:

```
| ?- send(contract, dept_location(100, L)).
L = 'Basement Annex' ;

no
```

But a request for the same information directed at `employees` still returns the old value:

```
| ?- send(employees, dept_location(100, L)).
L = '2nd floor Annex' ;

no
```

Once a clause has been refuted in a particular state, it will no longer be inherited by that state or by any of its child states. Should a new clause be added to the state, it will be inherited by all child states. Using a "refute" fact in this way greatly facilitates maintenance of a program.

Concepts of the Inheritance Mechanism

The inheritance mechanism is based on the following key concepts:

1) a hierarchy of states of knowledge;

2) inheritance of clauses from state to state; and

3) disabling the inheritance of a clause by *refuting* it.

The concepts of the frame formalism correspond to these concepts as follows:

a *frame* corresponds to a state of knowledge;

a *slot* corresponds to a clause attached to a state of knowledge;

inheritance of slot values from frame to frame corresponds to inheritance of clauses from state to state; and

the ability of a local slot value to *override* an inherited slot value corresponds to the ability to refute an inherited clause and replace it with a new clause.

The concepts of the object oriented formalism correspond to the concepts of the inheritance mechanism as follows:

a *class* corresponds to a state of knowledge;

a *method* corresponds to a clause attached to a state of knowledge;

an *object* corresponds to a clause attached to a state of knowledge;

inheritance of methods from class to class corresponds to inheritance of clauses from state to state.

the ability of a local method to *override* an inherited method corresponds to the ability to refute an inherited clause and replace it with a new clause.

The Meeting Example

To make this clear, it is worth considering how the inheritance mechanism can be used to implement the simple examples from earlier in the chapter. Here is a version of the meeting example. The meeting state has two children: `meeting_38`, that inherits the default time from `meeting`, and `meeting_39` that has its own time.

```
%   the tree of states:
child_of(meeting, activity).
child_of(meeting_38, meeting).
child_of(meeting_39, meeting).

%   clauses associated with "meeting":
time(meeting, 'Wed at 2pm').
place(meeting 'Board Room').

%   clauses associated with "meeting_38":
attendees(meeting_38, [ronald,cindy,fred]).

%   clauses associated with "meeting_39":
topic(meeting_39, 'release 3.0').
attendees(meeting_39, [martha,ronald,cindy]).
refute(meeting_39, time(meeting, _)).
time(meeting_39, 'Thurs at 9am').
```

Notice that the time inherited from `meeting` is refuted in `meeting_39`. This refutation prevents `meeting_39` from having two contradictory times. Notice also that all of these clauses are free of control side effects.

How could you use "send" to request the time of `meeting_39`? Can you write a rule that takes the name of a meeting as an argument and prints out all available information about that meeting?

The Birds Example

Here is a version of the birds example.

```
%  the tree of states:
child_of(canaries, birds).
child_of(penguins, birds).


%  clauses associated with "birds":
mode_of_transportation(birds, flying).


%  clauses associated with "canaries":
color(canaries, yellow).

%  a database of individual canaries:
individual(canaries, tweety).
individual(canaries, steve).


%  clauses associated with "penguins":
color(penguins, 'black and white').
refute(penguins, mode_of_transportation(birds, _)).
mode_of_transportation(penguins, waddling).

%  a database of individual penguins:
individual(penguins, ralph).
```

The following query will find all individual birds whose mode of transportation is `waddling`:

```
¦ ?- child_of(Child, birds),
       send(Child, mode_of_transportation(waddling)),
       send(Child, individual(I)).

Child = penguins
I = ralph ;

no
```

The "child_of" subgoal generates a candidate state that is a child of the birds state. The second subgoal checks to see if the mode of transportation associated with the candidate state is waddling. If it is, then the third subgoal generates all individuals associated with that state. This query can backtrack through all child states of the birds state.

Implementation of "send"

The "send" procedure is implemented as follows.

```
%  send: direct a query at a state
send(State, Q) :-
    Q =.. [X|Y],          % decompose query into a list
    send0(State, State, [X|Y]).

%  Qstate is the state to which
%  the original query was sent.
send0(Qstate, State, [X|Y]) :-
    Q =.. [X,State|Y],   % synthesize query with state
    Q,                    % run query
    not( refuted(Qstate, State, Q) ).

send0(Qstate, State, [X|Y]) :-
    %  generate a parent state:
    child_of(State, ParentState),
    %  try query in the parent state:
    send0(Qstate, ParentState, [X|Y]).


%  consider Q refuted if it is refuted in a
%  state higher than or equal to the state of
%  the original query.
refuted(Qstate, State, Q) :-
    refute(Nstate, Q),
    %  Nstate where Q is refuted
    %  must be higher than or equal to query state:
    higher_or_equal(Nstate, Qstate),
    %  but lower than or equal to State where Q is asserted:
    higher_or_equal(State, Nstate), !.
```

```
higher_or_equal(X, X) :- !.
higher_or_equal(X, Y) :-
    child_of(Y, Z),
    higher_or_equal(X, Z).
```

The "refuted" rule can be read:

> *A clause is refuted*
> *from the point of view of the query at hand if*
>   *it is refuted in some state* Nstate
>   *higher than or equal to the state in which*
>   *the clause was originally asserted*
>   *and lower than or equal to the state to which*
>   *the query was directed.*

In the "refuted" rule, the relationship between the variables State, Nstate, and Qstate can be pictured as in Figure 6-6:

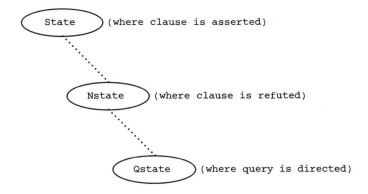

Figure 6-6

Algorithm of "send"

"send" takes a query Q, decomposes it into a list, and calls "send0." The first argument to "send0" is the name of the state to which the original query was sent. It remains the same on all subsequent recursive calls to "send0." The second argument to "send0" is the name of the state where the query is about to be attempted. On the first invocation of "send0," the second argument is the same as the first, but on each subsequent recursive call it becomes the parent of the previous state.

"Send0" synthesizes a query (Q) from its third argument, incorporating the current state as the first argument of the query. Then the query (Q) is executed, and if it succeeds, "send0" checks to make sure that the answer it returned was not refuted anywhere between the query state and the current state. If the user requests another answer, "send0" backtracks and looks for one in the same state where it found the previous answer. If there are no more answers in that state, "send0" recurses and looks for answers in the parent of that state. This process continues until the uppermost state is reached.

6.6 A Query Program for a Paper Inventory Database

We now consider several applications of the inheritance mechanism. The first is a form-driven database query program that allows a user to successively refine queries. The system being represented is the paper inventory of a printing company.

States as
Virtual
Databases

At the beginning of a user's session with this database query program, a database of the entire paper inventory is associated with a state called `paper`. When the user enters a query requesting information about paper inventory items that meet certain criteria, a new state is automatically asserted as a child of the `paper` state. Associated with the new state are the selection criteria entered by the user. The new state acts as a sort of *virtual database*, filtering the original database through its selection criteria. When a query is sent to the new state requesting paper inventory items, only those items meeting the selection criteria will be returned. An example will make this clear.

Suppose that in the uppermost state, `paper`, there are database items in the colors blue, red, white, and beige. The user writes a query asking to see only the red paper. As a result of this query, a child state of `paper` is asserted, with a name such as `red_paper`, for instance. The new `red_paper` state contains the selection criterion that the color attribute must be `red`. The situation is pictured in Figure 6-7:

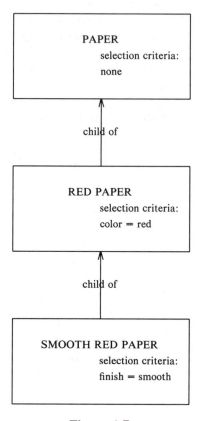

Figure 6-7

If the user asks to see inventory items in the `paper` state, all items in the database will be printed. But if the user asks to see items in the `red_paper` state, only red items will be printed.

Suppose that a user directs a query to the `red_paper` state specifying only items whose finish is smooth. As a result of this query, a child state of `red_paper` is asserted, with a name such as `smooth_red_paper`. `smooth_red_paper` contains the selection criterion that the finish attribute be `smooth`. This new state inherits all selection criteria of its ancestors, so that if the user asks to see items in the `smooth_red_paper` state, only smooth, red items will be printed.

States form a history of the session

Each state limits the database associated with its parent according to its selection criteria. After the user has made several queries in a session with the program, the tree of states that has been asserted constitutes a kind of *history* of the session. The "showstates" procedure displays all existing states, and the "character" procedure displays all selection criteria associated with a state. These procedures make it easy for a user to write a new query to narrow down answer set of a previous query.

Using "q"

The interface of this program is form driven. The user queries the database with the "q" procedure. "q" takes two arguments: the name of an existing state, and the name of a new state to be asserted as a child of the existing state. The "q" procedure then displays a form with all attribute names of the paper inventory database. If a selection criterion has already been set in the existing state for one of these attributes, then it is automatically printed in the appropriate slot of the form. If a selection criterion has not been set for an attribute, then nothing is printed, and the user has a chance to enter one. If the user hits return instead of entering a value, then no selection criteria will be applied to that attribute.

The paper inventory database has five attributes describing the grade, weight, color, and finish of the paper, and the type (i.e. whether the paper comes in sheets or rolls). Here is the database:

The paper inventory database

```
%  State  Type    Grade   Weight Finish  Color
pi(paper, sheet,  opaque, 60,    smooth, blue).
pi(paper, sheet,  opaque, 45,    vellum, green).
pi(paper, sheet,  index,  50,    vellum, red).
pi(paper, sheet,  opaque, 70,    gloss,  white).
pi(paper, roll,   opaque, 100,   smooth, beige).
pi(paper, roll,   opaque, 70,    gloss,  red).
pi(paper, roll,   opaque, 110,   smooth, blue).
pi(paper, roll,   offset, 160,   gloss,  red).
```

"show" is a procedure that displays all inventory items associated with a state. "show" takes the name of a state as its one argument.

```
¦ ?- show(paper).
```

sheet opaque 60 smooth blue
sheet opaque 45 vellum green
sheet index 50 vellum red
sheet opaque 70 gloss white
roll opaque 100 smooth beige
roll index 70 gloss red
roll opaque 110 smooth blue
roll offset 160 gloss red
yes

Querying the Database (Asserting a New State)

To assert a new state under `paper` called `red_roll`, containing all paper inventory items that are red and of type `roll`, a user types:

```
%        Existing  New
¦ ?- q(paper,    red_roll).
```

There are no selection criteria associated with the `paper` state, so the user is prompted for all five attribute values.

type?   roll
grade?
weight?
color?   red
finish?

The user typed in `roll` in response to the *type?* prompt, `red` in response to the *color?* prompt, and hit return in response to the other three prompts. As a result of this call to the "q" procedure, the new state `red_roll` is asserted as a child of `paper`. The user can examine it with the procedures "show" and "character."

```
¦ ?- show(red_roll).
```

paper roll index 70 gloss red
paper roll offset 160 gloss red
yes

```
| ?- character(red_roll).
```

type: *roll*
grade:
weight:
color: *red*
finish:
yes

Asserting
`heavy_red_roll`

Suppose that the user employs "q" again to find items that are red, of type roll, and of weight 160. A child state of `red_roll` called `heavy_red_roll` is asserted.

```
%        Existing   New
| ?- q(red_roll, heavy_red_roll).
```

type?   *roll*
grade?
weight?   160
color?   *red*
finish?

Since `heavy_red_roll` inherits all attribute values set for `red_roll`, "q" did not prompt the user for either *type* or *color*, but instead displayed the values for those attributes that were set in `red_roll`. The user entered the value 160 in response to the *weight?* prompt, and hit return in response to the other two prompts.

```
| ?- show(heavy_red_roll).
```

paper roll offset 160 gloss red
yes

```
| ?- character(heavy_red_roll).
```

type: *roll*
grade:
weight: 160
color: *red*
finish:
yes

"showstates"

After many queries have been written, the user may not remember all of the existing states. "showstates" is a procedure that displays all currently asserted states:

```
| ?- showstates.
```

paper

  red_roll

   heavy_red_roll

Usefulness of the Query Program

The original program was implemented for estimators at a printing plant. Estimators often work with a partial paper specification, in the sense that more than one type of paper may be acceptable for a given job. The ultimate choice of paper is greatly influenced by what is in stock, because it is cheaper to use paper already in stock than to order new paper. The query program enables an estimator to discover all types of paper currently in stock that are suitable for a particular job. The version of the program presented here is greatly simplified from the original.

Implementation of the Query Program

The paper inventory program is implemented by associating a set of attribute values with each state. If an attribute value is an uninstantiated variable, then there is no selection criterion for that attribute in the state. If an attribute value is an atom, however, it acts as a selection criterion for the state. The attribute values associated with the `paper` state are all uninstantiated variables, since this state has no selection criteria. Attribute values are asserted as "av" facts:

```
%  selection criteria for the "paper" state:

%  State     Attribute   Value
av(paper,    type,       S).
av(paper,    grade,      G).
av(paper,    weight,     W).
av(paper,    finish,     T).
av(paper,    color,      C).
```

Inheriting
attribute
values

All attributes values of the `paper` state are inherited by its child states. Inside the "show," "query," and "character" procedures, the relationship between a state and a particular attribute value is governed by a one-to-one integrity constraint. So, once one of these procedures has found the value of an attribute, it will not look for an additional value of the same attribute. Thus, when a new attribute value is added to a child state, it has the effect of *overriding* the attribute value inherited from the parent state.

Result of
creating
`red_roll`

As a result of the query q(paper, `red_roll`) above, the following clauses are added to the current program:

```
child_of(red_roll, paper).

%  selection criteria for the "red_roll" state:
%  State      Attribute  Value
av(red_roll, type,      roll).
av(red_roll, color,     red).
```

Notice that the attribute values are atoms, not uninstantiated variables as they were for the paper attributes above. The values of the type and color attributes associated with `red_roll` override the values of those attributes inherited from the `paper` state. The following queries to "send" show that the other three attribute values for `red_roll`, however, are still inherited from the `paper` state.

```
¦ ?- send(red_roll, av(type, V)).
V = roll               % from "red_roll"

¦ ?- send(red_roll, av(grade, V)).
V = _1                 % from "paper"

¦ ?- send(red_roll, av(weight, V)).
V = _1                 % from "paper"

¦ ?- send(red_roll, av(finish, V)).
V = _1                 % from "paper"

¦ ?- send(red_roll, av(color, V)).
V = red                % from "red_roll"
```

As a result of the `q(red_roll, heavy_red_roll)` call above, the following clauses are added to the current program:

```
child_of(heavy_red_roll, red_roll).

av(heavy_red_roll, weight, 160).
```

The `heavy_red_roll` state inherits the values of the type and color attributes from the `red_roll` state, and the values of the grade and color attributes from the `paper` state, but has its own local value of the weight attribute.

"show" takes the name of a state as an argument, and prints all paper inventory items associated with that state.

```
show(State) :-
    % get selection criteria:
    send(State, av(type,  S) ),
    send(State, av(grade, G) ),
    send(State, av(weight,W) ),
    send(State, av(finish,T) ),
    send(State, av(color, C) ),
    !,
    % get tuple that meets selection criteria:
    pi(paper, S, G, W, T, C),
    % print tuple:
    write(S), write(' '),
    write(G), write(' '),
    write(W), write(' '),
    write(T), write(' '),
    write(C), nl,
    % go back for another tuple:
    fail.
```

"show" directs queries to the target state, `State`, to get each attribute value. The cut ensures that once a set of five attribute values has been collected, the procedure will not try to find any alternative values. "show" then backtracks through the "pi" database, printing each tuple that meets the selection criteria.

"q"

The "q" program asserts a new state under an existing state, and then prompts the user for the selection criteria of this new state.

```
%  make a child state under an existing state
q(ExState, Child) :-
    assert( child_of(Child, ExState) ),
    send(ExState, av(type,  S) ),
            fill(Child, type,   S),
    send(ExState, av(grade, G) ),
            fill(Child, grade,  G),
    send(ExState, av(weight,W) ),
            fill(Child, weight, W),
    send(ExState, av(finish,T) ),
            fill(Child, finish, T),
    send(ExState, av(color, C) ),
            fill(Child, color,  C), !.

fill(State, Attname, Attvalue) :-               % (1)
    write(Attname), write('?'), write('    '),
    %  if Attvalue is uninstantiated, get it from user:
    var(Attvalue),
    getfield(Attvalue),
    (       var(Attvalue)
            ;
            %  if user entered a value, assert it:
            nonvar(Attvalue),
            assert( av(State, Attname, Attvalue) )
    ), !.

fill(_, Attname, Attvalue) :-                   % (2)
    %  if Attvalue is instantiated, print it.
    nonvar(Attvalue),
    write(Attvalue), nl, !.
```

Notice the behavior of the "fill" procedure. The first subgoals of "fill" rule (1) write the attribute name, a question mark, and a tab. If Attvalue is instantiated, then rule (1) fails, and rule (2) prints the attribute value. If Attvalue is uninstantiated, a call to "getfield" (Sec. 3.7) instantiates it to the value typed in by the user, or leaves it uninstantiated if the user hits return without entering a value. If the user typed in a value, then an "av" fact containing the value is asserted.

The "character" procedure shows all current selection criteria associated with a state.

```
character(World) :-
    send(World, av(type,  S) ),
        write('type: '),
        ( nonvar(S), write(S) ; true ), nl,
    send(World, av(grade, G) ),
        write('grade: '),
        ( nonvar(G), write(G) ; true ), nl,
    send(World, av(weight,W) ),
        write('weight: '),
        ( nonvar(W), write(W) ; true ), nl,
    send(World, av(finish,T) ),
        write('finish: '),
        ( nonvar(T), write(T) ; true ), nl,
    send(World, av(color, C) ),
        write('color: '),
        ( nonvar(C), write(C) ; true ), nl,
    !.
```

6.7 Describing Database Change

A *dynamic database* is one that needs to be changed from time to time to reflect the changing structure of the system that it describes. One way to implement a dynamic database is to edit the database destructively whenever a change needs to be made. Unfortunately, such destructive editing removes the possibility of returning to an earlier state of the database, and makes the analysis of database changes difficult.

The *frame axiom* is an alternative concept for implementing a dynamic database. When a change needs to be made, the original database is left intact, and the change itself is recorded. The current form of the database is obtained by looking up the original form and applying whatever changes have been made. Here is a formulation of the frame axiom, where U is any relation, and state S+1 is the result of performing an action A in state S:

The frame
axiom

Relation U *holds in a state S+1*
that results from performing action A *in state* S
   if U *holds in state* S
   and if A *does not affect* U.

In other words, a state of the database inherits each clause of the previous state unless it has been explicitly changed during the transition into that state.

The inheritance mechanism can be used to represent a dynamic database in accordance with the frame axiom. The initial state of the database is uppermost in the tree of states. Each new state of the database is asserted as a child state of the previous state. Thus, a changing database is represented by a tree of states growing downward (Figure 6-8):

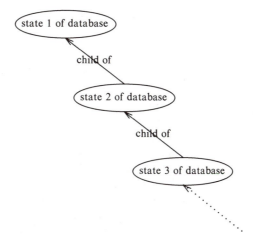

Figure 6-8

When a new state of the database is asserted as a child of an existing state, each clause associated with the existing state is either

  1) inherited by the child state (left unchanged),

  2) superseded by a new value (changed), or

  3) refuted (deleted).

New clauses can also be asserted in the new state.

**The Blocks
World**

The *blocks world* is an example often used to illustrate the frame axiom. Describing the blocks world accurately requires the representation of a dynamic database of block positions on the top of a table. The techniques necessary to represent the blocks world can be applied in other areas that require a dynamic database.

This version of the blocks world is based on a database of "on/3" facts that assert the positions of blocks. on(S, A, B) means that block A is on top of block B in state S. The "place" procedure allows a user to move the blocks in the world to other locations, thereby moving to a new state of the "on" database. The initial state of the "on" database is called 1, the next state is called 2, and so on.

*Characteristics
of the "on"
relation*

"on" is a relation that holds between two blocks in a state, or between a block and the table. "on" is defined to be asymmetric, irreflexive, and intransitive. All blocks are the same size, so "on" between two blocks is governed by a one-to-one integrity constraint. That is, if block A is already on block B, then no other block can be on block B. The table is allowed to have more than one block on it.

The primary purpose of the "place" procedure is *data acquisition*—it *acquires* changes to the database from the user. "place" applies integrity constraints to protect the "on" database from irrational changes. For instance, if block A is already on block B, and the user tries to put block C on block B, "place" will refuse to move any blocks and give the user a warning. Thus, "place" maintains "on" between two blocks as a one-to-one relation at the point that the user tries to change the database. "place" also enforces other integrity constraints, such as disallowing the introduction of a block that is not present in the current state.

In this example of the blocks world, the initial database consists of the following facts.

```
on(1, a, table).
on(1, b, table).
on(1, c, a).
on(1, e, c).

current_state(1).
```

The "current_state" fact contains the name of the latest state of the database.

Picture of a State

"show_state" is a screen oriented procedure that draws a picture of the blocks associated with a state of the database. The initial state appears as:

```
| ?- show_state(1).
```

```
                   -----
                   | e |
                   -----

                   -----
                   | c |
                   -----

                   -----         -----
                   | a |         | b |
                   -----         -----
         ---------------------------------------
                   t   a   b   l   e
```

The code for "show_state" is given in Appendix II.

Changing the Database with "place"

"place" changes the database by asserting a child state of the current state. It asserts new data in the child state, and then destructively changes the value of "current_state" to be the child. The first argument to "place" is the block to be moved, and the second argument is the location to which the block will be moved.

For example, if the current state is 1, then this query:

```
| ?- place(e, table).                     % query (1)
```

will cause the following clauses to be added to the program:

```
current_state(2).

on(2, e, table).
refute(2, on(_, e, c)).
```

It also causes current_state(1) to be retracted from the program.

Finding out   The following query will show where all blocks are in state 2 of the
where the   database:
blocks are

```
| ?- send(2, on(X, Y)).
X = e
Y = table ;                    % from state 2


X = a
Y = table ;                    % from state 1


X = b
Y = table ;                    % from state 1


X = c
Y = a ;                        % from state 1


no
```

The same information is easier to understand when presented
visually:

```
| ?- show_state(2).
```

```
                        -----
                        | c |
                        -----

    -----               -----               -----
    | e |               | a |               | b |
    -----               -----               -----
-----------------------------------------------
            t    a    b    l    e
```

Here is what the database looks like after several more changes.

```
| ?- place(a, b).             % query (2)
yes

| ?- place(c, e).             % query (3)
yes

| ?- current_state(X).
X = 4

| ?- show_state(4).
```

```
          -----        -----
          | c |        | a |
          -----        -----
          -----        -----
          | e |        | b |
          -----        -----
-----------------------------------------
           t   a   b   l   e
```

Implementation of "place"

```
%  disallow an unknown block to be used:
place(Block, Dest) :-
    %  check if either Block or Dest is not present:
    (       not( on(_, Block, _) )
            ;
            Dest \== table,
            not( on(_, Dest, _) )
    ),
    write('illegal block reference'), nl, !.

%  disallow change if Dest is a block
%  that already has a block on it:
place(Block, Dest) :-
    Dest \== table,
    current_state(State),
    send(State, on(Occupant, Dest)),
    write(Occupant),
    write(' is already on '),
    write(Dest), nl, !.
```

```
% database is changed here:
place(Block, Dest) :-
    current_state(State),                           % (1)
    NewState is State + 1,                          % (2)
    assert( child_of(NewState, State) ),            % (3)
    %
    send(State, on(Block, UnderBlock)),             % (4)
    assert( refute(NewState, on(_, Block, UnderBlock)) ),
    assert( on(NewState, Block, Dest) ),            % (6)
    retract( current_state(State) ),                % (7)
    assert( current_state(NewState) ), !.           % (8)
```

Acquisition-time integrity constraints

The first "place" rule disqualifies blocks not already present in the world. The second rule constrains a user from moving a block on top of a block that already has a block on it. If the first two rules fail, it means that the integrity constraints governing the database will not be violated by the proposed change. The change is effected in the third "place" rule. Subgoals (2) and (3) of this rule establish a new state in the "child_of" database. Subgoal (4) discovers where `Block` is currently, and subgoal (5) refutes this location. Subgoal (6) adds the new location of `Block` to the new state. Finally, subgoals (7) and (8) destructively edit the value of "current_state."

Moving a column of blocks

In its present form, "place" allows a column of blocks to be moved at once; that is, there is no constraint against moving a block if it happens to have another block on top of it. This is exactly what occurs in response to the query (2) (`place(a, b)`) above. Any blocks that are on top of the moved block inherit the new position of the moved block. Another integrity constraint rule could be added to ensure that blocks are moved one at a time.

Evaluation of the Inheritance Mechanism

The inheritance mechanism is an implementation of the concept of inheritance, and is useful for representing situations that involve multiple states of knowledge related hierarchically to one another. Thus, the inheritance mechanism provides a framework for the translation of knowledge expressed in the frame formalism or object oriented formalism into Prolog. An existing Prolog clause can be adapted to the mechanism just by adding an extra argument containing the name of a state of knowledge to the head of the clause. The examples in this section demonstrate that using the inheritance mechanism can result in a readable axiomatization of a system that is free of control side effects.

A disadvantage of the inheritance mechanism is that the implementation is not efficient when a query to "send" must consider long branches of states. In its present form, the mechanism allows a child state to have more than one parent (this is called *multiple inheritance* in the object oriented formalism). For instance, Figure 6-9 shows a situation in which state Z inherits clauses from both state Y and state X:

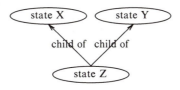

Figure 6-9

The inefficiency of "send" is exacerbated when a target state has more than one parent.

"send" as a
Metalanguage
Predicate

In Sec 0.9, it was stated that on the level of the object language, the meaning of the answer to a Prolog query is that the relation described by the query either holds or does not hold. But on the level of the metalanguage, the meaning of the answer to a query is that

> *The query is or is not provable*
> *by means of the interpreter's problem solving strategy*
> *according to the clauses currently asserted.*

We could say that the meaning of the answer to a query is governed by a *metalanguage predicate* with two implicit parameters: 1) the problem solving strategy to be used is that of the Prolog interpreter, and 2) the set of clauses to be consulted is limited to those clauses that are currently asserted.

Use of the inheritance mechanism changes the metalanguage meaning of the answer to a query slightly. When the "send" procedure evaluates a query, the meaning of the answer is that

The query is or is not provable
by means of the interpreter's problem solving strategy
according to the clauses associated with
a particular state of knowledge.

The name of a state of knowledge that appears in the first argument to "send" stands for the set of clauses associated with that state. Thus, the inheritance mechanism makes the set of clauses to be used in the evaluation of a query explicit. The implementation of "send" (like the implementation of "findall") should be regarded as augmenting the process structure of the Prolog interpreter.

Bibliographic Notes

The approach to knowledge representation in this chapter is strongly influenced by Hayes [1977], [1979], and [1985]. Hayes discusses the importance of model theory to knowledge representation.

A good introduction to semantic networks is in Brachman [1983] and Brachman et al. [1983]. Winograd [1980] discusses the limitations of semantic networks, while pointing out the advantage of frames. The point that both semantic networks and frames can be viewed as alternative syntaxes for predicate logic is made in Kowalski [1979], Hayes [1977] and [1979], and Nilsson [1980].

Goldberg and Robson [1983] provides a thorough introduction to the object oriented programming language, Smalltalk-80. The first object oriented language is SIMULA; for a fascinating history of its development, see Nygaard and Dahl [1978]. Hewitt [1977] discusses the control structures of an object (actor) based programming system. The notion of abstract data types is explained in Aho et al. [1983].

A great deal of work has been done on how other knowledge representation concepts can be expressed in a logic programming language. Regarding semantic nets, see Kowalski [1979]. Regarding frames, see Hayes [1979] and Nakashima [1984]. As for object oriented programming, see Shapiro and Takeuchi [1983], Zaniolo [1984], and Tokoro and Ishikawa [1984]. Kowalski [1986] discusses many other knowledge representation concepts.

Hayes [1979] discusses how the concept of inheritance in the frame formalism can be treated in logic; the inheritance mechanism in this chapter was inspired by his idea.

The frame axiom for dynamic databases is considered in Kowalski [1979] pp. 133-138. Issues of knowledge acquisition in the context of logic programming are covered in Kowalski [1979] and Kitakami et al. [1984].

Exercises

1. The "is_a" relation in the Prolog version of the `bird` example in Sec. 6.2 should be transitive to express the full meaning of the semantic network. In other words, the following query should produce two answers:

```
| ?- is_a(tweety, X).
X = canary ;

X = bird ;

no
```

Redefine the "is_a" predicate so that it is transitive. (Warning: making "is_a" transitive may have adverse side effects on other rules in the program that reference "is_a" as a subgoal, such as "flies" and "color.")

2. Write a program to represent the semantic network shown in Figure 6-10:

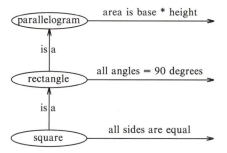

Figure 6-10

3. This exercise is concerned with the the paper inventory program of Sec. 6.6. Write a query to the uppermost state, `paper`, to see all paper inventory items.

Use the program "q" to create a new state under `paper` called `roll`, that contains only paper inventory items of type `roll`.

Use the programs "show" and "character" to examine items in the `roll` state.

Use "q" to create a new state under `roll` called `smooth`, that contains only paper inventory items of type `roll` and of finish `smooth`. Use "show" to examine items in the `smooth` state.

Use your interpreter's debugging facilities to study how "send" works.

Using "findall" (see Appendix II), write a program called "count," that counts the number of paper inventory items associated with a state. Modify the "q" program so that when a new state is asserted, the number of items in it is automatically reported back to the user.

4. Think of other application areas that can appropriately be represented as a hierarchy of states, where information in a general state is inherited by a specific state. Choose one of these application areas, and use the inheritance mechanism to implement it.

7

Expert Consultation

7.1 Systems for Expert Consultation

In its narrowest meaning, the term *expert system* is used to describe one of a small number of programs written by recognized *knowledge engineers*. The purpose of one of these programs is to reproduce the problem solving ability of an expert. A knowledge engineer is a person trained in the art of extracting knowledge from experts and translating it to a computer-understandable form. Most expert systems do not replace human experts entirely, but are used instead to amplify the knowledge and effectiveness of nonexpert personnel.

According to an alternative, behavioral definition, an expert system is any program used for expert consultation. This definition is weaker than the first one, for it embraces programs that are used like expert systems, but that may not have had a bona-fide "expert" involved in their construction.

Some developers of expert systems doubt that there will be a real long-term need for knowledge engineers. According to this argument, computer tools will become friendly enough to be used directly by experts. In many ways this would be a preferable development, since it avoids the possible inaccuracies or distortions that may occur when the knowledge engineer interprets the expert's knowledge. However, the experts involved must be willing to learn how to use computer tools and knowledge representation languages.

Programs that behave like expert systems but that are not derived from the knowledge of an expert are also known as *knowledge based systems* or *expert consultation systems*. In terms of the software technology itself, however, it makes little difference whether an expert was consulted prior to the writing of a program or not. Our major concern here is with the software technology. In this chapter, we use the term *expert consultation system*, and intend to include all variations of expert systems mentioned above.

Parts of an Expert Consulation System

Any expert consultation system requires the following three components:

1) a *knowledge representation language* that can represent complex domain knowledge in an intuitive fashion;

2) a *problem solving strategy* that can manipulate represented knowledge to solve problems as skillfully as human experts; and

3) a *user interface* that provides a natural way to access the knowledge of the program, and is able to explain its answers to both naive and expert users.

Prolog is suitable for the development of expert consultation systems because it has a knowledge representation language (Horn clauses) and a general-purpose problem solving strategy based on resolution. Concepts from other knowledge representation formalisms, alternative problem solving strategies, and various kinds of user interfaces can all be implemented in Prolog. Knowledge representation concepts are discussed in Chapter 6. The rest of this chapter is concerned with intelligent user interfaces and problem solving strategies.

User Interface

Many different approaches to user interfaces have been presented in earlier chapters. These include a conventional database query language (Sec. 5.5), a program that augments its knowledge by asking the user for unknown information (Secs. 3.6 and 4.3), a form-driven interface to a database (Sec. 6.7), and the graphical representation of information in a database (Sec. 6.8). One approach to a screen-oriented form driven interface is discussed in Appendix II.

An important aspect of the user interface for many expert consultation systems is the ability to explain how answers were found. Such ability is necessary to establish the credibility of the program in the minds of its users; without explanation, a user has no reason to accept the validity of an answer. An answer can be explained by showing the chain of inferences used by the program to find the answer.

Two programs are presented in the rest of this chapter that save the inference path of a query, and can show it to the user on demand. The first program, "ev" (for "evaluate"), demonstrates the simplest way to save the inference path of a query. The next program, "vis" (for "visible Prolog"), is an extension of "ev" that prints messages explaining the evaluation of a query as it goes along. Both "ev" and "vis" are useful in debugging other programs, because they enable a programmer to see exactly how a program produced its results. You may find that "vis" is a more useful debugging tool than the debugging facilities of some versions of Prolog.

Problem Solving Strategy

The Prolog interpreter uses a *backward-chaining* problem solving strategy: it starts from the goal and works backward until it reaches facts. (The idea of backward chaining is introduced in Sec. 0.6 and discussed in Chaps. 3 and 5.) Some other problem solvers (for instance, that of the OPS-5 language) are based on a *forward-chaining* strategy. In Sec. 5.2, we demonstrated how a forward-chaining strategy can be implemented in Prolog (i.e. in the bottom up parser, "bup_obj"). Certain problems can be solved more elegantly with a forward-chaining strategy (e.g. equation solving, or parsing languages that contain left recursive constructions such as Japanese).

An alternative problem solving strategy

A detailed explanation of the problem solving strategy of the Prolog interpreter is given in Sec. 3.1. The "ev" procedure discussed in the next section simulates this problem solving strategy exactly. Thus, "ev" can be regarded as an implementation of Prolog written in Prolog. The same techniques used to implement "ev" can also be used to implement a procedure that applies an *alternative problem solving strategy* to the evaluation of a Prolog query. Such a procedure, called "ldi" (for "loop detecting interpreter"), is presented in the last section of this chapter. "ldi" can successfully evaluate a query in certain circumstances that cause the Prolog interpreter to fail or go into an infinite loop, such as left recursive procedures.

7.2 Saving the Inference Path

"ev"

"ev" (for "evaluate") is a procedure that takes a query as an argument and evaluates it. If the evaluation is successful, "ev" prints the
query with its variables instantiated, and then asks if the user would
like to see the proof path or another answer. When there are no
further answers to the query, "ev" fails.

Using "ev"

Consider how "ev" responds to a query to the following database concerned with corporate ownership:

```
owns(ibm, rolm).
owns(rolm, datapoint).
owns(att, teletype).

| ?- ev(owns(ibm, X)).
owns(ibm, rolm)
enter  h  to see proof path, or  ;  for another answer.
```

Since this query can be successfully evaluated, "ev" prints it with X
unified with rolm. If the user types "h" at this point, then "ev" will
explain how it evaluated the query.

```
h
owns(ibm, rolm) is asserted.
```

The
explanation

The explanation is generated by the following method: Whenever a
query is unified with a fact in the current program, the query is
printed followed by "*is asserted.*" Whenever a query is unified
with a rule in the current program, the query is printed followed by
a "*?.*" Each subgoal of the rule is then printed according to the same
scheme, but indented from the original query.

The following session with "ev" contains further examples of its explanations. Notice that the form of the explanation reflects the form
of the clauses used to evaluate the query. "holds" is a transitive relation based on the "owns" database above. "holds" expresses the idea
that one company may own another indirectly through an intermediate company.

```
holds(X, Y) :-
    owns(X, Y).

holds(X, Y) :-
    owns(X, Z),
    holds(Z, Y).

¦ ?- ev(holds(ibm, X)).
```

holds(ibm, rolm)   % first answer
enter h to see proof path, or ; for another answer.
h

holds(ibm, rolm) ?
    owns(ibm, rolm) is asserted.

holds(ibm, rolm)
enter h to see proof path, or ; for another answer.
;

holds(ibm, datapoint)   % second answer
enter h to see proof path, or ; for another answer.
h

holds(ibm, datapoint) ?
    owns(ibm, rolm) is asserted.
    holds(rolm, datapoint) ?
        owns(rolm, datapoint) is asserted.

holds(ibm, datapoint)
enter h to see proof path, or ; for another answer.
;
no

Notice that "ev" prints the query again after responding to h.

How "ev"
Works

"ev" takes a query as its only argument and passes the query on to
"ev0." "ev0" returns a structure of the form

```
p(Query, ProofPath)
```

in its second argument, where `Query` is the original query, and `ProofPath` is a structure describing the steps necessary to prove the query. In the simplest case, when the query can be proved by a fact alone, `ProofPath` is unified with the word `assertion`. If the query is proved by a rule, then `ProofPath` is unified with a recursive "p" structure that contains each of the subgoals of the rule.

After `ProofPath` has been instantiated, it is passed on to the "check_with_user" procedure. "check_with_user" asks the user if he or she would like to see the proof path. If the answer is affirmative, "show_path" is called; otherwise, "check_with_user" fails, and "ev0" backtracks to get another answer.

*Implementation
of "ev"*

```
%  evaluate a query.
ev(X) :-
    ev0(X, P),
    check_with_user(X, P).

check_with_user(X, P) :-
    write(X), nl,
    write('enter  h  to see proof path, or ; for another answer'),
    nl,
    get0(A), get0(_),    % get char + newline
    A = 104,             % ascii 'h'
    show_path('', P),    % '' means no indentation.
    !,
    check_with_user(X, P).

%  base case: last clause was a fact.
%    +        -
%    Query    Path
ev0(true,   assertion) :- !.

%  compound query; return P1 joined to P2 by a comma
ev0((A,B), (P1,P2)) :-
    !,
    ev0(A, P1),
    ev0(B, P2).

%  simple query; return p() structure
ev0(A, p(A,P1)) :-
clause(A, Body),
    ev0(Body, P1).
```

```
%  show execution path:
%          +        +
show_path(Indent, p(Clause,assertion)) :-
    write(Indent), write(Clause),
    write(' is asserted.'), nl, !.

%  first subgoal in a compound query
show_path(Indent, p(Clause,(Subgoal,Subgoals)) ) :-
    cat(Indent, '   ', NewIndent),
    show_path(NewIndent, Subgoal),
    !, show_path(NewIndent, Subgoals).

%  remaining subgoals in a compound query
show_path(Indent, (Subgoal,Path)) :-
    show_path(Indent, Subgoal),
    !, show_path(Indent, Path).

show_path(Indent, p(Clause,Path)) :-
    write(Indent), write(Clause), write(' ?'), nl,
    cat(Indent, '   ', NewIndent),
    !, show_path(NewIndent, Path).

%   +   +  _
cat(X, Y, Z) :-              % concatenate two atoms.
    name(X, Xlist),
    name(Y, Ylist),
    append(Xlist, Ylist, Zlist),
    name(Z, Zlist), !.
```

Proving a Fact

The best way to understand how "ev" works is to examine the input and output of its subgoals. Consider what happens when "ev0" is given a query that is provable by a fact:

```
| ?- ev0(owns(ibm,X), ProofPath).
```

"ev0" calls "clause," which unifies X with rolm and Body with true, since owns(ibm, rolm) is a fact.

The next call to "ev0" is equivalent to the following query:

```
¦ ?- ev0(true, P1).
P1 = assertion
```

This query is answered by the first "ev0" rule. The value of P1 is passed through to become part of the "p" structure returned by the previous call to "ev0":

```
ProofPath =  p(owns(ibm,rolm), assertion)
```

Proving a Rule

Suppose that "ev0" is given a query that is only provable by a rule, such as:

```
¦ ?- ev0(holds(ibm,X), Path).                              (1)
```

This call matches the third "ev0" rule. The "clause" subgoal is equivalent to the following query:

```
¦ ?- clause(holds(ibm,X), Body1).                          (2)
Body1 = owns(ibm, X)
```

The "ev0" subgoal is equivalent to:

```
¦ ?- ev0(owns(ibm, X), P1).                                (3)
P1 =  p(owns(ibm,rolm), assertion)
```

This is the same query that was analyzed above. Query (1) to "ev0" now returns:

```
Path = p(holds(ibm,rolm), p(owns(ibm,rolm), assertion))
```

Showing the Proof Path

Asking to see the proof path causes a series of calls to "show_path," equivalent to the following queries:

```
¦ ?- show_path('', p(holds(ibm, rolm),
                     p(owns(ibm, rolm), assertion))).
holds(ibm, rolm) ?
```

```
¦ ?- show_path('    ', p(owns(ibm, rolm), assertion)).
   owns(ibm, rolm)  is asserted.
```

**Limitations of
"ev"**

The version of "ev" shown above makes no attempt to reproduce the effect of cut. If you give "ev" a query to a procedure containing a cut, it will treat cut as a subgoal that is always true. A cut will not stop it from backtracking.

7.3 Visible Prolog

With a few small changes, we can make a version of "ev" that explains all control decisions taken by the interpreter as it evaluates a query. The explanation is consistent with the stack oriented abstract machine presented in Chap. 3.

The resulting procedure, called "vis" (for "visible Prolog"), provides detailed output useful for tracing the execution of programs. When a query is being unified with a clause in the current program, "vis" prints *subgoal=* followed by the query, and *dbentry=* (database entry) followed by the program clause. If the unification is successful, "vis" prints *S* (for "success"); otherwise it prints *F*. Messages about the subgoals of a rule are indented from the message about the head of the rule. When "vis" can find no further clauses that have the same predicate name and the same number of arguments as the query, it prints an *:End of X database* message. Here is an example query.

```
| ?- vis(holds(ibm, X)).

% Head of first "holds" rule

subgoal=holds(ibm,_0)  dbentry=holds(_38,_42) S
   subgoal=owns(ibm,_0)  dbentry=owns(ibm,rolm) S

holds(ibm,rolm)
enter  h  to see proof path, or ; for another answer
;

   subgoal=owns(ibm,_0)  dbentry=owns(rolm,datapoint) F
   subgoal=owns(ibm,_0)  dbentry=owns(att,teletype) F
   :End of  owns  database.
```

```
% Head of second "holds" rule

subgoal=holds(ibm,_0)  dbentry=holds(_38,_42) S
   subgoal=owns(ibm,_78)  dbentry=owns(ibm,rolm) S
   subgoal=holds(rolm,_0)  dbentry=holds(_339,_343) S
      subgoal=owns(rolm,_0)  dbentry=owns(ibm,rolm) F
      subgoal=owns(rolm,_0)  dbentry=owns(rolm,datapoint) S

holds(ibm,datapoint)
enter  h  to see proof path, or ; for another answer
;

         subgoal=owns(rolm,_0)  dbentry=owns(att,teletype) F
         :End of   owns   database.
      subgoal=holds(rolm,_0)  dbentry=holds(_339,_343) S
         subgoal=owns(rolm,_379)  dbentry=owns(ibm,rolm) F
         subgoal=owns(rolm,_379)  dbentry=owns(rolm,datapoint) S
         subgoal=holds(datapoint,_0)  dbentry=holds(_702,_706) S
            subgoal=owns(datapoint,_0)  dbentry=owns(ibm,rolm) F
            subgoal=owns(datapoint,_0)  dbentry=owns(rolm,datapoint) F
            subgoal=owns(datapoint,_0)  dbentry=owns(att,teletype) F
            :End of   owns   database.
         subgoal=holds(datapoint,_0)  dbentry=holds(_702,_706) S
            subgoal=owns(datapoint,_742)  dbentry=owns(ibm,rolm) F
            subgoal=owns(datapoint,_742)  dbentry=owns(rolm,datapoint)F
            subgoal=owns(datapoint,_742)  dbentry=owns(att,teletype)F
            :End of   owns   database.
         :End of  holds   database.
         subgoal=owns(rolm,_379)  dbentry=owns(att,teletype) F
         :End of   owns   database.
      :End of  holds   database.
      subgoal=owns(ibm,_78)  dbentry=owns(rolm,datapoint) F
      subgoal=owns(ibm,_78)  dbentry=owns(att,teletype) F
      :End of   owns   database.
   :End of   holds   database.
   no
```

Notice how much time is spent looking for a nonexistent third answer.

**From "ev" to
"vis"**

The implementation of "vis" is very similar to that of "ev." "vis0" (the equivalent of "ev0") has a new first argument containing the number of spaces to indent. The major difference between "ev" and "vis," however, lies in the third "vis0" rule. Instead of just calling "clause" with a query as its first argument (as "ev0" did), "vis0" makes a copy of the query. All arguments to this new query are variables. This new query is passed to "find_clause," and the body of a unifying clause is returned. For instance, if the original query is owns(ibm, _0), the new query will be owns(_1, _2). "find_clause" may instantiate variables in the new query. After the call to "find_clause," the original query and the query returned by "find_clause" are printed, and then unification of the two clauses is attempted. If the unification succeeds, S (for "success") is printed and "vis0" is called recursively with the body of the clause returned by "find_clause." Otherwise, "find_clause" backtracks to find another clause in the current program.

*Implementation
of "vis"*

```
vis(X) :-
    vis0('', Q, Path),
    check_with_user(Q, Path).

check_with_user(Q, Path) :-
    write(Q), nl,
    write('enter h to see proof path, or ; for another answer'),
    nl,
    get0(A), get0(_),   % get char + newline
    A = 104,            % ascii 'h'
    show_path('', Path),
    check_with_user(Q, Path),
    !.

% base case for a fact
%    +Indent  +Query  -Path
vis0(_,       true,   assertion) :- !.

% compound query
vis0(Indent, (Q1,Q2), (Path1,Path2)) :-
    !,
    vis0(Indent, Q1, Path1),
    vis0(Indent, Q2, Path2).
```

```
%  simple query
vis0(Indent, Q1, p(Q1,Path)) :-
    %  make Q2:
    %  (Q2 is a copy of Q1, but all args are vars.)
    Q1 =.. [Pred|Args1],
    length(Args1, Length),
    makelist(Length, Args2),
    Q2 =.. [Pred|Args2],
    !,
    find_clause(Indent, Q2, Body, Pred),
    write(Indent), write('subgoal='), write(Q1),
    write('  dbentry='), write(Q2), write('  '),
    (   %  success if Q1 unifies with Q2:
        Q1 = Q2, write(' S'), nl
        ;
        %  failure if they do not unify:
        not(Q1 = Q2), write(' F'), nl, fail
    ),
    cat(Indent, '  ', NewIndent), % indent subgoals
    vis0(NewIndent, Body, Path).

%  find next clause, or print end of database message.
%              +       +   -      +
find_clause(_,      Q, Body, _) :-
    clause(Pred, Body).
find_clause(Indent, _, _,     Pred) :-
    write(Indent),
    write(': End of  '), write(Pred),
    write('  database.'), nl,
    !, fail.

makelist(0, []) :- !.
makelist(N, [X|R]) :-
    NN is N - 1,
    makelist(NN, R), !.
```

"show_path" and "cat" are the same as in "ev" above.

7.4 A Loop Detecting Interpreter

**Procedures
That Cycle**

At several points in the book, we have uncovered Prolog procedures that look like they ought to work (they have a clear declarative semantics), but that cause the Prolog interpreter to enter an infinite loop.

For instance, there is a procedure called "xancestor" in Sec. 1.5:

```
xancestor(A, B) :-         % (1)
    parent(A, B).


xancestor(A, B) :-         % (2)
    xancestor(A, C),
    parent(C, B).
```

"xancestor" is identical with "ancestor" (which does work) except that the order of subgoals in rule (2) is *left recursive*. Because the recursive call to "xancestor" comes before the "parent" subgoal, the variable C is uninstantiated at the point that "xancestor" is called.

When the Prolog interpreter tries to evaluate a query to "xancestor," it finds the correct answers, but then continues recursing until it runs out of memory.

**A Robust
Problem
Solver**

"ldi" (for "loop-detecting interpreter") is a version of "ev" that is capable of safely evaluating a query to a left recursive program like "xancestor." The technique used to make "ldi" a robust problem solver is similar to that used in the "tsi_travel3" program in Sec. 4.2: "ldi" keeps a record of the head of every clause it encounters in the evaluation of a query. Encountering the same clause head four times will cause it to fail. This feature prevents "ldi" from descending into infinite recursive loops.

To illustrate what "ldi" can do, let us consider a query to "xancestor." Assume that the following "parent" database is asserted:

```
parent(jb, lc).
parent(jb, gg).
parent(gg, wm).
```

The Prolog interpreter gets lost in an infinite recursion after finding the three answers:

```
¦ ?- xancestor(jb, Z).
Z = lc ;

Z = gg ;

Z = wm ;

warning: out of stack space.
```

But "ldi" is able to evaluate the same query safely:

```
¦ ?- ldi(xancestor(jb,X)).

xancestor(jb, lc)
enter  h  to see proof path, or ; for another answer
h
xancestor(jb, lc) ?
    parent(jb, lc)  is asserted.

xancestor(jb, lc)
enter  h  to see proof path, or ; for another answer
;

xancestor(jb, gg)
enter  h  to see proof path, or ; for another answer
h
xancestor(jb, gg) ?
    parent(jb, gg)  is asserted.

xancestor(jb, gg)
enter  h  to see proof path, or ; for another answer
;
```

```
xancestor(jb, wm)
enter  h  to see proof path, or ; for another answer
h
xancestor(jb, wm) ?
    xancestor(jb, gg) ?
        parent(jb, gg)  is asserted.
    parent(gg, wm)  is asserted.

xancestor(jb, wm)
enter  h  to see proof path, or ; for another answer
;

no
```

Algorithm of "ldi"

The implementation of "ldi" is very similar to that of "ev." "ldi0" (the equivalent of "ev0") has a new first argument that is a list of the subgoals encountered thus far in the evaluation of a query. The third "ldi0" rule has a new subgoal: not(unifiable(Q1, Trail, 3)). Trail is the list of subgoals. Q1 is the current subgoal. "unifiable" checks whether Q1 can be unified with three members of Trail in a row; if it can, then "ldi0" fails and backtracks. The number three here is arbitrary. If it were reduced to two, "ldi" would not be able to find answers in certain left recursive situations. If it were increased to four, "ldi" would be able to find additional answers in certain rarely encountered left recursive situations, but would also require much more time and memory.

```
% loop-detecting interpreter.
ldi(Q) :-
    ldi0([], Q, Path),
    check_with_user(Q, Path).

check_with_user(Q, Path) :-
    write(Q), nl,
    write('enter h to see proof path, or ; for another answer'),
    nl,
    get0(A), get0(_),    % get char + newline
    A = 104,             % 104 is an ascii 'h'
    show_path('', Path),
    check_with_user(Q, Path),
    !.
```

```
%  base case for a fact
%      +        +        -
%    Trail  Query    Path
ldi0(_,     true,   assertion) :- !.

%  second clause: compound query
ldi0(Trail, (Q1,Q2),  (P1,P2) ) :-
    !,
    ldi0(Trail, Q1, P1),
    ldi0(Trail, Q2, P2).

%  third clause: simple query
ldi0(Trail, Q1,  p(Q1,P)) :-
    % fail if 3 members of Trail list are unifiable with Q1:
    not(unifiable(Q1, Trail, 3)),
    clause(Q1, Body),
    ldi0([Q1|Trail], Body, P).

%  succeed if first arg
%  unifies with N of the members of second arg, a list.
unifiable(_, _, 0) :- !.
unifiable(A, [A|R], N) :-
    NN is N - 1,
    !, unifiable(A, R, NN).
```

"ldi" works in largely the same way as "ev." What is different is the way that Trail, the first argument to "ldi0," picks up elements as the procedure recurses deeper. The evaluation of the following query:

```
| ?- ldi(xancestor(jb,X)).
```

involves the following calls to "ldi0," showing how the first argument grows.

```
| ?- ldi0([], xancestor(jb,X), P1).
```

xancestor(jb, 1c)   % first answer printed by "ldi"

xancestor(jb, gg)   % second answer printed by "ldi"

```
| ?- ldi0([xancestor(jb,X)], xancestor(jb,C1), P2).
```

xancestor(jb,wm)   % third answer printed by "ldi"

```
¦ ?- ldi0([xancestor(jb,C1),xancestor(jb,X)], xancestor(jb,C2), P3).

¦ ?- ldi0([xancestor(jb,C2),xancestor(jb,C1),xancestor(jb,X)],
          xancestor(jb, C3),  P4).

¦ ?- not(unifiable(xancestor(jb,C3),
                   [xancestor(jb,C2),
                    xancestor(jb,C1),
                    xancestor(jb,X)],
                    3)).
```
no

During the evaluation of the query, the `Trail` list (the first argument of "ldi0") kept growing until it contained three `xancestor(jb,_)` elements, all of which are unifiable with one another. When an attempt is made to add a fourth such element (i.e. `xancestor(jb,C3)`), then the `not(unifiable(Q1,Trail,3))` subgoal fails, and "ldi" stops recursing. Note that this is exactly the point—when another answer is requested after the first three answers have been found—that the Prolog interpreter would go into an infinite loop.

"ldi" as a Metalanguage Predicate

As mentioned in Sec. 0.9 and Sec. 6.5, the meaning of an answer to a Prolog query is governed by a metalanguage predicate with two implicit parameters: 1) the problem solving strategy is that of the Prolog interpreter, and 2) the set of clauses used in the evaluation of the query is limited to the clauses that are currently asserted. In Sec. 6.5, we discussed how "send" is a metalanguage predicate that makes explicit the set of clauses to be used in the evaluation of a query. In the same sense, "ldi" is a metalanguage predicate that makes the problem solving strategy explicit. Thus, the meaning of the answer to a query evaluated with "ldi" is that

The query is or is not provable
by means of a loop detecting problem solving strategy
according to the clauses currently asserted.

7.5 Conclusion: Prolog Style

**The Nature of
a Computer
Program**

We use the term *system* to mean some limited part of the world that the programmer wants to represent (i.e. the application domain of a program). The job of a programmer writing an application program in any language is to embody the structure of the relevant system in the program. An application program is composed of two components: 1) a description of the structure of the system, and 2) procedures capable of transforming and realizing the meaning of that description. A programmer using a procedural language such as C is usually responsible for both components. As discussed in Sec. 6.1, a computational formalism is made up of 1) a descriptive language, and 2) a process structure (i.e. a set of procedures) capable of realizing the meaning of expressions of the descriptive language. Therefore, a programmer using a computational formalism can concentrate on describing the system in the formalism's descriptive language, and rely on the formalism's process structure to realize its meaning. This view of using a computational formalism is accurate only for those cases in which the formalism is strong enough to describe the system.

*Three Phases
of Learning
Prolog*

Viewed as a computational formalism, Prolog is made up of a descriptive language and a process structure (i.e. the interpreter) for realizing the formal meaning of expressions of that descriptive language. The process of learning to program in Prolog can be divided into three phases. In the first phase, a programmer learns the strength of Prolog as a computational formalism by writing programs that consists of purely declarative clauses. To put this another way, the programmer must learn the exact nature of Prolog's process structure (i.e. the actions of the interpreter) when no side effects (i.e. cut, "assert," "retract," "write," etc.) are involved. (This is why so much emphasis is put on the Prolog interpreter's problem solving strategy in this chapter and Chap. 3.)

Sooner or later, however, a programming situation is bound to occur that cannot be handled by Prolog's basic process structure. For instance, a situation may call for some kind of computation that is not possible in Prolog without the use of side effects. In such a situation, a programmer cannot rely on the interpreter to provide all of the process structure needed by the program. Thus, in the second phase of learning Prolog, a programmer learns how to use side effects to achieve complicated control structures in a Prolog program. This phase requires adopting the behavioral view of the language (Sec.

4.3). During this phase, programmers may be tempted to put side effects into almost every clause in a program.

A Prolog procedure that does not rely on side effects has a clear declarative meaning, and is wholly part of the descriptive part of the program. A Prolog procedure with side effects, however, has no declarative meaning. If side effects occur in an application-specific procedure (as, for instance, "loc" in Sec. 3.6), then that procedure must be considered to be some kind of mixture of description and process. Such a procedure degrades Prolog as a computational formalism by blurring the distinction between description and process.

If side effects occur in a general-purpose procedure (as, for instance, "findall" in Appendix II or "send" in Chap. 6), then that procedure can be considered to be part of the process structure of the application program. Prolog augmented by such procedures is actually a stronger computational formalism than Prolog by itself, because, when such procedures are available, more complicated systems can be described with purely declarative Prolog clauses.

Therefore, in the third phase of learning Prolog, a programmer must learn the discipline of isolating side effects into general-purpose procedures, in order to preserve the purely descriptive nature of application-specific code. Thus, whenever the computational formalism of Prolog seems inadequate for the programming situation at hand (or for the system that needs to be represented), there is always a choice between 1) degrading the formalism by adding side effects to application clauses, or 2) extending the formalism by writing general-purpose procedures. The following two rules of Prolog style are intended to encourage the second alternative.

Two Rules of Prolog Style

The first rule of Prolog programming style is:

Keep the descriptive part of a program distinct from the program's process structure.

Put another way, this rule is: *Do not put control side effects (which are procedural elements) into clauses that describe the application.* Following this rule goes a long way in preserving the clarity and maintainability of a program.

Declarative
boundary

The second rule of Prolog programming style is:

> *Establish a declarative boundary between the descriptive part of the program and the process structure, in such a way that application-specific clauses are wholly descriptive.*

On the process structure side of the boundary, the procedure does whatever is necessary to establish the relation. On the description side of it, a reference to a procedure that augments the process structure appears as a relation with a declarative meaning. Because the procedure has side effects that change the interpreter's problem solving strategy, part of this declarative meaning is on the level of the metalanguage. The existence of the boundary makes it possible to include a call to the procedure as a subgoal in a descriptive clause without compromising the declarative semantics of that clause.

For any particular application program, it remains a formidable design problem to decide where to make the declarative boundary between description and process. In general, a program written in a computational formalism can be easy to understand and maintain if the form of the program is *isomorphic* to the form of the system it describes (that is, if every variation in the form of the system has a corresponding variation in the form of the descriptive part of the program, and vice versa). So, when it is necessary to extend Prolog as a formalism, it is important to do so in such a way to enable isomorphism between the descriptive clauses and the system they describe. Ideally, above the level of the declarative interface, there should be isomorphism between the form of the program and the form of the system. Below the level of the declarative interface, the program may be a sort of behavioral free-for-all.

Examples of the Declarative Boundary

It is worthwhile to consider some examples of declarative boundaries. Suppose that the problem is to write a clause that defines person M to be a *single mother* of person C, if M is the mother of C, M lives with C, M is divorced, and M is not remarried. Assume that the "mother" database is very large. We would like to add control information to the rule so that when the interpreter evaluates a query to the rule in which C is instantiated and M is uninstantiated, it does not waste time looking for more than one value of M.

First solution   One solution is:

```
%                 One  Many
single_mother1(M,    C) :-
    nonvar(C),
    mother(M, C),
    !, % C has only one mother; disallow backtracking.
    lives_with(M, C),
    divorced(M),
    not( remarried(M) ).

single_mother1(M, C) :-
    var(C),
    mother(M, C),
    lives_with(M, C),
    divorced(M),
    not( remarried(M) ).

mother(susan, bobby).
mother(kathleen, fred).
mother(isadora, michele).
mother(barbara, wendy).
mother(barbara, steve).

lives_with(susan, bobby).
lives_with(isadora, michele).
lives_with(barbara, wendy).
lives_with(barbara, steve).

divorced(kathleen).
divorced(isadora).
divorced(barbara).

remarried(kathleen).
```

To verify that "single_mother1" solves the problem, use the debugging facilities of your interpreter to evaluate a query such as:

```
| ?- single_mother1(Who, wendy).
Who = barbara ;

no
```

The output of the debugging facilities will show that the interpreter does not backtrack to look for a second mother for Wendy.

In this first solution, the declarative boundary is on the level of "single_mother1." The implementation of "single_mother1" has no declarative meaning because it includes control side effects, but a call to "single_mother1" does have a declarative meaning. "single_mother1" is best considered a procedure that does whatever is necessary to establish the *single mother* relation between its arguments in an efficient manner.

Second solution

Another solution is:

```
single_mother2(M, C) :-
    om_mother(M, C),
    lives_with(M, C),
    divorced(M),
    not( remarried(M) ).

%  one-to-many front end to "mother" database:
%        One   Many
om_mother(M,    C) :-
    nonvar(C),
    mother(M, C), !.

om_mother(M, C) :-
    var(C),
    mother(M, C).
```

In this solution, the declarative boundary is on the level of "om_mother." "om_mother" is a procedure that does whatever is necessary to establish the *mother* relation between its arguments in an efficient manner. Because a call to "om_mother" has a declarative meaning, the body of the "single_mother2" rule also has a declarative meaning, and so is on the description side of the boundary.

The second solution is slightly preferable to the first because the declarative boundary is on a lower level. Furthermore, "om_mother" could be used in other clauses as an efficient front end to the "mother" database. But both solutions suffer from a common flaw: they violate the first rule of style. In the first solution, control side effects are added to an application-specific "single_mother1" clause. In the second solution, control side effects are added to an application-specific "om_mother" clause.

Third solution   There is a third solution that keeps the process structure entirely separate from the description. It requires a declaration that the arguments of the "mother" relation are governed by a one-to-many integrity constraint, and a problem solver that is capable of utilizing this information:

```
single_mother3(M, C) :-
    mother(M, C),
    lives_with(M, C),
    divorced(M),
    not( remarried(M) ).


%  declare one-to-many property of the "mother" relation:
%        Relation                One       Many
one_many(mother(Mother, Child), Mother,   Child).


%  problem solver that knows about one-to-many relations:
ps(true) :- !.

ps( (A,B) ) :-               % compound query
    !,
    ps(A),
    ps(B).

ps(A) :-    % special case: A is a one-to-many relation
    one_many(A, X, Y),
    !,
    om_ps(A, X, Y).

ps(A) :-    % A is not a one_to_many relation
    clause(A, Body),
    ps(Body).
```

```
%  evaluate a one-to-many relation efficiently:
%         One   Many
om_ps(A, X,    Y) :-
   nonvar(Y),
   clause(A, Body),
   ps(Body), !.


om_ps(A, X, Y) :-
   var(Y),
   clause(A, Body),
   ps(Body).
```

Notice the similarity of "ps" (for "problem solver") with "ev0" in Sec. 7.2. "ps" has an extra clause to deal with queries that are governed by a one-to-many integrity constraint. The form of the "om_ps" procedure is very similar to the form of "om_mother."

In the third solution, the declarative boundary is on the level of "ps." "ps" is a procedure that does whatever is necessary to establish the following property of its argument (a query):

> *The query is provable*
> *according to currently asserted clauses,*
> *using a strategy that takes advantage of knowledge about which*
> *relations are governed by a one-to-many integrity constraint.*

Declarative control information

As a result of the extra trouble it took to write "ps," the "single_mother3" rule is now completely on the description side of the boundary, and there is no need for a front-end procedure for the "mother" database. The "one_many" fact is also on the description side of the boundary, since it declares a property of another part of the description. The meaning of this fact is on the level of the metalanguage; it contains a type of *declarative control information* that is utilized by "ps."

Other Examples

There have been other programming problems in the course of the book that demonstrate how following the two rules of style yields a clean, easy to read, and reusable solution. Compare the "loc" procedure of Sec. 3.6, which violates the first rule, with same problem solved by "find_or_ask" in Sec. 4.3, which does not. Compare the "total_sal" procedure of Sec. 3.7, with the same problem solved by "findall" and "sum_up." Finally, compare the "meeting" example of Sec. 6.3, with the same problem solved by "send" in Sec. 6.4. In the "meeting" example solved by "send," all of the application-specific clauses are structurally isomorphic to the system they describe, and the details of how this is accomplished are hidden inside of "send."

Prolog as an Effective Computational Formalism

Prolog is not an ideal computational formalism, because there are many programming situations that the interpreter cannot handle without additional control information. But by following the two rules of style, it is possible for a programmer to turn Prolog into an effective computational formalism for any particular application. Establishing a declarative boundary in a program gives a clear indication of which parts of the program are intended to be description, and which parts are intended to be process. As the last example demonstrates, even control information can be included in the descriptive part of the program.

The discipline of Prolog programming amounts to extending the abilities of the interpreter when necessary by writing procedures, but doing it in a way that preserves "feel" of it as a computational formalism. The advantage to the programmer of adhering to this discipline is being able to think about the structure of applications at a high level.

Bibliographic Notes

The conventional definition of an expert system can be found in Hayes-Roth et al. [1983]. The behavioral definition is in Kowalski [1984].

Many expert system tools offer the ability to explain their answers. The style of *how* explanation given by "ev" was inspired by a similar ability in the APES language (Hammond and Sergot [1984]).

The "ev" procedure is similar to "eval" in Coelho et al. [1982]. Various kinds of loop-detecting interpreters are discussed in Brough and Walker [1984].

The discussion of Prolog style in the conclusion was inspired by a similar discussion in Kowalski [1984].

Exercises

1. Enter a "travel/4" database that contains cyclic data, and then use "ldi" to evaluate a query to "can_travel4." What happens?

Try "ldi" with some other problematic programs you have come across. Does one of these programs work with the loop detecting interpreter where it does not work with the normal interpreter? Why or why not?

2. A call to "findall" (Sec. 3.7) declares the relation between a query and all answers to that query; a call to "send" (Sec. 6.4) declares whether a query is provable according to the clauses associated with a state. What relation does a call to "place" (Sec. 6.5) declare? Could "place" be rewritten so as to have a clearer declarative meaning?

3. "ps" in Sec. 7.5 is now capable of optimizing queries to a relation declared to be "one_many." Extend "ps" so that it can optimize queries to relations declared to be "one_one" and "many_one" (see Sec. 1.7).

Appendix I

Basic Terminology

Arity

The number of arguments of a structure or predicate is known as its arity.

Atom

An atom is a nonnumeric constant. It is usually written as a single word outside of quotes. Examples:

```
hello   *   '#$%'   'New York'
```

Single quotes are used to delimit atoms composed of multiple words, or atoms that begin with a capital letter.

Axiom

In propositional logic or first order predicate logic, an axiom is a wff that is assumed to be true. A set of axioms that describe the structure of a field of knowledge is known as a *theory* (see Secs. 0.4 and 0.5). When a Prolog program is used to describe the structure of a system, each clause in the program can be considered to be an axiom.

Axiomatization

In predicate logic, an axiomatization (or *axiomatic definition*) of a relation is a set of axioms from which all true instances of the relation can be derived by application of the rules of inference.

Built-in Predicate

A particular version of Prolog comes with certain built-in predicates which do not have to be explicitly consulted before they are used. Commonly available built-in predicates are discussed in Secs. 3.3 through 3.10. See your reference manual for an exact list of available built-in predicates.

Clause	See *Horn Clause*.
Constant	A constant is either an integer (1, 20, -10), a floating point number (3.1417), or an atom.
Consult	During a session with the Prolog interpreter, a file of Prolog clauses is consulted in order to make those clauses part of the current program. Most versions of Prolog have the built-in predicate "consult/1" to perform this operation.
Cut	Cut (written as !) is a built-in predicate which always succeeds, but which prevents backtracking (see Sec. 3.2).
Determinate	A procedure is determinate if it succeeds only once. A compound query (or the body of a rule) is determinate if, after it has been evaluated, the interpreter is unable to backtrack to any of the subgoals within it.
Fact (or Unit Clause)	A fact is a Horn clause with no conditions—that is, with an empty body (see Sec. 1.2). Examples:

```
king(louis, france).
have_beaks(birds).
employee(nancy, data_processing, 55000).
```

Functor	A functor is the name and associated arity of a structure. Some researchers use "functor" in a more casual way to mean just the name of a structure or the name of a predicate (see Parsaye [1983]). Noncomputational logicians have used "functor" in a variety of other ways; for instance, Hodges [1977] refers to logical connectives such as "and," "or," and "not" as *truth functors*.
Goal	See *Query*.
Horn Clause	A Horn clause is either a fact, a rule, or a query (goal).
Inference	The process of reaching a conclusion from some assumptions is called *making an inference*.
Inference Rule	In propositional calculus or predicate calculus, an inference rule specifies the syntactic form of a valid inference (see Secs. 0.4 and 0.5). An example of an inference rule is *modus ponens*:

From p --> q and p, infer q.

See Table 0-2 for other rules. Resolution is an inference rule for the clausal form of predicate logic (see Sec. 0.6).

Instantiation   A Prolog variable is instantiated when it assumes a constant or structure as its value during the evaluation of a query.

Lexicon   The lexicon of a formal language is the set of symbols used to write statements in that language.

List   A list is a special type of structure written as a set of zero or more terms between square brackets. If there are no terms in a list, it is said to be empty, and is written as [ ]. In this first set of examples, all members of each list are explicitly stated.

```
[aa,bb,cc]    [X,Y]    [Name]    [[x,y],z]
```

In the second set of examples, only the first several members of each list are explicitly stated, while the rest of the list is represented by a variable on the right hand side of the lexical symbol ¦ :

```
[X¦Y]    [a,b,c¦Y]    [[x,y]¦Rest]
```

¦ is known as the *list constructor*. The elements to the left of ¦ are called the *head* of the list. The variable on the right hand side of ¦ is called the *tail* of the list; it represents a list of any length.

Operator   An operator is the name of a predicate or structure that can be written in infix, prefix, or postfix form (see Sec. 3.10). "+" is an example of a structure name declared to be an infix operator.

Predicate   A predicate is a relation that holds between a fixed number of arguments. A predicate is identified by its name and its arity (i.e. number of arguments). A reference to a predicate is written as:

```
name(arg1, arg2, ...argN)
```

In Prolog, a predicate is defined by a procedure.

Procedure   A procedure is a set of clauses in which the head of each clause has the same predicate name and the same number of arguments. For instance, in Chap. 1, these two clauses:

```
ancestor(A, B) :-                        % (1)
    parent(A, B).


ancestor(A, B) :-                        % (2)
    parent(C, B),
    ancestor(A, C).
```

constitute the "ancestor/2" procedure. The predicate "ancestor/2" is defined by this procedure.

Rule

A rule is a Horn clause with one or more conditions. Example:

```
has_stiff_neck(ralph) :-
    hacker(ralph).
```

In this rule, `hacker(ralph)` is the one and only condition, and `has_stiff_neck(ralph)` is the conclusion.

Stream

Data available in a sequential form is referred to as a stream. In a program, an input/output channel used to communicate with disk files or with the outside world can be thought of as a stream. A recursive data structure such as a list can also be thought of as a stream.

Structure

(Also known as *compound term*.) A structure is a complex data object identified by its name and its arity. A structure is written as a name followed by one or more arguments inside of parentheses. Here is an example of a "father/1" structure:

```
father(george)
```

`father` is the structure name, and `george` is the first and only argument. The argument to a structure can be another structure, as in

```
father(father(george))
```

An atom can be considered to be a structure with no arguments.

Subgoal

A subgoal is a condition in the body of a rule or in a compound query.

Term   An argument to a predicate or structure must be a term. A term is either a constant, a variable, or a structure.

Theory   A theory of propositional or predicate logic is a set of axioms that describe the structure of a field of knowledge (see Secs. 0.4 and 0.5). When a Prolog program is used to describe the structure of a system, that program can be considered to be a theory.

Unification   Unification is the process of matching a subgoal with the head of a clause during the evaluation of a query. A subgoal unifies with the head of a clause if 1) they have the same name, 2) they have the same arity, and 3) all of the arguments can be unified. The rules governing the unification of arguments are:

                1) Two constants unify with one another if they are identical.

                2) A variable unifies with a constant or a structure. As a result of the unification, the variable is instantiated to the constant or structure.

                3) A variable unifies with another variable. As a result of the unification, they become the same variable.

                4) A structure unifies with another structure if they have the same name, the same number of arguments, and if all of the arguments can be unified.

Query (Goal) In terms of Prolog's declarative semantics, a query is a question put by the user to the Prolog system about whether a particular instance of a relation holds. In terms of Prolog's procedural semantics, a query can be considered a procedure call.

                A simple query is written as the name of a predicate, arguments inside of parentheses, and a period. For example, this query:

                ```
                | ?- father(edward, ralph).
                ```

                refers to the predicate "father/2."

                If a query has no variables in it, the system will respond either *yes* or *no*. If a query has variables, the system will try to find values of those variables for which the query is true. After the system has found one answer, the user can ask the system to look for additional answers to the query by typing ";".

A compound query consists of two or more simple queries connected by the "and" connector (comma) or the "or" connector (semicolon). Each component of a compound query is called a subgoal. For example, the following compound query is intended to find Ralph's grandfather:

```
| ?- father(G, F), father(F, ralph).
```

Because the two subgoals of this compound query are connected by "and," both subgoals must be true simultaneously for the compound query as a whole to be true. F is a shared variable which is constrained by unification to have the same value in each of the two subgoals.

Variable

A variable is a type of Prolog term that can take on a constant or a structure as its value. A variable is written as a word beginning either with a capital letter outside of quotes, or with the character _. Examples:

```
X    Name    _c    _305
```

Appendix II

Useful Programs

Miscellaneous Procedures

```
%  Reverse the order of elements in a list.
%  Method #1:
%        +        -
reverse([C¦L1], L2) :-
    reverse(L1, Out),
    append(Out, [C], L2).
reverse([], []).


%  Method #2:
%        +    +   -
reverse(L1, [], L1).
reverse(L1, [X¦L2], L3) :-
        reverse([X¦L1], L2, L3).


%  The second version is queried as follows:
%  ¦ ?- reverse([], [a,b,c], R).
%  R = [c,b,a]


%  X to the power of Y is R.
%      +  +  -
power(0, 0, 0) :- !.
power(X, 0, 1) :- !.
power(X, 1, X) :- !.
power(X, Y, R) :- power(X, Y, 1, R).
```

```
power(A, 0, Final, Final) :- !.
power(A, P, Accum, Final) :-
        NP is P -1,
        NewAccum is Accum * A,
        power(A, NP, NewAccum, Final).
```

Answer Set Collection Procedures

```
%
%                       FINDALL
%          ?           +         -
findall(Element, Query, _) :-
    Query,
    gettmplist(List),
    append(List, [Element], Newlist),
    assert( tmplist(Newlist) ),
    fail.
findall(_, _, List) :-
    retract( tmplist(List) ), !.


gettmplist([]) :-
    not(tmplist(_)), !.
gettmplist(List) :-
    retract( tmplist(List) ), !.


%                   UNIQUE VALUE LIST
%  This procedure gets all answers
%  to a query, but eliminates duplicates.
%                      ?         +       -
unique_value_list(Element, Query, List) :-
    Query,
    gettmplist(List),
    (    member(Element, List),
         assert( tmplist(List) )
         ;
         not( member(Element, List) ),
         assert( tmplist([Element|List]) )
    ), fail.
unique_value_list(_, _, List) :-
    retract( tmplist(List) ), !.
```

Low level Input/Output Procedures

```
%
%                     GETFIELD/4 (used in Apx III)
%
% Write Prompt and Default (if there is one).
% Get Answer from the user.
% Condition is some sort of query
% which may involve Answer.
% Evaluate Condition;
% if it fails, run "getfield" again.
%        +       -      ?       +
getfield(Prompt, Answer, Default, Condition) :-
    write(Prompt), nl,
    (   nonvar(Default),
        write('['), write(Default), write('] ')
        ;
        var(Default)
    ),
    get0(C),
    (   C = 10, % 10 is newline on UNIX and VMS
        Answer = Default
        ;
        C \== 10,
        getchars(C, List),
        name(Answer, List)
    ),
    Condition, !.


% Condition failed in the "getfield" rule above,
% so try again:
getfield(Prompt, Answer, Default, Condition) :-
    !, getfield(Prompt, Answer, Default, Condition).

getchars(10, []) :- !. % 10 is newline
getchars(C, [C|Rest]) :-
    get0(C1), getchars(C1, Rest), !.
```

"show_state"

```
%                     SHOW STATE
% Part of blocks world program in Sec. 6.7.
% "show_state/1" takes the name of a state as
% an argument, and prints a picture of where
% all blocks are in that state.

show_state(State) :-
    % clear the screen:
    clears,
    % print "table" on line 20:
    show_table(20),
    % make a list of all blocks on the table:
    findall(Block, send(State, on(Block, table)), List),
    % start printing blocks at col. 10 line 17:
    first_layer(State, 10, 17, List),
    % leave the cursor below the picture:
    cursor(1, 22), !.

% print a layer of blocks directly on the table:
first_layer(State, X, Y, []).
first_layer(State, X, Y, [Block|List]) :-
    % print first block:
    toblock(X, Y, Block),
    % move up:
    NY is Y - 3,
    % print all blocks on top of Block:
    stack(State, X, NY, Block),
    % move right:
    NX is X + 10,
    !, first_layer(State, NX, Y, List).

% print all blocks on top of Block:
stack(State, X, Y, Block) :-
    % get the block above Block, if there is one:
    send(State, on(Above, Block)),
    toblock(X, Y, Above),
    % move up:
    NY is Y - 3,
    !, stack(State, X, NY, Above).
stack(_, _, _, _). % there is no block above Block.
```

```
                    toblock(X, Y, Block) :-
                        cursor(X, Y), write('___'),
                        NY is Y + 1,
                        cursor(X, NY), write('¦'),
                        write(Block), write('¦'),
                        NNY is Y + 2,
                        cursor(X, NNY), write('---'), !.


                    show_table(Y) :-
                        cursor(1, Y),
                        write('------------------------------'),
                        nl,
                        write('          t a b l e'),
                        nl.
```

A Screen-Oriented Database Query Program

```
        %                    QUERYDB
        %
        %  This program is executed with a query like:
        %        ¦ ?- querydb(Name).
        %  where Name is a predicate name.
        %  A "schema/2" fact must exist for each database
        %  to be queried; the first arg is predicate name,
        %  and the second arg is a list of screen prompts,
        %  one for each field.

        %  Example schema facts:
        %        Predicate  Prompts
        schema(employee, ['Name','Code','Position','Salary']).
        schema(department, ['Code','Name','Manager']).

        %  Example databases to be queried:
        employee(brian, 100, operator, 20000).
        employee(nancy, 200, acct_exec, 71000).
        employee(ralph, 100, manager, 71500).

        department(100, data_processing, ralph).
        department(200, sales, jb).
```

```prolog
%         +
querydb(Pred) :-
    schema(Pred, Prompts),
    clears,     % clear the screen
    cursor(1, 2),
    repeat,
    loop(Pred, Prompts, Return),
    Return = x, !.


% loop: print all prompts in col 25.
% Get query parameters from user,
% then call "try_query"
%     +       +        -
loop(Pred, Prompts, Return) :-
    show_prompts(25, 4, Prompts),
    % explain what appears on the screen:
    cursor(25, 2), clearl,
    write('Enter Parameters:'),
    get_parameters(40, 4, Prompts, Params),
    % make the query:
    Query =.. [Pred|Params],
    !, try_query(Pred, Prompts, Params, Return, Query).


% try_query: execute the query,
% show answers in col 40,
% then prompt for next action.
try_query(Pred, Prompts, Params, Return, Query) :-
    Query,      % allow backtracking
    % explain what appears on the screen:
    cursor(25, 2), clearl, write('Answers:'),
    show_answers(40, 4, Params),
    % prompt for next action:
    cursor(25,23), clearl,
    write('m (more answers) c (change params) x (exit)'),
    getfield(Answer),
    cursor(25, 23), clearl,
    (   Answer = c,
        loop(Pred, Prompts, Return)
        ;
        Answer = x, Return = x
    ).
    % If Answer is not c or x, backtrack to Query above.
```

```
%  Query failed in "try_query" clause above, so:
try_query(Pred, Prompts, _, Return, _) :-
    %  prompt for next action:
    cursor(25, 23), clearl,
    write('No (more) answers. c (change params) x (exit)'),
    getfield(Answer),
    cursor(25, 23), clearl,
    (   Answer = x, Return = x
      ;
        %  if Answer is not x:
        loop(Pred, Prompts, Return)
    ).


%              +  +  +
show_prompts(_, _, []).
show_prompts(X, Y, [Prompt|Prompts]) :-
    cursor(X, Y), write(Prompt), clearl,
    NY is Y + 2,        % move down two lines
    !, show_prompts(X, NY, Prompts).


%              +  +  +
show_answers(_, _, []).
show_answers(X, Y, [Answer|Answers]) :-
    cursor(X, Y), clearl,
    %  do nothing if Answer is uninstantiated:
    ( var(Answer) ; write(Answer) ),
    NY is Y + 2,        % move down two lines
    !, show_answers(X, NY, Answers).


%                +  +  +  _
get_parameters(_, _, [], []).
get_parameters(X, Y, [Prompt|Prompts], [Param|Params]) :-
    cursor(X, Y),
    %  if user hits return as first char,
    %  Param will remain uninstantiated:
    getfield(Param),
    NY is Y + 2,        % move down two lines
    !, get_parameters(X, NY, Prompts, Params).
```

```
%   position cursor on vt100 compatible terminal:
cursor(X, Y) :-
    put(27),    % escape
    put(91),    % [
    write(Y),
    put(59),    % ;
    write(X),
    put(72).    % H

%   clear screen:
clears :-
    cursor(1, 1),
    put(27),    % escape
    put(91),    % [
    put(74).    % J

%   clear to end of line:
clearl :-
    put(27),    % escape
    put(91),    % [
    put(75).    % K

%   For "getfield/1," see Sec. 3.9.
```

Appendix III

Case Study

A Factory Scheduling Program

You are the manager of a small manufacturing plant. The plant processes job orders. A typical job must be processed by four types of machines, but may require a special setup on one or more of the machines.

For any shift, there is a pool of operators to run the machines, but some of the machines can only be operated by certain operators. The operators work on flexible schedules, so that a different number of operators may show up to work on any given day. Sometimes operators leave work early.

The foreman's responsibility is to plan how to utilize the resources of the plant (i.e. operators and machines) so as to process all outstanding jobs in an efficient manner. Some jobs must be processed as soon as possible, while others can be held until there is not much other work to do. As manager, you must make sure that the foreman is using the machines to their full potential. You must also maintain an accurate description of the amount of resources required (i.e. the cost) to process any type of job order. After a careful requirements analysis, you decide that the foreman's productivity could be greatly enhanced by a computer program to aid in the selection of an optimum resource schedule for a shift. The success of this computer program, however, will clearly depend on how easily it integrates with the foreman's work habits; if it not easy for him to use, he will probably end up ignoring it or working around it. Therefore, a great deal of attention must go into the user interface of the computer program, to make sure that the foreman can use it to do all of the things he does when working with his current manual schedules. In order to design the user interface, it is necessary to observe the foreman's work habits carefully.

How the
foreman works

Typically, the foreman arrives at least one hour before the shift starts. He begins by sorting through all outstanding work, including jobs that were only partially processed by the previous shift. He must choose a set of jobs to work on during the shift, taking into account the relative importance of all jobs. He reviews the operational state of the machines that day, as well as which operators are supposed to show up for work. He considers various alternative schedules for the jobs, machines, and operators, and chooses the schedule that will result in the most work being processed during the shift. The processing capacity of a machine usually depends on the number of operators assigned to it, so the tricky point of scheduling is assigning and reassigning operators to various machines throughout the shift.

The foreman has selected an overall schedule by the time that the operators arrive, at which point he gives each operator an individual schedule. When something unexpected happens during the shift (such as an operator leaving early or a machine going down), the foreman must make a new schedule to utilize remaining resources in the best way.

The
Prototype

You decide that the place to start is to make a prototype of the scheduling program to be used by the foreman. The main purpose of the prototype is to develop an interface that the foreman can really use, and to test the assumptions that the foreman has been making about the processing capacities of machines. The production version of the scheduling program must be able to handle a great variety of situations, including different types of jobs, various combinations of machines, etc. To get the prototype working as soon as possible, however, it seems appropriate to limit its functionality to some subset of the needed functionality of the production program. Thus, the prototype will only be able to schedule jobs that require sequential processing by four machines, without any special setup on any of the machines. Here follows a description of the prototype.

*Representing
the situation*

The time resolution of the prototype is one hour. This means that the assignment of work to a machine and the assignment of operators to a machine can only be changed by the foreman once per hour; this is a simplifying assumption made to get the prototype working. The production scheduling program may require a finer time resolution of perhaps a quarter of an hour.

The prototype is hardwired to function only for one shift during the day. This shift starts at 8AM (represented by "8" in the program) and continues until 1PM (represented by "13"). Each job is referred to by a unique identifier, which may be the name of the customer. The movement of a job from machine to machine through the plant is tracked by both machine name and *station*. A station is a place where work accumulates after being processed by one machine and before being processed by the next. The machines are named *alpha*, *beta*, *gamma*, and *delta*. The stations are named *1*, *2*, *3*, *4*, and *5*. The entire process of the plant is represented in Figure III-1:

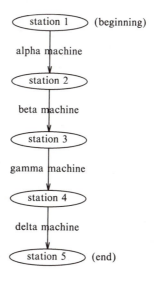

Figure III-1

The quantity of a job is measured in *units*, and the capacity of a machine is measured in *units per hour*. Suppose that at the beginning of hour 8, there are 15 units of a job identified as "consolidated" (i.e. the customer name) at station 2, and that the capacity of the beta machine is 12 units per hour. Then at the end of hour 8, there should be 3 units of the "consolidated" job left at station 2, and 12 units of the "consolidated" job newly arrived at station 3.

Jobs   The position of some units of a job at a particular station is represented by a fact of the form:

```
%    Hour   Station   ID            Units
     job(8,    2,       consolidated, 15).
```

which states that at hour 8, there are 15 units of the "consolidated" job at station 2. At the beginning of the shift, the scheduling program looks up all "job" facts currently asserted, and computes a schedule specifying how they can be processed during the shift. Once the foreman accepts the schedule, he can then use the program to simulate the processing of work through the plant on an hour-by-hour basis. (In the production program, the amount of processing predicted by the program will always be checked against actual processing.) When the scheduling program processes an hour, it asserts new "job" facts showing the position of each job after the processing that occurred during the last hour. Suppose that the capacity of the beta machine is 12 units per hour during hour 8. When the scheduling program processes hour 8, it asserts two new "job" facts to show the position of the "consolidated" job at the beginning of hour 9:

```
%    Hour   Station   ID            Units
     job(9,    2,       consolidated, 3).
     job(9,    3,       consolidated, 12).
```

Operators   When an operator arrives at the beginning of the shift, a fact of the following form is asserted into the database:

```
%          Arrival   Name
operator(8,          jack).
```

Should an operator leave before the end of the shift, then a "refute" fact should be added to the database to prevent that operator from further consideration:

```
% Jack leaves at 11AM:
refute(11, operator(_, jack)).
```

The foreman needs to know how many operators are at work during any hour of the shift. Expressing "operator" facts in the above form makes it possible to use the inheritance mechanism of Chap. 7 to keep track of the number of operators during any hour of the shift. The names of hours are related to one another in a "child_of" database:

```
child_of(9, 8).
child_of(10, 9).
...
```

The following rule finds the total number of operators during any hour of the shift:

```
%                 +     -
max_operators(Time, Number) :-
    % make a list of all operators still here at Time:
    findall(X, send(Time, operator(X)), List),
    length(List, Number).
```

Machine capacities

Each of the machines has a capacity of units per hour that depends on the number of operators assigned to it. For instance, the capacity of the delta machine is eight units per hour per operator assigned. The simple way to represent this information is in a rule of the form:

```
%           Name    Operators   -
machine_cap(delta, Number,    Capacity) :-
    Capacity is Number * 8.
```

However, the scheduling program sometimes needs to test the capacity of a machine with various assignments of operators. The problem with the "machine_cap" rule above is that Number must be instantiated or the "is" subgoal will produce an error. The version of "machine_cap" below generates a possible value for Number (not to exceed the total number of operators on the shift) if it is uninstantiated. This is accomplished by adding an extra argument containing the total number of operators, and using the "num_gen" rule to generate values of Number:

```
%               +       +       ?        -
machine_cap(delta, MaxOps, Number, Capacity) :-
    (    var(Number), num_gen(MaxOps, Number)
         ;
         nonvar(Number),
    ),
    %  8 units/hour/operator:
    Capacity is Number * 8.


% generate integer N between 1 and Max, inclusive:
%          +     -
num_gen(Max, N) :-
    num_gen0(Max, 1, N).
%           +       +       -
num_gen0(Max, Seed, Seed).
num_gen0(Max, Seed, N) :-
    NewSeed is Seed + 1,
    NewSeed =< Max,
    num_gen0(Max, NewSeed, N).
```

If Number was uninstantiated in a query to "machine_cap," then
backtracking will cause "num_gen" to generate each possible value of
Number from 1 to MaxOps.

Roadmap of the Program

The relation of the components of the scheduling program to one
another is shown below in Figure III-2 (*Roadmap of the Scheduling
Program*). The foreman starts the program with a query to "start,"
which takes the first hour of the shift as an argument. "start" allows
the foreman to add new work, and then enters the basic user interface loop of the program: a recursive procedure called "process_shift."
Initially, "process_shift" shows the foreman an abbreviated menu of
high level actions. One of these actions, schedule, will build a
schedule for the entire shift. The foreman must always build a
schedule first, because all other actions require a current schedule.
If no schedule has been built, the program will not allow the
foreman to perform any other action.

The components of the program can be divided into several
categories, specified in Table III-1:

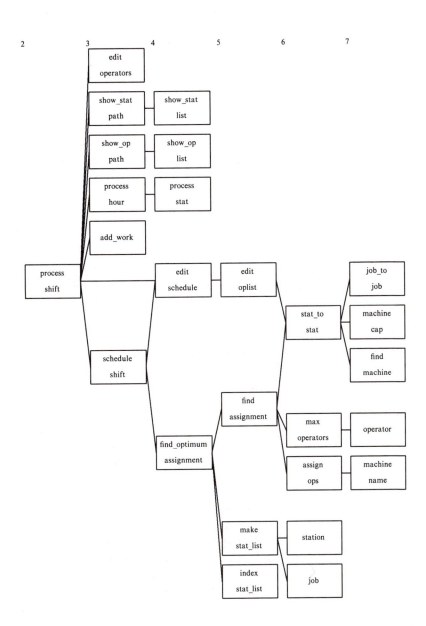

Figure III-2

Category	Procedures
user interface:	start process_shift schedule_shift process_hour add_work
display:	show_last_stat show_op_path
editing:	edit_schedule edit_operators
scheduling:	find_optimum_assignment find_assignment assign_ops stat_to_stat job_to_job

Table III-1

Example Sessions

Below, two of the foreman's sessions with the prototype are reproduced in full with explanations. At the beginning of each session, there are five operators who have reported to work, and two jobs to be processed:

```
%   Hour  Station  ID        Units
job(8,    1,       dow,      18).
job(8,    1,       mcgraw,   25).
```

Notice that the nature of the user interface is such that whenever the program asks the foreman a question, it is always ready with a default answer. The default answer is written in between [and] after the question, and to accept the default answer, all the foreman has to do is hit return. (See the "getfield/4" procedure in Appendix II for how this is accomplished.) Most of the questions have a limited number of answers, and if the foreman types an unacceptable answer, the question will repeat. Some of the questions display a list of valid answers. Notice also that questions on the outermost level of the user interface are written flush with the left margin, and questions on deeper levels of the user interface are indented.

SESSION 1

```
Add new work? (yes or no)
[no]                          % user hits return
                              % to accept default of "no"


(Hour is 8)
(new schedule is needed)
action? ('schedule','process','help' to see other actions)
[schedule]                            % user hits return
Building the schedule...
```

At this point, some time goes by while the program computes the schedule. When it is finished, it prints out the schedule of operator assignments to machines for the entire shift, as well as a table showing the position of each job at the end of the shift:

```
    The following assignment of operators:
Hour    Machine Ops  Machine Ops  Machine Ops  Machine Ops
8       alpha   5    beta    0    gamma   0    delta   0
9       alpha   3    beta    2    gamma   0    delta   0
10      alpha   1    beta    2    gamma   2    delta   0
11      alpha   0    beta    1    gamma   2    delta   2
12      alpha   0    beta    0    gamma   2    delta   3


    will result in the following state of work at hour 13:
Station ID      Amount  ID      Amount  ID      Amount
1       mcgraw  0       dow     0
2       mcgraw  0       dow     0
3       mcgraw  0       dow     0
4       mcgraw  0       dow     3
5       mcgraw  25      dow     15


    'accept' to accept schedule, 'edit' to change schedule
    [accept]                          % user hits return



(Hour is 8)
action? ('schedule','process','help' to see other actions)
[process]                             % user hits return
```

By hitting return to accept the default answer **process**, the foreman instructs the program to simulate the effect of processing work during the first hour, from 8 to 9. New "job" facts are asserted that show the position of each job at hour 9.

```
(Hour is 9)
action? ('schedule','process','help' to see other actions)
[process] help

     Actions include:
          schedule (schedule the rest of the shift)
          process (process the next hour)
          help
          show work (recompute and show current work)
          show operators (current assignment of operators)
          show schedule (schedule for rest of shift)
          end day

(Hour is 9)
action? ('schedule','process','help' to see other actions)
[process] show work

     Work at Hour 9
Stat    ID        Amount  ID       Amount   ID       Amount
1       mcgraw    0       dow      18
2       mcgraw    25      dow      0
3       mcgraw    0       dow      0
4       mcgraw    0       dow      0
5       mcgraw    0       dow      0

     Add new work? (yes or no)
     [no]                                   % user hits return


(Hour is 9)
action? ('schedule','process','help' to see other actions)
[process] show operators

     Operators at Hour 9
alpha   3         beta    2        gamma    0        delta    0

     Add or remove operators (add, remove, continue)?
     [continue]                             % user hits return
```

Above, the foreman elected to view the state of work and operator assignments at hour 9. Below, the foreman hits return in response to each question in order to process the hours remaining in the shift:

```
(Hour is 9)
action? ('schedule', 'process', 'help' to see other actions)
[process]                                       % user hits return


(Hour is 10)
action? ('schedule', 'process', 'help' to see other actions)
[process]                                       % user hits return


(Hour is 11)
action? ('schedule', 'process', 'help' to see other actions)
[process]                                       % user hits return


(Hour is 12)
action? ('schedule', 'process', 'help' to see other actions)
[process]                                       % user hits return


End of shift at hour 13.

State of work:
Station ID       Amount  ID      Amount  ID      Amount
1        mcgraw  0       dow     0
2        mcgraw  0       dow     0
3        mcgraw  0       dow     0
4        mcgraw  0       dow     3
5        mcgraw  25      dow     15
```

At the end of the shift, the program automatically prints out the state of work. Since the foreman added no new work during the execution of the program, and did not change any operator assignments, the final state of work is the same as the final state predicted when the schedule was first made.

In the second session, the foreman explores some of the other capabilities of the prototype, such as adding new work in the middle of the shift, adding a new operator in the middle of the shift, and editing the assignment of operators.

SESSION 2

```
(Hour is 8)
Add new work? (yes or no)
[no]                                            % user hits return


(Hour is 8)
(new schedule is needed)
action? ('schedule','process','help' to see other actions)
[schedule]                                      % user hits return
Building new schedule...
```

```
      The following assignment of operators:
```

Hour	Machine	Ops	Machine	Ops	Machine	Ops	Machine	Ops
8	alpha	5	beta	0	gamma	0	delta	0
9	alpha	3	beta	2	gamma	0	delta	0
10	alpha	1	beta	2	gamma	2	delta	0
11	alpha	0	beta	1	gamma	2	delta	2
12	alpha	0	beta	0	gamma	2	delta	3

```
      will result in the following state of work at hour 13:
```

Station	ID	Amount	ID	Amount	ID	Amount
1	mcgraw	0	dow	0		
2	mcgraw	0	dow	0		
3	mcgraw	0	dow	0		
4	mcgraw	0	dow	3		
5	mcgraw	25	dow	15		

```
      'accept' to accept schedule, 'edit' to change schedule
      [accept]                              % user hits return


(Hour is 8)
action? ('schedule','process','help' to see other actions)
[process]                                       % user hits return


(Hour is 9)
action? ('schedule','process','help' to see other actions)
[process] helpp
```

```
You typed helpp
Valid actions:
    schedule
    process
    help
    show work
    show operators
    show schedule
    end day
```

Notice that when the foreman misspells "help," the program points out the misspelling, shows a list of valid answers, and repeats the question:

```
action? ('schedule','process','help' to see other actions)
[process] help

    Actions include:
        schedule (schedule the rest of the shift)
        process (process the next hour)
        help
        show work (recompute and show current work)
        show operators (current assignment of operators)
        show schedule (schedule for rest of shift)
        end day

(Hour is 9)
action? ('schedule','process','help' to see other actions)
[process] show work
```

```
    Work at Hour 9
Stat    ID      Amount  ID      Amount  ID      Amount
1       mcgraw  0       dow     18
2       mcgraw  25      dow     0
3       mcgraw  0       dow     0
4       mcgraw  0       dow     0
5       mcgraw  0       dow     0
```

```
    Add new work? (yes or no)
    [no] yes

        Name of job, or "end"
        [end] citoh
```

```
Amount of work
[0] 12
Job added


Name of job, or "end"
[end]                                      % user hits return
```

```
Work has been added since current schedule was built.
Building new schedule...
```

Whenever the foreman types the command show work at the top level, the program displays the position of all jobs at the current hour, and then gives him a chance to enter new work. In this case, a rush job of 12 units identified as "citoh" arrived just before 9AM, so the foreman enters it. The program realizes that new work has arrived, and so automatically decides to build a new schedule. In the schedule below, notice that the new job was given priority over the existing jobs.

```
    The following assignment of operators:
```

Hour	Machine	Ops	Machine	Ops	Machine	Ops	Machine	Ops
9	alpha	4	beta	1	gamma	0	delta	0
10	alpha	2	beta	1	gamma	2	delta	0
11	alpha	0	beta	1	gamma	2	delta	2
12	alpha	0	beta	1	gamma	2	delta	2

```
    will result in the following state of work at hour 13:
```

Station	ID	Amount	ID	Amount	ID	Amount
1	citoh	0	mcgraw	0	dow	0
2	citoh	0	mcgraw	0	dow	0
3	citoh	0	mcgraw	0	dow	10
4	citoh	0	mcgraw	7	dow	8
5	citoh	12	mcgraw	18	dow	0

```
    'accept' to accept schedule, 'edit' to change schedule
    [accept]                                % user hits return



(Hour is 9)
action? ('schedule','process','help' to see other actions)
[process]                                   % user hits return
```

```
(Hour is 10)
action? ('schedule','process','help' to see other actions)
[process]                                    % user hits return


(Hour is 11)
action? ('schedule','process','help' to see other actions)
[process] show operators

    Operators at Hour 11
alpha    0        beta    1       gamma    2       delta    2

    Add or remove operators (add, remove, continue)?
    [continue] add

        Name of operator to add, or "end" to continue
        [end] mary
        Operator added

        Name of operator to add, or "end" to continue
        [end]                                % user hits return
```

Whenever the foreman types the command **show operators** at
the top level, the program displays the current assignment of operators, and then gives him a chance to add or remove operators. In
this case, an operator named Mary arrived just before 11AM, and so
the foreman adds her name to the database. Below, the foreman
builds a new schedule before continuing. Notice how much more
work will get processed by the end of the shift as a result of having
six instead of five operators.

```
(Hour is 11)
action? ('schedule','process','help' to see other actions)
[process] schedule


    The following assignment of operators:
Hour     Machine Ops    Machine Ops    Machine Ops    Machine Ops
11       alpha    0     beta    2      gamma    2      delta    2
12       alpha    0     beta    1      gamma    2      delta    3
```

```
     will result in the following state of work at hour 13:
Station ID        Amount  ID        Amount  ID        Amount
1        citoh    0       mcgraw    0       dow       0
2        citoh    0       mcgraw    0       dow       0
3        citoh    0       mcgraw    0       dow       5
4        citoh    0       mcgraw    7       dow       13
5        citoh    12      mcgraw    18      dow       0


     'accept' to accept schedule, 'edit' to change schedule
     [accept] edit
```

For some reason, the foreman is unhappy with the automatically
computed schedule, and so elects to change it. In edit mode, the
program shows work and operator assignments for each hour left in
the shift, and allows the foreman to change the operator assignments.
For hour 11, the foreman puts one operator on the beta machine instead of two, and three operators on the delta machine instead of
two. The foreman accepts the current operator assignments for hour
12.

```
     Projected Work in the Factory at Hour 11:
Stat     ID       Amount  ID        Amount  ID        Amount
1        citoh    0       mcgraw    0       dow       0
2        citoh    0       mcgraw    7       dow       18
3        citoh    12      mcgraw    3       dow       0
4        citoh    0       mcgraw    15      dow       0
5        citoh    0       mcgraw    0       dow       0


     Operators Currently Assigned:
alpha    0        beta     2        gamma    2        delta    2


     Machine: alpha    Number of Operators:
     [0]                                  % user hits return


     Machine: beta    Number of Operators:
     [2] 1


     Machine: gamma    Number of Operators:
     [2]                                  % user hits return


     Machine: delta    Number of Operators:
     [2] 3
```

```
                  Projected Work in the Factory at Hour 12:
     Stat     ID        Amount   ID         Amount   ID        Amount
     1        citoh     0        mcgraw     0        dow       0
     2        citoh     0        mcgraw     0        dow       10
     3        citoh     0        mcgraw     7        dow       8
     4        citoh     12       mcgraw     3        dow       0
     5        citoh     0        mcgraw     15       dow       0


                  Operators Currently Assigned:
     alpha    0          beta      1        gamma    2        delta    3


                  Machine: alpha    Number of Operators:
                  [0]                               % user hits return


                  Machine: beta    Number of Operators:
                  [1]                               % user hits return


                  Machine: gamma    Number of Operators:
                  [2]                               % user hits return


                  Machine: delta    Number of Operators:
                  [3]                               % user hits return



                  Projected Work in the Factory at Hour 13 (end):
     Stat     ID        Amount   ID         Amount   ID        Amount
     1        citoh     0        mcgraw     0        dow       0
     2        citoh     0        mcgraw     0        dow       0
     3        citoh     0        mcgraw     0        dow       10
     4        citoh     0        mcgraw     7        dow       8
     5        citoh     12       mcgraw     18       dow       0
```

At the end of the editing session, the program recomputes and displays the anticipated position of all work at the end of the shift. Notice that because the foreman changed the assignment of operators computed by the program, less work will be processed than with the automatically generated schedule. If the foreman was unhappy with the results of his edited schedule, he could edit it again or have the program build a new schedule automatically.

```
(Hour is 11)
action? ('schedule','process','help' to see other actions)
[process]                                        % user hits return


(Hour is 12)
action? ('schedule','process','help' to see other actions)
[process]                                        % user hits return


End of shift at hour 13.

State of work:
Station ID      Amount  ID       Amount  ID      Amount
1       citoh   0       mcgraw   0       dow     0
2       citoh   0       mcgraw   0       dow     0
3       citoh   0       mcgraw   0       dow     10
4       citoh   0       mcgraw   7       dow     8
5       citoh   12      mcgraw   18      dow     0
```

Use of the Program

The nature of the program enables the foreman to try "what if" scenarios in various different ways. For instance, he might build more than one schedule for the whole shift, with low priority jobs included or not included, or change the order of jobs in the database (the order of jobs determines their priority). He might also try varying the number of operators. He can experiment with the effect of adding new work in the middle of the shift, or of adding or removing operators in the middle of the shift.

Incremental refinement

When the prototype is tested, data about the actual capacities of machines in various circumstances will be collected and compared with the program's predictions. The present "machine_cap" database is only an approximation, subject to incremental refinement as better data is collected.

The Program

Scheduling Algorithm

The algorithm for finding an optimum schedule is worth considering in detail. "find_optimum_assignment" is the declarative interface between the scheduling component and the rest of the program. The assignment of operators to machines for the entire shift is described in the variable `OpPath`. Associated with `OpPath` is `StatPath`, which describes the position of jobs at stations during the shift. The information in `StatPath` is a result of the assignments in `OpPath`. `FStats` (final station list) is the last element in `StatPath`, and it describes the position of all jobs at the end of the shift. "index_statlist" is a procedure that evaluates `FStats` and assigns it an index value. The more work that has been processed by the end of the shift, the higher the value of the index.

*"find_*
*optimum_*
assignment"

"find_optimum_assignment" starts by asserting an "optimum_schedule" fact with an index value of 0. It then calls "find_assignment" which returns a trial schedule in OpPath and an associated `FStats` and `StatPath`. The index value of `FStats` is computed and compared with the index value of the "optimum_schedule" fact. If the index of `Fstats` is higher, then the current "optimum_schedule" fact is replaced by one containing current values of `OpPath` and `StatPath`. Then the procedure backtracks to "find_assignment," and gets another trial schedule. If the index value of the new schedule is higher than that of the current "optimum_schedule" fact, then the "optimum_schedule" fact is replaced by one containing the new schedule. (Note the similarity between this technique and one of the solutions to exercise 4.1.) This process continues until "find_assignment" has generated every possible schedule, at which point the second "find_optimum_assignment" rule returns the schedule contained in the last "optimum_schedule" fact asserted.

"assign_ops"

"find_assignment" calls "assign_ops" to find an assignment of operators for an hour of the shift. The algorithm of "assign_ops" is based on several heuristic assumptions. First, all available operators must be assigned to some machine during each hour of the shift. Second, if there is any work at a station, then at least one operator must be assigned to the machine that processes work coming from that station. These two heuristics eliminate many useless schedules from consideration. If the foreman wants to ignore jobs at an intermediate station for several hours of the shift, he can either:

1) remove the relevant job facts from the database and recompute the schedule, or

2) edit the program generated schedule and take all operators off of a machine.

"find_assignment" recurses once for each hour of the shift. After calling "assign_ops" to find an assignment of operators for an hour, it calls "stat_to_stat" to compute the work that will be done during that hour as a result of the assignment. (Later, the procedure may backtrack to "assign_ops" to get another assignment.) Like "assign_ops," "stat_to_stat" recurses once for each station. "stat_to_stat" calls "job_to_job," which recurses once for each job at a station. "job_to_job" always gives the maximum capacity of a machine to the first job in the list of jobs it receives, and then gives whatever capacity is left to other jobs in the list.

Evaluation of the Scheduling Algorithm

In its current form, the scheduling component of the program is not capable of finding an optimum schedule in the face of every possible contingency the foreman may encounter. It operates competently only for what are considered normal situations in the plant. However, to deal with extraordinary situations, it provides many entry points where the foreman can juggle critical factors to influence the scheduling algorithm. An important entry point that the prototype does not provide is the ability to edit the "job" database.

Reading the Code

Below is the code of the program. Each component is labeled as to its level and category (i.e. user interface, display, etc.). The roadmap included earlier should make it easier to follow.

Naming convention

There are many procedures the names of which end with the character "0." This is a naming convention which indicates that the procedure is called by another procedure with the same name but without the "0." For instance, "make_statlist0" is called by "make_statlist." The purpose of "make_statlist" is to set up the arguments for "make_statlist0"; "make_statlist0" does the real work.

```
% The Factory Scheduling Program

% Variable Name Conventions:

% Stat       Name of a station, i.e. 1,2,3,4, or 5
% StatA, StatB   StatB is the next station after StatA

% Stats      Stationlist:
%            List of what amount of each job is at each
```

```
%               station of the form: [at(Stat,Jobs),...]

% IStats       Initial station list
% FStats       Final station list (at end of processing)

% StatPath     List of station lists, one for each hour

% Jobs         List of jobs of the form: [job(ID,Amount),...]
% JobsX        List of jobs at hour X
% JobsY        List of jobs at hour Y, where Y = X + 1
% JobsA        List of jobs at station A
% JobsB        Jobs at station B (B is the station after A)
% JobsXA       List of jobs at hour X, station A

% ID           Unique identifier of a job

% OpList       List of the number of operators assigned
%              to each machine, i.e. [op(Machine,Number),...]

% OpPath       List of OpLists, one for each hour


% IHour        Initial Hour
% FHour        Final Hour

% Index        Relative measurement of how much work
%              has been processed by end of shift

% RCapacity    Remaining capacity of a machine in a time
%              period, after some work has been processed.


%%%%%%%%%%%%%%%%%%%%%%%%%%%%%%%%%%%%%%%%%%%%%%%%%%%%%%%%%
%        USER INTERFACE PROCEDURES
%

%        START (level 1; user interface)
current_hour(8).
```

```
%       +
start(Hour) :-
  retract(current_hour(_)), assert(current_hour(Hour)),
  nl, pr('(Hour is ', Hour, ')'),
  %
  getfield('Add new work? (yes or no)', Answer, no,
       member(Answer,[yes,no])),
  ( Answer = yes, add_work(Hour, _) ; Answer = no ), !,
  process_shift(menu, schedule, Hour, [], []).



%----------------------------------------------------------
%          PROCESS SHIFT (level 2; user interface)
%
%  "process_shift" is the highest level user interface loop.
%  There is one rule for each menu entry.
%  The last subgoal in each rule is a recursive call.

end_of_shift(13).          % hour that the shift ends.

%  End condition:
%                      +      + +      +            +
process_shift(menu, _, Hour, StatPath, OpPath) :-
  end_of_shift(Hour),
  pr('End of shift at hour ', Hour, '.'),
  make_statlist(Hour, FStats),
  nl, pr('State of work:'),
  show_last_stats([FStats]), !.

process_shift(menu, Default, Hour, StatPath, OpPath) :-
  nl, pr('(Hour is ', Hour, ')'),
  ( Default = schedule, pr('(new schedule is needed)')
    ;
    true
  ),
  getfield('action? (schedule,process,help to see other actions)',
       Answer, Default,
       ( OpPath = [],     % if OpPath is empty:
         ( Answer = schedule
           ;
           pr('You must make a schedule!'),
           fail
         )
         ;
```

```
                    OpPath \== [],     % if OpPath is not empty:
                 (   member(Answer, [schedule,process,help,
                      'show work','show operators','show schedule',
                      'end day'])
                     ;
                     pr('You typed ', Answer),
                     pr('Valid actions:'),
                     element_pr('   ',[schedule,process,help,
                      'show work','show operators','show schedule',
                      'end day']),
                     fail
                 )
             )          % end of Condition arg to "getfield"
       ),
       !, process_shift(Answer, process, Hour, StatPath, OpPath).

process_shift(schedule, Default,   Hour, _, _) :-
   schedule_shift(Hour, StatPath, OpPath),
   !, process_shift(menu, Default, Hour, StatPath, OpPath).

process_shift(process, Default, Hour, [Stats|StatPath],
               [OpList|OpPath]) :-
   NewHour is Hour + 1,
   retract(current_hour(Hour)), assert(current_hour(NewHour)),
   %  assert job/4 facts at the new hour:
   process_hour(NewHour, Stats),
   !, process_shift(menu, Default, NewHour, StatPath, OpPath).

process_shift(help, Default,   Hour, StatPath, OpPath) :-
   pr(' Actions include '),
   element_pr('    ',
             ['schedule (schedule the rest of the shift)',
              'process (process the next hour)',
              'help',
              'show work (recompute and show current work)',
              'show operators (current assignment)',
              'show schedule (schedule for rest of shift)',
              'end day']),
   !, process_shift(menu, Default, Hour, StatPath, OpPath).
```

```
process_shift('show work', Default,  Hour, [Stats|StatPath],
                 [OpList|OpPath]) :-
  %  make NewStats to replace Stats for Hour:
  make_statlist(Hour, CStats),
  max_operators(Hour, MaxOps),
  stat_to_stat(MaxOps, CStats, OpList, NewStats),
  %
  pr(' Work at Hour ', Hour),
  write('Stat      '),
  statlist_header(4),
  show_statlist(CStats),
  getfield(' Add new work? (yes or no)', Answer, no,
           member(Answer,[yes,no]) ),
  %
  ( Answer = yes, add_work(Hour, WorkFlag)
    ;
    Answer = no, WorkFlag = no_new_work
  ),
  !,
  ( WorkFlag = new_work,
    pr(' Work has been added since schedule was built.'),
    pr(' Building new schedule...'),
    process_shift(schedule, Default, Hour, [], [])
    ;
    WorkFlag = no_new_work,
    process_shift(menu, Default, Hour,
                 [NewStats|StatPath], [OpList|OpPath])
  ).

process_shift('show operators', Default, Hour, StatPath,
                 [OpList|OpPath]) :-
  pr(' Operators at Hour ', Hour),
  show_oplist(OpList),
  getfield(' Add or remove operators (add, remove, continue)',
           Answer, continue,
                 member(Answer,[add,remove,continue]) ),
  ( ( Answer = add ; Answer = remove ),
    edit_operators(Hour, Answer)
    ;
    Answer = continue
  ),
  !, process_shift(menu, Default, Hour, StatPath,
                 [OpList|OpPath]).
```

```
process_shift('show schedule', Default, Hour, StatPath,
              OpPath) :-
  nl,
  pr('Current assignment of operators:'),
  show_op_path(Hour, OpPath), nl,
  %
  end_of_shift(End),
  pr('will result in the following state of work at hour ',
     End, ':'),
  show_last_stats(StatPath), nl,
  !, process_shift(menu, Default, Hour, StatPath, OpPath).


%--------------------------------------------------------
%          SCHEDULE SHIFT (level 3; user interface)
%
%  Construct a schedule for the rest of the shift,
%  from Hour until end of shift
%                  +      -        -
schedule_shift(Hour, StatPath, OpPath) :-
  end_of_shift(FHour),
  find_optimum_assignment(Hour, FHour, IStats, NStatPath, NOpPath),
  %
  % IStats contains work at Hour, before processing starts.
  nl,
  pr(' The following assignment of operators:'),
  show_op_path(Hour, NOpPath), nl,
  %
  pr(' will result in the following state of work at hour ',
     FHour, ':'),
  % display the last station list in the new StatPath:
  show_last_stats(NStatPath), nl,
  %
  getfield(' accept to accept schedule, edit to change schedule',
           Answer, accept,
           ( member(Answer, [accept,edit])
             ;
             pr('invalid response'), fail)
           ),
  ( Answer = accept,
    StatPath = NStatPath,
    OpPath = NOpPath
    ;
    Answer = edit,
```

```
            edit_schedule(Hour, IStats, NStatPath, NOpPath,
                           StatPath, OpPath)
    ).



%----------------------------------------------------------
%        PROCESS HOUR (level 3; user interface)
%
% Assert job structures with nonzero amounts as facts.
%           +      +
process_hour(Hour, [at(Stat,Jobs)¦Stats]) :-
  process_station(Hour, Stat, Jobs),
  !, process_hour(Hour, Stats).
process_hour(_, []).

%                    +       +       +
process_station(Hour, Stat, [job(ID,Amount)¦Jobs]) :-
  (  Amount \== 0,
     assert( job(Hour, Stat, ID, Amount) )
     ;
     Amount = 0
  ),
  !, process_station(Hour, Stat, Jobs).
process_station(_, _, []).



%----------------------------------------------------------
%        ADD WORK (level 3; user interface)
%        +      -
add_work(Hour, Flag) :-
  % check ID against approved job list.
  getfield('     Name of job, or "end"', ID, end, true),
  (  ID = end,
     Flag = no_new_work
     ;
     ID \== end,
     getfield('     Amount of work', IAmount, 0,
              IAmount > 0 ),
     assert( job(Hour, 1, ID, IAmount) ),
     pr('Job added'),
     Flag = new_work,
     add_work(Hour, _)
  ).
```

```
%%%%%%%%%%%%%%%%%%%%%%%%%%%%%%%%%%%%%%%%%%%%%%%%%%%
%         SCHEDULING PROCEDURES
%
%         FIND OPTIMUM ASSIGNMENT of operators for a shift.
%         (level 4; scheduling)
%                          +      +      -   -   -
find_optimum_assignment(IHour, FHour, _, _, _) :-
  % make IStats, the initial station list:
  make_statlist(IHour, IStats),
  assert( optimum_schedule(IStats, 0, IStats, [IStats], []) ),
  %
  % backtrack through all possible assignments for shift:
  find_assignment(IHour,FHour,IStats,FStats,StatPath,OpPath),
  index_statlist(FStats, Index),
  optimum_schedule(_, OptimumIndex, _, _, _),
  ( Index > OptimumIndex,
    once( retract( optimum_schedule(_, _, _, _, _) ) ),
    assert( optimum_schedule(FStats, Index, IStats,
                                StatPath, OpPath))
    ;
    Index =< OptimumIndex
  ), fail.
find_optimum_assignment(_, _, Stats, StatPath, OpPath) :-
  retract( optimum_schedule(_, _, Stats, StatPath, OpPath) ), !.


%----------------------------------------------------------
%         MAKE STATLIST (level 5; scheduling)
%  Find out which work is at each station at Hour:
%                  +      -
make_statlist(Hour, Stats) :-
  findall(S, station(S), SList),
  unique_value_list(ID0, job(_,_,ID0,_), IDList),
  make_statlist0(Hour, IDList, SList, Stats), !.
```

```
make_statlist0(_, _, [], []).
%              +      +      +           -
make_statlist0(Hour, IDList, [S|SList], [at(S,Jobs)|Stats]) :-
  findall(job(ID1,Amount),
          (  member(ID1, IDList),
             ( job(Hour, S, ID1, Amount)
               ;
               not( job(Hour, S, ID1, Amount) ),
               Amount = 0     % 0 if no "job" fact exists
             )
          ),     % end of 2nd arg to "findall"
          Jobs),
  !, make_statlist0(Hour, IDList, SList, Stats).



%-----------------------------------------------------------
%          INDEX STATION LIST (level 5; scheduling)
%  Compute an index value for a station list
%  which reflects how much work has been processed.
%  For each station, multiply station name times
%  amount of work at that station.

index_statlist([], 0).
%                +                   -
index_statlist([at(Stat,Jobs)|Stats], SIndex) :-
  index_joblist(Jobs, JIndex),
  !, index_statlist(Stats, SIndex0),
  SIndex is SIndex0 + (Stat * JIndex).

index_joblist([], 0).
index_joblist([job(_,Amount)|Jobs], JIndex) :-
  !, index_joblist(Jobs, JIndex0),
  JIndex is JIndex0 + Amount.
```

```
%-------------------------------------------------------
%        FIND ASSIGNMENT (level 5; scheduling)
%
%  This is the basic engine of building a schedule.
%  It computes OpPath (an assignment of operators
%  for the period IHour to FHour), and StatPath
%  (the amount of work that will be processed
%  as a result of the assignment).
%  It recurses once for each hour of the shift.

% Stop when final hour is reached:
%                 +        +        +        -        -    -
find_assignment(FHour, FHour, FStats, FStats, [], []).

find_assignment(IHour,              % +initial hour
                FHour,              % +final hour
                StatsX,             % +work processed previous hour
                FStats,             % -work at end of shift
                [StatsY|StatPath],  % -
                [OpList|OpPath]     % -
               ) :-
  IHour < FHour,
  max_operators(IHour, MaxOps),
  %
  %  backtrack through all assignments for the hour:
  assign_ops(IHour, MaxOps, StatsX, OpList),
  stat_to_stat(MaxOps, StatsX, OpList, StatsY),
  NewHour is IHour + 1,
  find_assignment(NewHour, FHour, StatsY, FStats, StatPath,
                  OpPath).


%-------------------------------------------------------
%        ASSIGN OPERATORS (level 6; scheduling)
%
%  Given Stats (a list of how much work is at each station),
%  return OpList (an assignment of operators).
%  Recurse once for each station.
```

```
assign_ops(Hour,                      % +
           Ops,                       % +operators to assign
           [at(StatA,JobsA)|Stats],% +station list
           [op(Mach,Num)|OpList]   % -operator assignments
          ) :-
  Ops > 0,    % do not use this rule if 0 operators
  machine_name(Mach, StatA, StatB),
  ( empty(JobsA),          % remaining jobs have 0 amounts
    Num = 0,
    NewOps is Ops
    ;
    not(empty(JobsA)),
    machine_cap(Mach, Ops, Num, _),    % generate Num.
    %
    % assign at least 1 op if there is work at StatA:
    Num > 0,    % disallow default capacity of 0
    NewOps is Ops - Num
  ),
  assign_ops(Hour, NewOps, Stats, OpList).


% Assign 0 operators if there are 0 operators
% left to assign (2nd arg), and if JobsA is empty;
% Stats (3rd arg) must have at least 2 elements:
assign_ops(Hour,                            % +
           0,                               % +ops
           [at(StatA,JobsA),at(StatB,JobsB)|Stats],% +
           [op(Mach,0)|OpList]              % -
          ) :-
  empty(JobsA),
  machine_name(Mach, StatA, _),
  assign_ops(Hour, 0, [at(StatB,JobsB)|Stats], OpList).


% Must assign all operators. "assign_ops" fails and
% backtracks if Ops (2nd arg) is not 0 at the last at(_,_)
% in station list:
assign_ops(_, 0, [at(_,_)], []).



%       EMPTY JOBLIST (used in "assign_ops")
% Check that all job(_,_) structures have a zero amount:
empty([job(_,0)|Jobs]) :-
  empty(Jobs).
empty([]).
```

```
%----------------------------------------------------------
%         STATION TO STATION (level 6; scheduling)
%
% Given StatsX (the position of work at hour X),
% and OpList (an assignment of operators),
% compute StatsY (the position of work at hour Y, Y=X+1).
% Recurse once for each station.

%              +       +       +       -
stat_to_stat(MaxOps, StatsX, OpList, StatsY) :-
  % set up empty ArrivingWork list:
  unique_value_list(job(ID,0),  job(_,_,ID,_), ArrivingWork),
  stat_to_stat0(MaxOps, ArrivingWork, StatsX, OpList, StatsY).

% last at(_,_) in station list:
stat_to_stat0(_,                            % +
            ArrivingWork,                   % +
            [at(_,JobsX)],                  % +
            OpList,                         % +
            [at(_,JobsY)]                   % -
                  ) :-
  job_to_job(0, ArrivingWork, JobsX, JobsY, _), !.


stat_to_stat0(MaxOps,                       % +
  ArrivingWork,                             % +
  [at(StatA,JobsXA),at(StatB,JobsXB)|StatsX], % +work hour X
  OpList,                                   % +
  [at(StatA,JobsYA),at(StatB,JobsYB)|StatsY] % -work hour Y
              ) :-
  % find NumberOps and Machine for stats A & B in OpList:
  find_machine(OpList, Machine, StatA, StatB, NumberOps),
  machine_cap(Machine, MaxOps, NumberOps, Capacity),
  job_to_job(Capacity, ArrivingWork, JobsXA, JobsYA, ProcessedWork),
  !, stat_to_stat0(MaxOps,
              ProcessedWork,
              [at(StatB,JobsXB)|StatsX],
              OpList,
              [at(StatB,JobsYB)|StatsY]).
```

```
%----------------------------------------------------------
%          JOB TO JOB (level 7; scheduling)
%
%   Given Capacity (the capacity of a machine),
%   JobsX (a list of work from the last hour), and a list of
%   arriving work from processing already done this hour,
%   return JobsY (a new list of work for the next hour).
%   Recurse once for each job.

job_to_job(_, [], [], [], []).

job_to_job(Capacity,                          % +
     [job(Name,AmountAW)|ArrivingWork], % +Arriving work
     [job(Name,AmountX) |JobsX],        % +Jobs at hour X
     [job(Name,AmountY) |JobsY],        % -Jobs at hour Y
     [job(Name,AmountPW)|ProcessedWork] % -Processed work
          ) :-
  Capacity > 0,
  actually_processed(AmountX, Capacity, AmountPW),
  AmountY is AmountX - AmountPW + AmountAW,
  RCapacity is Capacity - AmountPW,
  !, job_to_job(RCapacity, ArrivingWork,
                JobsX, JobsY, ProcessedWork).


job_to_job(0,                                 % +Capacity
     [job(Name,AmountAW)|ArrivingWork], % +Arriving work
     [job(Name,AmountX) |JobsX],        % +Jobs at hour X
     [job(Name,AmountY) |JobsY],        % -Jobs at hour Y
     [job(Name,0)       |ProcessedWork] % -Processed work
          ) :-
  %  add in amount of arriving work:
  AmountY is AmountX + AmountAW,
  %  the amount of work processed is 0:
  !, job_to_job(0, ArrivingWork, JobsX, JobsY, ProcessedWork).
```

```
%----------------------------------------------------------
%          FIND MACHINE (level 7; scheduling)
%
%  Given OpList (operator assignment list)
%  and the names of two stations, StatA and StatB,
%  return Mach (the name of the machine
%  that processes work between these stations),
%  and Num (the number of operators on the machine).
%               +                   -      +      +      -
find_machine([op(Mach,Num)|OpList], Mach, StatA, StatB, Num) :-
  machine_name(Mach, StatA, StatB), !.
find_machine([_|OpList], Mach, StatA, StatB, Num) :-
  find_machine(OpList, Mach, StatA, StatB, Num), !.


%----------------------------------------------------------
%          ACTUALLY PROCESSED WORK (level 8; scheduling)
%
%  If Quantity of work < available Capacity,
%  then #Processed = Quantity;
%  otherwise, #Processed = Capacity:
%                         +  +  -
actually_processed(Q, C, P) :- Q < 0,        P = 0, !.
actually_processed(Q, C, P) :- Q - C > 0,    P = C, !.
actually_processed(Q, C, P) :- Q - C =< 0,   P = Q, !.


%%%%%%%%%%%%%%%%%%%%%%%%%%%%%%%%%%%%%%%%%%%%%%%%%%%%%%%%%%%%
%          DATABASES AND DATABASE INTERFACES

%----------------------------------------------------------
%          MACHINE CAPACITY DATABASE (level 7; scheduling)
%
%  Machine capacities per hour; Number is number of operators.
%          +Name   +        ?        -
machine_cap(alpha, MaxOps, Number, Capacity) :-
  (  %  if Number is a var, generate Number:
     var(Number), num_gen(MaxOps, Number)
     ;
     nonvar(Number), Number > 0
  ),
  %  5 units/hour/operator:
  Capacity is Number * 5.
```

```
machine_cap(beta, MaxOps, Number, Capacity) :-
  (  var(Number),
     num_gen(MaxOps, Number)
     ;
     nonvar(Number), Number > 0
  ),
  (  Number = 1, Capacity = 15
     ;
     Number = 2, Capacity = 20
     ;
     Number > 2,
     Capacity is 20 + ((Number - 2) * 2)
     %  more than 2 ops: 2 additional units per hour.
  ).

machine_cap(gamma, _, Number, Capacity) :-
  %  gamma needs exactly two operators:
  (  var(Number), Number = 2
     ;
     nonvar(Number), Number >= 2
  ),
  Capacity = 20.

machine_cap(delta, MaxOps, Number, Capacity) :-
  (  var(Number), num_gen(MaxOps, Number)
     ;
     nonvar(Number),  Number > 0
  ),
  %  8 units/hour/operator:
  Capacity is Number * 8.

%  default:
machine_cap(_, _, 0, 0).


%-----------------------------------------------------------
%        MAXIMUM NUMBER OF OPERATORS (level 6; scheduling)
%               +     -
max_operators(Hour, Number) :-
  %  make a list of all operators still on the job at Hour:
  findall(X, send(Hour, operator(X)), List),
  length(List, Number), !.
```

```
%           OPERATOR DATBASE (level 7; scheduling)
%
% These facts are asserted by timeclock interface.
% 8 = 8AM (hour that operator arrived)
operator(8, jack).
operator(8, martha).
operator(8, susan).
operator(8, barney).
operator(8, fred).

% doug arrives late:
%operator(9, doug).

% barney and fred are leaving at 11AM:
%refute(11, operator(8, barney)).
%refute(11, operator(8, fred)).


%-------------------------------------------------------
%           STATION DATABASE (level 6; scheduling)
%
% A station is a place where work accumulates
% before and after being processed by a machine.
% 1 == completely unprocessed;
% 5 == finished.

station(1).    % begin.
station(2).
station(3).
station(4).
station(5).    % end.


%-------------------------------------------------------
%           MACHINE NAME DATABASE (level 7; scheduling)
%
% "alpha" machine processes work between station 1 and station 2:
machine_name(alpha, 1, 2).
machine_name(beta,  2, 3).
machine_name(gamma, 3, 4).
machine_name(delta, 4, 5).
```

```
%-----------------------------------------------------------
%          JOB DATABASE (level 6; scheduling)
%
%  Each job to be processed
%  is added to the program in the following form:
%   Hour   Station   ID        Units
job(8,      1,        dow,      18).
job(8,      1,        mcgraw,   25).



%-----------------------------------------------------------
%          TIME DATABASE
%
%  This database enables "send" to find
%  the correct # of operators for an hour.
child_of(9, 8).
child_of(10, 9).
child_of(11, 10).
child_of(12, 11).
child_of(13, 12).
child_of(14, 13).


%%%%%%%%%%%%%%%%%%%%%%%%%%%%%%%%%%%%%%%%%%%%%%%%%%%%%%
%          DISPLAY PROCEDURES
%
%          SHOW OP PATH (level 3; display)
%  Display operator assignments through
%  the hours of the shift.
show_op_path(_, []).
show_op_path(Hour, [OpList¦OpPath]) :-
  length(OpList, Num),            % Num = number of machines.
  write('Hour     '),
  op_path_header(Num),
  show_op_path0(Hour, [OpList¦OpPath]).

op_path_header(0) :- nl.          % newline here.
op_path_header(Length) :-
  Length > 0,
  write('Machine    Ops    '),
  NewLength is Length - 1,
  op_path_header(NewLength).
```

```
        show_op_path0(_, []).
        show_op_path0(Hour, [OpList|OpPath]) :-
          write(Hour), write('    '),    % tab
          show_oplist(OpList),
          NewHour is Hour + 1,
          show_op_path0(NewHour, OpPath).

        show_oplist([]) :- nl.        % newline here.
        show_oplist([op(Machine,Ops)|OpList]) :-
          write(Machine), write('     '),    % tab
          write(Ops), write('    '),
          show_oplist(OpList).


        %----------------------------------------------------------
        %       SHOW LAST STATION LIST (level 3; display)
        %
        % Skip through until the last Stats, then call show_statlist.
        show_last_stats([Stats|StatPath]) :-
          StatPath \== [],
          show_last_stats(StatPath).
        show_last_stats([Stats]) :-    % last element in StatPath list.
          write('Station    '),
          statlist_header(4),
          show_statlist(Stats).

        statlist_header(0) :- nl.
        statlist_header(Length) :-
          Length > 0,
          write('ID    Amount    '),
          NewLength is Length - 1,
          statlist_header(NewLength).


        %----------------------------------------------------------
        %       SHOW STATLIST (level 4; display)
        %
        show_statlist([]).
        show_statlist([at(Stat,Jobs)|Stats]) :-
          write(Stat), write('     '),    % tab
          show_joblist(Jobs), nl,
          show_statlist(Stats).
```

```
show_joblist([]).
show_joblist([job(ID,Amount)|Jobs]) :-
  write(ID), write('      '), write(Amount), write('      '),
  show_joblist(Jobs).


%%%%%%%%%%%%%%%%%%%%%%%%%%%%%%%%%%%%%%%%%%%%%%%%%%%%%%
%        EDITING PROCEDURES
%
%        EDIT OPERATORS (level 3; editing)
edit_operators(Hour, add) :-
     getfield('      Name of operator to add, or end to continue',
          Answer, end, true),
     (  Answer = end
     ;
     Answer \== end,
     assert( operator(Hour, Answer) ),
     write('      Operator added'),
     edit_operators(Hour, add)
   ).


edit_operators(Hour, remove) :-
  getfield('      Name of operator to remove, or end',
       Answer, end, true),
  (  Answer = end
     ;
     Answer \== end,
     assert( refute(Hour, operator(_, Answer)) ),
     write('      Operator removed'),
     edit_operators(Hour, remove)
   ).


%-----------------------------------------------------------
%        EDIT SCHEDULE (level 4; editing)
edit_schedule(Hour,                % +
              IStats,              % +work at Hour
              [StatsX|StatPathX],  % +current StatPath
              [OpListX|OpPathX],   % +current OpPath
              [StatsY|StatPathY],  % -edited StatPath
              [OpListY|OpPathY]    % -edited OpPath
              ) :-
  edit_oplist(Hour, IStats, StatsY, OpListX, OpListY),
  NewHour is Hour + 1,
  edit_schedule(NewHour, StatsY, StatPathX, OpPathX, StatPathY,
             OpPathY).
```

```
                % StatsY returned by edit_oplist is 2nd arg to recursive call

        edit_schedule(Hour, IStats, [], [], [], []) :-
            nl,
            pr('    Projected Work in the Factory at End of Shift:'),
            write('Stat    '),
            statlist_header(4),
            show_statlist(IStats), !.

        %       EDIT OPLIST (level 5; editing)
        %
        % Front end to "edit_oplist0."
        %          +     +     -     +     -
        dit_oplist(Hour, IStats, NewStats, OpListX, OpListY) :-
            nl,
            pr('    Projected Work in the Factory at Hour ', Hour, ':'),
            write('Stat    '),
            statlist_header(4),
            show_statlist(IStats),
            %
            nl,
            pr('    Operators Currently Assigned:'),
            show_oplist(OpListX),
            nl,
            %
            max_operators(Hour, MaxOps),
          edit_oplist0(MaxOps, OpListX, OpListY),
            %
            % compute NewStats (result of the new assignment of ops):
            stat_to_stat(MaxOps, IStats, OpListY, NewStats).

        edit_oplist(_, _, [], [], []).
```

```
%         EDIT_OPLIST0
% Edit all operator assignments at a particular hour.
edit_oplist0(MaxOps,                    % +
             [op(Mach,NumX)|OpListX],% +
             [op(Mach,NumY)|OpListY] % -
                      ):-
    machine_name(Mach, StatA, StatB),
    pr('    Machine: ',Mach,' between ',StatA,' and ',StatB,'    '),
    %  test new value:
    getfield('Number of Operators:', NumY, NumX,
         ( NumY >= 0, NumY =< MaxOps ) ),
    !, edit_oplist0(MaxOps, OpListX, OpListY).


edit_oplist0(_, [], []) :- !.



%%%%%%%%%%%%%%%%%%%%%%%%%%%%%%%%%%%%%%%%%%%%%%%%%%%%%%
%         LOW LEVEL I/O PROCEDURES
%         PRINT
%  Write 1-7 arguments followed by newline:
pr(A) :- write(A), nl.
pr(A,B) :- write(A), write(B), nl.
pr(A,B,C) :- write(A), write(B), write(C), nl.
pr(A,B,C,D) :- write(A), write(B), write(C), write(D), nl.
pr(A,B,C,D,E) :-
    write(A), write(B), write(C), write(D), write(E), nl.
pr(A,B,C,D,E,F) :-
    write(A), write(B), write(C), write(D), write(E),
    write(F), nl.
pr(A,B,C,D,E,F,G) :-
    write(A), write(B), write(C), write(D), write(E),
    write(F), write(G), nl.


%%%%%%%%%%%%%%%%%%%%%%%%%%%%%%%%%%%%%%%%%%%%%%%%%%%%%%
%         MISCELLANEOUS PROCEDURES
%
%         ELEMENT PRINT
element_pr(Offset, [A|R]) :-
    write(Offset), write(A), nl, element_pr(Offset, R).
element_pr(_, []).
```

```
%          NUMBER GENERATOR
% Generate integer N between 1 and Max, inclusive:
num_gen(Max, N) :-
    num_gen0(Max, 1, N).
num_gen0(Max, Seed, Seed).
num_gen0(Max, Seed, N) :-
    NewSeed is Seed + 1,
    NewSeed =< Max,
    num_gen0(Max, NewSeed, N).


%          SUM OF A LIST OF NUMBERS
sum([], 0).
sum([F|R], Total) :-
    sum(R, Sub),
    Total is F + Sub.


%          CLEANUP
cleanup :-    % get rid of all jobs asserted after 8am.
    job(Hour, A, B, C),
    Hour > 8,
    retract( job(Hour, A, B, C) ), fail.
cleanup :-    % reset hour
    retract(current_hour(_)), assert(current_hour(8)).


%          FILE DEPENDENCIES
:-consult('send').            % the inheritance mechanism
```

Appendix IV

Versions of Prolog

CProlog

Availability

CProlog is available in C source code form from:

Department of Architecture
University of Edinburgh
20 Chambers Street
Edinburgh, U.K. EH1 1JZ

It is easily ported to almost any 32-bit computer running UNIX, and has also been ported to some other computers that have C compilers. It will not, however, run on 16-bit machines. There is an extensive library of CProlog-compatible Prolog code (the SCORE Prolog library) available through Stanford University Computer Science Department and other sources.

Syntax and Built-in Predicates

The syntax of CProlog is the same as that of DEC-10 Prolog. CProlog's built-in predicates are almost identical to those of DEC-10 Prolog. All of the examples in this book will work without modification in CProlog.

Types

The fundamental types of CProlog are atoms, integers, floating point numbers, and structures. When the arguments to an arithmetic expression are exclusively integers, then the result of evaluating that expression (for instance with "is") will also be an integer. If floating point numbers occur in an arithmetic expression, then the result of evaluating the expression will be a floating point number. In the case of division, however, there are two separate operators. The result of a division performed with / is always a float, and the result of a division performed with // is always an integer. Floating point numbers can be written in exponential notation, i.e. 6.1E10.

Characters written in between single quotes, as in 'abc', form an atom. Writing characters in between double quotes is an alternative notation for a list of characters (sometimes called a "string"). Thus, when the interpreter sees "abc", it translates it into [97,98,99].

Directives

Directives are commands to the interpreter that are embedded in a Prolog source file, and executed at the point that the source file is consulted. A directive begins with the characters :- against the left hand margin. If the following directive were included in a source file:

```
:-write('hello there'), nl.
```

it would write the message *hello there* followed by a newline to the standard output stream at the point that the file is consulted. Typically in CProlog, directives are used to declare operators and to specify dependencies between source files. If the following two directives appear in a source file called "a.pl":

```
:-op(700, xfy, ->).
:-consult('b.pl').
```

then at the point that "a.pl" is consulted, -> will be made into an infix operator (see Sec. 3.10), and source file "b.pl" will also be consulted.

Development Environment

CProlog has no internal editor, and so the programmer must rely on the support of the UNIX environment to develop a program. The typical development cycle might proceed as follows. Initially, the programmer writes the program with a text editor, say "vi." Then the programmer runs CProlog and consults the file. When a bug is discovered in the program, the programmer can end the CProlog session, re-edit the file, run CProlog again, and consult the file again. However, this might become tedious with a long program file, because consulting takes a long time. CProlog provides a built-in predicate, "system/1," that executes an operating system command from within a Prolog session. This predicate enables the programmer to re-edit the source file from within Prolog, with a command such as:

```
| ?- system("vi a.pl").
```

Notice that "system" requires that the operating system command be in the form of a list of characters. As a result of the query above, a separate editor process will be started on top of the current Prolog process. When the programmer finishes editing the file and leaves the editor, control returns to the Prolog process and the interpreter prints:

yes

If the file "a.pl" has already been consulted prior to the "system" query above, then it must be reconsulted at this point with a query such as:

```
| ?- reconsult('a.pl').
```

If a file is consulted twice, then the set of currently asserted clauses will contain two instances of every clause in the file. Reconsulting a file is a way to avoid this problem. When reconsulting a file, the interpreter checks each predicate in the file to see if there are any currently asserted clauses that belong to that predicate (i.e. have the same name and arity). If there are any such clauses, then the interpreter gets rid of all of them and replaces them with the clauses in the file being reconsulted. Thus, if a programmer changed the definition of a clause in the file, the new definition will supersede the old one.

To take maximum advantage of the "reconsult" facility (i.e. to minimize the time spent reconsulting), it is recommended that a programmer organize a program into several short files rather than one large file.

Debugger

The C-Prolog debugger is capable of writing an explanatory message at four points in the execution of a procedure:

1) when the first clause of a procedure is considered ("Call");

2) when a procedure has been evaluated successfully ("Exit");

3) when the system backtracks to consider the second or subsequent clause of the procedure ("Back to");

4) when the system reaches the end of a set of clauses defining a procedure ("Fail").

There are two ways to turn on the debugger. Typing:

```
¦ ?- trace.
```

will cause the debugger to begin showing the maximum level of debugging information for the next query. That is, a message will be printed for each of the four points in each procedure encountered. Typing:

```
¦ ?- notrace.
```

will turn the debugger off.

The other way to use the debugger is to set a spypoint on one or more procedures. This will cause the debugger to be turned on automatically whenever a call to a procedure with a spypoint on it is encountered. For instance, typing

```
¦ ?- spy connects/3.
```

will cause a spypoint to be placed on the "connects/3" procedure. Typing:

```
¦ ?- nospy connects/3.
```

will remove that spypoint.

An example session

Here is an example of using the debugger to watch the execution of a simple procedure. Whenever a question mark appears at the end of a debug line, the debugger is giving the user a chance to enter a debug command. In the session below, the user hits return in response to each question mark, signaling the debugger to continue printing debugging information at the maximum level of detail.

```
flight(peoples, newark, raleigh).
flight(peoples, raleigh, nashville).
```

```
| ?- trace.
yes

| ?- flight(peoples, X, Y).
   (1) 0 Call: flight(peoples,_309,_324) ?
   (1) 0 Exit: flight(peoples,newark,raleigh) ?

X = newark,
Y = raleigh ;
   (1) 0 Back to: flight(peoples,_309,_324) ?
   (1) 0 Exit: flight(peoples,raleigh,nashville) ?

X = raleigh,
Y = nashville ;
   (1) 0 Back to: flight(peoples,_309,_324) ?
   (1) 0 Fail: flight(peoples,_309,_324) ?


no
```

In messages printed by the debugger, all variables are shown as their internal names. When the user types ; to reject an answer, the most recently activated query is made to fail, and all variables that were instantiated by the success of the most recently activated query are uninstantiated. Notice that the CProlog debugger shows such variables in their uninstantiated form when it prints a "Back to" message.

Interpreting a debug line

A debug line such as

```
* (1) 0 Call: flight(peoples,_309,_324) ?
```

can be interpreted as follows:

* means that a spypoint is currently set on the "flight/3" procedure.

(1) is a unique identification of the particular invocation of this procedure.

0 represents the number of direct ancestor goals that this particular subgoal has. This will show, for instance, the depth that a recursive procedure has reached.

Call: indicates that this is where the procedure is first entered.

flight(peoples,_309,_324) is the subgoal itself.

? is a prompt indicating that the debugger is waiting for a debugging command.

Once the debugger has been turned on, either with "trace" or by encountering a spypoint, then it will prompt the user for a command after printing each message. If the user types return in response to this prompt, the debugger will continue at the maximum level of detail. Other debugging commands include:

Debugging Commands

`<return>`	The debugger will print debug lines for all procedures (this is the debugger's maximum level of detail).
`s`	(skip). The debugger will print nothing more until an "Exit" or "Fail" from this procedure call.
`l`	(leap). The debugger will print nothing more until the next call to a procedure that has a spypoint set.
`n`	(nodebug). Turns off the debugger until the system returns to the top level prompt.
`a`	(abort). Stops execution of the program and returns to the top level prompt.

To use the debugger to view only the execution of a single procedure, the programmer would set a spypoint on that procedure, start the program running, and type 1 (leap) in response to each of the debugger's prompts. The 1 command causes the debugger not to print anything until the next time a spied procedure is encountered.

s (skip) can be used to skip to the exit or failure of a procedure. Suppose that the debugger prints a message at the call point of a procedure that is thoroughly debugged, such as "member." Using the s command is a way to avoid seeing all of the tedious detail about exactly how "member" succeeds or fails.

Compiler

CProlog has no compiler.

Saved States

Consulting a Prolog source file requires a certain amount of time. It is possible to avoid this time by consulting the program once, and then using the "save" command to save the current state of the Prolog system into a binary file, including all currently asserted clauses. CProlog will accept the name of one saved state file as a command line argument at the point that it is invoked from the operating system. In the example session below, the user consults a file, makes a saved state file, and then leaves Prolog:

```
| ?- consult('a.pl').
yes

| ?- save('a.save').
yes

| ?- halt.            % to end session
```

To run CProlog again and restore the saved state, the user need only call CProlog from the operating system with the name of the saved state file as a argument:

```
$ cprolog a.save
```

For a large program, restoring a saved state is usually much quicker than consulting the source files. Saved state files, however, tend to be large.

An interesting feature of saved states is that any unevaluated queries in the Prolog session will also be saved, and evaluated as soon as the saved state file is restored. In the example below, the user specifies that a query to the "start" procedure should be evaluated upon the restoration of the saved state:

```
| ?- save('a.pl'), start(8).
yes
```

Thus, saved states can be used to make an "executable" version of a Prolog program in which the existence of the Prolog interpreter is completely hidden from the user of the program.

Foreign Language Attachment

Additional built-in predicates can be added to CProlog by modifying the C source code and recompiling.

Extensions

CProlog contains an extension for writing top down parsers in the Definite Clause Grammar (DCG) formalism. Here is how a simple grammar from Chapter 6 would appear in the DCG notation:

```
% Grammar in Prolog code, from Chapter 6:
%    nonterminals:
%   In  Out  Name
obj(I,  O,    sentence) :-
    obj(I,  R,    nounphrase),
    obj(R,  O,    verbphrase).
obj(I,  O,   nounphrase) :-
    obj(I,  R,    article),
    obj(R,  O,    noun).
obj(I,  O,   verbphrase) :-
    obj(I,  R,    verb),
    obj(R,  O,    nounphrase).

%    terminals:
%   In          Out  Name
obj([the|R],    R,    article).
obj([cow|R],    R,    noun).
obj([tail|R],   R,    noun).
obj([shakes|R],R,    verb).
obj([walks|R],  R,    verb).

% Grammar in DCG notation:
sentence    --> nounphrase, verbphrase.
nounphrase --> article, noun.
verbphrase --> verb, nounphrase.

article --> [the].
noun    --> [cow].
noun    --> [tail].
verb    --> [shakes].
verb    --> [walks].
```

The DCG notation has many features which make it easy to write grammars. For a full description, see Warren and Pereira [1980].

Quintus Prolog

Availability

Quintus Prolog is available from Quintus Computer Systems, Inc. It runs on a number of machines under both the UNIX and VMS operating systems. An extensive library of utility programs are distributed with the product. Quintus Prolog is notable for its very high execution speed.

Syntax and Built-in Predicates

The syntax of Quintus Prolog is the same as that of DEC-10 Prolog. All of the examples in this book will work without modification in Quintus Prolog. It has most of the same built-in predicates as DEC-10 Prolog, as well as some new ones. Notable additions are in the area of file control.

In addition to "see," "tell," etc. described in Sec. 4.5, there are the following predicates that use stream identifiers to keep track of open files:

`open(F,M,S)` F is a filename. M is one of the following three atoms representing modes: `read`, `write` or `append`. This predicate opens the file in the manner prescribed and instantiates S to a unique stream identifier.

`set_input(S)` S must be a unique stream identifier returned from a call to "open/3" with a mode argument of read. This predicate will associate the file identified by S with the current input stream.

`set_output(S)` S must be a unique stream identifier returned from a call to "open/3" with a mode argument of write or append. This predicate will associate the file identified by S with the current output stream.

`close(S)` S must be a unique stream identifier returned from a call to "open/3." This predicate closes the file identified by S.

Example:

```
| ?- open('ap.data', read, S1),
     set_input(S1),
     repeat,
     read(R),
     process(R),
```

```
R = end_of_file,
close(S1),
set_input(user).
```

It is worth noting that when "set_input" is used to redirect the input steam from an open file inside of a query, the input stream will automatically revert to the terminal when the query is over. This is not true in CProlog if the user opens a file with "see" in a query; if the user did not close the file with "seen" in the same query, then the interpreter will continue to take input from the open file, and the Prolog session will end when the end of file is encountered.

The built-in predicate "current_stream/3" can be used to get the stream identifiers and modes of any open files. There are versions of the other input/output predicates (i.e. "write," "read," etc.) that take a stream identifier as an argument, and write to or read from the file associated with that identifier.

There is a formatted write predicate, "format/2," with format codes similar to those understood by the "printf" function in C.

"consult" in Quintus Prolog means the same as "reconsult" in CProlog; that is, for each predicate in the consulted file, the system will remove any currently asserted clauses belonging to that predicate before adding the clauses from the file. This is intended to protect a programmer from asserting the same clauses more than once. Declaring a procedure to be "multifile" will defeat this behavior.

Types

The fundamental types of Quintus Prolog are atoms, integers, floating point numbers, and structures. As in CProlog, when the arguments to an arithmetic expression are exclusively integers, then the result of evaluating that expression (for instance with "is") will also be an integer. If floating point numbers occur in an arithmetic expression, then the result of evaluating the expression will be a floating point number. In the case of division, however, there are two separate operators. The result of a division performed with / is always a float, and the result of a division performed with // is always an integer. Floating point numbers can be written in exponential notation, i.e. 6.1E10.

As in CProlog, writing characters in between double quotes is an alternative notation for a list of characters.

Directives

If the clauses of a certain predicate are going to be asserted and retracted during the execution of a procedure, that predicate must be declared to be dynamic in a directive of the form:

```
:- dynamic king/2.
```

If the "king/2" predicate is not declared to be dynamic, then "assert" and "retract" on it will fail with an error message. Also, "clause" (Sec. 4.9) will only work on dynamic predicates.

Development Environment

Quintus Prolog can be run either as a stand alone process or through a special EMACS editor interface. When Quintus Prolog is run with EMACS, there are typically two windows on the screen: the upper window contains a Prolog source file, and the lower window contains the Prolog process embedded in an EMACS editor buffer. From the source file window, there are EMACS commands to incrementally consult or compile clauses into the active Prolog process. For instance, if all clauses for a certain procedure are grouped together in one part of the source file, one EMACS command will find all of these clauses and consult or compile them. EMACS has been extended in other ways to give it knowledge of Prolog syntactical forms.

In the Prolog process window, all output from the Prolog system is automatically inserted into an EMACS buffer. When the session is over, this buffer is usually thrown away, but can be explicitly saved into a file. The buffer acts as a sort of history mechanism for the session, and there is an EMACS command to find and re-execute a query that was entered previously in the session.

In CProlog, when the interpreter encounters a query to a predicate that is not currently asserted, it just fails. Quintus Prolog allows a programmer to define the behavior of the system upon encountering an unknown predicate. By default, a query to an unknown predicate will turn on the debugger. Using debugger commands, a programmer can consult or compile the file containing the predicate (or enter it from the keyboard), and tell the system to retry the query.

Debugger

The Quintus Prolog debugger is essentially similar to the CProlog debugger, except that there are many more debugger commands available.

Compiler

Quintus Prolog includes both an incremental compiler and an interpreter. Interpreted code and compiled code can be freely intermixed in the same Prolog session. The compiler is incremental in the sense that new clauses can be compiled into a running Prolog process at any point. Compiled code executes much faster than interpreted code, but interpreted code has more debugging information in it. Typically, a procedure would be interpreted during development, and then compiled once it is thoroughly debugged.

Saved States

Saved states in Quintus Prolog function in much the same way as in CProlog. In UNIX versions, a Prolog process can be started and a saved state restored just by entering the name of the saved state on the operating system command line.

Foreign Language Attachment

Procedures written in foreign computer languages can be incrementally attached to a Prolog process and called from within the Prolog session like any other built-in predicate. Support for the following languages is available: C, Pascal, Assembler, Fortran, Cobol, and Lisp. For each language, facilities exist to map the data structures of the language to and from Prolog data structures for the purpose of passing arguments.

Extensions

Quintus Prolog includes the DCG extension described in the section on CProlog above.

Miscellaneous

When clauses are consulted or compiled, they are examined by a style checker. The style checker issues warnings about various conditions usually associated with errors, such as the occurrence of a "singleton" variable in a clause (i.e. a variable that occurs only once). This type of warning can help identify spelling errors.

First argument
indexing

Compiled procedures in Quintus Prolog automatically have first argument indexing, except for those declared to be dynamic. This
means that when a query to a procedure is being evaluated, a hash
table is used to speed up access to clauses of that procedure that
have the same first argument as the query. If the first argument is a
structure, then clauses are indexed on the basis of the structure
name.

Tail recursion
optimization

Quintus Prolog automatically applies *tail recursion optimization* to a
recursive procedure that is determinate at the point that the recursive subgoal is called. Tail recursion optimization is a way of
economizing on the amount of stack space needed to evaluate a
query to a procedure. When operative, it ensures that no further
stack units are allocated to evaluate the recursive subgoal of a procedure. Instead, the recursive subgoal reuses the stack units allocated for its parent goal. Thus, a procedure can recurse to any
depth utilizing a constant number of stack units.

As an example of how to take advantage of tail recursion optimization, consider the following two versions of the recursive "sum_up"
procedure that adds up a list of numbers:

```
%         +     _
sum_up1([], 0).
sum_up1([N|R], Total) :-
    sum_up1(R, Subtotal),
    Total is N + Subtotal.

%         +     +       _
sum_up2([], Total, Total).
sum_up2([N|R], Subtotal, Total) :-
    NewSubtotal is N + Subtotal,
    sum_up2(R, NewSubtotal, Total).

| ?- sum_up1([2,2], T1).
T1 = 4

| ?- sum_up2([2,2], 0, T2).
T2 = 4
```

The compiler will not apply tail recursion optimization to the
"sum_up1" procedure because at the point that the recursive subgoal
(i.e. sum_up1(R, Subtotal)) is called, there is still another
subgoal to be evaluated. The compiler will apply tail recursion

optimization to the "sum_up2" procedure because at the point that the recursive subgoal (i.e. `sum_up2(R, NewSubtotal, Total)`) is called, all previous subgoals (i.e. `NewSubtotal is N + Subtotal`) are determinate, and there are no further subgoals after the recursive subgoal.

Silogic Knowledge Workbench

Availability

Silogic Knowledge Workbench is available from Silogic, Inc. It runs on a variety of UNIX computers. Although the product is based on CProlog, it includes many additional facilities and extensions.

Syntax and Built-in Predicates

The syntax of Knowledge Workbench is compatible with DEC-10 Prolog. All examples in this book will work without modification. Knowledge Workbench has most of the same built-in predicates as DEC-10 Prolog and many new ones. Notable additions are in the area of UNIX-like file control and UNIX system calls.

The following predicates use stream identifiers to keep track of open files:

`fopen(F,M,S)`
F is a filename. M is one of the following three atoms representing modes: `r` (read), `w` (write), or `a` (append). This predicate opens the file in the manner prescribed and instantiates S to a unique stream identifier.

`gets(S,L)`
S is a stream identifier associated with a file that was opened for reading. L is a list of characters. This predicate instantiates L to the next line of input from the file associated with S.

`puts(S,L)`
S is a stream identifier associated with a file that was opened for writing or appending. L is a list of characters. This predicate puts the characters in L into the file associated with S.

`fclose(S)`
This predicate closes the file associated with stream identifier S.

Example:

```
¦ ?- fopen("ap.data", r, SI),
     fopen("ap.report", w, SO),
     gets(SI, X),
     process(X, Y),
     puts(SO, Y),
     puts(SO, "end of report"),
     fclose(SI),
     fclose(SO).
```

The predicate "name_stream/2" returns the names and stream identifiers of all open streams.

Knowledge Workbench includes the following built-in predicates that interface to UNIX system calls:

```
chdir
chmod
chown
fork
getpid
getenv
kill
nice
etc.
```

Knowledge Workbench provides the built-in predicates "argc," which returns the number or arguments on the command line when it was called from the operating system, and "argv," which returns a list of the command line arguments. There is a formatted write predicate, "writef/2," which takes format codes similar to those understood by "printf" in C.

The arithmetic evaluators ("is," "<," etc.) will evaluate a number of functions in addition to the usual arithmetic operators, including:

```
sqrt(X)      % square root of X
exp(X)       % e to the power of X
log(X)       % log base e of X
log10(X)     % log base 10 of X
sin(X)
cos(X)
tan(X)
```

```
asin(X)
acos(X)
atan(X)
etc.
```

Types

The fundamental types of Knowledge Workbench are atoms, integers, floating point numbers, and structures. As in CProlog, when the arguments to an arithmetic expression are exclusively integers, then the result of evaluating that expression will also be an integer. If floating point numbers occur in an arithmetic expression, then the result of evaluating the expression will be a floating point number. The result of a division performed with / is a float, and the result of a division performed with // is an integer.

As in CProlog, writing characters in between double quotes is an alternative notation for a list of characters.

There is an alternative notation for ascii code values which consists of 0 and ´ written in front of a character. The following two lists are equivalent:

```
[97,98,99]        [0´a, 0´b, 0´c]
```

For purposes of compile-time optimization, Knowledge Workbench supports the following type declarations in "mode" directives (see "Directives" below):

compound   This argument is a compound term.

list(X)   This argument is a list; if X is the
             name of a type, then it is a list of
             terms of that type.

atomic   This argument is an atom or a
             number.

atom   This argument is an atom.

```
number        This argument is a float or an in-
              teger.

integer       This argument is an integer.
```

A programmer can define additional types using the "type" directive.

Directives

Knowledge Workbench makes a distinction between program predicates and data predicates. The clauses of a program predicate
cannot be asserted and retracted. All clauses loaded by means of the
built-in predicate "load" are program predicates by default. A predicate must be declared to be "data" if its clauses are going to be
changed dynamically. For instance, the following directive will make
"running_total/1" into a data predicate:

```
:-data running_total/1.
```

For compile-time optimization, the direction (i.e. input or output)
and type of arguments to a predicate can be declared with a "mode"
directive. A predicate can also be declared to be determinate with a
"mode" directive. For example, in the "total" rule below, the first argument must always be an input compound term, and the second argument is always an output integer:

```
%        +                          -
total( customer(_,Rate,Days), Owed) :-
    Owed is Rate * Days.
```

The following "mode" directive instructs the compiler about the nature of the arguments to "total":

```
:-mode total( +compound, -integer).
```

If "total" is intended to be determinate (i.e. to succeed only once),
the compiler could be informed of this fact by adding a plus sign in
front of the name of the predicate in the "mode" directive:

```
:-mode +total( +compound, -integer).
```

The "mode" directive describing a predicate should occur in the same
source file that the predicate is defined. It has no effect if the source
file is consulted instead of compiled.

There are several other directives that can be used to inform the compiler about the nature of a predicate for purposes of optimization. A "writeless" predicate contains no calls to "assert" or "retract." The order of clauses of an "orderless" predicate is not important. All of the arguments of a "modeless" predicate are bidirectional. There are no cuts in the clauses of a "cutless" predicate. The clauses of an "ioless" predicate contain no calls to input/output predicates.

Development Environment

The built-in predicate "load" is like "consult," except that it can load both object (compiled) and source files, and it will refuse to load clauses that belong to an already loaded procedure. "reload" is like "reconsult": for each procedure in the file, it will remove any current clauses before asserting new clauses for that procedure.

Knowledge Workbench can be run as a stand alone process, in which case the development cycle is much like that of CProlog. Suppose that the programmer loads a source file called "a.pl," and then discovers a bug in it. The following compound query will start an editor process on top of the Prolog process, and then reload the file once the editing session is complete:

```
| ?- shell("vi a.pl"), reload('a.pl').
```

Knowledge Workbench can also be run as a subprocess under EMACS, in which case all output from the Prolog session is inserted into an EMACS buffer. EMACS has been extended to support Prolog sessions.

Knowledge Workbench allows a programmer to define the behavior of the system upon encountering an unknown predicate. By default, a query to an unknown predicate will turn on the debugger.

Debugger

The Knowledge Workbench debugger is essentially similar to the CProlog debugger. However, to trace the evaluation of a query, the query is given as a argument to the built-in predicate "trace/1." For example, the following call will trace a query to "employee/3":

```
| ?- trace(employee(X, Y, Z)).
```

Besides "Call," "Exit," "Back to," and "Fail," the debugger can print messages at three additional points in the evaluation of a query:

5) before unification is attempted between the active query and the head of a clause ("Head");

6) when the unification of the active query and the head of a clause has failed ("Miss");

7) after unification between the active query and the head of a clause has succeeded ("Neck").

These additional messages make it easy to see the results of attempted unification of a query with the head of a clause. Knowledge Workbench has many more debugger commands available than CProlog.

Compiler

Knowledge Workbench has an external compiler that operates similarly to the C compiler. By convention, Prolog source files end with the extension `.pl` and object (compiled) files end with the extension `.po`. The compiler is an operating system command called "plc"; it takes source files as arguments and produces object files. Object files can be incrementally loaded into a running Prolog process with the built-in predicate "load." Compiled procedures cannot be interactively debugged.

Saved States

Saved states work largely the same as in CProlog. However, unevaluated queries are not included in a saved state. To run a program automatically upon the restoration of a saved state, a programmer needs to define a program called "main/1." If there is a "main/1" defined, then when a saved state is restored, the following compound query will be executed:

```
| ?- argv(L), main(L), !.
```

(`argv(L)` is a reference to the command line arguments of the Prolog process.) If the user ever interrupts the Prolog process, execution will begin again from this compound query, and Prolog will not return to the top level prompt. If no "main/1" is defined, then Prolog will go to the top level prompt when the saved state is restored.

A Prolog process can be started and a saved state restored just by entering the name of the saved state on the operating system command line.

Foreign Language Attachment

Knowledge Workbench allows C functions to be attached to a Prolog process; each C function appears as a built-in predicate from within Prolog. The mechanism is as follows: The interface between a C function and Prolog is specified in a file that ends with the extension `.pmi`. The operating system command "pmic" takes a `.pmi` file as an argument and generates a `.pmo` file. Then the operating system command "pld" takes a `.pmo` file and corresponding C object files as arguments, and generates a Prolog saved state. When the saved state is restored, the C functions can be called through their specified interface.

Extensions

Knowledge Workbench comes with a disk-based relational database system. Prolog programs can be kept on disk as external knowledge bases. If an external knowledge base is attached to a running Prolog process, then all clauses in the external knowledge base can be referenced in the same way as normally loaded Prolog clauses. Knowledge Workbench will also interface to some existing commercial relational database systems.

Certain operations can be performed on clauses in an external knowledge base that cannot be performed on clauses loaded into memory. For instance, the built-in predicate "aggregate" will perform operations such as count, average, minimum, maximum, and sum on one argument of a predicate that is part of an external knowledge base. Regular expression pattern matching is also available for the arguments of a predicate in an external knowledge base. For instance, suppose that the "employee/3" predicate is part of an external knowledge base that is attached to the current Prolog process, and that the first argument of "employee/3" is an atom containing an employee name. Then the following query will return the argument values of all "employee/3" clauses whose first argument ends with the characters "Smith":

```
¦ ?- employee( Name ?: 'Smith$', _, _).
Name = 'William G. Smith' ;

Name = 'Susan Smith'
```

($ specifies the end of a line in a regular expression.)

Knowledge Workbench has a transaction facility that enables a programmer to make certain operations atomic. The sense of an atomic operation is that either the whole thing succeeds, or none of it succeeds. The transaction facility is particularly useful for programs that must modify external knowledge bases. Transaction operations are implemented with the built-in predicates "tbegin" (transaction begin), "tcommit" (transaction commit), "tabort" (transaction abort), "detract" (delayed retract), and "dessert" (delayed assert). After a call to "tbegin," no calls to "dessert" or "detract" have any permanent effect on an external knowledge base until a call to "tcommit." A call to "tcommit" causes all outstanding calls to "dessert" and "detract" to be executed. Transactions may be nested.

Knowledge Workbench includes the DCG extension described in the section on CProlog above.

Miscellaneous

"plint" is an operating system command that checks the style of a Prolog program and points out singleton variables, predicates defined in more than one file, etc. "plxref" is an operating system command that produces a report about which procedures call which other procedures in a Prolog source file.

Prolog-2

Availability

Prolog-2 is available from Expert Systems International. It runs on an IBM PC or compatible under the MS-DOS operating system.

Syntax and Built-in Predicates

The syntax of Prolog-2 is the same as that of DEC-10 Prolog with the following exceptions: Prolog-2 recognizes comments between /* and */; % is not a comment character. A directive is written after the characters ?-. After the top-level interpreter has found an answer to a query, it prints it followed by the prompt *more (y/n)?* Typing y at this point is equivalent to typing a semicolon in other versions of Prolog, in that it causes the interpreter to look for another answer.

All of the examples in the book will work without modification in Prolog-2. It has all of the same built-in predicates as DEC-10 Prolog, either in the core system itself or in a DEC-10 compatibility library. There are many additional built-in predicates.

All Prolog-2 input/output is based on streams. The usual input/output predicates "see," "tell," etc. create and open streams automatically. A stream may be a *window* (see below). The following built-in predicates provide more precise control over streams:

create_stream(N,A,T,D)

> N must be a unique stream name. A is an access code: read, write, or readwrite. T is the data type of characters coming through the stream: either byte (8-bit) or ascii (7-bit). D is a structure describing the stream. If it is a "window/3" structure, then "create_stream" makes a new window according to the parameters of the structure. It may also be a "file/1" structure whose argument is the name of a file.

open(N,A)

> N is the name of a stream that has been created by "create_stream." A (access) is one of read, write, or readwrite. "open/2" opens the named stream for the type of access specified.

screen(V,C)

> To display a window on the screen, a *viewport* must be opened to it. V is the name of a viewport to be opened. C is a control structure that specifies what is to be done to the viewport. If C is a "create/11" structure, one of whose arguments is the name of a window that was made with "create_stream" and opened with "open/2," then this predicate opens a viewport to that window.

state(T,_,N)

> If a window has been created with "create_stream," opened with "open/2," and made to appear on the screen with "screen/2," then a call to "state/3" can be used to make that window into the current input stream and/or the current input stream. (Note that "state/2" has many other functions besides controlling the current input and output streams.) N is the name of an open stream which is a window. T is either input or output.

close(N)

> N is the name of an open stream. This predicate closes the stream. The stream still exists, however, and can be re-opened with "open/2."

If N is the name of a window, all viewports to that window are destroyed, and the contents of the window are lost.

`delete_stream(N)`N is the name of a stream made with "create_stream." This predicate deletes the named stream.

Arithmetic functions

The arithmetic evaluators ("is," "<," etc.) will evaluate a number of functions in addition to the usual arithmetic operators, including:

```
sqrt(X)      % square root of X
exp(X)       % e to the power of X
log(X)       % log base e of X
X ^ Y        % X to the power of Y
length(X)    % length of string X
sin(X)
cos(X)
tan(X)
asin(X)
acos(X)
atan(X)
etc.
```

Types

The fundamental types of Prolog-2 are atoms, integers, floating point numbers, structures, and strings.

If the arguments to an arithmetic expression are exclusively integers, then the result of evaluating that expression will also be an integer. If floating point numbers occur in an arithmetic expression, then the result of evaluating the expression will be a floating point number. The result of a division performed with / is a float, and the result of a division performed with // is an integer.

Strings

In Prolog-2, a string is used in most of the places that a list of characters would be used in other versions of Prolog. Characters written inside of double quotes are interpreted as a string and not as a list of characters. Since a string is stored internally as a character array, strings are more memory efficient than lists of characters. Many of the built-in predicates that take a list of characters as an argument in other Prologs (i.e. "name" in Sec. 4.9) expect a string as an argument in Prolog-2. There is a special built-in predicate, "is_string/2," for operating on strings. "is_string" takes one of the following string functions as its second argument, evaluates it, and returns the result in its first argument:

String
functions

```
% concatenate two strings:
X & Y

% insert string Y into string X at position P:
insert(X,Y,P)

% delete N characters from string X at P:
delete(X,P,N)

% extract N characters from string X at P:
substring(X,P,N)

etc.
```

Example

```
?- Z is_string substring("california",2,4).
Z = "lifo"
```

Directives

An important consideration in designing a Prolog-2 module (see below) is whether the predicates defined therein are *public* or *private*. A public predicate can be referenced from outside of its module, whereas a private predicate can only be referenced from inside of the module. By default, all predicates in a module are public. All predicates in a module can be specified to be private with a "private/0" (no arguments) directive, or to be public with a "public/0" directive. A particular predicate can be specified to be private with a "private/1" directive, or to be public with a "public/1" directive.

For compile-time optimization, the direction (i.e. input or output) of arguments to a predicate can be declared with a "mode" directive. For example, in the "total" rule below, the first argument must always be input, and the second argument is always output:

```
%      +                -
total( customer(_,Rate,Days), Owed) :-
    Owed is Rate * Days.
```

The following "mode" directive instructs the compiler about the nature of the arguments to "total":

```
?-mode total(+, -).
```

In a source code file that is to be compiled into a module, all references to predicates not defined in the file (other than built-in predicates) must be specified as such in an "external" directive.

Development Environment

The Prolog-2 environment is organized into *modules*. A module can be either consulted Prolog code, compiled Prolog code, or the object code of a routine written in another language. Modules can be attached to a Prolog process either explicitly with a call to the built-in predicate "open_module," or automatically when the process is started up. Prolog-2 has its own virtual memory scheme, and part of the specification of a module is whether it should be kept completely in real memory or partly in real memory and partly in virtual memory. The ability to use virtual memory modules makes it possible to write very large programs, at the cost of execution speed. Many utility programs, such as the top level interpreter, editor and debugger, exist in their own modules, so that they do not occupy memory space when they are not being used.

Modules

Inside of a module, predicates are specified to be either *public* or *private*. A public predicate can be referenced from outside of its module, whereas a private predicate can only be referenced from inside of the module. At a given time in a Prolog session, there is a *current output module* and a *current input module*. The current output module is where newly asserted clauses are placed.

Editor

Prolog-2 has a built-in full screen editor which is useful for making small fixes to existing programs. When invoked, it shows the programmer a menu of editable modules, and when a module is selected, it shows a menu of predicates within that module. When the programmer selects a predicate, it brings up the text of all clauses that belong to that predicate on the screen, and functions like a text editor. It has a strong knowledge of Prolog syntax, and so is able to catch syntax errors early. Like almost everything else in Prolog-2, the editor can be customized.

Debugger

The Prolog-2 debugger is similar to the CProlog debugger, except that there are more commands available. When the debugger is invoked, it appears in its own window, so there is no danger of confusing input and output to the debugger with input and output to the running program.

Compiler

The Prolog-2 compiler is invoked via a built-in predicate, but operates on an external source file and produces an external object code module. The debugger will not work on compiled code. The compiler does first argument indexing (hashing) on any predicate with more than four clauses, unless the programmer suppresses this behavior with a "hash/2" directive.

Saved States

save_exe(File, Query) saves the Prolog system together with the current database into an executable file and ends the current Prolog session. When the executable file is called from the operating system, the saved state is restored and Query is evaluated. Note that the top level Prolog interpreter module is not included in the saved state.

Foreign Language Attachment

Prolog-2 provides a way to attach a procedure written in another language to a Prolog process. The procedure must be compiled to object code, and then a special machine code calling routine must be added to the object code. Calling routines are available for several different high level languages. There is no automatic mapping of Prolog data structures to the data structures of other languages; instead, the format of Prolog-2's internal data structures is specified. A programmer must write routines in the foreign language to make use of Prolog-2's data structures.

Extensions

Prolog-2 includes the DCG extension described in the section on CProlog above.

Miscellaneous

Prolog-2 includes a lexical analysis tool that is of comparable flexibility and power to the UNIX utility "lex." The lexical analysis tool makes it possible to write text manipulation programs without having to write a lexical analyzer (such as "readsent" in Sec. 6.1) in Prolog itself.

Windows

Prolog-2 has its own windowing system. A window is a type of stream that can be manipulated like other types of streams (i.e. files, devices). A window is associated with a memory buffer, and includes characteristics like color, type of border, etc. To display a window on the screen, a *viewport* must be opened to it with a call to "screen/2" (see above). If there are several layers of overlapping windows being displayed on the screen simultaneously, the depth of each window (i.e. how far it is from the topmost window) can be adjusted.

In an interpreted module, first argument indexing can be specified for a predicate with a "hash/3" directive.

Prolog-2 has tail recursion optimization (see "Miscellaneous" in the section on Quintus Prolog above). It can be toggled on or off with a call to "state/3."

Prolog-2 has a *garbage collector* that reclaims memory automatically during the evaluation of a query. There are also built-in predicates that force the system to garbage collect. Garbage collection can be toggled on or off with a call to "state/3."

There is a built-in predicate, "lint," that checks the syntax and style of a Prolog source file.

Arity Prolog

Availability

Arity Prolog is available from Arity Corporation. It runs on an IBM PC or compatible under the MS-DOS operating system.

Syntax and
Built-in
Predicates

The syntax of Arity Prolog is the same as that of DEC-10 Prolog. All of the examples in the book will work in Arity Prolog; however, the newline character in "getfield" (Sec. 3.9 and Appendix II) should be changed from 10 to 13 for MS-DOS. | can be used as a synonym for ; to connect subgoals. Arity Prolog has a new syntactic feature called a *snip*. In a compound query, a snip is a set of subgoals written in between [! and !]. The interpreter will not backtrack to any of the subgoals inside of the snip (that is, it is as if all of the subgoals inside of the snip were passed as arguments to "once"; see Sec. 3.2).

Arity Prolog has most of the same built-in predicates as DEC-10 Prolog. In addition to "see," "tell," etc. described in Sec. 3.5, there are the following predicates that use stream identifiers (called *handles*) to control files:

create(S,F)   F is a file name. S is a stream identifier. This predicate creates a new file for writing.

open(S,F,A)   F is a file name. S is a stream identifier. A (access mode) is one of r, w, a, rw, or ra, where r means read, w means write, and a means append. This predicate opens the file in the prescribed mode.

close(S)   S is a stream identifier returned from a call to "open" or "create."

There is a version of each of the standard input/output predicates (such as "get," "read," "put," "write," etc.) with two arguments, one of which is a stream identifier. Here is an example of reading terms from a file opened with "open":

```
?- open(S1,'ap.data', r),
   repeat,
   read(S1, R),
   process(R),
   R = end_of_file,
   close(S1).
```

Arithmetic functions

The arithmetic evaluators ("is," "<," etc.) will evaluate a number of functions in addition to the usual arithmetic operators, including:

```
random       % number between 0 and 1
abs(X)       % absolute value of X
sqrt(X)      % square root of X
exp(X)       % e to the power of X
log(X)       % log base 10 of X
ln(X)        % log base e of X
X ^ Y        % X to the power of Y
sin(X)
cos(X)
tan(X)
asin(X)
acos(X)
atan(X)
etc.
```

Types

The fundamental types of Arity Prolog are atoms, integers, floating point numbers, structures, and strings. Writing characters in between double quotes is an alternative notation for a list of characters.

If the arguments to an arithmetic expression are exclusively integers, then the result of evaluating that expression will also be an integer. If floating point numbers occur in an arithmetic expression, then the result of evaluating the expression will be a floating point number. The result of a division performed with / is a float, and the result of a division performed with // is an integer.

Strings

Characters written inside of dollar signs are interpreted as a *string*. A string may have newline characters embedded in it. Since a string is stored internally as a character array, strings are more memory efficient than lists of characters; however, unification of strings is much slower than unification of atoms. A string will not unify with an atom that has the same characters, but the built-in predicate == will evaluate a string and an atom with the same characters as equal:

```
?- $california$ = california.
no

?- $california$ == california.
yes
```

The following are special built-in predicates for dealing with strings:

```
%  input/output:
read_string(MaxLength, String)      % from current input
read_string(S, MaxLength, String)   % from stream S
read_line(S, String)                % from stream S
write(String)                       % like write(Atom)

%  conversion:
string_term(String, Term)
atom_string(Atom, String)
int_text(Integer, String)
float_text(Float, String)
list_text(List, String)             % [97,98] to $ab$

%  other:
string_search(Pattern, String, Position)
substring(String, Position, Length, Substring)
string_length(String, Length)
concat(S1, S2, S3)                  % S3 is S1 con-
                                    % catenated with S2
```

Development Environment

Arity Prolog has two features to support the development of large programs: 1) virtual memory; and 2) the partition of the program into *worlds*. The virtual memory manager swaps clauses back and forth between physical memory and disk in 16K pages. A world can be composed of up to 256 pages. A single program can have up to 256 worlds. Unlike a Prolog-2 module, an Arity Prolog world is just a way of organizing clauses inside of a single program, and cannot be attached and detached from various programs. A world is either a *data world* or a *code world*. A data world is exclusively made up of databases of facts. A fact is added to the current data world with any of the built-in predicates "recorda," "recordz," "record_after," or "replace," and is removed from the current data world with "erase." A code world is made up of predicates that may include both facts and rules. A clause is added to the current code world with "assert," and removed from the current code world with "retract" (see Sec. 4.7).

The default world (for both data and code) in a Prolog session is called "api"; the "api" world always exists. A new world is made with a call to the built-in predicate "create_world." Once a world has been created, a call to "data_world" will make it the current data world (that is, it will be the world that "recorda," "erase," etc. operate on). A call to "code_world" will make a world the current code world (that is, it will be the world that "assert" and "retract" operate on). To optimize the use of virtual memory, a programmer can put all predicates that relate to a certain subject into a world, and then make that world the current world whenever the predicates in that world need to be queried. A call to "delete_world" removes a world with all of its clauses.

edit(F)

The built-in predicate "edit" takes a file name as its only argument. It looks at a DOS environment variable called "editor" for the name of an editor. It suspends the Prolog process and invokes the external editor with the file. When the editing session is over, it resumes the Prolog process, and automatically reconsults the file. (The meaning of "reconsult" is the same as in CProlog.)

Debugger

The Arity Prolog debugger is largely the same as the CProlog debugger. A debug line such as

```
(api,api) ** (0) CALL: flight(peoples,_0039,_0040) ? >
```

can be interpreted as follows:

(api,api) is the name of a code world followed by the name of a data world.

** means that a spypoint is currently set on the "flight/3" procedure.

(0) is a unique identification of the particular invocation of this procedure.

CALL: indicates that this is where the procedure is first entered.

flight(peoples,_0039,_0040) is the subgoal itself.

? > is a prompt indicating that the debugger is waiting for a debugging command.

The Arity Prolog debugger has many more commands available than the CProlog debugger.

Compiler

Arity Prolog has a compiler.

Saved States

The built-in predicate "save/0" will save all changes made to any of the worlds of a program since the last call to "save/0." The changes are saved in a binary file. The built-in predicate "restore/0" will eliminate all changes made to the current program since the last call to "save/0."

The built-in predicate "save/1" takes a filename as its argument. "save/1" will save a binary image of the current state of the Prolog interpreter, putting the clauses of each world into a separate file. "restore/1" takes a filename as its argument that was previously used in a call to "save/1." "restore/1" restores the state of the Prolog interpreter described in the file.

Extensions

Arity Prolog includes the DCG extension described in the section on CProlog above. Other extensions include a version of the SQL database query language, and an expert systems development package.

Miscellaneous

Arity Prolog provides two ways to speed up access to databases of facts: b-tree indexing and hash table indexing.

B-trees

A b-tree can be used to store a database of facts sorted according the values of one of its arguments. New facts are added to the database with the built-in predicate `recordb(Tree, SortField, Fact)`, where `Tree` is the name of the tree, `Fact` is a fact, and `SortField` is one of the arguments in `Fact`. If `Tree` does not already exist, it is created. Note that a database created with "recordb" will not appear as a set of facts in the program, and cannot be queried directly. All queries to such a database must be made through the built-in predicate "retrieveb/3," whose arguments are the same as those of "recordb/3." A fact can be removed from the database with the built-in predicate "removeb/3."

Hash tables

A hash table can be used to store a database so that all facts that have the same value of one argument are kept together. The hash table can greatly increase the efficiency of a query to the database if the hashed argument is instantiated in the query. New records are added to the database with the built-in predicate `recordh(Table, SortField, Fact)`, where `Table` is the name of the table, `Fact` is a fact, and `SortField` is one of the arguments in `Fact`. If `Table` does not already exist, it is created. A database created with "recordh" will not appear as a set of facts in the program, and cannot be queried directly. All queries to such a database must be made through the built-in predicate "retrieveh/3." A fact can be removed from the database with the built-in predicate "removeh/3." In other versions of Prolog, a hash table can only be built for the first argument of a clause, whereas Arity Prolog's built-in predicates for hashing allow a hash table to be built for any argument.

Arity Prolog has a garbage collector that is automatically invoked when the number of available stack units reaches a critical point. It can also be explicitly invoked by a call to the built-in predicate "gc."

UNSW Prolog

Availability

UNSW (University of New South Wales) Prolog is a public domain
version of the language that runs on almost all UNIX computers. It
is available from someone who already has the source code. Prolog-
86 is a version of UNSW Prolog for the MS-DOS and CP/M operating systems available from MICRO-AI. Prolog-86 runs on an IBM
PC and all compatibles. It can only utilize a limited amount of
memory, but executes very fast. Chalcedony Prolog is a version of
UNSW Prolog for the MS-DOS and Apple MacIntosh operating
systems available from Chalcedony.

Syntax and
Built-in
Predicates

The syntax of Prolog-86 is largely the same as that of DEC-10
Prolog, but there are some important differences. To be able to use
the programs in this book, it is recommended that you modify the
file "prolog.lib" (or "prolog_lib") that comes with Prolog-86 to include
the DEC-10 compatibility library given at the end of this section.
Without this library, many of the programs must be modified to
work under Prolog-86 (for instance, wherever lists of characters are
used).

Prolog-86's top level prompt is :. If a user types in a clause to this
prompt that ends in a period, it is interpreted as an assertion (not a
query), and is added to the current set of clauses. To query the
current set of clauses, a user should type in a clause that ends in a
question mark. This feature makes it very convenient to add clauses
interactively (that is, the user does not have to type   con-
sult(user). to be able to enter new clauses), but is confusing if
the user is accustomed to any other version of Prolog.

If a user types in a query that contains variables, the Prolog-86 interpreter will automatically print all values of the variables that
make the query true, without pausing after each answer and waiting
for the user to type a semicolon. The problem with this behavior is
that if there are more answers than will fit onto the screen, the first
answers may disappear before the query stops. The situation is particularly difficult if a query has an infinite number of answers. The
best way to deal with this behavior is to write a top level interpreter
that takes a query as an argument, and pauses after printing each
answer to the query.

The basic list constructor notation in Prolog-86 is as follows:

```
[a,b,..R]
```
which means the same as
```
[a,b¦R]
```

Prolog-86 will accept ¦ as a list constructor, but translates it into the .. notation. ¦ can be used as a synonym for ; to connect subgoals.

Prolog-86 has some of the same built-in predicates as DEC-10 Prolog, and some additional ones. Built-in predicates that deal with characters are discussed in the section on "Types" below.

"consult" in Prolog-86 means the same as "consult" in CProlog. Any filenames entered on the command line when Prolog-86 is invoked from the operating system will automatically be consulted. "load" in Prolog-86 means the same as "reconsult" in CProlog.

The built-in predicate "ratom" reads a single atom from the current input stream, and (unlike "read") does not require that the atom end with a period. The built-in predicate "print" will print any number of arguments followed by a newline, and the built-in predicate "prin" will print any number of arguments not followed by a newline.

The arithmetic evaluators ("is," "<," etc.) will interpret the ^ operator; 2 ^ 3 means two to the third power.

Types

The fundamental types of Prolog-86 are atoms, integers, structures, and characters. Instead of the input predicate "get0," which returns the ascii code value of a character from the current input stream, Prolog-86 has "getc," which returns a character from the current input stream. Instead of "put," which takes the ascii code value of a character as its argument, Prolog-86 has "putc," which takes a character as its argument. The built-in predicate `ascii(Character, Code)` converts a character into an ascii code value and vice versa. Unlike "name" in other versions of Prolog, which takes a list of ascii codes as its second argument (see Sec. 4.9), "name" in Prolog-86 takes a list of characters as its second argument and converts it into an atom, or vice versa. (See below for how to define a version of "name" that behaves like "name" in other versions of Prolog.)

Unlike CProlog, writing characters in between double quotes is not
an alternative notation for a list of characters, but is interpreted (like
characters in between single quotes) as an atom.

Directives

If a user types in a query followed by an exclamation mark, the
query will be evaluated but no output will be printed. A query followed by an exclamation mark is known as a *command*. When a file
is being consulted, the interpreter treats everything in the file in exactly the same way that it would treat it if the user typed it in
directly. Thus, if a fact in a source file ends with a question mark,
then when the file is consulted, that fact will be interpreted as a
query and the query will be evaluated before any of the rest of the
file is consulted. If a fact ends in an exclamation mark, it will be
evaluated as a command (i.e. no output will be printed) before any
of the rest of the file is consulted. The interpreter will also treat a
query preceded by : _ and followed by a period as a command.

Development Environment

Prolog-86 has no internal editor, and so the programmer must rely
on the support of the operating system environment to develop a program.

UNSW Prolog provides a built-in predicate, "ed/1," for editing a
procedure during a Prolog session. Before running Prolog, the name
of a UNIX editor must be defined in the shell variable "EDITOR."
During a Prolog session, "ed/1" is called with the name of a
currently defined procedure as its argument. "ed/1" writes all of the
clauses for that procedure out to a temporary file, and runs the
specified editor on the temporary file as a child process of the Prolog
process. When the editing session is complete, the old clauses for
that procedure are replaced by the clauses in the temporary file, and
the temporary file is removed.

Debugger

The Prolog-86 debugger is vaguely similar to the CProlog debugger.
However, there are no spypoints, no interactive debugging commands, and no way to trace the execution of all procedures without
specifying them by name. The debugger is invoked by a call to
"trace/1," which takes either the name of a single procedure or a list
of procedure names as a argument. Whenever one of the traced procedures is encountered in the evaluation of a query, the debugger
will print a message at the usual four points: call, exit, fail, and redo.
There is no unique identification of a procedure call in a message

from the debugger, but the number of ancestors of a particular subgoal is indicated by the presence of ¦ characters in front of the subgoal itself. This gives an interesting graphic appearance to the execution of a query to a recursive procedure. Here is some sample output from a query to "member":

```
: trace member?
**yes


: member(a, [c,b,a])?
C ¦ >member(a, [c, b, a])
C ¦ ¦ >member(a, [b, a])
C ¦ ¦ ¦ >member(a, [a])
E ¦ ¦ ¦ <member(a, [a])
E ¦ ¦ <member(a, [b, a])
E ¦ <member(a, [c, b, a])
**yes
```

C at the beginning of the line indicates the call point, and E at the beginning of the line indicates the exit point.

Compiler

Prolog-86 has no compiler.

Saved States

Prolog-86 has nothing like the binary saved states of CProlog. The built-in predicate "save/1" takes a filename as an argument, and writes all currently asserted clauses into the file in human readable form. However, when there are variables in clauses, they will be shown with their internal names.

Foreign Language Attachment

If the source code to UNSW Prolog is available, C functions can be added as additional built-in predicates.

Miscellaneous

There is a built-in predicate "eof" that becomes true whenever an input predicate encounters an end of file condition in the current input stream.

Here is a DEC-10 compatibility library for Prolog-86 that will make it possible to run the examples in the book:

```
% Compatibility Library for Prolog-86;
% Add to file "prolog.lib" or "prolog_lib"

% use this instead of built-in "name":
dec10name(Atom, IList) :-
    nonvar(IList),
    char__list(IList, CList),
    name(Atom, CList), !.

dec10name(Atom, IList) :-
    atom(Atom),
    name(Atom, CList),
    char__list(IList, CList), !.

get0(I) :- getc(C), ascii(C, I), !.
put(I) :- ascii(C, I), putc(C), !.

:- op(700, xfy, =<).
X =< Y :- X <= Y.

:- op(700, xfx, ==).
X == Y :- not( X = Y ).
```

Turbo Prolog

Availability

Turbo Prolog is available from Borland International. It runs on an IBM PC or compatible under the MS-DOS operating system.

Turbo Prolog is a compiler (not an interpreter) which is notable for its fast compile time, fast execution time, and flashy development environment. A Turbo Prolog program looks considerably different from other Prolog programs, because it must always begin with a number of compiler directives. The general form of a program is as follows:

```
trace                        /* optional             */
project "project_name"       /* optional             */
include "other_source_file"  /* optional             */
```

```
        domains                    /* optional; defines    */
            person = symbol        /* new domain types      */
            shift = symbol

        database                   /* optional;             */
            works(person, shift)   /* declares predicates   */
                                   /* that can be asserted  */
                                   /* and retracted         */

        predicates                 /* necessary; declares   */
            knows(person,person)   /* the domain of each arg*/

        goal                       /* optional              */
            knows(A, B).

        clauses                    /* usually necessary;    */
            works(bill, day).      /* actual code goes here */
            works(nancy, day).

        knows(X, Y) :-
            works(X, S),
            works(Y, S),
            X <> Y.
```

If a program has a "goal" directive, then when the program is executed, the run-time system will evaluate that goal once and end. If a program has no "goal" directive, then when the program is executed, the user will be able to enter queries. The meaning of the other directives is discussed below.

Syntax and Built-in Predicates

The syntax of Turbo Prolog is largely the same as that of DEC-10 Prolog. Many of the examples in the book can be made to work in Turbo Prolog.

The word `if` can be used as a synonym for `:-`, or `;`, and `and` is a synonym for `,`. Turbo Prolog recognizes comments between `/*` and `*/`; `%` is not a comment character.

Turbo Prolog has a few of the same built-in predicates as DEC-10 Prolog. Here are the Turbo Prolog built-in predicates equivalent to some common DEC-10 built-in predicates:

DEC-10	Turbo Prolog	Explanation
`is/2`	`=/2`	arithmetic evaluation
`var/1`	`free/1`	succeeds if argument is an uninstantiated variable
`nonvar/1`	`bound/1`	succeeds if argument is not an uninstantiated variable
`\==/2`	`<>/2`	succeeds if arguments are not exactly the same
`get0/1`	`readchar/1`	reads a characters from the current input device

Turbo Prolog has no predicate that is equivalent to "=/2" in Dec-10 Prolog (i.e. that will unify any two terms). It is not possible to define operators in Turbo Prolog.

Turbo Prolog has the built-in predicates "asserta," "assertz," and "retract" for manipulating the current program, but (unlike in other versions of Prolog discussed here) the arguments to any of these three must be facts, not rules. Any predicate whose clauses are going to be asserted and retracted must be declared to be a *database predicate* with a "database" compiler directive. For example, the predicate "works/2" is declared to be a database predicate in the example source file above.

The built-in predicate "write" takes any number of arguments. There is a built-in predicate "writef" which requires a format string as its first argument, but can take any number of arguments after that. Turbo Prolog has no predicate equivalent to "read/1" in DEC-10 Prolog. However, it does have "readln/1" which reads a line of characters, and "readterm/2" which reads a term. "readterm/2" requires a *domain specification* as its first argument, which controls what types of terms it can read (see the section on types below).

Instead of the built-in predicates "see," "tell," etc. there are the following predicates for controlling files:

openread(N,F)   F is an MS-DOS file name. N is an internal name selected by the
openwrite(N,F)   programmer with which to refer to the open file. "openread" opens
openappend(N,F)   the file for reading. "openwrite" opens the file for writing. "openap-
openmodify(N,F)   pend" opens the file for appending. "openmodify" opens the file for
                       reading and writing. A random access file can be updated by open-
                       ing it with "openmodify" and using "filepos/3" to position the file
                       pointer.

writedevice(N)   N is the internal name of a file opened with "openwrite," "openmo-
                       dify," or "openappend." This predicate makes the file into the current
                       output device, so that the output of any call to "write" or "writef" will
                       go into the file.

readdevice(N)   N is the internal name of a file opened with "openread." This predi-
                       cate makes the file into the current input device, so that the input of
                       any call to "readchar/1," "readln/1," "readint/1," "readreal/1," or
                       "readterm/2" will come from the file.

closefile(N)   N is the internal name of an open file. This predicate closes the file.

Arithmetic   The arithmetic evaluators ("=," "<," etc.) will evaluate a number of
functions   functions in addition to the usual arithmetic operators, including:

```
abs(X)          % absolute value of X
sqrt(X)         % square root of X
exp(X)          % e to the power of X
log(X)          % log base 10 of X
ln(X)           % log base e of X
sin(X)
cos(X)
tan(X)
arctan(X)
etc.
```

Types

Turbo Prolog is different from other versions of Prolog in that the
domain type of each argument of each predicate must be declared.
Turbo Prolog comes with the following simple domain types:

```
char
integer
real
string
symbol
file
```

A char is a single character. A symbol is an atom. Strings and symbols may be used interchangeably, although they are stored differently. Here is a simple example of how new domain types can be defined in terms of the simple domain types, and how domain types are used in predicate declarations:

```
domains
    name = symbol
predicates
    transaction(name, real)
clauses
    transaction(bob, 37.50).
    transaction(mary, 4.75).
    transaction(sue_ellen, 50.00).
```

Because of the domain declaration name = symbol, name becomes a new domain type that is the same as a symbol. When this program is executed, if the user tries a query to "transaction" with inappropriate domain types, Turbo Prolog will produce a domain type error.

Structures can be defined as new domain types in terms of the simple domain types. Here is a version of the "transaction" program from Sec. 2.2. Both arguments to "transaction" are structures:

```
domains
    name = symbol
    amount = integer
    cust_str = customer(name,amount,integer)
    date_str = date(integer,integer,integer)
predicates
    transaction(cust_str, date_str)
clauses
    transaction( customer(smith,29,4), date(87,4,22) ).
    transaction( customer(lee,35,7), date(86,10,30) ).
```

If a predicate has a list as one of its arguments, the domain of that argument must be declared as *object**, where object is the domain of each element in the list. As an example, here is a version of "member" that will work with a list that includes either integers or reals:

```
domains
    int_list = integer*
predicates
    member(integer, int_list)
clauses
    member(X, [X|_]).
    member(X, [_|Y]) :- member(X, Y).
```

This last example points out a disadvantage of Turbo Prolog's strong typing: If the user tries a query to "member" with a list that has atoms, reals, or structures in it, Turbo Prolog will produce a domain type error, and fail to execute the program. Practically, this means that the programmer must think of every possible type of element that might occur in a list that will be the argument to "member," and include it in the domain declaration. Thus, the need for domain declarations drastically reduces the possibility of reusing code in different applications. The need for domain type declarations also makes it impossible to write metalanguage predicates; see "Miscellaneous" below.

Domain type declarations seem to have a large effect on how Turbo Prolog's unification algorithm works. In general, the unification of a term in a query with a term in a program clause can only occur if the two terms were declared to be of compatible domain types when the program was compiled.

Strings   Turbo Prolog has the following built-in predicates for string manipulation:

readln(String)   This predicate reads a line from the current input device, and returns it as a string.

frontchar(String,FrontChar,Rest)
This predicate takes the first character off the front of the string and returns the rest of the string in Rest.

frontstr(N,String,Begin,End)
N is an integer, and String is a string of at least N characters. This predicate returns the first N characters of String in Begin (also a string), and the rest of the characters in String in End.

fronttoken(String,Token,Rest)
If String is instantiated, this predicate finds the first word or number contained in String and returns it in Token. It returns the rest of the string in Rest.

`str_len(String,Length)`
> This predicate returns the number of characters in `String`.

Conversion
> Turbo Prolog has the following built-in predicates for conversions between types:

```
str_char(String, Character)
str_int(String, Integer)
str_real(String, Real)

/* convert between an ascii code and a character: */
char_int(Character, Integer)

/* convert a string to all caps, or all lower case: */
upper_lower(UpperString, LowerString)
```

Development Environment

When Turbo Prolog comes up, it takes over the screen with four resizeable windows: an editor window, a dialog window in which the program runs, a message window for compiler warnings, etc., and a trace window for the output of the debugger. A command line at the top of the screen acts as a high level menu, and makes it easy to go from writing a program to compiling it to executing it.

The Turbo Prolog compiler can create object files that are linkable with the MS-DOS linker. Thus, it is possible to write a large program as a set of *modules*, and then link them together into an executable program. The interface between modules is controlled by declaring global domains and global predicates (i.e. predicates that can be referred to from outside of the module in which they were defined). A program made up of more than one module is called a *project*; a project is defined in a *librarian* file. Each source file that is part of a project must have a "project" compiler directive; see the first example source file above.

Debugger

The Turbo Prolog debugger is invoked by including the "trace" compiler directive in a source file, after which all predicates in the file will be traced on execution of the program. Tracing can be toggled on or off with a query to the built-in predicate trace/1." In the trace window, the debugger prints messages which are similar to the messages printed by the CProlog debugger. At the same time, the debugger positions the cursor in the edit window over the clause that is currently being evaluated. This last feature is very useful, in that it shows exactly where the program is at any given time.

Saved States

Turbo Prolog has nothing like the binary saved states of CProlog. The built-in predicate "save/1" takes a filename as an argument, and writes all currently asserted facts for database predicates into the file in human readable form. (A predicate is declared to be a database predicate with a "database" compiler directive; see the first example source file above.) Note that the file created by "save/1" is not a Prolog source file, and cannot be compiled. The facts in this file can be read back into the current program with a call to "consult/1."

Foreign Language Attachment

Turbo Prolog allows procedures written in Pascal, C, Fortran or Assembler to be attached to a Prolog program. The foreign language procedure must be declared as a global predicate in the Prolog program. Once both the Prolog program and the foreign language procedure have been compiled to object modules, the MS-DOS linker can be used to link them together into an executable program. Facilities exist to map the data structures of the language to and from Prolog data structures for the purpose of passing arguments.

Extensions

Turbo Prolog includes extensions for screen oriented input/output, color, windows, turtle graphics, and sound.

Miscellaneous

If the "trace" compiler directive is not present when a program is compiled, the compiler will apply tail recursion optimization to recursive procedures that are determinate when the recursive subgoal is called.

Because of Turbo Prolog's strong typing, none of the metalevel predicates such as "once," "find_or_ask," getfield/4," "send," etc. will work as defined in the book. Consider how "once" (Sec. 3.2) could be implemented in Turbo Prolog, since it is the simplest example. The usual code for "once" is:

```
once(P) :-
    P, !.
```

First of all, the Turbo Prolog compiler objects to a variable becoming a subgoal. Secondly, every possible argument to once must be declared in the predicate declaration of "once." Suppose that the program contained the predicates "knows/2" and "works/2," and that we want to be able to use "once" with either of these predicates when the program is executed. The following program will do the job:

```
domains
    person = symbol
    shift = symbol
    query = knows(person,person) ; works(person,shift)
predicates
    knows(person,person)
    works(person, shift)
    once(query)
clauses
    works(bill, day).
    works(nancy, day).

    knows(X, Y) :-
        works(X, S),
        works(Y, S),
        X <> Y.

    once( works(A,B) ) :-
        works(A, B), !.

    once( knows(C,D) ) :-
        knows(C, D), !.
```

It should be clear that this implementation of "once" is not reusable in different applications. Perhaps it would be possible to write a sort of pre-processor for Turbo Prolog that would automatically expand the general definition of a metalanguage predicate like "once" into a set of application-specific clauses.

The approach to Prolog programming advocated in this book requires the ability to extend Prolog's process structure by writing general-purpose procedures (see Secs. 6.1 and 7.5). In general, it is not possible to pursue this approach in Turbo Prolog.

Appendix V

Answers to Exercises

Answers to Exercises

Chapter 1

3.
```
group(henry, compiler).
group(nancy, compiler).
group(susan, network).

knows(PersonA, PersonB) :-
    group(PersonA, Group),
    group(PersonB, Group).
```

4. "knowing" is symmetric and many-to-many. "knowing," in the social sense, is also irreflexive. The "knows" program above, however, is reflexive. It can be made irreflexive by adding one more subgoal that depends on a built-in predicate introduced in Chap. 3:

```
knows(PersonA, PersonB) :-
    group(PersonA, Group),
    group(PersonB, Group),
    PersonA \== PersonB.
```

5. Here is another example of a transitive relation:

```
%               Subassembly Assembly
included_in(capacitor,   disk_drive).
included_in(disk_drive,  computer).
included_in(computer,    computer_system).
```

```
%                 Manufacturer   Part
manufactures(sprague,       capacitor).
manufactures(atasi,         disk_drive).
manufactures(convergent,    computer).
manufactures('AT&T',        computer_system).


%            Supplier     User          Part
supplies(sprague,     atasi,        capacitor).
supplies(atasi,       convergent,   disk_drive).
supplies(convergent,  'AT&T',       computer).


uses_parts_from(User, Supplier, Part) :-
    supplies(Supplier, User, Part).


uses_parts_from(User, Supplier1, Part) :-
    supplies(Supplier2, User, _),
    uses_parts_from(Supplier2, Supplier1, Part).
```

6. "competitor" should be symmetric, and it is symmetric. However, like "knows" above, it should be irreflexive. It can be made irreflexive in the same way that "knows" was.

Chapter 2

1.
```
| ?- X is 10, Y is X * 3.
X = 10
Y = 30



| ?- X is 10, Y is X * 3, Y is 300.
no
```

When the third subgoal of the last query is evaluated, Y is already instantiated, so this subgoal amounts to a test of the value of Y. This exercise emphasizes that there is no destructive assignment in Prolog.

2.

```
area(Base, Height, Area) :-
    Area is Base * Height.

¦ ?- area(10, 2, A).
A = 20


¦ ?- area(10, H, 20).
arithmetic error
```

The program is not reversible.

4. There are two easy solutions. The first follows the form of "has_length"; it is left recursive, and counts words on the way back from the end of the list:

```
%           +      +            -
find_word(Word, [Word¦List], Count) :-
    find_word(Word, List, SubCount),
    Count is SubCount + 1.

find_word(Word, [XWord¦List], Count) :-
    find_word(Word, List, Count).

find_word(_, [], 0).
```

The second solution is right recursive, and uses an extra argument to accumulate a count on the way toward the end of the list. When the end of the list is encountered, the accumulated count is passed to the fourth argument. (This solution is actually more efficient than the first solution in versions of Prolog that perform tail recursion optimization; see Appendix IV.)

```
%           +      +             +           -
find_word(Word, [Word¦List], Accumulator, Count) :-
    NewAccumulator is Accumulator + 1,
    find_word(Word, List, NewAccumulator, Count).

find_word(Word, [XWord¦List], Accumulator, Count) :-
    find_word(Word, List, Accumulator, Count).

find_word(_,    [],          Accumulator, Accumulator).
```

```
% example query:
¦ ?- find_word(the, [the,dog,in,the,barn], 0, C).
C = 2
```

5.
```
has_length([none¦R], Count) :-
    has_length(R, Count).

has_length([F¦R], Count) :-
    has_length(R, SubCount),
    Count is SubCount + 1.

has_length([], 0).
```

6. Possible answers to this exercise are discussed in detail in Chap. 4.

7.
```
grand_total([cust(_,Rate,Days)¦Rest], Total) :-
    grand_total(Rest, SubTotal),
    Total is SubTotal + Rate * Days.

grand_total([], 0).
```

8.
```
parent(henry,   jack).
parent(jack,    richard).
parent(richard, charles).
parent(charles, jane).

anc(X, Y, [X,Y]) :-
    parent(X, Y).

anc(X, Y, [X¦Rest]) :-
    parent(X, Z),
    anc(Z, Y, Rest).
```

10.
```
%              +                       -
bt_to_list(bt(N,D,P,S,Before,After), FinalList) :-
    bt_to_list(Before, BeforeList),
    bt_to_list(After, AfterList),
    append(BeforeList, [e(N,D,P,S)¦AfterList], FinalList).

bt_to_list(end, []).
```

11. In "rev_print," the pattern matching that occurs when the heads of the clauses are unified specifies when the clauses should be applied. In "xancestor," there is no pattern matching that occurs when the heads of the clauses are unified, so the interpreter must activate the body of a clause to determine if it should be applied.

Chapter 3

1.

```
¦ ?- travel(amtrak, new_york, X, _), !,
    travel(amtrak, X, Y, _).
```

2.

```
area(Base, Height, Area) :-
    nonvar(Base), nonvar(Height),
    Area is Base * Height.

area(Base, Height, Area) :-
    nonvar(Base), nonvar(Area),
    Height is Area / Base.

area(Base, Height, Area) :-
    nonvar(Height), nonvar(Area),
    Base is Area / Height.
```

If two of the three arguments are uninstantiated, the problem can still be solved by using a procedure that generates integers. See "num_gen" in Appendix III.

3. A complete answer set should include just mary and brian. Query A is complete and inefficient. Query B is incomplete and inefficient. Query C is incomplete and efficient. Query D is complete and efficient.

```
license(X) :-
    drivers_training(X),
    age(X, 16).

license(X) :-
    age(X, Age), Age >= 17.
```

4.
```
address_in_ny(milford_plaza).
address_in_ny(confucius_plaza).

connects(A, B, taxi) :-
    address_in_ny(A),
    address_in_ny(B),
    not( connects(A, B, bus) ),
    not( connects(A, B, train) ).



condition(Machine, normal) :-
    not( annuciator_on(Machine, Annunciator) ).



customer(X, 'AT&T') :-
    has_phone(X),
    not( customer(X, mci) ),
    not( customer(X, sprint) ).
```

5.
```
¦ ?- repeat,
    write('enter name of classmate: '),
    read(Name),
    (   Name = end % avoid asserting "classmate(end)"
        ;
        assert( classmate(Name) )
    ),
    Name = end,
    !,
    classmate(Name),
    write(Name), nl,
    fail.
```

6. First possibility: the database is a set of facts.

```
transaction(smith, air_travel, 139).
transaction(rodriguez, charitable_contribution, 25).
subtotal(0).
```

```
%                    +      -
transaction_sum(Name, Sum) :-
    transaction(Name, _, Amount),
    once( retract( subtotal(Sub) ) ),
    NewSub is Sub + Amount,
    assert( subtotal(NewSub) ),
    fail.

transaction_sum(Name, Sum) :-
    retract( subtotal(Sum) ),
    assert( subtotal(0) ).
```

Second possibility: the database is a list of structures. For convenience of testing, this list is asserted into the program in a "list" fact.

```
list([t(smith, air_travel, 139),
      t(rodriguez, charitable_contribution, 25)]).
```

```
%                      +                    ?
rtransaction_sum([t(Name,_,Amount)|Rest], Name, Sum) :-
    rtransaction_sum(Rest, Name, SubTotal),
    Sum is SubTotal + Amount.

rtransaction_sum([t(XName,_,Amount)|Rest], Name, Sum) :-
    XName \== Name,
    rtransaction_sum(Rest, Name, Sum).

rtransaction_sum([], _, 0).
```

```
| ?- list(L), rtransaction_sum(L, smith, Total).
Total = 139
```

8.

```
travel_list([t(amtrak,     new_york, boston,     train),
             t(nj_transit,new_york,  princeton, train),
             t(amtrak,     boston,    portland,  train),
             t(greyhound,  boston,    portland,  bus),
             t(amtrak,     new_york,  washington,train),
             t(peoples,    new_york,  washington,plane),
             t(peoples,    burlington,new_york,  plane)]).
```

```
can_travel(CityA, CityB, List) :-
    member(t(_,CityA,CityB,_), List).

can_travel(CityA, CityB, List) :-
    member(t(_,CityA,CityC,_), List),
    can_travel(CityC, CityB, List).

¦ ?- travel_list(TL), can_travel(new_york, portland, TL).
```

9.
```
%       Many    One
group0(henry, compiler).
group0(nancy, compiler).
group0(susan, network).

group(Name, Group) :-
    nonvar(Name),
    group0(Name, Group), !.

group(Name, Group) :-
    var(Name),
    group0(Name, Group).

group(Name, Group) :-
    not( group0(Name, Group) ),
    (    var(Name),
         write('name? '),
         read(Name)
         ;
         nonvar(Name)
    ),
    (    var(Group),
         write('group? '),
         read(Group)
         ;
         nonvar(Group)
    ),
    assert( group0(Name, Group) ).
```

11.
```
:-op(500, xfy, --).
:-op(499, xfy, ->).

can_travel5(A, B, A--Type->B) ) :-
    travel(_, A, B, Type).

can_travel5(A, B, A--Type->Rpath) ) :-
    travel(_, A, C, Type),
    can_travel5(C, B, Rpath).
```

Chapter 4

1. Here are new versions of the database and procedures that include mileage:

```
%         From        To          Via         Miles
travel(manhattan,  newark,    bus,        15).
travel(manhattan,  queens,    lirr,        5).
travel(newark,     bronx,     limousine, 25).
travel(bronx,      queens,    bus,         8).
travel(manhattan,  bronx,     subway,      4).
travel(newark,     princeton, limousine, 35).
travel(manhattan,  princeton, bus,        50).


%  Symmetric front end to the "travel/4" database
s_travel(A, B, Mode, Miles) :- travel(A, B, Mode, Miles).
s_travel(A, B, Mode, Miles) :- travel(B, A, Mode, Miles).


%             +       + +   _
tsi_travel3(Trail, A, B, Miles-m(Mode,B)) :-          % (1)
    A \== B,
    s_travel(A, B, Mode, Miles).


%             +       + +   _
tsi_travel3(Trail, A, B, Miles-m(Mode1,C,Mode2)) :-  % (2)
    A \== B,
    s_travel(A, C, Mode1, Miles1),             % generate C
    not( member(C, Trail) ),        % test C
    tsi_travel3([C|Trail], C, B, Miles2-Mode2),
    Miles is Miles1 + Miles2.
```

Recursive solution:

```
r_best_path(A, B, Path) :-
    findall(Mode, tsi_travel3([],A,B,Mode), List),
    keysort(List, SortedList),
    SortedList = [Path|_].
```

Backtracking Solution:

```
optimum_path(_, 100000).

best_path(A, B, Path) :-
    tsi_travel3([], A, B, Miles-Path),
    once( optimum_path(OpPath, OpMiles) ),
    (   Miles < OpMiles,
        once( retract( optimum_path(_, _) ) ),
        assert( optimum_path(Path, Miles) )
        ;
        Miles >= OpMiles
    ),
    fail.

best_path(A, B, Path) :-
    retract( optimum_path(Path, _) ),
    assert( optimum_path(_, 100000) ).
```

If the implementation of "keysort" in your version of Prolog is at all
efficient, the recursive solution should execute more quickly. The
backtracking solution will use less memory. The recursive solution is
based on a data stream approach, and the backtracking solution is
based on a behavioral approach.

2. The following "askable" fact covers the case when origin is unknown:

```
% orgin unknown:
askable(travel(A,B,Mode), 'enter the origin:', A) :-
    nonvar(Mode), nonvar(B).
```

The following version of "find_or_ask" can handle any number of
unknown arguments. The second argument to "askable2" is a list of
prompts, one for each argument to "travel":

```
askable2(travel(Orig,Dest,Mode),
         ['origin? ', 'destination? ', 'mode? ']).

find_or_ask2(Query) :-
    Query.
find_or_ask2(Query) :-
    not( Query ),     % use this rule if Query fails
    askable2(Query, PromptList),
    Query =.. [Pred|ArgList],
    check_each(ArgList, PromptList),
    assert( Query ).

check_each([Arg|ArgList], [Prompt|PromptList]) :-
    (     var(Arg),
          write(Prompt),
          read(Arg)
          ;
          nonvar(Arg)
    ),
    !, check_each(ArgList, PromptList).

check_each([], _).
```

Chapter 5

1. "readsent" will accept a sentence on more than one line. If you
type in more than one sentence on a single line, it will only get the
first sentence. What happens to the rest of the characters on the line
depends on input buffering in your version of Prolog.

2. The way to write "getline" so that it returns a list of words from a
line of input may be different on different versions of Prolog. Here is
a simple solution that works in CProlog, with the disadvantage that
it returns the newline character as the last word in the list:

```
%          _
getline([W|Lw]) :-              % read a line
    get0(C),
    readword(C, W, C1),
    restsent(W, C1, Lw), !.
```

```
% prev word and next char are input; read rest of line.
%         +   +   -
restsent(W, _, []) :-
    fullstop(W), !. % end if prev word was a fullstop.
restsent(W, C, [W1|Lw]) :-
    readword(C, W1, C1),
    restsent(W1, C1, Lw).

% take initial char, read a word, give back next char.
%           +   -   -
readword(C, W, _) :-
    newline(C),
    !,
    name(W, [C]).        % construct a word from the char C.
readword(C, W, C1) :-
    punctuation(C),
    !,
    name(W, [C]),        % construct a word from the char C.
    get0(C1).
readword(C, W, C1) :-
    valid_char(C),
    !,
    get0(C2),
    restword(C2, Lc, C1),   % get further chars.
    name(W, [C|Lc]).        % construct a word.
readword(C, W, C1) :-
    get0(C2),           % C is not acceptable. Get new char;
    readword(C2, W, C1).    % and try again.

% fill out a word, until an unacceptable char is found.
%          +   -        -   -
restword(C, [C|Lc], C1) :-    % aggregate chars into list
    valid_char(C),
    !,
    get0(C2),
    restword(C2, Lc, C1).
restword(C, [], C).           % end word if C is not valid

% characters that stand by themselves as words:
punctuation(44).              % ,
punctuation(59).              % ;
punctuation(58).              % :
```

```
punctuation(63).              % ?
punctuation(33).              % !
punctuation(46).              % .

newline(10).                  % newline on UNIX, VMS, etc.

% spans of chars that are valid:
valid_char(I) :- I > 96, I < 123.    % a-z
valid_char(I) :- I > 64, I < 91.     % A-Z
valid_char(I) :- I > 47, I < 58.     % 0-9

% characters that terminate a line:
fullstop('
').                           % newline
```

A simpler solution might be to write a version of "getfield/1" (Sec. 3.9) that returns a list of all characters on a line, and then write another procedure that breaks this list up into individual words.

6. Both "(" and ")" should be declared to be punctuation. If both ":" and "-" are declared to be valid characters, then ":-" will come out of "readsent" as a word, as long as there is a space or newline immediately following it.

8. It is fairly difficult to add a "sum" command without some major redesign of the program. The best approach is to associate the command with the final action that takes place when a query is evaluated. Thus, the "show" command should cause the final action to be a call to "print_tlist" (as it is now by default). The "sum" command should cause the final action to be a call to a new routine, named for instance "sum_tlist." "sum_tlist" would add up all the values that occur in its Printlist argument, and print the total.

Chapter 6

1. "is_a" can be made safely transitive by defining an explicit "is_a0" database, and by writing a recursive "is_a" procedure that references the "is_a0" database:

```
is_a0(canary, bird).
is_a0(tweety, canary).
```

```
is_a(X, Y) :-
    is_a0(X, Y).

is_a(X, Y) :-
    is_a0(X, Z),
    is_a(Z, Y).
```

However, "flies" and "color" are themselves transitive (recursive) in a way that depends on "is_a." To prevent a query to one of these procedures from recursing infinitely, the "is_a" subgoal in the body of each recursive rule should be changed to an "is_a0" subgoal:

```
flies(bird).
flies(X) :- is_a0(X, Y), flies(Y).

color(canary, yellow).
color(X, Y) :- is_a0(X, Z), color(Z, Y).
```

2.
```
is_a0(square, rectangle).
is_a0(rectangle, parallelogram).

property(parallelogram, 'area is base * height').
property(rectangle, 'all angles are 90 degrees').
property(square, 'all sides are equal').
property(Node, Property) :-
    is_a0(Node, AnotherNode),
    property(AnotherNode, Property).
```

3.
```
count(State, Count) :-
    % get selection criteria:
    send(State, av(type,  S) ),
    send(State, av(grade, G) ),
    send(State, av(weight,W) ),
    send(State, av(finish,T) ),
    send(State, av(color, C) ),
    !,
    % count all tuples that meet selection criteria:
    findall(S, pi(paper,S,G,W,T,C), List),
    has_length(List, Count).
```

Note: in the call to "findall," it does not actually matter what is collected into List, because we are only concerned with how many items there are in List.

Chapter 7

1. An example of a database with cyclic data is:

```
travel(amtrak,    new_york,  boston,    train).
travel(greyhound, boston,    new_york,  bus).
```

When the normal interpreter evaluates a query to "can_travel4" such as:

```
¦ ?- can_travel4(new_york, X).
```

it will produce a pattern of answers like:

```
X = boston ;
X = new_york ;
X = boston ;
X = new_york ;
   . . .
```

The same query evaluated through "ldi" will produce the same answers. "ldi" will only detect a loop if the same subgoal occurs three times in a row. The query above gets into an oscillating loop that "ldi" cannot detect. The best solution to this oscillation problem is found in the "tsi_travel3" procedure of Chap. 4. Can you write a general-purpose problem solver that can detect oscillating answer sets, using the same technique that was used in "tsi_travel3"?

2. Since a successful call to "place" actually causes a state transition, the meaning of a call to "place" would be clearer if the names of the states involved appeared as arguments; for instance:

```
%       +         +          ?            -
place(Object, Destination, CurrentState, NewState) :-
   . . .
```

3.

```
% declare one-to-many property of the "mother" relation:
%       Relation                One       Many
one_many(mother(Mother, Child), Mother,   Child).

% declare one-to-one property of the "soc_sec_number" relation:
%       Relation                        One   One
one_one(soc_sec_number(Name, Number), Name, Number).

% problem solver that knows about
% one-to-many and one_to_one relations:
ps(true) :- !.

ps( (A,B) ) :-              % compound query
    !,
    ps(A),
    ps(B).

ps(A) :-    % special case: A is a one-to-many relation
    one_many(A, X, Y),
    !,
    om_ps(A, X, Y).

ps(A) :-    % special case: A is a one-to-one relation
    one_one(A, X, Y),
    !,
    oo_ps(A, X, Y).

ps(A) :-    % A is not a one-to-many or one-to-one relation
    clause(A, Body),
    ps(Body).

% evaluate a one-to-many relation efficiently:
%       One  Many
om_ps(A, X,   Y) :-
    nonvar(Y),
    clause(A, Body),
    ps(Body), !.

om_ps(A, X, Y) :-
    var(Y),
    clause(A, Body),
    ps(Body).
```

```
%  evaluate a one-to-one relation efficiently:
%          One  One
oo_ps(A, X,   Y) :-
    clause(A, Body),
    ps(Body), !.
```

Many-to-one relations can be achieved by declaring them to be "one_many" and reversing the order of the arguments.

Bibliography

Aho, A. V., and Ullman, J. D. [1979]. *Principles of Compiler Design*, Addison-Wesley, Reading, Ma.

Aho, A. V., Hopcroft, J. E., and Ullman, J. D. [1983]. *Data Structures and Algorithms*, Addison-Wesley, Reading, Ma.

Apt, K. R., and van Emden, M. H. [1982]. "Contributions to the Theory of Logic Programming," *Journal of the ACM* 29:3

Bobrow, D. G. [1984]. "If Prolog is the Answer, What is the Question?," *Proc. International Conference on Fifth Generation Computer Systems*, Tokyo, Japan, November 6-9. Institute for New Generation Computer Technology, pp. 138-148

Bowen, D., Znidarsic, D., et al. [1985]. *Quintus Prolog Reference Manual*, Quintus Computer Systems, Palo Alto, Ca.

Bowen, K. A., and Kowalski, R. A. [1982]. "Amalgamating Language and Metalanguage in Logic Programming," in *Logic Programming* (K. L. Clark and S. A. Tarnlund, eds.), Academic Press, London, pp. 153-172

Bowen, K. A., and Weinberg, T. [1985]. "A Meta-Level Extension of Prolog," *Proc. Symposium on Logic Programming*, Boston, Ma., July 15-18. IEEE Computer Society Press, New York, pp. 48-53

Boyer, C. B. [1968]. *A History of Mathematics*, Princeton University Press, Princeton, N. J.

Brachman, R. J., Fikes, R. E., and Levesque, H. J. [1983]. "Krypton: A Functional Approach to Knowledge Representation," *Computer* 16:10, pp. 67-74.

Brachman, R. J. [1983]. "What IS-A Is and Isn't: An Analysis of Taxonomic Links in Semantic Networks," *Computer* 16:10, pp. 30-36.

Brough, D. R., and Walker, A. [1984]. "Some Practical Properties of Logic Programming Interpreters," *Proc. International Conference on Fifth Generation Computer Systems*, Tokyo, Japan, November 6-9. Institute for New Generation Computer Technology, pp. 149-158

Bundy, A. [1983]. *The Computer Modelling of Mathematical Reasoning*, Academic Press, London

Bundy, A., and Welham, B. [1981]. "Using Meta-level Inference for Selective Application of Multiple Rewrite Rules in Algebraic Manipulation," *Artificial Intelligence* 16:2

Campbell, J. A. [1984]. *Implementations of Prolog*, Ellis Horwood, Chichester, England

Chang, C., and Lee, R. C. [1973]. *Symbolic Logic and Mechanical Theorem Proving*, Academic Press, New York

Chikayama, T. [1983]. "ESP—Extended Self-contained Prolog—as a Preliminary Kernel of Fifth Generation Computers," *New Generation Computing* 1:1, pp. 11-24

Clark, K. L. [1978]. "Negation as Failure," in *Logic and Data Bases*, (H. Gallaire and J. Minker, eds.), Plenum Press, New York, pp. 293-324

Clark, K. L., and Gregory, S. [1985]. "Notes on the Implementation of Parlog," *Journal of Logic Programming* 2:1, pp. 17-42

Clark, K. L., McCabe, F. G., and Gregory, S. [1982]. "IC-PROLOG Language Features," in *Logic Programming*, (K. L. Clark and S. A. Tarnlund, eds.), Academic Press, London, pp. 253-266

Clark, K. L., and McCabe, F. G. [1984]. *micro-PROLOG: Programming in Logic*, Prentice-Hall, Englewood Cliffs, N. J.

Clark, K. L., and Tarnlund, S. A. (eds.) [1982]. *Logic Programming*, Academic Press, London

Clocksin, W. F., and Mellish, C. S. [1984]. *Programming in Prolog*, Springer-Verlag, Berlin

Coelho, H., Cotta, J. C., and Pereira, L. M. [1982]. *How to Solve it with Prolog*, Laboratio Nacional de Engenharia Civil, Lisbon

Colmerauer, A. [1978]. "Metamorphosis Grammars," in *Natural Language Communication with Computers* (L. Bolc, ed.), Springer-Verlag, Berlin, pp. 133-189

Colmerauer, A. [1985]. "Prolog in 10 Figures," *Communications of the ACM* 28:12, pp. 1296-1310

Copi, I. M. [1986]. *Introduction to Logic*, Macmillan, New York

Cory, H. T., Hammond, P., Kowalski, R. A., Kriwaczek, F., Sadri, F., and Sergot, M. J. [1984]. "The British Nationality Act as a Logic Program," Logic Programming Research Reports, Department of Computer Science, Imperial College, London, England

Dahl, V., and Abramson, H. [1984]. "On Gapping Grammars," *Proc. Second International Logic Programming Conference*, Uppsala, Sweden, July 2-6. Ord and Form, pp. 77-88

Darvas, F. [1980]. "Logic Programming in Chemical Information Handling and Drug Design," *Proc. Logic Programming Workshop*, July 14, p. 261

Davis, M. [1983]. "The Prehistory and Early History of Automated Deduction," in *Automation of Reasoning 1* (J. Siekmann and G. Wrightson, eds.), Springer-Verlag, Berlin

Davis, R. E. [1982]. "Runnable Specification as a Design Tool," in *Logic Programming* (K. L. Clark and S. A. Tarnlund, eds.), Academic Press, London, pp. 141-152

Ennals, J. R. [1984]. *Beginning Micro-PROLOG*, Ellis Horwood, Chichester, England

Gallaire, H., Minker, J., and Nicolas, J. M. [1978]. "An Overview and Introduction to Logic and Data Bases," in *Logic and Data Bases* (H. Gallaire and J. Minker, eds.), Plenum Press, New York, pp. 3-32

Gazdar, G., Klein, E., Pullum, G. K., and Sag, I. A. [1985]. *Generalized Phrase Structure Grammar*, Harvard University Press, Cambridge, Ma.

Goldberg, A., and Robson, D. [1983]. *Smalltalk-80 The Language and its Implementation*, Addison-Wesley, Reading, Ma.

Goldstein, I. P., and Roberts, R. B. [1979]. "Nudge, a Knowledge-based Scheduling Program," in *Frame Conceptions and Text Understanding* (D. Metzing, ed.), de Gruyter, Berlin, pp. 26-45

Hamilton, A. G. [1978]. *Logic for Mathematicians*, Cambridge University Press, Cambridge, England

Hammond, P., and Sergot, M. [1984]. *apes: Augmented Prolog for Expert Systems Reference Manual*, Logic Based Systems, Richmond, Surrey, England

Hayes, P. J. [1977]. "In Defence of Logic," *Proc. IJCAI-77*, MIT, Cambridge, Ma., August 22-25. International Joint Conferences on Artificial Intelligence, pp. 559-565

Hayes, P. J. [1979]. "The Logic of Frames," in *Frame Conceptions and Text Understanding* (D. Metzing, ed.), pp. 46-60

Hayes, P. J. [1985]. "The Second Naive Physics Manifesto," in *Readings in Knowledge Representation* (R. Brachman and H. Levesque, eds.), Morgan Kaufmann, Los Altos, Ca., pp. 467-486

Hayes-Roth, F., Waterman, D. A., and Lenat, D. B. (eds.) [1983]. *Building Expert Systems*, Addison-Wesley, Reading, Ma.

Hermes, H., and Markwald, W. [1974]. "Foundations of Mathematics," in *Fundamentals of Mathematics* (H. Behnke, F. Bachmann, K. Fladt, and W. Suss, eds.), MIT Press, Cambridge, Ma., pp. 1-88

Hilbert, D. [1904]. "On the Foundations of Logic and Arithmetic," in *From Frege to Godel*, van Heijenoort (ed.), Harvard University Press, Cambridge, Ma.

Hodges, W. [1977]. *Logic*, Penguin, New York

Hogger, C. J. [1984]. *Introduction to Logic Programming*, Academic Press, London

Horn, R. E. [1983]. "An Overview of Trialectics with Applications to Psychology and Public Policy," in *Trialectics Toward a Practical Logic of Unity* (R. E. Horn ed.), Information Resources, Lexington, Ma., pp. 1-39

Kahn, K. M., and Carlsson, M. [1984]. "How to Implement Prolog on a Lisp Machine," in *Implementations of Prolog* (J. A. Campbell, ed.), pp. 117-134

Kaplan, R. M., and Bresnan, J. [1984]. "Lexical-Function Grammar: A Formal System for Grammatical Representation," in *The Mental Representation of Grammatical Relations* (J. Bresnan, ed.), MIT Press, Cambridge, Ma., pp. 173-281

Kawanobe, K. [1984]. "Current Status and Future Plans of the Fifth Generation Computer Systems Project," *Proc. International Conference on Fifth Generation Computer Systems*, Tokyo, Japan, November 6-9. Institute for New Generation Computer Technology, pp. 3-17

Kay, M. [1985]. "Parsing in Functional Unification Grammar," in *Studies in Natural Language Processing*, Cambridge University Press, Cambridge, England

Kitakami, H., Kunifuji, S., Miyachi, T., and Furukawa, K. [1984]. "A Methodology for Implementation of a Knowledge Acquisition System," *Proc. International Symposium on Logic Programming*, Atlantic City, N. J., February 6-9. IEEE Computer Society Press, New York, pp. 131-143

Kluzniak, F., and Szpakowisz, S. [1985]. *Prolog for Programmers*, Academic Press, London

Kowalski, R. A. [1974]. "Predicate Logic as a Programming Language," *Proc. IFIP-74*, North Holland, Amsterdam, pp. 569-574

Kowalski, R. A. [1979a]. *Logic for Problem Solving*, Elsevier-North Holland, New York

Kowalski, R. A. [1979b]. "Algorithm = Logic + Control," *Comm. of the ACM* 22, pp. 424-431

Kowalski, R. A., and Kuehner, D. G. [1971]. "Linear Resolution with Selection Function," *Artificial Intelligence* 2, pp. 227-260

Kowalski, R. A., et al. [1984]. *Fifth Generation Software*, Course Outline, Programming Logic Systems, Milford, Ct.

Kriwaczek, F. [1982]. "Some Applications of PROLOG to Decision Support Systems," MSc Thesis, Imperial College, London

Kriwaczek, F. [1984]. "A Critical Path Analysis Program," in *micro-PROLOG: Programming in Logic* (K. L. Clark and F. G. McCabe), pp. 277-293

Li, D. [1984]. *A PROLOG Database System*, Research Studies Press, Letchworth, England

Lloyd, J. W. [1984]. *Foundations of Logic Programs*, Springer-Verlag, New York

Loveland, D. W. [1968]. "Mechanical Theorem Proving by Model Elimination," *Journal of the ACM* 15:2

Manna, Z. and Wladinger, R. [1985]. *The Logical Basis of Computer Programming*, Addison-Wesley, Reading, Ma.

Matsumoto, Y., Kiyono, M., and Tanaka, H. [1984] "Facilities of the BUP Parsing System," *Proc. Natural Language Understanding and Logic Programming*, Rennes, France, September 18-20, pp. 71-80

McCabe, F. G., and Clark, K. L. [1985]. *micro-PROLOG 5.2 Programmer's Reference Manual*, Logic Programming Associates, London, England

McCarthy, J., and Hayes, P. J. [1969]. "Some Philosophical Problems from the Standpoint of Artificial Intelligence," in *Machine Intelligence 4* (B. Meltzer and D. Mitchie, eds.), Edinburgh University Press, Edinburgh, pp. 463-502

McCord, M. C. [1982]. "Using Slots and Modifiers in Logic Grammars for Natural Language," *Artificial Intelligence* 18, pp. 327-367

McCord, M. C. [1985]. "Modular Logic Grammars," *Proc. 23rd Annual Meeting of the Association for Computational Linguistics*, Chicago, Il., July 8-12, pp. 104-117

McDermott, D. [1983]. "DUC: A Lisp-Based Deductive System," Technical Report, Department of Computer Science, Yale University

Mendelson, E. [1979]. *Introduction to Mathematical Logic*, D. Van Nostrand, New York

Minsky, M. [1979]. "A Framework for Representing Knowledge," in *Frame Conceptions and Text Understanding* (D. Metzing, ed.), pp. 1-25

Miyachi, T., Kunifuji, S., Kitakami, K., Furukawa, K., Takeuchi, A., and Yokota, H. [1984]. "A Knowledge Assimilation Method for Logic Databases," *Proc. International Symposium on Logic Programming*, Atlantic City, N. J., February 6-9. IEEE Computer Socicty Press, New York, pp. 118-125

Moto-oka, T. et al. [1981]. "Challenge for Knowledge Information Processing Systems," in *Fifth Generation Computer Systems* (T. Moto-oka, ed.), pp. 3-92

Nagel, E., and Newman, J. R. [1964]. *Godel's Proof*, New York University Press, New York

Naish, L. [1985]. "All Solutions Predicates in Prolog," *Proc. Symposium on Logic Programming*, Boston, Ma., July 15-18. IEEE Computer Society Press, New York, pp. 73-77

Nakashima, H. [1984]. "Knowledge Representation in Prolog/KR," *Proc. International Symposium on Logic Programming*, Atlantic City, N. J., February 6-9. IEEE Computer Society Press, New York, pp. 126-130

Nicolas, J. M., and Gallaire, H. [1978]. "Data Base: Theory vs. Interpretation," in *Logic and Data Bases* (H. Gallaire and J. Minker, eds.), Plenum Press, New York, pp. 33-54

Nilsson, N. J. [1980]. *Principles of Artificial Intelligence*, Tioga, Palo Alto, Ca.

Nygaard, K., and Dahl, O. J. [1978]. "The Development of the SIMULA Languages," *SIGPLAN Notices* 13:8, pp. 245-272

O'Keefe, R. A. [1985]. "On the Treatment of Cuts in Prolog Source-Level Tools," *Proc. Symposium on Logic Programming*, Boston, Ma., July 15-18. IEEE Computer Society Press, New York, pp. 68-72

Parsaye, K. [1983]. "Database Management, Knowledge Base Management, and Expert System Development in Prolog," *Proc. ACM Database Week*, San Jose, Ca., pp. 179-183

Pereira, F. C. N. (ed.) [1985]. *CProlog User's Manual Version 1.4*, Department of Architecture, University of Edinburgh, Edinburgh

Pereira, F. C. N., and Warren, D. H. D. [1980]. "Definite Clause Grammars for Language Analysis—A Survey of the Formalism and a Comparison with Augmented Transition Networks," *Artificial Intelligence* 13, pp. 231-278

Pereira, F. C. N., and Warren, D. H. D. [1983]. "Parsing as Deduction," *Proc. 21st Annual Meeting of the Association for Computational Linguistics*, MIT, June 15-17. Association for Computational Linguistics, pp. 137-144

Poe, M. D. [1984]. "Control of Heuristic Search in a Prolog-Based Microcode Synthesis Expert System," *Proc. International Conference on Fifth Generation Computer Systems*, Tokyo, Japan, November 6-9. Institute for New Generation Computer Technology, pp. 589-595

Pollard, C. [1984]. *Generalized Phrase Structure Grammars, Head Grammars, and Natural Languages*, PhD Thesis, Stanford University, Stanford, Ca.

Reichenbach, H. [1947]. *Elements of Symbolic Logic*, Macmillan, New York

Reiter, R. [1978]. "On Closed World Data Bases," in *Logic and Data Bases* (H. Gallaire and J. Minker, eds.), Plenum Press, New York, pp. 55-76

Roberts, G. M. [1977]. *An Implementation of PROLOG*, M.Sc. Thesis, University of Waterloo, Ontario, Canada

Robinson, J. A. [1965]. "A Machine-Oriented Logic Based on the Resolution Principle," *Journal of the ACM* 12, pp. 23-41

Robinson, J. A. [1979]. *Logic: Form and Function*, Elsevier-North Holland, New York

Roussel, P. [1975]. *PROLOG: Manuel de Reference et d'Utilisation*, University of Aix-Marseilles, Luminy, France

Sergot, M. [1982]. "Prospects for Representing the Law as Logic Programs," in *Logic Programming* (K. L. Clark and S. A. Tarnlund, eds.), Academic Press, London, pp. 3-18

Shapiro, E. Y. [1983a]. *Algorithmic Program Debugging*, The MIT Press, Cambridge, Ma.

Shapiro, E. Y. [1983b]. "A Subset of Concurrent Prolog and its Interpreter," *ICOT Technical Report* TR-003, Institute for New Generation Computing, Tokyo

Shapiro, E. Y. [1984]. "Guest Editor's Preface," *New Generation Computing* 2:4, pp. 305-308

Shapiro, E. Y., and Takeuchi, A. [1983]. "Object Oriented Programming in Concurrent Prolog," *New Generation Computing*, 1:1, pp. 25-48

Shieber, S. M., Uszkoreit, H., Pereira, F. C. N., Robinson, J. J., and Tyson, M. [1983]. "The Formalism and Implementation of PATR-II," in *Research on Interactive Acquisition and Use of Knowledge*, Artificial Intelligence Center, SRI International, Menlo Park, Ca.

Siekmann, J., and Wrightson, G. (eds.) [1983a]. *Automation of Reasoning 1 Classical Papers on Computational Logic 1957-1966*, Springer-Verlag, Berlin

Siekmann, J., and Wrightson, G. (eds.) [1983b]. *Automation of Reasoning 2 Classical Papers on Computational Logic 1967-1970*, Springer-Verlag, Berlin

Simmons, R. F. [1984]. *Computations from the English*, Prentice-Hall, Englewood Cliffs, N. J.

Swinson, P. S. [1980]. "Prescriptive to Descriptive Programming a Way Ahead for Caad," *Proc. Logic Programming Workshop*, July 14, pp. 262-273

Taylor, A. E. [1955]. *Aristotle*, Dover, New York

Tick, E., and Warren, D. H. D. [1984]. "Towards a Pipelined Prolog Processor," *New Generation Computing* 2:4, pp. 323-346

Tokoro, M. and Ishikawa, Y. [1984]. "An Object-Oriented Approach to Knowledge Systems," *Proc. International Conference on Fifth Generation Computer Systems*, Tokyo, Japan, November 6-9. Institute for New Generation Computer Technology, pp. 623-631

Uehara, K., Ochitani, R., Kakusho, O., and Toyoda, J. [1984]. "A Bottom-Up Parser Based on Predicate Logic: A Survey of the Formalism and its Implementation Technique," *Proc. International Symposium on Logic Programming*, Atlantic City, N. J., February 6-9. IEEE Computer Society Press, New York, pp. 220-227

Uehara, K., Ochitani, R., Mikami, O., and Toyoda, J. [1984]. "An Integrated Parser for Text Understanding: Viewing Parsing as Passing Messages among Actors," *Proc. Natural Language Understanding and Logic Programming*, Rennes, France, September 18-20, pp. 59-70

Uehara, T., and Kawato, N. [1983]. "Logic Circuit Synthesis Using Prolog," *New Generation Computing* 1:2, pp. 187-193

Warren, D. H. D, and Pereira, F. C. N. [1981]. "An Efficient Easily Adaptable System for Interpreting Natural Language Queries," DAI Research Paper No. 155, Department of Artificial Intelligence, University of Edinburgh, Edinburgh

Warren, D. H. D., Pereira, L. M., and Pereira, F. C. N. [1977]. "PROLOG—The Language and its Implementation Compared with LISP," *SIGPLAN Notices* 12:8

Winograd, T. [1980]. "Extended Inference Modes in Reasoning by Computer Systems," *Artificial Intelligence* 13, 1980, pp. 5-26

Yasukawa, H. [1983]. "LFG in Prolog—Toward a Formal System for Representing Grammatical Relations," *ICOT Technical Report* TR-019, Institute for New Generation Computing, Tokyo

Zaniolo, C. [1984]. "Object-Oriented Programming in Prolog," *Proc. International Symposium on Logic Programming*, Atlantic City, N. J., February 6-9. IEEE Computer Society Press, New York, pp. 265-271

Zaumen, W. T. [1983]. "Computer-Assisted Circuit Evaluation in Prolog for VLSI," *Proc. ACM Database Week*, San Jose, Ca., pp. 179-183

van Emden, M. H., and Kowalski, R. A. [1976]. "The Semantics of Predicate Logic as Programming Language," *Journal of the ACM* 23:4, pp. 733-742

van Heijenoort, J. (ed.) [1967]. *From Frege to Goedel: A Source Book in Mathematical Logic 1879-1931*, Harvard University Press, Cambridge, Ma.

Index

F

File control, 151, 163, 394-95, 399,
    407-8, 412-13, 425
"findall," 163-64, 171, 201, 323, 327,
    330, 340, 349, 372, 379
    as an extension of Prolog's process
      structure, 256, 262, 302
    implementation, 338
"find_or_ask," 198-200, 202, 328
Formal meaning:
    of a descriptive program, 255-56,
      322
    of a symbol, 258, 259-61
Frame axiom, 294-95, 303
Frame formalism, 266-70
    compared with object oriented for-
      malism, 273
    compared with the inheritance
      mechanism in Prolog, 280
    program in Prolog, 268
Frege, G., 15-16, 48
Function:
    analysis of, 28, 53
    arithmetic, 96-97, 400, 408, 413,
      419, 425
    definition, 29
    semantic definition, 30, 54
    successor, 35-36
    syntax of, 26

G

"getfield," 161-62, 293, 339, 342-43,
    367-71, 382-84

H

Hayes, P. J., 63, 274, 302, 329
Head of a list, 103
Head of a rule, 72-73, 162
    quantification of a variable in, 74
    unification with, 122-25
Horn clause, 6
    as a form of predicate logic, 43
    quantification of a variable in, 45,
     91
    written in Prolog, 51-52

I

Implicit database, 75, 113
Inconsistency, 39
Inference rule, 10, 23-24, 36, 254
    resolution, 39, 44-48
Infinite domain of interpretation, 35
Infinite loop, 222, 307, 317-18, 320
Inheritance:
    concept of, 263-64
    mechanism in Prolog, 273-302,
     348-49
    of messages in the object oriented
     formalism, 271-72
    of slot values in the frame for-
     malism, 267
Instantiation of a variable, 70
Integrity constraints, 87-89, 140, 158,
    177, 179-80, 269, 277, 291,
    296, 300, 326-28
Interpretation, 20, 31-33, 254, 259,
    274
    of algebraic rules, 13-14, 16
    domain of, 27-28
    Herbrand, 39-42
    in predicate logic, 31-33
    in propositional logic, 20, 23
Isomorphism, 3, 324, 329

K

Knowledge representation, 54-55, 62, 254
  in C, 261
  in a computational formalism, 255-56
Kowalski, R. A., 39, 48-49, 54, 60-61, 63, 116, 167, 274, 302, 329

L

Laws of logic, 7, 58
Left recursive procedure, 83-84, 107, 222-23, 252-53, 307, 317
Lexical analyzer, 203-208, 235
"ldi" (loop detecting interpreter), 307, 317-21, 330
  as a metalanguage predicate, 321
List processing, 105-11
List constructor, 103
Logical connective, 18-19
Loop detection, 317, 321

M

Meaning:
  declarative, 55, 74, 76, 135-36, 148, 262, 275
  of a descriptive program, 255-56, 322
  external, 258-61
  informal, 17, 21-22, 25
  procedural, 77-79, 84, 148
  of a symbol, 258, 261-62
Meeting example, 267-70, 273-74, 281
Metalanguage, 144-45, 301-2, 321, 324 427, 430
  definition, 24-25, 63
  functions of, 58

predicates, 60
  of Prolog, 58-59
  syntactic relation with object language, 58
Method in the object oriented formalism, 270-74, 281
Method of a bottom-up parser, 215-216
Method of a top-down parser, 214
micro-Prolog, 63, 92, 229-38
  syntax of, 230
Minsky, M., 266
Model:
  Herbrand, 41-42, 46
  in predicate logic, 33-34
  in propositional logic, 20, 23
Model theory, 302
"name," 161-62, 206, 232, 311, 339

N

Negation:
  explicit, 146
  in predicate logic, 27
  in propositional logic, 14-15, 18
Negation as failure, 144-145
Nonterminal, 208
"not," 143, 144
"num_gen" (number generator) 350, 377-78, 385

O

"obj" (top-down parser), 208-214, 229, 241-42
Object language, 25, 57-59, 145
Object oriented formalism, 264, 270-73, 276, 280-81, 302
"once," 144, 171, 371
Ontological assumptions of predicate